Sustainability Matters

UNIVERSITY OF CALGARY
Press

Sustainability Matters
Prospects for a Just Transition in Calgary, Canada's Petro-City

NOEL KEOUGH with **GEOFF GHITTER**

University of Calgary Press
2500 University Drive NW
Calgary, Alberta
Canada T2N 1N4
press.ucalgary.ca

LIBRARY AND ARCHIVES CANADA CATALOGUING IN PUBLICATION

Title: Sustainability matters : prospects for a just transition in Calgary, Canada's petro-city
    / Noel Keough with Geoff Ghitter.
Names: Keough, Noel, author. | Ghitter, Geoff, author.
Description: Chapters 4 to 13 comprise an adapted and updated collection of essays
    previously published in Calgary's Fast Forward Weekly from 2010 to 2015. | Includes
    bibliographical references and index.
Identifiers: Canadiana (print) 20210217030 | Canadiana (ebook) 20210217138 |
    ISBN 9781773852485 (softcover) | ISBN 9781773852492 (Open Access PDF) | ISBN
    9781773852508 (PDF) | ISBN 9781773852515 (EPUB)
Subjects: LCSH: Sustainable urban development—Alberta—Calgary. | LCSH: Sustainable
    living—Alberta—Calgary. | LCSH: City planning—Environmental aspects—Alberta—
    Calgary. | LCSH: Calgary (Alta.)—Environmental conditions.
Classification: LCC HT243.C32 C34 2021 | DDC 307.76097123/38—dc23

The University of Calgary Press acknowledges the support of the Government of Alberta
through the Alberta Media Fund for our publications. We acknowledge the financial support
of the Government of Canada. We acknowledge the financial support of the Canada Council
for the Arts for our publishing program. Financial support for printing was received from
the Sustainability Certificate Program at U of C.

Printed and bound in Canada by Marquis Book Printing
♻ This book is printed on Enviro Smooth White paper

Copyediting by Jo Hildebrand
Cover image: © 2021, Denis Gadbois, *Peace Bridge Mesmerized*, Calgary, Alberta, photograph.
Interior photographs by Noel Keough
Cover design, page design, and typesetting by Melina Cusano

Table of Contents

Introduction   1
> *Noel Keough*

1: A New Story of Cities and Urban Life   9
> *Noel Keough*

2: The Origins and Evolution of Sustainable Development   23
> *Noel Keough*

3: Colonization and Resource Extraction on the Canadian Frontier   37
> *Geoff Ghitter and Noel Keough*

4: Where Would You Put 600,000 People?   49

Head for the Hills: Municipal Development Plan Stress-Test Failure | 51

Curbing Sprawl through Inner City Renovation | 53

Density: Designing at a Human Scale | 55

Resilience: A Cautionary Tale from New Orleans to Cuba | 58

To Weather Future Storms, Calgary Needs Resilience | 60

Green Urbanism: A Necessary Evolution of Cities | 62

5: Where Do We Grow from Here?   75

A Pricey Ride to School: The Hidden Costs of Suburban Sprawl | 77

Big Box Boondoggle: Why Small and Local Is Beautiful | 79

Fiscal Cliff: Calgary's Growth Management Strategy under Siege | 81

No Limits, No More: It's Time for an Urban Growth Boundary | 84

Pride and Prejudice—Or Why Developers and Builders Want to Control City Hall | 86

Lessons from the Left Coast | 88

6: Sustainable Mobility: Bikes, Trams, and (Fewer) Automobiles   97

Trams: The Missing Link in Calgary's Transportation System | 99

Loving Transit: If You Build It (Right), They Will Come | 101

Looking Ahead to the Past: A Tale of Three Tram Cities | 103

In Praise of the Bicycle: Pedalling to the Rescue in the Climate
     Emergency | 106

Everything Old Is New Again: The Right Stuff on the East Coast | 109

7: Peak Auto: A Tragedy in the Making   119

Auto Dependence: The Numbers Don't Add Up | 120

The Life and Times of the Deadly American Automobile | 122

The Road Less Travelled: Life beyond the Private Automobile | 125

The Winding Road to the Airport Tunnel: A Case of the Tail Wagging
     the Dog | 127

Ring Road Rethink: Finding Opportunity in Crisis | 130

8: A Culture of Sustainability   143

Give Peace a Chance | 145

I and We: The Case for Social Cohesion | 147

Libraries: What Are They Good for? | 149

On Dandelions: Speaking Truth to Flowers | 151

9: The Wheels Are Off the Growth Machine   161

Economic Growth Is No Longer Delivering the Goods | 162

The Current Crisis: It's More Than the Economy | 165

Minding Our Own Business: Co-operative Solutions to a New Economy | 167

Growing Pains: Economically, the End May Be Nigh | 169

The Growth Machine: Second Thoughts on Calgary's Booms and Busts | 172

Beyond Growth: Time for a Radical Economic Development Strategy | 174

The Wealth of Our Nation | 176

10: The Energy Question

191

Diversity Is the Key: Confronting Our Energy Habits | 192

Pipedream Nightmare: A Crisis Entirely of Our Own Making | 195

Ostrich Alberta: Our Heads in the Tar Sands | 198

The 400 ppm Threshold Breached—And the Tragic Irony of Our Petro-State | 201

Do the Math: Fossil Fuel Divestment, Stranded Assets, and the Dawn of the Solar Age | 203

King Coal and the Carbon Calamity: Time to Face our Dirty Little Secrets | 206

11: Justice, Fairness, and Inclusion

221

Home Suite Home: A Primer on Secondary Suites | 223

Affordable Living: The House Hunter's New Mantra | 225

Cultural Diversity, Social Inclusion, and Sustainability: Opportunity Knocks | 228

How Much Is Enough? Buy Nothing Day an Opportunity for Reflection and Redirection | 230

12: Governance: The Sine Qua Non of Sustainability

243

Beyond the Law of the Jungle: Good Ideas for Good Governance | 244

The Gift That Keeps On Giving: Lessons in Governance from the Nordic Lights | 247

Sacred Trust: Without It, We're Lost | 249

Democracy on the Ropes: Money, Access, and the Perversity of First-Past-the-Post | 252

Booms, Busts, and Budgets | 254

Silent Spring 2012: Sustainability Vision Betrayed | 257

13: Our Petro-State at a Crossroads   269

Tax Is Not a Four-Letter Word | 270

Where Has All the Money Gone? The Great Alberta Giveaway | 273

Alberta's Inconvenient Truths | 275

Sleepwalking into Crisis: Has Canada Lost Its Way? | 277

Capitalism and Climate Change: God Bless Us One and All! | 279

14: Five Reasons Why Sustainability Matters   289
    Noel Keough

Bibliography   303

Acknowledgements   347

Authors   349

Index   351

Introduction

Journalists recognize that at heart they are storytellers. Academics tend not to see ourselves as mere storytellers—but we are. In 2010 we took up an invitation to write a regular column on sustainability matters for Calgary's *Fast Forward Weekly*. We listened to the public conversations Calgarians were having—the collective stories they were telling and retelling. We came to appreciate the power of the stories we tell ourselves, and we realized that even as people begin to lose faith in their stories, without new stories they are reluctant to abandon the comfort of the old.

Facts and figures on their own rarely have the power to move people. In *Sustainability Matters*, we articulate, interpret, and critique stories that we in the West have been telling ourselves for some time now—like the story that all good things come from economic growth, or that technology will solve all our problems. But many of us now believe that we are at an epochal moment in the history of our city and of our species and that, more than ever, we need to craft a new story. This book is a small contribution to that effort.

The original motivation for the collection of essays that form the core of this book (chapters 4 to 13) was to engage Calgarians in discussion, debate, and exploration of current events as they unfolded week to week. We were putting into practice what we believe is an obligation of all academics—to be engaged intellectuals. As such, our goal was to write in an inclusive manner that speaks to all Calgarians, including academics and post-secondary and post-graduate students.

Our goal for the current collection remains the same—to engage and educate readers. These essays offer more than debate and opinion; they also present evidence via government and not-for-profit reports and websites, as well as peer-reviewed academic books and journals, for readers to investigate issues in more depth.

A core attribute of sustainability analysis is systems thinking. In these essays, we attempt to connect the dots. To illuminate causes, we probe behind the political flashpoints of the day, which can tend to focus on the symptoms. We make the argument that local phenomena like sprawl, auto dependence, affordability, lack of economic diversification, and broken governance are all connected; they are not isolated issues to be dealt with in their respective bureaucratic silos. We argue further that none of these local issues can be divorced from global challenges such as climate change, income inequality, and economic crisis. Instead, they are systemic manifestations of fundamentally unsustainable patterns of human settlement.

The public debates of the time dictated our topics. But as the *Fast Forward* column evolved, we began to see a pattern. The early essays took on some of the most immediate sustainability issues in the city of Calgary, including land use planning and transportation, and the politics and economics of these processes. As the column matured, we found ourselves exploring the technical, ecological, and political dimensions of issues like energy and economic diversification—issues that were still core to our petro-city but were generally perceived as rooted in provincial- and national-scale politics and economics. Our stories got bigger.

In the later essays, we widened our lens once again. Rather than continue to hammer away at the day to day of city politics, we were compelled to connect these debates to issues of global significance. Cities, after all, are not isolated islands. We invited Calgarians to reflect on local issues in a global context and to consider the Sustainable Calgary principle that our bid to achieve sustainability cannot be at the expense of our neighbours—whether they be the family next door or on the other side of the planet. We connected our stories to the stories being told in the global village.

This book is a place-based exploration of the concept of sustainability from the vantage point of Calgary—a fast-growing, wealthy, car-dependent, sprawling, culturally diverse, cosmopolitan urban centre. The book is also the story of a unique period in our city's history. In the first two decades of the twenty-first century, our political conversation has reflected an understanding of sustainability, but we have struggled mightily to turn that knowledge into action.

The themes articulated in this book transcend Calgary. We offer these matters of sustainability in the city of Calgary as a microcosm of the issues faced by cities around the world, particularly those of the more affluent nations. Furthermore, to the extent that cities are imagined as the engines of growth and creativity in the global human enterprise (more than half of humanity is now urbanized), the issues faced by Calgarians transcend urbanism. In this sense, Calgary—its governance, energy regime, diversity, economic development, and ecological health—is a microcosm not only of cities but of the global village.

The structure of the book emerged rather organically as a praxis—a dialogue of theory and practice. Pedagogically, the book is informed by the tradition of radical education whose practitioners, most notably Brazilian educator Paulo Freire, counsel educators to start where the people are.[1] So while critical theory inspires the book, most citizens are not critical theorists and do not necessarily adhere to radical critiques of the status quo. To paraphrase Freire, educators should aspire to stretch the thread that joins an educator to his or her audience, but not to break the thread.

Our essay series started with instrumental, liberal, practical proposals for change that would find the light of day within a neoliberal capitalist economic reality. For example, confining debate and discussion to proposals for good urban design may frustrate the critical theorist, but it is the ground on which much of the debate in Calgary begins. Our challenge, moving from essay to essay, was to leverage those starting points and nudge debate onto more critical theoretical terrain. We attempted to do this both within the individual essays and through the arc of the essay series. The reader can judge whether we have been successful.

If critical urban theorists are to bridge the theory-practice divide and contribute to change, then we have to make our theoretical discourse accessible. The arc of these essays reflects a growing confidence in building that bridge. We walked the line between the average citizen discounting our words as academic impracticality and academic colleagues doing the same with the charge of simplistic analysis. Engaging citizens through a journalistic medium, we experimented with the art of storytelling in a way that we hope achieved, in some degree, what Leonie Sandercock, an urban planner and academic, advocates as the power of storytelling in planning practice and pedagogy.[2] The book also straddles two fields of inquiry that rarely communicate with one another: the literature on cities, processes of urbanization, and critical urban theory, on the one hand, and the sustainable development discourse that originates in the international development enterprise, on the other.

Chapter 1 outlines, in broad strokes, the challenge of urban sustainability. We review critical commentary on the modern city and processes of urbanization as well as the diverse prescriptions for change that have been proposed since the publication of the World Commission on Environment and Development's *Our Common Future*, popularly known as the Brundtland Report, which introduced sustainable development to the global policy debate.[3] We suggest that contemporary themes in critical urban theory are the most productive lens through which to understand cities and processes of urbanization.

For over a quarter century, sustainable development has been a prominent theme in the global conversation about the future of our economy, human societies, our planet, and the cities that most people call home. In chapter 2, we provide a brief overview of the emergence and evolution of the concept of "sustainable development"—its definition, critiques of the conventional use of the term, how and why it has been popularized, frameworks we use to understand it, and some of the tools that have been devised to operationalize the concept in cities. In chapter 3, we provide a brief introduction to the city of Calgary, including key moments in its evolution and a critique of its current trajectory. We introduce a set of five principles of sustainability that emerged from a deliberative citizen-led process. These principles help frame the discussion and debate that we hope will be provoked by the book.

Chapters 4 to 13 comprise an adapted and updated collection of essays that we wrote and published in Calgary's *Fast Forward Weekly* from 2010 to 2015. In these essays, we cover a wide range of topics in a style that is provocative, myth-busting, and evidence-based. Each chapter presents a set of essays under wide-ranging themes that play out not only in Calgary but in most of the world's cities and communities. These themes include public transit, the private automobile, economic growth, sprawl, arts and culture, environment, social justice, governance, and—of particular importance in Calgary—energy. Within the essays, readers will find references to other cities that are facing some of the same challenges as Calgary, as well as stories of cities and city districts that, while still falling short of the ideal, are widely acknowledged as early adopters and innovators in the sustainability transition. The final chapter takes up the question of why sustainability matters and proposes five defining features of sustainability as a philosophy for the age of ecology.

This book takes the point of view that conventional approaches to how humans make a living on our planet, approaches crafted within the confines of a capitalist economic system, are not working. For all its flaws, the 1992 Earth Summit in Rio de Janeiro convened the global community to create an agenda for sustainable development, because the evidence was undeniable that conventional approaches were failing all species, including our own. Over the past thirty years, the concept of sustainable development has been ubiquitous, and there is much criticism that it can mean anything to anybody. Our position is that sustainability is a radical concept and that an assessment of conventional approaches through a sustainability lens obliges us to take up the challenge as citizens to help create communities, cities, nations, and a global village that are sustainable for the long term.

Through these essays, we invite readers to examine the specific historical forces that have shaped issues like sprawl in Calgary. In the spirit of Peter Marcuse's call to expose, propose, and politicize, many of the essays name and challenge the existing power structures, chief among them the private sector development industry, that maintain the unsustainable trajectory of Calgary's urban growth.[4] We advocate for an uncompromising and ethically defensible approach to dealing with issues of economic and cultural marginalization in Calgary—echoing past and current formulations of the "right to the city," as first articulated by Henri Lefebvre and, more recently, by Peter Marcuse.[5] We focus on making the connections across social, ecological, and economic domains in order to decipher the contradictions, crisis tendencies, and lines of potential or actual conflict that claim the headlines in Calgary, none more so than the future of our energy industry in the face of climate change. Many of the essays go beyond identification of the tensions and critiques of the current reality and propose alternatives, including renewable energy transitions, transportation futures that decentre the private automobile, non-market housing models, co-operative forms of economy, and non-consumerist models of urban life.

Leveraging issues of the day, the essays introduce a variety of theoretical concepts that invite citizens to consider issues on a more abstract and critical plane. Embedded in essays on the role of arts and culture and the idea of the "creative city" are critiques of the evolution from a managerialist mode of urban governance to an entrepreneurial mode. Such an evolution sidelines issues of social justice and ecological decay, resulting in what David Harvey calls "a stimulating if often destructive maelstrom of urban-based cultural, political, production and consumption innovations" and what Richard Florida calls "the creative city."[6] Harvey was one of the first urbanists to argue that urbanization is first and foremost about endless growth and the centralization of capital.[7]

We used our bi-monthly platform to introduce conceptual tools, including Harvey Molotch's notion of the urban growth machine; Clarence Stone's urban regime theory; and interpretations of gentrification by theorists like Lees, Slater and Wyley, and Ley and Dobson.[8] These offerings invite readers to look beyond the local headlines, coffee shop discussions, and civic forums of debate in order to better understand the forces that shape Calgary and the opportunities for change.

A word on terminology. Already we have introduced the original formulation of the Brundtland Report's *sustainable development*. We have also used the stand-alone term *sustainability*. To further qualify *sustainability*, we now introduce the notions of "strong" and "weak" sustainability, signifying a divergence of theory and practice since the release of the Brundtland Report.

We equate "weak sustainability" with what we argue is the compromised concept of sustainable development. In our view, the concept holds too much of the old paradigm of development: it maintains allegiance to the idea of economic growth, a technocentric view of where solutions lie, and an unwillingness to address issues of power and neocolonialism in the current world order. Weak sustainability also encompasses the notion of complete substitutability of forms of capital: for example, if we cause the extinction of honeybees, we can substitute that loss with technology.

"Strong sustainability," in contrast, forcefully challenges whether economic growth is still a viable strategy; argues that change will have to reach deep into social, cultural, and political ways of being on the planet; and calls out inequality, abuse of power, and the neocolonial nature of the current world order. Strong sustainability holds to the notion that very little of nature is substitutable. We use the shorthand "sustainability" to mean "strong sustainability."[9]

NOTES

1   Paolo Freire, *Pedagogy of the Oppressed*, 30th anniversary ed., trans. Myra Bergman Ramos (New York: Continuum, 2005).

2   Leonie Sandercock, "Out of the Closet: The Importance of Stories," *Planning Theory and Practice* 4, no. 1 (2003): 11–28.

3   World Commission on Environment and Development, *Our Common Future* (Oxford: Oxford University Press, 1987), https://sustainabledevelopment.un.org/content/documents/5987our-common-future.pdf.

4   Peter Marcuse, "Critical Planning: An Interview with Peter Marcuse," *Critical Planning* 15 (Summer 2008): 111–20.

5   Henri Lefebvre, *The Production of Space* (Hoboken, NJ: Wiley-Blackwell, 1992); Peter Marcuse, "From Critical Urban Theory to the Right to the City," *City* 13, nos. 2–3 (2010): 185–97.

6   David Harvey, *Spaces of Capital: Towards a Critical Geography* (London: Routledge, 2012), 362; Richard Florida, *The Rise of the Creative Class: Revisited,* 10th anniversary ed. (Philadelphia: Basic Books, 2014).

7   David Harvey, *Rebel Cities: From the Right to the City to the Urban Revolution* (London: Verso, 2013).

8   Harvey Molotch, "The City As a Growth Machine: Toward a Political Economy of Place," *American Journal of Sociology* 82, no. 2 (1976): 309–32; Clarence N. Stone, *Regime Politics: Governing Atlanta 1946–1988* (Lawrence: University of Kansas Press, 1989); Loretta Lees, Tom Slater, and Elvin Wyly, *Gentrification* (London: Routledge, 2007); David Ley and Cory Dobson, "Are There Limits to Gentrification? The Contexts of Impeded Gentrification in Vancouver," *Urban Studies* 45, no. 12 (2008): 2471–98.

9   For a thorough discussion of the concepts of strong and weak sustainability, see Eric Neumayer, *Weak Versus Strong Sustainability: Exploring the Limits of Two Opposing Paradigms,* 4th ed. (Cheltenham, UK: Edward Elgar, 2013). William Rees's discussion of the expansionist (weak sustainability) and ecological (strong sustainability) world views is also an excellent source. William Rees, "Achieving Sustainability: Reform or Transformation?" *Journal of Planning Literature* 9, no. 4 (1995): 343–61.

Works Cited

Florida, Richard. *The Rise of the Creative Class: Revisited.* 10th anniversary ed. Philadelphia: Basic Books, 2014.

Freire, Paolo. *Pedagogy of the Oppressed.* 30th anniversary ed. Translated by Myra Bergman Ramos. New York: Continuum, 2005.

Harvey, David. *Rebel Cities: From the Right to the City to the Urban Revolution.* London: Verso, 2013.

———. *Spaces of Capital: Towards a Critical Geography.* London: Routledge, 2012.

Lees, Loretta, Tom Slater, and Elvin Wyly. *Gentrification.* London: Routledge, 2007.

Lefebvre, Henri. *The Production of Space.* Hoboken, NJ: Wiley-Blackwell, 1992.

Ley, David, and Cory Dobson. "Are There Limits to Gentrification? The Contexts of Impeded Gentrification in Vancouver." *Urban Studies* 45, no. 12 (2008): 2471–98.

Marcuse, Peter. "Critical Planning: An Interview with Peter Marcuse." *Critical Planning* 15 (Summer 2008): 111–20.

———. "From Critical Urban Theory to the Right to the City." *City* 13, nos. 2–3 (2010): 185–97.

Molotch, Harvey. "The City As a Growth Machine: Toward a Political Economy of Place." *American Journal of Sociology* 82, no. 2 (1976): 309–32.

Neumayer, Eric. *Weak Versus Strong Sustainability: Exploring the Limits of Two Opposing Paradigms.* 4th ed. Cheltenham, UK: Edward Elgar, 2013.

Rees, William. "Achieving Sustainability: Reform or Transformation?" *Journal of Planning Literature* 9, no. 4 (1995): 343–61.

Sandercock, Leonie. "Out of the Closet: The Importance of Stories." *Planning Theory and Practice* 4, no. 1 (2003): 11–28.

Stone, Clarence N. *Regime Politics: Governing Atlanta 1946–1988.* Lawrence: University of Kansas Press, 1989.

World Commission on Environment and Development. *Our Common Future.* Oxford: Oxford University Press, 1987. https://sustainabledevelopment.un.org/content/documents/5987our-common-future.pdf.

1

A New Story of Cities and Urban Life

As communities around the world confront the imperative for a sustainability transition, recurring stories have emerged as core sustainability challenges, whether our concern is Calgary, cities in general, or the global village. One such story is the notion that we have entered an era of uneconomic growth. A flawed accounting system, by definition, presents any growth as good growth, but the increasingly pressing externalities of economic growth make it uneconomic. In Calgary, as in many cities across Canada and around the world, the fiscal cliff of deferred maintenance is just one example of an externality.

In this era of neoliberal economics, public debate is fixated on short-term budget deficits. Such discussion seems not only blind to long-term public infrastructure deficits but also to ecological and social deficits. The growing wealth and income inequalities in Calgary speak to the social deficit, which is also evident in automobile-related death and injury and in public health issues related to sedentary lifestyles, including heart disease, diabetes, and obesity. The mounting ecological deficit (most evident in our oversized ecological footprint) includes the loss of wildlife habitat to urban sprawl, increased greenhouse gases due to the burning of fossil fuels, and the appropriation of natural resources from around the globe to support an unsustainable consumerist lifestyle.

A core issue for so many urban challenges is the artificial divide between public and private spending and the ideological bias that private spending is good for the economy but public spending is not. In fact, most critical urban systems are based on a combination of both. The transportation system, for example, relies on public spending on roads and private spending for the rolling stock—the automobile. We need to link city economies to sustainability priorities and understand economic development as a means to an end. Just any old kind of investment or innovation is not enough. Sustainability provides an end that benefits everyone; it is a moral and ethical compass for cities.

Most sustainable development discourse asserts that urbanization is inevitable and irreversible in the foreseeable future; indeed, most of the world's people now live in cities. Richard Florida has popularized the notion that cities are the economic and cultural engines of growth, creativity, and innovation, a thesis that is not without its critics.[1] In response to the challenge of sustainable development, critiques of classic North American suburban development and of automobile-dependent urban transportation have proliferated.[2] These critiques have led to more compact, people-centred, and green urban and community design options.[3] Andres Duany, Elizabeth Plater-Zyberk, and Jeff Speck describe and critique urban sprawl and are co-founders of the urban design movement known as New Urbanism, which calls for a return to neotraditionalist, pre-auto urban and neighbourhood design.[4] William McDonough and Michael Braungart have helped popularize the concepts of ecological design and industrial ecology and their application to energy-efficient building design, redesign of mass transit, and systems of industrial production.[5] In the social domain, many recognize the importance of a sense of community, vibrant neighbourhoods, and designing to the notion of human scale as necessary ingredients for safe, healthy, and vibrant cities.[6] David Satterthwaites' *Earthscan Reader in Sustainable Cities* and Stephen Wheeler and Timothy Beatley's *Sustainable Urban Development Reader* curate this diverse body of city and urbanization literature.[7]

Civic debates about the future of the city have been taken up via a dizzying array of proposed city typologies that have moved in and out of favour since the 1992 Rio Earth Summit convened global leaders to agree on an agenda for sustainable development. Our cities have been variably referred to as ecological, creative, liveable, sustainable, just, resilient, in transition, smart, post-carbon, new urbanist, and circular.[8] Many of these monikers make an appearance in this book's essays, often used as foils to champion or challenge visions for Calgary's future.

Meanwhile, the global discourse, policy, and practice of city-making inspired by the Brundtland Report are reflected in publications of groups such as the German Advisory Council of Global Change, International Council for Local Environmental Initiatives (ICLEI), and UN-Habitat. The focus tends to be on how we can improve the sustainability of urban living by integrating the domains of environment, society, and economy through common policy framings, such as the triple bottom line.[9] Contemporary global city coalitions are rallying around notions of sustainability (ICLEI and the Global Environmental Facilities Sustainable Cities Impact Program), resilience (the 100 Resilient Cities, of which Calgary is a member), and climate change (C40 Cities Climate Leadership Group). None of these initiatives imagine life beyond capitalism or the logic of economic growth.

Geographic traditions of critical analysis of the evolution, function, and spatial character of cities proper, of processes of urbanization, and of the conventional framing of sustainable cities are more compatible with the notion of strong sustainability. Geographers in the radical Marxist tradition have focused on the ways in which the built environment inhibits or enhances opportunities for a flourishing and just urban life. David Harvey, Mike Davis, Edward Soja, and Doreen Massey are some of the most well known.[10] The critical urbanist perspective has been clearly summarized by Neil Brenner, David Marcuse, and Margit Mayer in their volume on critical approaches to urbanism:

> In the most general terms, critical approaches to urban studies are concerned: (a) to analyze the systemic, yet historically specific, intersections between capitalism and urbanization processes; (b) to examine the changing balance of social forces, power relations, socio-spatial inequalities and political-institutional arrangements that shape, and are in turn shaped by, the evolution of capitalist urbanization; (c) to expose the marginalizations, exclusions, and injustices (whether of class, ethnicity, "race", gender, sexuality, nationality, or otherwise) that are inscribed and naturalized within existing urban configurations; (d) to decipher the contradictions, crisis tendencies, and lines of potential or actual conflict within contemporary cities; and on this basis, (e) to demarcate and politicize the strategically essential possibilities for more aggressive,

socially just, emancipatory and sustainable formations of urban life.[11]

The spectrum of prescriptions for making cities sustainable ranges from relatively minor reform to significant transformation of cities and urban life. While many acknowledge a sustainability crisis, a general sense of impotence prevails about how to deal with it. In Canada, this is exacerbated by the fact that cities are legal creatures of their provinces, leaving them constrained by provincial legislation that governs what they can and cannot do and with very limited fiscal tools to fund sustainability initiatives. Most policy and planning exercises begin from a vantage point relatively close to the status quo, the argument for this stance usually being practicality or pragmatism. The Bruntland Report, the Kyoto Protocol, and the City of Calgary Municipal Development Plan are all examples of this approach.[12] Solutions arrived at from this status quo perspective are rarely long term. They are piecemeal and incremental in the sense that they set their sights on a goal that may represent improvement but is not consistent with strong sustainability.

We maintain that cities need to orient planning and action toward a realistic end point that is sustainable in the long term. In this book, we propose practical transformative solutions to that end. We advocate going beyond improving how we "make do" in present circumstances in order to widen the horizon of change into future generations and to critically examine what needs to be done now to ensure long-term sustainability. In our view, the goal is not to sustain the current system but to craft and construct a better one—one that conforms to a framework of strong sustainability.

The call for more equitable and just cities is explicit in many of these essays and implicit in all of them. The simple fact is that during the past three decades of unprecedented economic growth in Calgary, injustice and inequity have increased. As pointed out in several of these essays, this trend is a global one. The symptoms of injustice and inequality are evident in deteriorating housing affordability and in homelessness, the extreme end of the affordability continuum; the institutionalization of food banks in some of the wealthiest cities in the world; and the number of people working full time and more, yet still living in poverty.

The utopian urban stories we tell ourselves, like Richard Florida's *Rise of the Creative Class,* turn out to be flawed, as Florida himself acknowledges in his 2017 book, *The New Urban Crisis.*[13] Members of the economics profession, from Nobel economist Paul Krugman to best-selling author Thomas Piketty, acknowledge the positive correlation of equity to overall economic health.[14] Writers like Naomi Klein argue that equity and justice are, in fact, prerequisites for dealing with the global catastrophe that is climate change.[15]

Throughout these essays, two conflicting metaphors for the city are invoked—the machine versus the living organism. These conflicting metaphors are evident in the observation that modern cities are economic "growth machines" and have been designed as car habitat rather than human habitat. While urban planners and designers have been inspired by the ideas of Jane Jacobs and Jan Gehl, traffic engineers still seem to be in the thrall of New York City's infamous development czar Robert Moses. While cities are increasingly imagined as urban ecologies, industrial ecologies, and social ecologies, it is engineers who command the largest budgets in cities and who are charged with laying the infrastructure (most importantly, highways and major roads) that constrains the intentions of urban planners and designers to create human habitat rather than car habitat. The emerging debates over data-driven, networked, smart cities and autonomous vehicles are some of the most high-profile manifestations of this ongoing dialectic. The Hollywood blockbuster *Blade Runner* is a popular media manifestation of these debates and anxieties about the future of cities.[16]

These competing metaphors of the city have been debated for at least one hundred years. Most famously, Lewis Mumford's *The City in History* draws this contrast in strong terms.[17] Mumford's bleak analysis fell out of favour as the ascendant city emerged as the dominant form of human settlement on our planet, but the city as machine is still arguably the dominant utopian/dystopian image driving city building. Critical debate about city as machine versus city as living organism obliges us to reflect on cities at a civilizational scale. The machine metaphor is rooted in Western philosophy, science, and industrialization. The founders of modern Western science, including Isaac Newton and René Descartes, helped entrench the clockwork universe in our imaginations. Subsequently, the Industrial Revolution ushered in the age of machines.

There is nothing more emblematic of the city-as-machine metaphor than the automobile. During the post–World War II period, which many now refer to as the geological era of the Anthropocene, we have seen both staggering increases in humanity's impact on the planet and the blossoming of the so-called love affair with the automobile.[18] In light of the effects of ground-level air pollution, global warming, and the shocking carnage of death and injury, the automobile surely stands out as one of the most destructive machines ever devised, and Calgary, like so many cities in North America, is utterly car dependent.

These essays also critically examine the paradoxical social and cultural dimensions of sustainability. In Calgary, as in cities around the world, we see this paradox reflected in the trend toward cosmopolitanism, the celebration of diversity, and the embrace of the cultural and material spectacle of cities. Cities are arguably the planet's greatest co-operative achievement. They are built on social and cultural capital and on attributes like trust, compassion, civility, and conviviality. Calgary has taken halting steps (witness the nasty race-infused and female-candidate-shaming 2017 civic elections) toward a more culturally inclusive city. Cowtown—the hard-driving, abrasive, insular city of the 1970 and 1980s—is fading as we celebrate growing cultural diversity, its valuation represented in the election of an immigrant, Muslim, visible-minority mayor. Beyond the cosmopolitan vibe, people are also drawn to cities for the material culture—the ubiquitous universe of products and experiences that are on display and on offer on a daily basis. The average city dweller is exposed to from four to ten thousand advertisements and product brands every day.[19] Home appliances, communications media, and the automobile are the most evident technologies that highlight the materiality and artificiality of this human enclave.

Governance, how we collectively organize society and make decisions, plays a prominent role in most of the issues discussed in these essays. Good governance—whether in voluntary organizations or the media, the private sector or the public sector—is about transparency, efficiency, effectiveness, meaningful participation, and, perhaps most importantly, fairness. In the essays on governance, we use the concept of the "urban regime" to understand municipal governance, highlighting the activities of a collection of influential actors, the most prominent among them being business leaders, land and real estate developers, and politicians. We examine aspects of governance at provincial, national, and global scales. We would go so far as to say that good governance is the sine qua non of sustainable cities.

Our political silos encourage us to think in a fragmented fashion. City governments have discrete responsibilities, as do other levels of government, but as citizens, our well-being, our practical lives, are not so easily apportioned. Ecologically speaking, we live in a connected world. As global citizens who happen to live in cities, we have an obligation to imagine city life within both nation-states and a planetary ecological system. In fact, it is in our self-interest to do so: as city dwellers, we of course influence global events, but global events also affect our cities. Cutting through the issue of governance is the constant struggle, at all levels, between the laissez-faire doctrine of neoliberal economics and the sustainability agenda's call for assertive collective governance.

What these essays demonstrate is that although we manage cities, for the most part, as bounded human settlements, it is an inescapable reality that the reach and impact of cities is unbounded. In ecological terms, cities and their hinterlands constitute one unified phenomenon. The resource consumption demands of the materialistic, artificial lifestyle that has evolved in cities is best represented by the concept of "ecological footprint." Calgary's footprint, the largest of any city in Canada, is of such a magnitude that we would need five or six planets for all of humanity to live as the average citizen of Calgary does.[20] This is clearly not sustainable.

At this period in history, when cities have become home for more than half of humanity, high-profile urbanites like Mayor Ann Hidalgo of Paris, former mayor Michael Bloomberg of New York, and former mayor Enrique Peñaloso of Bogotá—as well as Calgary's own mayor, Naheed Nenshi—proclaim their belief that cities are the answer to the problems that plague the world—that it is in cities that we nurture the human creativity and innovation through which these problems will be surmounted. Exploring the concept of "ecological footprint" obliges us to entertain the notion that perhaps at the core, the city is not a sustainable form of human habitat.[21] This is something that Lewis Mumford postulated—that the human invention of the city is a tool for the accumulation of power and wealth and that it is parasitic on its surrounding ecological systems.[22]

This is also a question that William Rees, co-creator of the ecological footprint concept, put on the table when he asked whether the term *sustainable city* is an oxymoron.[23] As Rees points out, our cities are wholly dependent upon a land area far greater than their political boundaries. While the popular imagination of the city is as an engine of growth, innovation, and creativity, cities are also parasitic on their hinterlands and those on the margins. The flow-through of energy and resources needed to maintain the incredible metabolism of cities requires a harvest of resources not only from their adjacent geographies but also from places around the globe. As the ecological footprint concept makes clear, a modern, affluent city like Calgary by necessity appropriates land and resources from every corner of the planet.

In recent years, it has become fashionable to project cities as the answer to the problems of the world, especially climate change. In this collection, we emphasize that it is equally important to be vigilant, skeptical, and demanding of evidence for or against that assertion. If cities are in fact the dynamos of the global economy—and more grandly, of the human experience on this planet—then it is the nature of cities that needs to be called to account for the predicament we find ourselves in. We should not shy away from the question of whether humanity can survive the rise of the city. Science, technology, and the economic engine of capitalism drive the city dynamo, but they are also the catalyst of the challenge of the Anthropocene and of a nasty future, according to the warnings of thoughtful individuals. In his 2010 Charles R. Bronfman Lecture in Canadian Studies, elder statesman Ed Broadbent warned of a return to barbarism in the wake of growing inequality and lack of progress on an environmental agenda.[24] In October 2017, the managing director of the International Monetary Fund, Christine Lagarde, spoke of "moving into a dark future" if we do not respond to climate change and inequality.[25] Activist and author Jane Jacobs writes at length of this threat in *Dark Age Ahead*.[26]

We find ourselves in a world that, unfortunately and tragically, vindicates the critical stance toward cities expressed in these pages. In 2013 Calgarians experienced the second-most expensive natural disaster in Canada's history, after the 2016 Fort McMurray fire, with much of our downtown submerged in floodwaters. Since 2017, we have seen the US president incite violence against his fellow citizens and stand in the United Nations threatening North Korea with genocide. We have recently been witness to the most catastrophic and deadly wildfires in history in California and Australia, as those regions continue to endure the worst droughts in thousands of years. In 2018 the Caribbean and southeast coast of the United States lived through three Category 5 hurricanes in less than a month, and Mexico was devastated by three earthquakes over the same period. As a result of all of these events, the cities of Havana, Houston, Mexico City, Oaxaca, Sonoma, San Juan, and Calgary have suffered loss of life and damages from which some of them may never fully recover. During the period in which these essays were written, ongoing violent conflicts have laid waste to cities like Aleppo, Syria, and Sana, Yemen. Urban issues are a microcosm of global issues, from climate change to water to state violence.

Cities—and the human experiment that has imagined them into existence—are at an epochal turning point. The core message of this collection of essays is this: we need a new story, a new narrative of what the human enterprise is about and what our species should aspire to. Clearly, the story that tells of continual economic growth based on exploitation of the planet is leading us to the edge of a precipice. In *Sapiens*, Yuval Noah Harari argues that we dominate the planet because seventy thousand years ago, a cognitive revolution, a rewiring of our brains, gave us the capacity to imagine and create new "fictional realities."[27] According to Harari, the stories that people invent and tell one another are the most powerful forces in the world and are at the root of the ecological and social challenges we face. He is convinced that in this time of crisis, we need completely new stories—a notion that is certainly not new. Ecologian Thomas Berry has written that "the deepest crises experienced by any society are those moments of change when the story becomes inadequate for meeting the survival demands of a present situation."[28] David Korten declares his simple message in the title of his 2015 book, *Change the Story, Change the Future*, echoing Riane Eisler, who argues that to change our realities, we have to change our myths.[29]

Cities can be at the forefront of addressing the critical issues that humanity faces, but this will only happen by design: there is nothing inherent in the nature of a city that ensures it. As Mumford writes, the new story of cities will require "a fresh dedication to the cosmic and ecological processes that enfold all being," thereby ensuring "to the highest degree possible, the illumination of consciousness, the stamp of purpose, the color of love."[30] To achieve this promise, we will have to craft a new story, one in which sustainability matters.

NOTES

1   Richard Florida, *The Rise of the Creative Class: Revisited,* 10th anniversary ed. (Philadelphia: Basic Books, 2014). For a forceful critique of Florida, see Jamie Peck, "Struggling with the Creative Class," *International Journal of Urban and Regional Research* 29, no. 4 (2005): 740–70.

2   See, for example, Peter Newman and Jeff Kenworthy, *The End of Automobile Dependence: How Cities are Moving Beyond Car-Based Planning* (Washington, DC: Island Press, 2015); J. H. Crawford, *Carfree Cities* (Utrecht, Netherlands: International Books, 2002); and Wolfgang Sachs, *For the Love of the Automobile: Looking Back into the History of Our Desires* (Berkeley: University of California Press, 1992).

3   Stephen Wheeler and Timothy Beatley, eds., *The Sustainable Urban Development Reader,* 3rd ed. (New York: Routledge, 2014).

4   Andres Duany, Elizabeth Plater-Zyberk, and Jeff Speck, *Suburban Nation: The Rise of Sprawl and the Decline of the American Dream* (New York: North Point Press, 2010).

5   William McDonough and Michael Braungart, *Cradle to Cradle: Remaking the Way We Make Things* (New York: North Point Press, 2002), and *The Upcycle: Beyond Sustainability—Designing for Abundance* (New York: North Point Press, 2013).

6   Jan Gehl, *Cities for People* (Washington, DC: Island Press, 2010); Jane Jacobs, *The Death and Life of Great American Cities* (New York: Random House, 1961).

7   David Satterthwaite, ed., *The Earthscan Reader in Sustainable Cities* (London: Earthscan, 1999); Wheeler and Beatley, *Sustainable Urban Development Reader.*

8   Tali Hatuka et al., "The Political Premises of Contemporary Urban Concepts: The Global City, the Sustainable City, the Resilient City, the Creative City, and the Smart City," *Planning Theory and Practice* 19, no. 2 (2018): 160–79.

9   German Advisory Council on Global Change, *Humanity on the Move: Unlocking the Transformative Power of Cities* (Berlin: WBGU, 2016); "Sustainable City," *ICLEI (International Council for Local Environmental Initiatives),* accessed 4 September 2020, http://old.iclei.org/index.php?id=35; UN-Habitat, *World Cities Report 2016:*

Urbanization and Development—Emerging Futures (Nairobi, Kenya: United Nations Human Settlement Programme, 2016), https://unhabitat.org/world-cities-report.

10   David Harvey, *Rebel Cities: From the Right to the City to the Urban Revolution* (London: Verso, 2013), and "Possible Urban Worlds," Megacities Lecture 4 (Amersfoort, Netherlands: Twynstra Gudde Management Consultants, 2009), http://www.kas.de/upload/dokumente/megacities/MegacitiesLectur4Worlds.pdf; Mike Davis, *Planet of Slums* (New York: Verso, 2007); Edward Soja, *Thirdspace: Journeys to Los Angeles and Other Real-and-Imagined Places* (Toronto: Wiley-Blackwell, 1996); Doreen Massey, *Space, Place and Gender* (Oxford: Polity Press, 1994).

11   Neil Brenner, David Marcuse, and Margit Mayer, *Cities for People, Not for Profit: Critical Urban Theory and the Right to the City* (New York: Routledge, 2011), 5.

12   World Commission on Environment and Development, *Our Common Future* (Oxford: Oxford University Press, 1987), https://sustainabledevelopment.un.org/content/documents/5987our-common-future.pdf; UN Framework Convention on Climate Change, *The Kyoto Protocol* (Geneva: United Nations, December 1997), https://unfccc.int/kyoto_protocol; City of Calgary, *Municipal Development Plan* (Calgary: City of Calgary, 2009), https://www.calgary.ca/pda/pd/municipal-development-plan/municipal-development-plan-mdp.html.

13   Richard Florida, *The New Urban Crisis: How Our Cities Are Increasing Inequality, Deepening Segregation, and Failing the Middle Class—And What We Can Do about It* (New York: Basic Books, 2017).

14   Paul Krugman, *End This Depression Now* (New York: W. W. Norton, 2012); Thomas Piketty, *Capital in the Twenty-First Century*, trans. Arthur Goldhammer (Cambridge, MA: Belknap, 2014).

15   Naomi Klein, *This Changes Everything: Capitalism and the Climate* (New York: Simon and Schuster, 2014).

16   Peter Suderman, "Blade Runner's 2019 Los Angeles Helped Define the American City of the Future," *Vox*, 2 October 2017, https://www.vox.com/culture/2017/10/2/16375126/blade-runner-future-city-ridley-scott.

17   Lewis Mumford, *The City in History: Its Origins, Its Transformations, Its Prospects* (New York: Harvest Books, 1968).

18   For a discussion of the Anthropocene, see Robinson Meyer, "The Cataclysmic Break That (Maybe) Occurred in 1950," *The Atlantic*, 16 April 2019, https://www.theatlantic.com/science/archive/2019/04/great-debate-over-when-anthropocene-started/587194/.

19   "How Many Ads Do You See Each Day?" *Gradschools.com*, 2020, https://www.gradschools.com/programs/marketing-advertising/how-many-ads-do-you-see-each-day.

20   Noel Keough, Bob Morrison, and Celia Lee, *State of Our City 2020: An Urgent Call for a Just Transition* (Calgary: Sustainable Calgary Society, 2020), 7, http://www.sustainablecalgary.org/publications.

21   "Ecological Footprint," *Global Footprint Network: Advancing the Science of Sustainability*, 2003–20, https://www.footprintnetwork.org/our-work/ecological-footprint/.

22   Mumford, *City in History.*

23   William Rees, "Is 'Sustainable City' an Oxymoron?" *Local Environment* 2, no. 3 (1997): 303–10.

24   Ed Broadbent, "Equality or Barbarism?" Charles R. Bronfman Lecture, University of Ottawa, 14 October 2010, *Toronto Star*, 16 October 2010, https://www.thestar.com/opinion/editorials/2010/10/16/equality_or_barbarism.html.

25   Agence France-Presse, "'We Will Be Toasted, Roasted and Grilled': IMF Chief Sounds Climate Change Warning," *The Guardian*, 25 October 2017, https://www.theguardian.com/environment/2017/oct/25/we-will-be-toasted-roasted-and-grilled-imf-chief-sounds-climate-change-warning.

26   Jane Jacobs, *Dark Age Ahead* (Toronto: Vintage Canada, 2005).

27   Yuval Noah Harari, *Sapiens: A Brief History of Humankind* (Oxford: Signal Books, 2016).

28   Thomas Berry, *The Dream of the Earth* (San Francisco: Sierra Club Books, 1990), xi.

29   David C. Korten, *Change the Story, Change the Future: A Living Economy for a Living Earth* (Oakland, CA: Berrett-Koehler, 2015); Riane Eisler, *The Chalice and the Blade: Our History, Our Future* (San Francisco: Harper, 1988).

30   Mumford, *City in History*, 575–76.

Works Cited

Agence France-Presse. "'We Will Be Toasted, Roasted and Grilled': IMF Chief Sounds Climate Change Warning." *The Guardian*, 25 October 2017. https://www.theguardian.com/environment/2017/oct/25/we-will-be-toasted-roasted-and-grilled-imf-chief-sounds-climate-change-warning.

Berry, Thomas. *The Dream of the Earth*. San Francisco: Sierra Club Books, 1990.

Brenner, Neil, David Marcuse, and Margit Mayer. *Cities for People, Not for Profit: Critical Urban Theory and the Right to the City*. New York: Routledge, 2011.

Broadbent, Ed. "Equality or Barbarism?" Charles R. Bronfman Lecture, University of Ottawa, 14 October 2010. *Toronto Star*, 16 October 2010. https://www.thestar.com/opinion/editorials/2010/10/16/equality_or_barbarism.html.

City of Calgary. *Municipal Development Plan*. Calgary: City of Calgary, 2009. https://www.calgary.ca/pda/pd/municipal-development-plan/municipal-development-plan-mdp.html.

Crawford, J. H. *Carfree Cities*. Utrecht, Netherlands: International Books, 2002.

Davis, Mike. *Planet of Slums*. New York: Verso, 2007.

Duany, Andres, Elizabeth Plater-Zyberk, and Jeff Speck. *Suburban Nation: The Rise of Sprawl and the Decline of the American Dream*. New York: North Point Press, 2010.

"Ecological Footprint." *Global Footprint Network: Advancing the Science of Sustainability*, 2003–20. https://www.footprintnetwork.org/our-work/ecological-footprint/.

Eisler, Riane. *The Chalice and the Blade: Our History, Our Future*. San Francisco: Harper, 1988.

Florida, Richard. *The New Urban Crisis: How Our Cities Are Increasing Inequality, Deepening Segregation, and Failing the Middle Class—And What We Can Do about It*. New York: Basic Books, 2017.

———. *The Rise of the Creative Class: Revisited*. 10th anniversary ed. Philadelphia: Basic Books, 2014.

Gehl, Jan. *Cities for People*. Washington, DC: Island Press, 2010.

German Advisory Council on Global Change. *Humanity on the Move: Unlocking the Transformative Power of Cities*. Berlin: WBGU, 2016.

Harari, Yuval Noah. *Sapiens: A Brief History of Humankind*. Oxford: Signal Books, 2016.

Harvey, David. "Possible Urban Worlds." Megacities Lecture 4. Amersfoort, Netherlands: Twynstra Gudde Management Consultants, 2009. https://www.kas.de/c/document_library/get_file?uuid=1463ff93-1eab-8877-edfc-ccef8540c262&groupId=252038.

———. *Rebel Cities: From the Right to the City to the Urban Revolution*. London: Verso, 2013.

Hatuka, Tali, Issachar Rosen-Zvi, Michael Birnhack, Eran Toch, and Hadas Zur. "The Political Premises of Contemporary Urban Concepts: The Global City, the Sustainable City, the Resilient City, the Creative City, and the Smart City." *Planning Theory and Practice* 19, no. 2 (2018): 160–79.

"How Many Ads Do You See Each Day?" *Gradschools.com*, 2020. https://www.gradschools.com/programs/marketing-advertising/how-many-ads-do-you-see-each-day.

Jacobs, Jane. *Dark Age Ahead*. Toronto: Vintage Canada, 2005.

———. *The Death and Life of Great American Cities*. New York: Random House, 1961.

Keough, Noel, Bob Morrison, and Celia Lee. *State of Our City 2020: An Urgent Call for a Just Transition*. Calgary: Sustainable Calgary Society, 2020. http://www.sustainablecalgary.org/publications.

Klein, Naomi. *This Changes Everything: Capitalism and the Climate*. New York: Simon and Schuster, 2014.

Korten, David C. *Change the Story, Change the Future: A Living Economy for a Living Earth*. Oakland, CA: Berrett-Koehler, 2015.

Krugman, Paul. *End This Depression Now*. New York: W. W. Norton, 2012.

Massey, Doreen. *Space, Place and Gender*. Oxford: Polity Press, 1994.

McDonough, William, and Michael Braungart. *Cradle to Cradle: Remaking the Way We Make Things*. New York: North Point Press, 2002.

———. *The Upcycle: Beyond Sustainability—Designing for Abundance*. New York: North Point Press, 2013.

Meyer, Robinson. "The Cataclysmic Break That (Maybe) Occurred in 1950." *The Atlantic*, 16 April 2019. https://www.theatlantic.com/science/archive/2019/04/great-debate-over-when-anthropocene-started/587194/.

Mumford, Lewis. *The City in History: Its Origins, Its Transformations, Its Prospects*. New York: Harvest Books, 1968.

Newman, Peter, and Jeff Kenworthy. *The End of Automobile Dependence: How Cities are Moving Beyond Car-Based Planning*. Washington, DC: Island Press, 2015.

Peck, Jamie. "Struggling with the Creative Class." *International Journal of Urban and Regional Research* 29, no. 4 (2005): 740–70.

Piketty, Thomas. *Capital in the Twenty-First Century*. Translated by Arthur Goldhammer. Cambridge, MA: Belknap, 2014.

Rees, William. "Is 'Sustainable City' an Oxymoron?" *Local Environment* 2, no. 3 (1997): 303–10.

Sachs, Wolfgang. *For the Love of the Automobile: Looking Back into the History of Our Desires*. Berkeley: University of California Press, 1992.

Satterthwaite, David, ed. *The Earthscan Reader in Sustainable Cities*. London: Earthscan, 1999.

Soja, Edward. *Thirdspace: Journeys to Los Angeles and Other Real-and-Imagined Places*. Toronto: Wiley-Blackwell, 1996.

Suderman, Peter. "Blade Runner's 2019 Los Angeles Helped Define the American City of the Future." *Vox*, 2 October 2017. https://www.vox.com/culture/2017/10/2/16375126/blade-runner-future-city-ridley-scott.

"Sustainable City." *ICLEI (International Council for Local Environmental Initiatives)*. Accessed 4 September 2020. http://old.iclei.org/index.php?id=35.

UN Framework Convention on Climate Change. *The Kyoto Protocol*. Geneva: United Nations, December 1997. https://unfccc.int/kyoto_protocol.

UN-Habitat. *World Cities Report 2016: Urbanization and Development—Emerging Futures*. Nairobi, Kenya: United Nations Human Settlement Programme, 2016. https://unhabitat.org/world-cities-report.

Wheeler, Stephen M., and Timothy Beatley, eds. *The Sustainable Urban Development Reader*. 3rd ed. New York: Routledge, 2014.

World Commission on Environment and Development. *Our Common Future*. Oxford: Oxford University Press, 1987. https://sustainabledevelopment.un.org/content/documents/5987our-common-future.pdf.

The Origins and Evolution of Sustainable Development

Over the past thirty years, sustainable development, more than any other concept (save neoliberalism), has shaped deliberations over the future of our planet, nation-states, and communities. The 1987 Brundtland Report attempted a grand synthesis—sustainable development as a compromise, a bricolage patched together to obtain enough political capital to move forward on the important agenda of alleviating poverty and environmental destruction while staying within the context of a capitalist world system.[1] Clearly, the Brundtland compromise is not working.

The concept of sustainable development emerged into public consciousness in 1992, but that moment in Rio de Janeiro was the result of a long and winding historical process. To understand the sustainability debates in Calgary, it is important to have at least a rudimentary understanding of that history. Our review of the origins and evolution of sustainable development follows four lines of inquiry. First, we summarize the Brundtland Report's prescription for sustainable development. Second, we explore the problematic nature of the term's association with sustained-yield natural resource management and with the international development paradigm. Third, we sketch the main tenets of the dominant sustainable development theory (ecological modernization) and critique what Aidan Davison calls its techno-systemic orientation.[2] We close with a sketch of the multilateral attempts to operationalize the Brundtland Report's call for sustainable development over the past thirty years, from Agenda 21 to the Millennium Development Goals and the current campaign for the UN Sustainable Development Goals, and argue that these fall short of the notion of strong sustainability.

North/South: The Great Divide

During preparations for and staging of the Earth Summit in Rio de Janeiro in 1992, the divide between the North and the South became all too apparent. On the one hand, the majority of influential governments from the North, along with the multinational economic power brokers (under the banner of the World Business Council for Sustainable Development), argued for market-oriented solutions to achieve a sustainable future. The problem of environmental degradation in the South, they argued, was a result of the South's overpopulation and lack of technology: the solution was to curb population growth, undertake a massive transfer of technology from the North to the South, and further integrate developing countries into the global capitalist market economy.

In contrast, the goal of many Southern governments and of much of the international NGO community was to put the role of consumption in the North front and centre on the Rio agenda. Their position was that poverty alleviation was a priority and was the number one reason to protect the environment, and that this was only possible by curtailing the material consumption of developed countries. Integral to the prescription for change was the alleviation of Third World debt and a more equitable distribution of power and resources in the world. They called for a redefinition of "development," serious attention to the scourge of militarization, the recognition that capitalism and communism do not exhaust the possible choices of political system, and the devolution of power to the community level.[3]

Something for Everyone in Brundtland's Sustainable Development

The Brundtland Report's definition of sustainable development and its general prescription for change remain the touchstone of sustainable development discourse: "meeting the needs of the present without compromising the ability of future generations to meet their own needs."[4] Four key principles are outlined in the report: (1) the overriding priority to address the needs of the poor, (2) limits to growth, (3) equity within and between generations, and (4) people's participation in decisions affecting their own lives.

The report states explicitly that it is "futile to attempt to deal with environmental problems without a broader perspective that encompasses the factors underlying world poverty and international inequality" and that in fact "inequality is the planet's main 'environmental' problem" as well as "its main 'development' problem."[5] Tensions arise, however, as one delves deeper into the report's proposed solutions.

The report explicitly recognizes the inequities in the international system: for example, in 1980–82, the 26 percent of the world's population living in the North were using 80 percent of the world's energy.[6] However, it then goes on to suggest that this problem can be alleviated by continued growth in the North and the redistribution of a mere 25 percent of the incremental growth of the North to the South.[7] Despite its initial recognition of limits to growth, the report states that, thanks to the wonders of human ingenuity embodied in technological advancement, "growth has no set limits in terms of population or resource use beyond which lies ecological disaster."[8]

Sustaining the Unsustainable

Sustainable development has been shackled, from its inception, by its indebtedness to sustained-yield resource management and the international development paradigm. The concept of "maximum sustained yield" (MSY) evolved out of a four hundred–year tradition of European forestry, with natural forests long a thing of the past.[9] MSY is a resource management approach crafted to squeeze the maximum possible production from forest (and later, ocean) ecosystems based on a deeply inadequate understanding of those ecosystems. Lester Brown, of the World Watch Institute, borrowing from the concept of MSY, first coined the term *sustainable development* in the late 1970s. The term was elaborated in *The World Conservation Strategy,* published in 1980, and placed firmly on the global agenda with the Brundtland Report.[10]

New and Improved Development?

Key to understanding the tensions around the concept of sustainable development is the critique of the second word in the term. Wolfgang Sachs argues that development practitioners have, since the beginning of the post–World War II period, mistakenly set out to promote the American way of life in large part as an antidote to the feared postwar influence of the Soviet Union in what was referred to as the Third World.[11] In his inaugural address in 1949, US president Harry Truman heralded the development era. "Greater production is the key to prosperity and peace," he said. "The United States is pre-eminent among nations in the development of industrial and scientific techniques" and thus duty-bound to "relieve the suffering" of the people of the "underdeveloped areas."[12]

Since Truman's address, "international development" has been the rallying cry behind massive economic, social, and political changes that have taken place in the so-called Third World. It has been a pervasive force in these communities for more than seventy-five years. A vast body of knowledge and hundreds of institutions, including dozens of United Nations agencies, have been created to oversee international development—its definition, evolution, and operationalization. Proponents of international development argue that the Bretton Woods institutions (the World Bank, the International Monetary Fund, and the World Trade Organization) were developed to mediate capitalism's impacts and ease the development transition of the South.[13] Others disagree. Anti-colonialists, post-colonialists, and post-development theorists pushed back against this benign characterization of the development enterprise.[14] Claude Alvarez captures the essence of this pushback in *Science, Development and Violence*, arguing that "the idea of 'development' has been closely identified with those of progress, modernity and emancipation," but that in fact it "is a label for plunder and violence."[15] In *Staying Alive: Women, Ecology and Development*, Vandana Shiva, an Indian environmental and human rights activist, espouses a critique of development strongly influenced by the Right Livelihood Award–winning Chipko movement of tribal women in India. She defines the links among the mistreatment of women by men, the colonized by the colonizers, and nature by humanity. Drawing parallels with the eighteenth-century enclosures in Britain, Shiva concludes that elite consensus on sustainable development is a rationale to accelerate the enclosure of the global commons.[16]

Co-opting the Environment Movement

According to Wolfgang Sachs, since the early 1970s, the environmental problem has been increasingly framed within the development discourse as an economically, socially, and culturally undifferentiated human impact on the biosphere. This discourse has marginalized the grassroots environmental movement's early critique of the role of corporate power and neocolonialist states, emphasizing instead the technical fix of global environmental management designed to maintain the current economic system.[17]

In Aidan Davison's characterization, "the first wave of environmental concern was deeply skeptical of the modernist model of progress and called for far-reaching spiritual, moral, and economic change in technological societies." This first wave, catalyzed by the publication in 1962 of Rachel Carson's *Silent Spring*, held an "antigrowth position with respect to the orthodoxy of unlimited economic growth and technological globalization."[18] The second wave of environmental concern, roughly from the first Earth Day in 1970 to the present, is referred to by John Dryzek as the "Promethean response."[19] By stealing fire from Zeus, the Greek god Prometheus increased the human capacity to manipulate nonhuman nature. The second wave's Promethean response, then, is based on unlimited confidence in the human ability to solve any problem through technology. It is characterized by regulatory initiatives to stabilize the global environment, wrest the agenda from activist first-wave environmentalists, and assure the citizenry that all is in good hands.[20] Its strategy is to ameliorate the direct effects of environmental degradation in the First World, thereby assuring First World citizens that the issue is being dealt with. Accordingly, as Davison notes, "since the 1980s, ecological crisis has been increasingly interpreted as a threat to human survival that can only be countered by redesigning nature."[21]

The publication of the December 1989 issue of *Scientific American* was a marquee event in this shift described by Sachs, Davison, and Dryzek. The issue, entitled "Managing Planet Earth," tackled everything from food scarcity to revolutions in materials science, side by side with full-page ads by corporations such as Ford, Shell Oil, and Union Carbide proclaiming their allegiance to sustainable development.[22]

The State of the Art of Sustainable Development

In *Technology and the Contested Meanings of Sustainability*, Davison argues that efforts to rehabilitate or recapture the concept of sustainable development are "ultimately futile" because, in his estimation, sustainable development is "conceptually incoherent and politically compromised."[23] This analysis accords with that of other writers, including Michael Redclift, who argues that the term *sustainable development* is an oxymoron, since the growth-oriented nature of development cannot be sustained on a finite planet.[24]

William Rees, a leading thinker on sustainable development, points to the something-for-everyone, schizophrenic nature of the Brundtland Report, but he argues for redefinition rather than abandonment of the concept.[25] He laments the fact that to date, the sustainable development–inspired prescription for change is more of what he calls the "expansionist paradigm": expanded free trade, deregulation, privatization, technology transfer, and an increased role for transnational corporations. This prescription is silent on the need to look at the underlying social and political problems (whose symptoms are environmental problems), such as inequity, unfair distribution, and overconsumption. Rees predicts that the biophysical reality will sooner or later force "ecological limits" onto the planning landscape. He reminds us that all production is consumption in a world governed by the second law of thermodynamics. He makes a useful distinction between strong and weak sustainability, with the latter, synonymous with the expansionist paradigm, assuming infinite substitutability of pieces of nature with human technology and the former acknowledging some capacity for technological substitution but rejecting the idea of technology's infinite capability. Brundtland's compromise has resulted in a weak and expansionist theory of sustainability still wedded to the development paradigm.

Ecological Modernization: An Emperor in Old Clothes

It is widely agreed that ecological modernization (EM), sometimes referred to as "green capitalism," has become the dominant theoretical framework of sustainable development. Arthur Mol and Eric Sonnenfeld, champions of EM, describe it as a theory of how industrial societies deal with environmental crisis.[26] Proponents of EM claim that it is a pragmatic answer to the sustainable development problematic. Together with Gert Spaargaren, Mol and Sonnenfeld identify three distinct phases of EM's development. It emerged in Germany, with a heavy emphasis on industrial technological innovation and modernization, an antagonism to bureacracy, a steadfast belief in markets, and a systems theory orientation with a limited notion of human agency. In the 1990s, EM evolved to a more balanced view of the roles of the market and state intervention and gave more attention to institutional and cultural dynamics. The third, contemporary stage has been labelled "reflexive ecological modernization" (REM).[27] Mol and his fellow travellers argue that REM has successfully responded to the critiques of EM by incorporating social learning, cultural politics, and governance into its theoretical frame.[28]

Aidan Davison offers a radical critique of EM, which he sees as a manifestation of "technological society." He argues that "*technological society* names a peculiar political and moral condition in which the greatest common good is understood as the greatest possible productivity of technosystems."[29] In Davison's view, EM "is founded on the pursuit of ecoefficiency," which is "encouraged by a technological optimism."[30] He writes that "the triumph of ecomodernism" has been to marginalize informed democratic debate and deliberation about the future we want and the role we want technology to play. Instead of critical examination of the good and the bad of modern society, it offers an "ahistorical agenda for engineering the future."[31] Davison laments the Brundtland Commission's role in all of this, which has been to "cement into the foundations of sustainable development policy the conviction that technology is the neutral instrument of social institutions."[32]

Fast forward almost twenty years, and Davison's earth-as-device analysis has advanced with a vengeance. We now entertain serious discussion of the eclipse of the human species by machines—a scenario popularized by Yuval Noah Harari in *Homo Deus*.[33] In *Radical Technologies: The Design of Everyday Life*, Adam Greenfield critically assesses the promise and the peril of fast-emerging technological change, from social media to blockchain, artificial intelligence, virtual reality, and robotization of the workplace, warning of the existential danger it poses for humanity.[34]

Twenty-five years after its emergence, ecological modernization remains the dominant sustainable development policy discourse. In 2002 world leaders met for Earth Summit II in Johannesburg to assess progress, and again in 2012 for Rio+20. In 2000 the UN Millennium Development Goals were launched to focus international efforts on the needs of the world's poorest, followed by the UN Sustainable Development Goals (SDGs), with the UN calling on all nations to focus on these seventeen goals.[35]

In July 2019 the first report on the SDGs restated trends that had already been acknowledged at Earth Summit II and Rio+20. "The world remains on a trajectory of increasing inequality," reported the UN Department of Economic and Social Affairs, "and it is facing armed conflicts, humanitarian and environmental crises, as well as economic, financial, and climate challenges. We, therefore, urgently need a surge in financing, investments and technological innovation."[36]

The report itself urged immediate action: "It is abundantly clear that a much deeper, faster and more ambitious response is needed to unleash the social and economic transformation needed to achieve our 2030 goals."[37] CO_2 levels continue to rise, biodiversity is declining, inequality is growing, prospects for achieving the SDGs are fading, and liberal democracy is faltering amidst the rise of dangerous nationalist politics. Yet in *The Age of Sustainable Development*, Jeffrey Sachs, perhaps the most prominent proponent of sustainable development and the SDGs, reaffirms the ecological modernist orientation of mainstream sustainable development practice communicated in the Brundtland Report, Agenda 21, Earth Summit II, Rio+20, and the SDGs. The sustainable development path, he writes, "aims for economic growth but also for social inclusion and environmental sustainability."[38]

Cities, which is where most of us live, and the processes of urbanization are humanity's most visible manifestation of the ecological modernization narrative. It is not hard to make the argument that urban policy is the poster child of ecological modernization. City governments remain preoccupied by competition, growth, and investment within the confines of the capitalist economic system. Technology is firmly entrenched at the vanguard of the ascendant Smart Cities agenda. Politicians who question the unfettered infiltration of technology into our lives and the logic of economic growth or who propose alternatives to capitalism face poor prospects indeed. We have our work cut out for us.[39]

NOTES

1   World Commission on Environment and Development (WCED), *Our Common Future* (Oxford: Oxford University Press, 1987), https://sustainabledevelopment.un.org/content/documents/5987our-common-future.pdf.

2   Aidan Davison, *Technology and the Contested Meanings of Sustainability* (Albany, NY: SUNY Press, 2001), 97.

3   My own experience in the preparations for the Rio Earth Summit as part of the Canadian Council for International Cooperation and Canadian Environment Network's Sustainable Development Working Group is consistent with this view of the process. Two members of that Working Group were Aaron Schneider and Sangit Roy, authors of *Policy from the People: A North-South NGO Policy Dialogue* (Ottawa: Canadian Council for International Cooperation, 1992).

4   WCED, *Our Common Future*, 8.

5   WCED, *Our Common Future*, 3, 6.

6   WCED, *Our Common Future*, 33, Table 1.2.

7   WCED, *Our Common Future*, 50.

8   WCED, *Our Common Future*, 45.

9   Jeremy Caradonna, *Sustainability: A History* (Oxford: Oxford University Press, 2014); Ulrich Grober, *Sustainability: A Cultural History,* trans. Ray Cunningham (Cambridge, UK: UIT Cambridge, 2013).

10 International Union for the Conservation of Nature and Natural Resources, World Wildlife Fund, and United Nations Environment Program, *The World Conservation Strategy: Living Resource Conservation for Sustainable Development* (Gland, Switzerland: IUCN, 1980).

11 Wolfgang Sachs, *The Development Dictionary: A Guide to Knowledge as Power* (London: Zed Books, 2010).

12 Harry S. Truman, "Inaugural Address of Harry S. Truman," 20 January 1949, *The Avalon Project: Documents in Law, History and Diplomacy,* Yale Law School, Lillian Goldman Law Library, 2008, https://avalon.law.yale.edu/20th_century/truman.asp.

13 John Cavanagh, Daphne Wysham, and Marcos Arruda, eds., *Beyond Bretton Woods: Alternatives to the Global Economic Order* (Boulder, CO: Pluto Press, 1994).

14 Anti-colonialists: Frantz Fanon, *The Wretched of the Earth*, trans. Richard Philcox (New York: Grove Press, 1963); Kwame Nkrumah, *Neo-Colonialism: The Last Stage of Imperialism* (London: Thomas Nelson, 1965); Ernesto Che Guevara, *The Motorcycle Diaries: A Journey around South America* (London: Verso, 1995). Post-

colonialists: Edward Said, *Orientalism* (London: Penguin Books, 1985); Robert Young, *Postcolonialism: A Very Short Introduction* (Oxford: Oxford University Press, 2003). Post-development theorists: Vandana Shiva, *Staying Alive: Women, Ecology and Development* (New York: South End Press, 2010); Claude Alvarez, *Science, Development and Violence: The Revolt against Modernity* (Oxford: University of Oxford Press, 1992); Wolfgang Sachs, *Planet Dialectics: Explorations in Environment and Development* (Toronto: Zed Books, 2000); Arturo Escobar, *Encountering Development: The Making and Unmaking of the Third World* (Princeton, NJ: Princeton University Press, 1995); David C. Korten, *The Post-Corporate World: Life after Capitalism* (West Hartford, CT: Kumerian Press and Berrett-Koehler, 1997).

15   Alvarez, *Science, Development and Violence*, vii, 1.

16   Shiva, *Staying Alive*. For more on this issue of commons enclosure, see Maria Mies, *The Subsistence Perspective: Beyond the Global Economy* (New York: Zed Books, 2000), and Elinor Ostrom, *Governing the Commons: The Evolution of Institutions for Collective Action* (Cambridge: Cambridge University Press, 2015).

17   Sachs, *Development Dictionary*.

18   Davison, *Technology and the Contested Meanings of Sustainability*, 13–14.

19   John Dryzek, "Growth Unlimited: The Promethean Response," in *The Politics of the Earth: Environmental Discourses* (Oxford: Oxford University Press, 2013), 52–72.

20   This latter sentiment was certainly my experience in meetings in Ottawa in the fall of 1992, organized by Environment Canada to brief non-governmental organizations on the outcomes and aftermath of the Earth Summit in Rio de Janeiro.

21   Davison, *Technology and the Contested Meanings of Sustainability*, 206.

22   "Managing Planet Earth," *Scientific American*, September 1989.

23   Davison, *Technology and the Contested Meanings of Sustainability*, 41.

24   Michael Redclift, *Sustainable Development: Exploring the Contradictions* (London: Routledge, 1987).

25   For some of William Rees's most insightful writing, see "The Ecology of Sustainable Development," *Ecologist* 20, no. 1 (1990): 18–23; "Is 'Sustainable City' an Oxymoron?" *Local Environment* 2, no. 3 (1997): 303–10; and "What's Blocking Sustainability: Human Nature, Cognition and Denial," *Sustainability: Science, Practice and Policy* 6, no. 2 (2010): 13–25.

26   Arthur P. J. Mol and David A. Sonnenfeld, "Ecological Modernization and the Global Economy," *Global Environmental Politics* 2, no. 2 (2002): 92–115.

27   Arthur P. J. Mol, David A. Sonnenfeld, and Gert Spaargaren, *The Ecological Modernization Reader: Environmental Reform in Theory and Practice* (London: Routledge, 2009).

28   For one critique of EM, see Ulrich Beck, Anthony Giddens, and Steve Lash, *Reflexive Modernization: Politics, Tradition and Aesthetics in the Modern Social Order* (Chicago: University of Chicago Press, 1995).

29   Davison, *Technology and the Contested Meanings of Sustainability*, 93.

30 Davison, *Technology and the Contested Meanings of Sustainability*, 5.

31 Davison, *Technology and the Contested Meanings of Sustainability*, 62.

32 Davison, *Technology and the Contested Meanings of Sustainability*, 24.

33 Yuval Noah Harari, *Homo Deus: A Brief History of Tomorrow* (Oxford: Signal Books, 2017).

34 Adam Greenfield, *Radical Technologies: The Design of Everyday Life* (New York: Verso, 2017).

35 "We Can End Poverty: Millennium Development Goals and Beyond 2015," *United Nations*, accessed 2 September 2020, https://www.un.org/millenniumgoals/; "Sustainable Development Goals," *United Nations*, accessed 2 September 2020, https://sustainabledevelopment.un.org/?menu=1300.

36 "Staying on Track to Realize the Sustainable Development Goals," *United Nations: Department of Economic and Social Affairs*, 3 January 2019, https://www.un.org/development/desa/en/news/sustainable/sustainable-development-goals.html.

37 United Nations, *The Sustainable Development Goals Report 2019* (New York: United Nations, 2019), 2, https://unstats.un.org/sdgs/report/2019/The-Sustainable-Development-Goals-Report-2019.pdf.

38 Jeffrey D. Sachs, *The Age of Sustainable Development* (New York: Columbia University Press, 2017), 43.

39 For further critique of the traces of ecological modernization in cities, see Julian Agyeman, *Introducing Just Sustainabilities: Policy, Planning and Practice* (London: Zed Books, 2013), and Samuel Mössner, Tim Freytag, and Byron Miller, "Editorial: Cities and the Politics of Urban Sustainability," *Die Erde: Journal of the Geographical Society of Berlin* 48, no. 4 (2017): 195–96.

Works Cited

Agyeman, Julian. *Introducing Just Sustainabilities: Policy, Planning and Practice*. London: Zed Books, 2013.

Alvarez, Claude. *Science, Development and Violence: The Revolt against Modernity*. Oxford: University of Oxford Press, 1992.

Beck, Ulrich, Anthony Giddens, and Steve Lash. *Reflexive Modernization: Politics, Tradition and Aesthetics in the Modern Social Order*. Chicago: University of Chicago Press, 1995.

Caradonna, Jeremy. *Sustainability: A History*. Oxford: Oxford University Press, 2014.

Cavanagh, John, Daphne Wysham, and Marcos Arruda, eds. *Beyond Bretton Woods: Alternatives to the Global Economic Order*. Boulder, CO: Pluto Press, 1994.

Davison, Aidan. *Technology and the Contested Meanings of Sustainability*. Albany: SUNY Press, 2001.

Dryzek, John. "Growth Unlimited: The Promethean Response." In *The Politics of the Earth: Environmental Discourses*, 52–72. Oxford: Oxford University Press, 2013.

Escobar, Arturo. *Encountering Development: The Making and Unmaking of the Third World*. Princeton, NJ: Princeton University Press, 1995.

Fanon, Frantz. *The Wretched of the Earth*. Translated by Richard Philcox. New York: Grove Press, 1963.

Greenfield, Adam. *Radical Technologies: The Design of Everyday Life*. New York: Verso, 2017.

Grober, Ulrich. *Sustainability: A Cultural History*. Translated by Ray Cunningham. Cambridge, UK: UIT Cambridge, 2013.

Guevara, Ernesto Che. *The Motorcycle Diaries: A Journey around South America*. London: Verso, 1995.

Harari, Yuval Noah. *Homo Deus: A Brief History of Tomorrow*. Oxford: Signal Books, 2017.

International Union for the Conservation of Nature and Natural Resources, World Wildlife Fund, and UN Environment Program. *The World Conservation Strategy: Living Resource Conservation for Sustainable Development*. Gland, Switzerland: IUCN, 1980.

Korten, David C. *The Post-Corporate World: Life after Capitalism*. West Hartford, CT: Kumerian Press and Berrett-Koehler, 1997.

"Managing Planet Earth." *Scientific American*, September 1989.

Mies, Maria. *The Subsistence Perspective: Beyond the Global Economy*. New York: Zed Books, 2000.

Mol, Arthur P. J., and David A. Sonnenfeld. "Ecological Modernization and the Global Economy." *Global Environmental Politics* 2, no. 2 (2002): 92–115.

Mol, Arthur P. J., David A. Sonnenfeld, and Gert Spaargaren. *The Ecological Modernization Reader: Environmental Reform in Theory and Practice*. London: Routledge, 2009.

Mössner, Samuel, Tim Freytag, and Byron Miller. "Editorial: Cities and the Politics of Urban Sustainability." *Die Erde: Journal of the Geographical Society of Berlin* 48, no. 4 (2017): 195–96.

Nkrumah, Kwame. *Neo-Colonialism: The Last Stage of Imperialism*. London: Thomas Nelson, 1965.

Ostrom, Elinor. *Governing the Commons: The Evolution of Institutions for Collective Action*. Cambridge: Cambridge University Press, 2015.

Redclift, Michael. *Sustainable Development: Exploring the Contradictions*. London: Routledge, 1987.

Rees, William. "The Ecology of Sustainable Development." *Ecologist* 20, no. 1 (1990): 18–23.

———. "Is 'Sustainable City' an Oxymoron?" *Local Environment* 2, no. 3 (1997): 303–10.

———. "What's Blocking Sustainability? Human Nature, Cognition and Denial." *Sustainability: Science, Practice and Policy* 6, no. 2 (2010): 13–25.

Sachs, Jeffrey D. *The Age of Sustainable Development.* New York: Columbia University Press, 2017.

Sachs, Wolfgang. *The Development Dictionary: A Guide to Knowledge as Power.* London: Zed Books, 2010.

———. *Planet Dialectics: Explorations in Environment and Development.* Toronto: Zed Books, 2000.

Said, Edward. *Orientalism.* London: Penguin Books, 1985.

Schneider, Aaron, and Sangit Roy. *Policy from the People: A North-South NGO Policy Dialogue.* Ottawa: Canadian Council for International Cooperation, 1992.

Shiva, Vandana. *Staying Alive: Women, Ecology and Development.* New York: South End Press, 2010.

"Staying on Track to Realize the Sustainable Development Goals." *United Nations: Department of Economic and Social Affairs,* 3 January 2019. https://www.un.org/development/desa/en/news/sustainable/sustainable-development-goals.html.

"Sustainable Development Goals." *United Nations.* Accessed 2 September 2020. https://sustainabledevelopment.un.org/?menu=1300.

Truman, Harry S. "Inaugural Address of Harry S. Truman." 20 January 1949. *The Avalon Project: Documents in Law, History and Diplomacy.* Yale Law School, Lillian Goldman Law Library, 2008. https://avalon.law.yale.edu/20th_century/truman.asp.

United Nations. *The Sustainable Development Goals Report 2019.* New York: United Nations, 2019. https://unstats.un.org/sdgs/report/2019/The-Sustainable-Development-Goals-Report-2019.pdf.

"We Can End Poverty: Millennium Development Goals and Beyond 2015." *United Nations.* Accessed 2 September 2020. https://www.un.org/millenniumgoals/.

World Commission on Environment and Development. *Our Common Future.* Oxford: Oxford University Press, 1987. https://sustainabledevelopment.un.org/content/documents/5987our-common-future.pdf.

Young, Robert. *Postcolonialism: A Very Short Introduction.* Oxford: Oxford University Press, 2003.

3

Colonization and Resource Extraction on the Canadian Frontier

The first eight thousand years of human settlement in Calgary is an Indigenous story. The land is known as *Moh'kinsstis* ('elbow'), the Blackfoot word used to describe the landscape at the confluence of what we now call the Bow and Elbow rivers. In oral history, Niitsitapi (the Blackfoot people) had "interwoven and integrated themselves with the land, environment, and other living beings in the territory given to them by Is tsi pa ta piyopi," the Creator or Source of Life.[1] The place we call Calgary is within the traditional territories of the Siksikaitsitapi (Blackfoot Confederacy), including the Siksika, Kainai, and Piikani; the Tsuut'ina, the Îyâxe Nakoda Nations, and the Métis Nation.

The story of the last 150 years in Alberta is one of European expansion, which meant the clearances of First Nations to reserves to make way for frontier settlement, agriculture, and oil. To support western expansion, the British Crown established eleven numbered treaties across Canada, Treaty 7 being the one in which the city of Calgary is located; each of these treaties involved relocation of First Nations to reserve lands. According to Treaty 7 Elders, "for the Crown, the most important aspect of the written treaty was the 'surrender' of land. However, all First Nations understand and maintain that the true meaning and intent of the process and lasting treaty relationships that followed were about 'sharing' the land and peaceful co-existence as separate nations" and that "the true spirit and intent of the Proclamations has been lost from our public understanding."[2] Since the 1874 signing of Treaty 7, all Calgarians have been Treaty peoples.

Calgary (named after Calgary Bay on the Isle of Mull, Scotland) was founded in 1875 as a rail hub along the trans-Canada rail line. The land surrounding Calgary was considered ideal for dryland farming and livestock grazing, and a strong agricultural economy emerged rapidly. Both the railway and wheat farming form the basis of what economic historian Harold Innes called "the staples economy thesis," which argues that Canadian society has been shaped by the desire to extract raw materials from Canada for export to Britain.[3] In 1894 Calgary incorporated as a city (population 10,000), and by 1912, owing to successive waves of European immigration beginning in the late 1890s, the population had swelled to 55,000. But as the prewar boom turned to bust, the hoped-for development did not fully materialize. Between 1913 and 1947, Calgary's growth was relatively moribund, with the city not reaching 100,000 people until 1945.[4]

The development trajectory of the city changed forever when, in 1947, Imperial Oil made a major oil discovery at Leduc, just south of Edmonton, the provincial capital. Subsequently, Calgary emerged as the financial and administrative centre of Canada's oil industry. At that time, Calgary, like many North American cities, was already experiencing a rapid increase in economic activity to meet the pent-up demand for housing, consumer goods, automobiles, and luxury items demanded by returning Second World War veterans.[5] The Leduc discovery stimulated billions of dollars more in energy-related investments, and within ten years, the population of both of Alberta's major cities had doubled. Catalyzed by these circumstances, Calgary became the fastest-growing, youngest, best-educated, and highest-income city in Canada.[6]

Postwar Suburbanization

The post–World War II pace of urban development reflected the optimism and wealth of that generation, and the resulting suburban form manifested these values and mimicked the North American trend toward suburbanization.[7] For many years, more than 100 percent of the city's population growth occurred in greenfield suburban development on Calgary's fringe, owing to out-migration from the inner city.

After the war, Calgary city planners faced a dilemma. Conditioned by decades of slow growth and low revenue and unconvinced that the new oil economy was permanent, decision-makers were reluctant to underwrite the exploding demand for urban services provoked by the oil rush. As an adaptive response, through a series of agreements beginning in 1955, the City retreated from its traditional role of developer/planner and ceded that function to the private sector. In return, the developers began paying for much of the needed suburban infrastructure.[8] Although seen by civic administrators as beneficial for the city, the agreements codified an arrangement whereby much of the City's ability to control growth was transferred to private developers. Over time, zoning, permitting, and the approval process at City Hall were streamlined in the name of efficiency and profit, and the bureaucracy was actively re-engineered to conform to the suburban vision.

By the 1980s, Calgary's development pattern was beginning to alarm city managers. They recognized a growing disconnection between land use and transit planning and the unsustainably high costs of future maintenance. In 1984 a legally mandated Municipal Development Plan (MDP) was drafted. However, the modest reforms it proposed were seen by the developers, and their allies on City Council and in administration, as threatening to the highly profitable status quo. In a showdown, the plan was rejected following intense lobbying by the development regime, which had a strong ally in Mayor Ralph Klein; the city planners who had created the plan were summarily replaced, and a new town plan, reverting to the established suburban model, was adopted in 1986.

Sustainability and Planning in the Post-Earth Summit Era

Stimulated by Local Agenda 21, the urban manifesto of the 1992 Earth Summit in Rio de Janeiro, new design approaches and participatory processes emerged in Calgary. The 1995 Sustainable Suburbs Study, the 1995 Go Plan (the Calgary transportation plan), and the 1998 MDP—documents emanating from these new influences—signalled that the City of Calgary had engaged with the new agenda. Yet owing to its fossil fuel–generated wealth, its rapid growth, its coming of age in the automobile era, and the entrenched trajectory of the development process, the city remained among North America's most sprawling cities in terms of suburban share of growth, automobile dependence, and rate of growth of the city's footprint.

Calgary's municipal government functions through an impressive array of strategies, plans, policies, and bylaws. Statutory documents include land use bylaws that set the basic building blocks shaping the street-by-street structure of the city: Area Redevelopment Plans and Local Area Plans for existing communities, Area Structure Plans for new communities, and the Municipal Development Plan and Calgary Transportation Plan for the city as a whole. Council adopts other plans and strategies from time to time, such as the Calgary Cycling Strategy, the Ecological Footprint Project, and the Triple Bottom Line Policy Framework, but these are non-statutory.

All of these documents, whether statutory or not, are enacted in conformity with the provincial Municipal Government Act, which establishes municipalities as wards of the provincial government. Two of the most important long-range planning documents to come out of the city in the last twenty years are the non-statutory 2006 imagineCalgary Plan for Long-Range Urban Sustainability and the statutory Plan It Calgary (comprising the 2009 Municipal Development Plan and Calgary Transportation Plan). Together, these two plans are meant to provide the framework for how Calgary will grow beyond 2050.

Plan It and imagineCalgary: Products of Civic Engagement

Galvanized by the failure of the 1998 MDP to achieve meaningful change, a new initiative designed to engage citizens in participatory planning and sustainable transitions, named imagineCalgary, began in 2003. Taking a cue from the Vancouver model, stakeholders and citizens embarked on what was billed as the most extensive public engagement process of its kind to that time, engaging approximately eighteen thousand citizens to help craft a hundred-year vision for the city.[9]

The imagineCalgary Plan was the result of an eighteen-month process that culminated in a presentation of the plan by Mayor David Bronconnier at the UN-Habitat Conference in Vancouver in June 2006. The process design was based on systems thinking and sustainability and was inspired by the work of Donella Meadows.[10] The final plan contained a hundred-year vision statement and a set of goals, targets, and strategies organized around five urban systems. Working groups for each of the urban systems were composed of a broad cross-section of stakeholders with representatives from the public sector, including all levels of government; the private sector and civil society, including NGOs representing social and community economic development; and environmental organizations. City Council unanimously endorsed imagineCalgary, and this new initiative established sustainability at the core of planning discourse and debate in the city and as the conceptual touchstone for the Plan It process.

The 2009 Municipal Development Plan and the complementary Calgary Transportation Plan, collectively known as Plan It, represented the City's first attempt to integrate transportation and land use planning.[11] Plan It contemplated urban growth and development over a sixty-year timespan, during which the population was forecast to double to 2.4 million. Plan It anticipated that half of the 1.2 million new inhabitants would settle in greenfield developments and half within established areas.[12] The plan oriented future development along transportation nodes and corridors using well-established "smart growth" and "new urbanism" templates featuring more compact, transit-oriented design, with attention to a high-quality public realm—sidewalks, parks, plazas, and street-oriented building façades.

Despite considerable good will in creating a broad-based consultation that resulted in imagineCalgary and Plan It, only modest changes resulted, and even those remain under siege. Developers used their substantial political capital in attempts to derail Plan It. In the final act of the Plan It process, in September 2009, the development industry's lobbying arm, the Urban Development Institute, was granted a private audience with Mayor Bronconnier in the final days leading up to the presentation of Plan It documents to Council. Civil society leaders, representing a broad range of stakeholders in the process, sought representation at these meetings but were denied. Council was brought into the discussions at the eleventh hour, and a deal was struck to further water down the plan's substance, whereupon Council passed Plan It by unanimous vote. Ten years on, the promise of Plan It has failed to alter the basic trajectory of suburban development. A 2018 report found that 91 percent of Calgary's population growth between 2006 and 2016 still occurred in greenfield—the highest percentage of suburban growth in Canada.[13]

Assessing Calgary's Progress toward Sustainability

In the wake of the Rio Earth Summit, a new citizen-based organization emerged in Calgary in 1996 to champion sustainability.[14] Sustainable Calgary Society initiated a public engagement process that resulted in two thousand citizens contributing to the State of Our City (SOOC) Community Sustainability Indicators Report. Sustainable Calgary invited citizens to consider a set of indicators that would represent sustainability in Calgary. A set of principles that guided this process is presented at the end of this chapter (figure 1). Since 1998, five SOOC reports have been published, the most recent in 2020. These reports provide a detailed assessment of Calgary's progress toward sustainability. Over time, the reports have found that, on the whole, Calgarians are building a strong, diverse, creative community in a clean natural environment and are relatively well educated and healthy; however, Calgarians' use of natural resources is wasteful and costly, and the inequities in the city are making life difficult for many.

Every SOOC report since 1998 has identified two critical challenges. First, Calgary is a city where inequality persists and deepens, and vulnerable groups in the city—First Nations people, new immigrants, low-income and disabled people—face economic and social marginalization. Conventional wisdom is that the economy has been Calgary's strong suit for at least the past two decades. In most of those years, Calgary led the nation in economic growth and was often best-in-class for building development permits and housing starts—and, until the oil price crash in 2014, unemployment rates. However, the Sustainable Calgary indicator initiative identified a very different set of economic indicators more attuned to affordability and equity, meaningful work and livelihood, and economic resilience and diversity. The second challenge identified by the reports is that Calgarians continue to pursue a lifestyle that consumes far too much of the earth's resources. As the 2011 report states, "We live hard and fast in Calgary and too many vulnerable people and too much of the natural world gets trampled in the process."[15]

With respect to our stewardship of nature, the 2020 SOOC report provides evidence that Calgary is living well beyond its means. Our ecological footprint continues to grow and is the largest of any Canadian city. If everyone on the planet consumed as we do, we would need four to six planets' worth of resources. Our energy consumption per capita has grown significantly over the last twenty years, and our large and growing per capita greenhouse gas emissions constitute a crisis. Our overall population density, while slowly increasing, is far from sustainable and leaves us almost completely dependent on the private automobile and vulnerable to long-term maintenance costs. Steady improvement in number of commuters taking transit to work through the first decade of the millennium has reversed in recent years. Transport spending in the City budget is tilted in favour of transit, but overall spending by all levels of government still favours road building. The only good news story here is how we deal with waste. Total waste to landfill is down by over 50 percent since 2001, with waste-diversion programs delivering results.[16]

Calgary's ecological footprint, a measure of the per capita land that would be required to supply all the resources consumed by a given population on a sustainable basis—food crops, pasture, forest products, seafood, CO_2 sequestration—was estimated at approximately 12.4 hectares per person in 2014. This was over 50 percent greater than the Canadian average and more than seven times the global fair share. In 2017 Calgary had a population density of 2,473 people per square kilometre, based on a population of 1,246,377 people and a built-up area of 504 square kilometres. The population density has increased 1.3 percent since 2001 but is still 23 percent less dense than the 3,228 people per square kilometre calculated for 1951. Calgarians own more vehicles per capita than in any other Canadian city, and we are second only to Edmonton in per capita vehicle kilometres travelled.

The 2020 State of Our City report also highlights positive sustainability trends over the last twenty years. Calgary has significantly reduced per capita water consumption and increased rates of recycling, has maintained relatively clean air in comparison to other Canadian cities, and has increased the number of community gardens. Its school system produces some of the best international test scores.

A Shifting Political Landscape

A watershed event occurred in Calgary in 2010. In a stunning upset of the conservative, developer-friendly history of individuals occupying the office of mayor, a young, liberal-minded Muslim emerged from the activist community and was elected mayor. Even more stunning, in 2015, the forty-year reign of the Conservative Party in Alberta came to an end as the social democratic New Democratic Party, led by a dynamic female leader, took control of the provincial government. Both leaders mobilized social, economic, and environmental change with some notable success. Yet both leaders found themselves championing oil and gas pipeline expansion, and in 2019 the Conservative agenda returned with a vengeance with the re-emergence of the Right under the United Conservative Party. Calgary's journey to sustainability remains a long and winding road; the reason is summed up in the title of Kevin Taft's 2017 book, *Oil's Deep State: How the Petroleum Industry Undermines Democracy and Stops Action on Global Warming—in Alberta and in Ottawa.*[17]

At the time of writing, Calgary is severely challenged by the global pandemic, and in the midst of the pandemic, one of the most potent social movements of the last twenty years, Black Lives Matter, emerged across North America, inciting thousands of Calgarians to take to the streets in protest and to join a powerful discussion via social and conventional media. It is unclear in these early days how the pandemic and Black Lives Matter will affect the political and economic trajectory of the city. What we do know is that these events are an exclamation point to unsustainable and unjust social and political structures and have shone a glaring light on the ravaging of the natural world by our current economic system, reinforcing our contention that now, more than ever, sustainability matters.

Figure 1: Sustainable Calgary Principles of Sustainability

1. *Maintain or enhance ecological integrity.* A sustainable community lives in harmony with the natural world. It protects the air, water, soil, flora, fauna, and ecosystems that it depends upon for its survival. These are the life support systems for all human communities.

2. *Promote social equity.* In a sustainable community, each and every citizen is afforded access to the benefits and opportunities that a community has to offer without social or economic discrimination.

3. *Provide the opportunity for meaningful work and livelihood for all citizens.* A strong, resilient, and dynamic local economy is essential for community sustainability. A sustainable economy provides the opportunity for meaningful work and livelihood for each and every citizen.

4. *Encourage democratic participation of all citizens.* We live in a democracy. The bedrock of a democracy is citizen participation in the functioning, planning, and decision-making of society. In a sustainable community, participation is both a right and a responsibility and should be available to every citizen.

5. *Maintain ethical relations with our neighbours.* In our bid to achieve sustainability, we need to find ways to work co-operatively with our neighbours in our urban village and the global village. Sustainability cannot be achieved at the expense of our neighbours—wherever they may be.

NOTES

1   Lorna Crowshoe and Fraser McLeod, *Indigenous Policy Framework for the City of Calgary* (Calgary: City of Calgary, Calgary Aboriginal Urban Affairs Committee, 2017), 8, https://www.calgary.ca/csps/cns/first-nations-metis-and-inuit-peoples/first-nations-metis-inuit-peoples.html.

2   Treaty 7 Elders and Tribal Council, *The True Spirit and Original Intent of Treaty 7*, with Walter Hildebrandt, Dorothy First Rider, and Sarah Carter (Montreal/Kingston: McGill-Queen's University Press, 1996), cited in Crowshoe and McLeod, *Indigenous Policy Framework*, 12.

3   For more on this, see Mel Watkins, "Comment Staples Redux," *Studies in Political Economy* 79, no. 1 (2007): 213–26.

4   This historical discussion has been informed by Lawrence Bussard, "Early History of Calgary" (Master's thesis, University of Alberta, 1935), https://archive.org/details/earlyhistoryofca00buss/page/n1/mode/2up; Hugh Dempsey, *Calgary: Spirit of the West: A History* (Saskatoon: Fifth House, 1994); and Max Foran and Heather Foran, *Calgary: Canada's Frontier Metropolis* (Los Angeles: Windsor, 1982).

5   Robert Stamp, *Suburban Modern: Postwar Dreams in Calgary* (Calgary: Touchwood, 2004).

6   For a more in-depth understanding of the unique social forces shaping Canadian cities, see Harry H. Hiller, ed., *Urban Canada,* 3rd ed. (Don Mills, ON: Oxford University Press, 2014).

7   Stamp, *Suburban Modern.*

8   Max Foran, *Expansive Discourses: Urban Sprawl in Calgary, 1945–78* (Athabasca, AB: Athabasca University Press, 2009).

9   John Punter, *The Vancouver Achievement: Urban Planning and Design* (Vancouver: University of British Columbia Press, 2003).

10 Donella H. Meadows, *Thinking in Systems: A Primer*, ed. Diana Wright (White River Junction, VT: Chelsea Green, 1998).

11 The updated 2020 Municipal Development Plan and Calgary Transportation Plan were approved by City Council in November 2020 and will go into effect after the third reading of the related bylaw. City of Calgary, "Calgary Transportation Plan," 2021, https://www.calgary.ca/transportation/tp/planning/calgary-transportation-plan/calgary-transportation-plan-ctp.html.

12 I (Keough) was intimately involved in these final days of the MDP debate. The 50/50 split between inner city and greenfield development represents a last-minute "compromise" forced by the suburban developers and their allies on Council, who threatened to scuttle the entire process if the division was not reduced from the 65/35 split originally contemplated.

13 David Gordon, *Still Suburban? Growth in Canadian Suburbs, 2006–2016*, with Lyra Hindrich and Chris Willms, Council for Canadian Urbanism Working Paper #2, August 2018, http://www.canadiansuburbs.ca/files/Still_Suburban_Monograph_2016.pdf.

For further analysis of the failure of sustainability planning in Calgary, see Byron Miller, "Sustainability Fix Meets Growth Machine: Attempting to Govern the Calgary Metropolitan Region," in *Governing Cities through Regions: Canadian and European Perspectives*, eds. Roger Keil et al. (Waterloo, ON: Wilfrid Laurier University Press, 2016), 213–38.

14 It should be noted that I (Keough) was intimately involved in both the imagineCalgary and Plan It processes and was a co-founder of Sustainable Calgary Society and lead researcher and/or co-author of each of the State of Our City reports.

15 Noel Keough, *State of Our City Report 2011: Sustainability in a Generation* (Calgary: Sustainable Calgary Society, 2011), 8, https://static1.squarespace.com/static/5ab716b9ee1759b04ca2703e/t/5bff5fd970a6ad4f2ff729e0/1543462882064/2011-SOOC-Report.pdf.

16 Noel Keough, Bob Morrison, and Celia Lee. *State of Our City 2020: An Urgent Call for a Just Transition* (Calgary: Sustainable Calgary Society, 2011), 7, http://www.sustainablecalgary.org/publications.

17 Kevin Taft, *Oil's Deep State: How the Petroleum Industry Undermines Democracy and Stops Action on Global Warming—in Alberta and in Ottawa* (Toronto: Lorimer, 2017).

Works Cited

Bussard, Lawrence. "Early History of Calgary." Master's thesis, University of Alberta, 1935. https://archive.org/details/earlyhistoryofca00buss/page/n1/mode/2up.

"Calgary Transportation Plan." *City of Calgary*, 2021. https://www.calgary.ca/transportation/tp/planning/calgary-transportation-plan/calgary-transportation-plan-ctp.html.

Crowshoe, Lorna, and Fraser McLeod. *Indigenous Policy Framework for the City of Calgary*. Calgary: City of Calgary, Calgary Aboriginal Urban Affairs Committee, 2017. https://www.calgary.ca/csps/cns/first-nations-metis-and-inuit-peoples/first-nations-metis-inuit-peoples.html.

Dempsey, Hugh. *Calgary: Spirit of the West: A History*. Saskatoon: Fifth House, 1994.

Foran, Max. *Expansive Discourses: Urban Sprawl in Calgary, 1945–78*. Athabasca, AB: Athabasca University Press, 2009.

———, and Heather Foran. *Calgary: Canada's Frontier Metropolis*. Los Angeles: Windsor, 1982.

Gordon, David. *Still Suburban? Growth in Canadian Suburbs, 2006–2016*. With Lyra Hindrich and Chris Willms. Council for Canadian Urbanism Working Paper #2, August 2018. http://www.canadiansuburbs.ca/files/Still_Suburban_Monograph_2016.pdf.

Hiller, Harry H., ed. *Urban Canada*. 3rd ed. Don Mills, ON: Oxford University Press, 2014.

Keough, Noel. *State of Our City Report 2011: Sustainability in a Generation*. Calgary: Sustainable Calgary Society, 2011. https://static1.squarespace. com/static/5ab716b9ee1759b04ca2703e/t/5bff5fd970a6ad4f2ff72 9e0/1543462882064/2011-SOOC-Report.pdf.

———, Bob Morrison, and Celia Lee. *State of Our City 2020: An Urgent Call for a Just Transition*. Calgary: Sustainable Calgary Society, 2020. http://www. sustainablecalgary.org/publications.

Meadows, Donella H. *Thinking in Systems: A Primer*. Edited by Diana Wright. White River Junction, VT: Chelsea Green, 1998.

Miller, Byron. "Sustainability Fix Meets Growth Machine: Attempting to Govern the Calgary Metropolitan Region." In *Governing Cities through Regions: Canadian and European Perspectives*, edited by Roger Keil, Pierre Hamel, Julie-Anne Boudreau, and Stefan Kipfer, 213–38. Waterloo, ON: Wilfrid Laurier University Press, 2016.

Punter, John. *The Vancouver Achievement: Urban Planning and Design*. Vancouver: University of British Columbia Press, 2003.

Stamp, Robert. *Suburban Modern: Postwar Dreams in Calgary*. Calgary: Touchwood, 2004.

Taft, Kevin. *Oil's Deep State: How the Petroleum Industry Undermines Democracy and Stops Action on Global Warming—in Alberta and in Ottawa*. Toronto: Lorimer, 2017.

Treaty 7 Elders and Tribal Council. *The True Spirit and Original Intent of Treaty 7*. With Walter Hildebrandt, Dorothy First Rider, and Sarah Carter. Montreal/Kingston: McGill-Queen's University Press, 1996.

Watkins, Mel. "Comment Staples Redux." *Studies in Political Economy* 79, no. 1 (2007): 213–26.

Where Would You Put 600,000 People?

In *Expansive Discourses: Urban Sprawl in Calgary, 1945–1978*, Max Foran argues that the 1950s saw a perfect storm of conditions for the creation of urban and suburban sprawl in Calgary. While the provincial government and City Hall handed the reins of development over to private developers, the oil boom, the dawn of the automobile age, and the desire to house returning war veterans increased the pace of growth of Calgary as a habitat for cars rather than for people.

In this chapter, we explore the issue of sprawl with specific reference to Calgary—the problems it creates, the strategies to combat it, and the challenges to implementing these strategies. The essays highlight the so-cial, economic, and ecological costs of sprawl and the benefits accruing to more compact development. Sprawl—low-density, automobile-dependent development based on segregation of land uses—eats up quality agricul-tural land and demands large per capita consumption of energy resources. It requires enormous expenditures to build and maintain infrastructure. Travel by car becomes almost indispensable while the creation of quality pedestrian environments is neglected, making it difficult to maintain an active lifestyle.

The 2009 Municipal Development Plan (MDP) was designed to curb sixty years of sprawl and create a more sustainable city. In two essays fo-cusing on greenfield, edge-of-city development and inner city community renovation, we assess to what extent the MDP is actually steering develop-ment in Calgary. Keystone Hills is one such development now underway on Calgary's northeast fringe. Its approval paved the way for the unpreced-ented approval of fourteen new suburban communities in the summer of 2019. These new suburban developments are being marketed as sustain-able, but are they really any more sustainable than the previous generation of suburban sprawl? And does sustainable urban planning simply mean increasing density? In addressing these questions, this chapter introduces the ideas of Jane Jacobs and Jan Gehl, two well-known champions of sus-tainable cities and neighbourhood design.

Two essays in this chapter introduce the concept of resilience as a characteristic of a sustainable city. Resilience is explained via the contrast between the responses to disaster in New Orleans following Hurricane Katrina and to an equally powerful hurricane that hit Cuba. Cuba proved to be much more resilient than New Orleans. The discussion of resilience seems prescient given Calgary's experience with catastrophic flooding in 2013. We argue that to prepare for future social, economic, and weath-er-related storms, Calgary needs to build resilience.

We end the chapter with "Green Urbanism," where we examine some of the best examples of sustainable cities beyond North America: Helsinki, Finland; Växjö, Sweden; Freiburg, Germany; and Curitiba, Brazil. These cities offer lessons for how to build compact, resilient, and sustainable cities.

HEAD FOR THE HILLS: MUNICIPAL DEVELOPMENT PLAN STRESS-TEST FAILURE

Imagine another 1.2 million people arriving in our city from all corners of the world. That is what Calgary's 2009 Municipal Development Plan (MDP) forecasts will happen by 2069. Where will we house these new arrivals? Where will they work, shop, go to school, and get medical care?

The answer for the past twenty years has been almost exclusively in greenfields—farmland and prairie on the edge of our city—with urban development spilling relentlessly out into the foothills. But all of this growth has come at a cost. Every home built in a suburban development has put our city deeper in the red. In 2014 the City of Calgary was forecasting a $1.9 billion shortfall for transit infrastructure spending alone.[1] According to Mayor Nenshi, under the current arrangement for tax revenue from these suburbs, we will never recoup the costs of building them.

The MDP was supposed to change all of that. In June 2012 City Council held a public hearing to consider a bylaw for the first new development under the new MDP—the Keystone Hills Area Structure Plan (ASP).[2] When completed, Keystone will cover eleven square kilometres and will house sixty thousand people in three distinct communities. It is located northwest of the junction of Stoney Trail and Deerfoot Trail—that's right, fifteen kilometres from downtown Calgary as the crow flies and a mere two kilometres from CrossIron Mills, the megamall located in the Municipal District of Rockyview.

If you look at this new community plan in isolation, it looks pretty good. The street grid, the bicycle and transit routes, and the design guidelines for the neighbourhood, including community activity and retail centres, will all contribute to a more walkable community. But as soon as you widen the lens to look at the plan's context, things come undone. As they say, "Location, location, location." Calgary's new communities are isolated pockets of habitation in a sea of multi-lane highways and interchanges far from the heart of the city. The further out from the city centre you go, the more these communities are hemmed in by the freeways required to service them. Keystone Hills doesn't change that.

In all likelihood, if you live in Keystone Hills, you will have little choice but to get in a car to venture beyond your community. If you want to go to the library or to a swimming pool, you will have to trek across the formidable Stoney Trail. Transit routes have been sketched in, but there is no date for the LRT extension and no commitment to put sufficient buses on those routes.

The United Nations' 2019 *Global Environmental Outlook 6* reports that the planet is becoming increasingly unhealthy due to biodiversity loss and climate change.[3] Meanwhile, the City's own sustainability assessment notes that the Keystone ASP does nothing to reduce our ecological footprint and will result "in greater demands on the earth's biosphere than the current citywide baseline."[4]

The City has made commitments to reduce greenhouse gas emissions by 80 percent by 2050, but the sustainability assessment estimates that Keystone Hills will produce greenhouse gas emissions greater than the current Calgary average.[5] There are lofty pronouncements of how to reduce energy consumption. They are called "guidelines"—friendly suggestions, really, to hardnosed, bottom-line, profit-seeking developers. They carry no legal weight.

A goal of the 2009 MDP is that new developments will not "compromise quality of life for current and future Calgarians."[6] We think the Keystone Hills ASP may do just that. A major study from Queens University published in 2012 estimates that adults' inactive lifestyles, caused in large part by auto-dependent cities, cost the Canadian health care system almost $7 billion annually, with Calgary's share being approximately $212 million.[7] That's a lot of compromised quality of life.

As is, this ASP will lock its communities into the old, financially unsustainable pattern of development for the next twenty-five years. It does not meet the expectations of Calgarians as expressed through the Plan It and imagineCalgary processes, and it undermines MDP goals and the City's financial stability. Has another battle for sustainability been lost?

Here's how we might improve future ASPs. First, include established communities in the land supply assessment. Currently, the City does not have an analysis of potential population growth in established communities and thus overestimates the need for new greenfield development. Second, if a case can still be made for new developable lands, establish energy intensity targets so that these communities will contribute to the City's resilience strategy.[8] Third, ask if this ASP makes financial sense.

Ensure that the ASP's acceptance or rejection is based on the real costs of growth, including full lifecycle costs. Fourth, ensure that people could live in the community without a car. Make transit a part of the core infrastructure, and make acceptance of this ASP contingent on the provision (in plans *and* budgets) of high-quality transit service that will make transit a realistic option for Keystone residents within five years of first occupancy. In the community of Arabianranta in Helsinki, for example, public transit is in place from day one.

Keystone Hills will be the suburban development template for decades. It is incumbent upon City Council and developers to get it right. Let's make sure we know where we are growing.

CURBING SPRAWL THROUGH INNER CITY RENOVATION

Charles Dickens' classic *A Tale of Two Cities* starts with the iconic line "It was the best of times, it was the worst of times." Though much less tumultuous than the events that frame Dickens' novel, Calgary has, for decades, been living with the paradox of having access to a resource motherlode that makes it the country's wealthiest city while facing unwelcome development pressures that threaten its sustainability.

The 2009 Municipal Development Plan, the core of Plan It, forecast a doubling of Calgary's population by 2069—that means 1.2 million new Calgarians. The big question is where to put all of these newcomers. Plan It's compromise is to put half of them on the edges of the city in new suburbs (greenfield development) and half of them in established communities.

The edge-of-city development is relatively straightforward. City Council has already approved area structure plans and community plans for hundreds of thousands of newcomers. Greenfield developers are well practiced at building suburbia. Meanwhile, Plan It envisions most of the growth in established communities to occur along transportation corridors. Calgary has a long-standing Transit Oriented Development (TOD) policy that supports that vision, calling for more density, mixed-use development (homes, shops, and offices), and an improved public realm (plazas, wider sidewalks, bicycle infrastructure).[9] This makes sense, but the devil is in the details. When the plan becomes a reality in a particular community is when the second-guessing starts. Everybody thinks it's a good idea in somebody else's community.

A good example of how this policy plays out is the community of Hillhurst-Sunnyside. In response to the TOD policy and in anticipation of development intensification, the City spent three years working with residents to remodel the community's Area Redevelopment Plan (ARP) to accommodate higher density.[10]

Very soon after the new ARP was accepted by Council in 2009, and faster than almost anybody imagined, Hillhurst-Sunnyside experienced an extreme makeover. Within two years, there were two eight-storey mixed-use condominium towers well under way, with another thirteen major projects at some stage of the development process—from first exploration with the community to actually making their way through City Hall approvals. These projects totalled over one million square feet (half the size of the Bow Tower, Calgary's largest office building) and 843 dwellings (an estimated 1,517 people)—an 18 percent growth in the community's population. By 2020, five such projects were complete and occupied, with another four under construction or awaiting development approval.

The community is feeling the heat. One of the promises of the ARP-TOD was that redevelopment would come with aggressive public space enhancement—a key feature of the TOD policy. Within months, that promise hit a glitch. Just as development was heating up, City Hall lawyers deemed the development levy envisioned to pay for public realm improvements to be unenforceable under the Municipal Government Act. Developers balked at paying it, and the City was left scrambling to introduce an enforceable alternative. At the same time, the old adage "Give them an inch and they will take a mile" is evident in the development process. Most new development proposals start by maximizing the allowable square feet of space and height on a given parcel of land. From there, almost invariably, developers make an argument for why they should get more.

Meanwhile, as development plans roll in, very little uptake is evident on all of the coulds, shoulds, and if-you-feel-like-its of the ARP. Things like green building design, car-sharing programs to reduce auto density, and affordable units are conspicuously absent.

Plan It, and imagineCalgary before it, made an unassailable case for why we need to intensify development in existing communities, and

Calgarians support this vision. If done well, intensification will make for better communities, but it could go sideways fast if the pace of development overwhelms City Hall's finite planning resources. Nobody wants that. With 600,000 new people coming to existing communities by 2069, these first makeovers in places like Hillhurst-Sunnyside have to get it right or the Plan It strategy will be dead in the water.

One solution is for the city to assign and locate city planners in the community long term, not unlike the idea of a beat cop, to get to know the community, its residents, and the development realities in intimate detail. Another solution is allocating more power to the people. In Hillhurst-Sunnyside, the innovative and wildly successful Bow to Bluff initiative, which is tackling a new public realm plan along the LRT route, has demonstrated the capacity of citizens to engage the community in the planning process.[11] So why not give communities a bigger role? They deserve to be at the table with the City and the developers every step of the way.

There is a lesser-known phrase in that opening sentence of *A Tale of Two Cities*: "it was the age of wisdom, it was the age of foolishness." The City made a wise decision when it adopted Plan It. To not back up the decision with diligence, adequate resources, and attention to detail would indeed be foolish.

DENSITY: DESIGNING AT A HUMAN SCALE

In early May each year, hundreds of Calgarians participate in dozens of Jane's Walks—neighbourhood tours led by citizens. The annual event honours the legacy of urban planning legend Jane Jacobs, whose 1961 book *The Death and Life of Great American Cities* challenged the conventional wisdom that had, for at least a decade, been remaking North American cities for the benefit of cars. Jane and other community activists took on Robert Moses, then the most powerful urban planner in North America, and saved what is today one of the most celebrated urban neighbourhoods in the world—Greenwich Village, New York. Jane went on to bring her community action approach to Toronto, where she inspired Torontonians to similarly reclaim their city's most precious neighbourhoods. Density was one of the key ingredients in Jane's recipe for success.

In 2010 another New Yorker was even more emphatic about density. In his controversial bestseller *Green Metropolis*, *New York Times* journalist David Owen argues passionately that density is the key ingredient to sustainability. Owen points out that in Manhattan, the nation's densest residential district, residents drive, consume, and pollute less than most Americans, resulting in a 30 percent smaller ecological footprint.[12]

Not only is high-density living greener; it's also healthier. Public health research shows that denser urban environments are safer and encourage healthy living. People can walk to the grocery store and kids can bicycle safely to school. Even during the 2020 pandemic, this is holding true. Singapore, the hyper-dense, quintessential modern city-state, with almost six million inhabitants, suffered only twenty-seven deaths in the first six months of the pandemic.[13]

Here at home, Calgary policy makers have embraced density for another reason: expansive, auto-oriented cities are expensive. Becoming denser would improve transit service, reduce car ownership costs, and create a more walkable city, all for half the cost to the City of suburbs-as-usual development. According to a 2009 study, *The Implications of Alternative Growth Patterns on Infrastructure Costs*, commissioned by the City of Calgary, this would, over sixty years, save taxpayers about $11 billion in capital costs and another $130 million annually in maintenance.[14] In 2009 taxes paid to subsidize urban sprawl added about $115 to the average property tax assessment.

But how dense is dense enough? In cities around the world, there are huge variations and cultural norms. A new immigrant from Manila, for example, might find the lack of people on the streets of Calgary kind of scary. Mumbai, India, is the densest city in the world at thirty thousand people per square kilometre. Those numbers are not the average Calgarian's cup of tea. So what about some of the most liveable cities in the world? Calgary's density is 2,473 people per square kilometre. Compare that to Helsinki at 2,883; Paris at 21,370; Stockholm at 4,219; and Amsterdam at 4,952.[15]

On a cautionary note, Danish sustainability expert Jan Gehl reminded us on a visit to Calgary that density alone does not make a city liveable, safe, sustainable, or healthy. If density is not paired with better transit, quality public space, and judicious approval of high-rise development, there is little to gain except lower taxes. Gehl implored the packed house at the Central Library theatre to focus on the human scale by creating quality social spaces that encourage people to gather and linger.[16]

In his 2010 book *Cities for People*, Gehl is emphatic that tall buildings and poor public spaces are not a recipe for lively cities.[17] He points out that, unlike David Owen's hyper-dense Manhattan, Jane Jacob's Greenwich Village and the old urban quarters of Paris, Barcelona, and Copenhagen are great examples of quality, compact urban neighbourhoods of four- to six-storey residential blocks.

In the end, it comes down to whether we choose to build our cities for cars or for people. Our roads, shopping malls, suburban homes, schools, and hospitals are all super-sized for the automobile. Fringe suburbs, no matter how many units per hectare, will never achieve one of the most attractive density benefits—reduced dependence on the automobile and a decrease in its attendant pollution, noise, and congestion.

In *Expansive Discourses*, local historian Max Foran identifies the early 1950s as the period when land developers arrived on the scene and City administration abdicated its responsibility to shape the city, to the benefit of developers.[18] They arrived just in time to ride the wave of a perfect storm of postwar economic expansion, the baby boom, Alberta's oil bonanza, easy mortgage credit, and the ascendancy of automobile-dependent residential urban sprawl across North America. The business model became entrenched and, to this day, has proven very profitable for a handful of land developers.

Looking out from McHugh Bluff above Sunnyside on a cool spring day, Jane's Walks enthusiasts had a bird's eye view of just about every era of Calgary's growth—from downtown to suburbia on Signal Hill—but the edge of the city was beyond view. Density—what is it good for? Tax savings, more walkable communities, more amenities in your neighbourhood, a new school perhaps (or your existing school saved from the chopping block), more kids in the playground around the corner, more coffee shops, restaurants, and health clinics—all within walking distance. We say, bring it on!

RESILIENCE: A CAUTIONARY TALE FROM NEW ORLEANS TO CUBA

The concept of "resilience" has two simple and related meanings. First, resilience is a system's capacity to withstand shock without permanent damage: resilient systems are pliable, like old Gumby toys or young hockey players. Second, resilience is the ability to recover from, or adjust easily to, misfortune or change: resilient systems are more adaptable, so they rebound faster and further after a calamity. But what happens when we apply these straightforward ideas to cities—to our city? Simple-sounding concepts can quickly become complex when discussing real places and real people in real time.

On one level, it means taking an informed peek into the future to see what kinds of disruptions we may have to contend with but have no control over. On another level, it means honestly assessing our ability to withstand short- and long-term shocks and to deal with adversity. On a third level, it means taking proactive action to enhance our strengths and address our shortcomings.

But resilience isn't just one thing. It is the accumulated benefit of many processes—small and large, material and social—that together provide alternatives for people to meet their needs when things change. Some elements of resilience concern physical infrastructure such as transit, energy distribution, and waste management. Others are related to the social sphere and the economy. A strong local business community is part of a resilient landscape. Institutions that encourage amenities such as community gardens, public art, public toilets, quality parks, and green space solidify community networks. The day-in and day-out collective activities of place-making build a sense of community and the social capital that resilient cities rely on in times of crisis.

A very instructive modern example illustrating the difference between rigid and resilient systems is the comparison of New Orleans after Hurricane Katrina in 2005 and Cuba after Hurricane Ivan in 2004. The more recent effects of Hurricane Maria on Puerto Rico in 2017 and Hurrican Dorian on the Bahamas two years later reinforce the point.

The results in New Orleans are well known. A lack of preparation, including the delay of expensive yet critical maintenance to the city's infrastructure—combined with ad hoc evacuation plans ("get in your car, if you have one") and a bumbling response from federal, state, and municipal agencies—turned a simple disaster into a monumental catastrophe played out on CNN for all the world to see. According to the US National Hurricane Center, the official estimate is 1,577 deaths in Louisiana due to Katrina.[19] Puerto Rican casualties are harder to confirm but the governor's office estimated almost 3,000.[20] According to research published by Dr. Adam Vinconne and colleagues in the journal *Medical Anthropology* in May 2011, we can expect almost half of the victims of such disasters to be seniors.[21]

Cuba's response to Ivan, a Category 5 hurricane that hit the Caribbean nation a year before Katrina, is less well known. According to United Nations emergency relief coordinator Jan Egeland, authorities in Cuba implemented a well-rehearsed disaster response plan. To ease concerns and encourage at-risk people to abandon their homes, tough anti-looting strategies were implemented. As a result, 1.5 million Cubans were evacuated to designated shelters prior to the hurricane's landfall, leading to minimal casualties despite the loss of twenty thousand homes.[22]

In New Orleans, it took weeks after the storm passed to organize a coordinated response: according to PBS Frontline, after nine days, five to ten thousand people were still stranded in the city.[23] In Cuba, electricity was mostly restored and the cleanup begun within days. Although damage to personal property and civic infrastructure was extensive, local communities weathered the storm because of foresight and advanced planning.[24] In Cuba, everyone knew what to do. In New Orleans, no one did. That was the difference.

Cuba is not an affluent society, but it is one that takes care of its citizens in an equitable manner. There is no great divide between the rich and the poor. It is a cohesive society. According to Bloomberg News, New Orleans is the most inequitable city in the US, with both racial and economic fault lines defining the city and, as it turns out, defining who is protected from natural disasters and who is not.[25] Because they had a plan in Cuba, community organizations and family life spontaneously regenerated and the essential characteristics of their communities were sustained in the crisis. In New Orleans, where social resilience was lacking, many communities simply disappeared. A photo essay by Ellyn Kail exposed one such neighbourhood.[26]

The threats facing Calgary are less tangible. There are no hurricanes here, but the flood of 2013 and the summer hailstorm in 2020 did demonstrate that nature can deliver nasty surprises, even in Calgary. The comparative lessons of Cuba and New Orleans are readily adaptable as we contemplate the city of our future. Unfortunately, a pragmatic look at Calgary's urban growth pattern forebodes trouble. Much as in New Orleans, a lack of willingness to make the required investment in social, physical, and community infrastructure will leave us vulnerable when one or more of the looming global threats emerges.

While socioeconomic disparities in Calgary are not what they are in New Orleans, we are moving in the wrong direction. Resilience is what allowed the Cubans to cope, and its lack resulted in the devastation in New Orleans.

TO WEATHER FUTURE STORMS, CALGARY NEEDS RESILIENCE

When it comes to Calgary's future, are you buying in or just passing through? This doesn't mean, Do you own a house? It means, Are you here for the long haul? It's an important question. When planning a city, there's a huge difference in the psychology of long-term versus short-term thinking.

Short-term thinking prioritizes fast profits and superficial solutions, and it elevates "I" over "us." Long-term thinking, on the other hand, results in equitably distributing wealth over time; seeking solutions that address causes, not symptoms; and honouring individuals and communities equally. It is not a crime to be a short-term thinker. If you are a speculator or property flipper or if you plan to make a pile of money in the oilpatch before skedaddling with bulging pockets—fine. The problem is that a city with this mindset is brittle and ill-prepared to cope with the massive social and environmental challenges we will all soon confront. While the short-term profiteers are caressing cocktails in the Caymans—assuming the islands are not under water—the rest of us will be left to deal with the aftermath.

Cities with a short-term mindset, like Calgary, are built for the here and now—streamlined and shaped to extract the maximum profit in the shortest time. In the short term, city problems (such as traffic congestion) are "solved" using bandaid solutions (such as building more roads). In contrast, a long-term city takes patience. Over time, benefits accumulate because solutions to urban problems are engineered into the city's internal logic. More roads to combat congestion are unnecessary because the long-term city does not create as much auto traffic. The demand for more police diminishes because, as Kate Pickett and Richard Wilkinson show in their 2011 book *The Spirit Level: Why Greater Equality Makes Societies Stronger*, a more equitable distribution of economic and political resources, combined with universal access to high-quality social spaces, produces fewer criminals.[27] More herbicides to control dandelions won't be needed because natural means of weed management, such as letting native grasses grow on boulevards and along transportation corridors, will do the job for free.

Calgary experienced a moment of vulnerability when gasoline prices spiked to $1.40 in 2008. Even with that relatively minor fluctuation, many who felt financially secure were suddenly in trouble. Why? Because there was (and still is) no plan B. Calgary's sprawling geography only works well within a narrow range of constraints. As we saw with the fuel-price spike, when a critical threshold was exceeded, the urban system had difficulty coping. If a sudden change were to become permanent, the system could collapse. In fits of collective amnesia, short-term thinkers routinely accuse advocates of long-term thinking of "social engineering," of being against the "free market." Or such advocates are drowned in a mean-spirited discourse with the sole aim of keeping property and business taxes as low as possible.

Resilience is the key—it's the quality that allows systems to persist and flourish even in the face of adverse changes to the economic, social, or environmental relations that power them. Peter Newman and his colleagues, in their seminal 2009 book *Resilient Cities: Responding to Peak Oil and Climate Change*, demonstrate that resilient cities are better able to cope with reductions in the resources that are used to make cities work.[28] Ten years later, this sentiment was echoed passionately in Douglas Kelbaugh's

The Urban Fix: Resilient Cities in the War Against Climate Change, Heat Islands and Overpopulation.[29]

Calgary is vulnerable when it comes to our transportation system. Consider a case cited by Newman and colleagues. In Atlanta, 2,960 litres of gasoline per person is needed every year to make the urban system work, while in Barcelona, individuals use only 242 litres per year.[30] Which city would cope better with rising energy prices? No contest. Calgary is more like Atlanta.[31]

In 2015 car ownership rates per one thousand people in Germany, Norway, and Sweden were 593, 611, and 540, respectively. Canada, on the other hand, had an ownership rate of 646 per one thousand people. The US rate was 821.[32] In the European countries, the public transportation system provides choice. You can live, work, and play in these countries without a car. In Calgary, where the ownership rate in 2019 was 740 per thousand people and transit accounted for only 14 percent of all work trips, it is hard to make that claim.[33] In 2011, 93 percent of Calgary households owned a car, according to City of Calgary research.[34] In comparison, according to Euromonitor International, in 2015 only 53 percent of Berlin households had at least one car. In Copenhagen and Tokyo, the rates were 62 percent and 60 percent, respectively.[35] In each of these three cities, the public transportation system provides choice. In Calgary, using public transportation takes a determined effort. With options comes resilience.

We cannot predict with precision the conditions that will confront us in the future, which reinforces the need to remain nimble. What matters are the values we instill and the ethic we embed in the bricks and mortar of our city. Calgary's Resilience Strategy is a move in the right direction.[36] As with so many city policies, its success or failure will rest on whether it is backed up with budgets and the day-to-day decisions of City Council. Are you here for the duration? Are you buying into Calgary's future or are you just kicking the tires?

GREEN URBANISM: A NECESSARY EVOLUTION OF CITIES

Modern urban life—at least, the technology that makes it all possible—has made a stranger of nature. Occasionally, nature intrudes into our lives through weather or natural calamity. While some urbanites like venturing into the wild to play or relax, for most of us, it's back to the urban silo when the weekend ends.

In the magical world of the city, needs are invisibly met. Flick a switch and presto! Night becomes day. Twist a faucet and clean, drinkable water gushes out, seemingly without limit. Flush a toilet and stinky sewage disappears out of sight and mind. At the store, shelves teem with fresh and preserved foods that appear, manna-like, each new day. The sheer ease with which all this happens makes it easy to forget that outside the silo lies a vast network of utilities and infrastructures that continuously extract raw materials from nature and transform them into useful products to be delivered to our homes, creating garbage and pollution in the process.

The problem is that our flick-and-flush existence conceals many of the destructive effects that our consumption patterns create, as well as the fragile state of the ecological systems that underpin them. Being physically removed from nature fosters psychological detachment—so much so that when confronted with alarming claims that could conflict with our daily safe, healthy, and abundant personal existence, we often ignore them—or worse, deny them.

This city-nature rift may explain why we continue to build as we do. A city of far-flung suburbs and drive-to malls is unsustainable, and everybody knows it—planners, politicians, ordinary citizens, and even developers (although they don't typically admit it publicly). But things are changing out there, and to adapt, we're going to have to change as well.

Building cities as we have in the past is not an option for deep thinkers like Timothy Beatley, professor of sustainable communities at the University of Virginia and author of more than fifteen books, including *Green Urbanism: Learning from European Cities* and *Green Urbanism Down Under*. He believes the future of our species is intimately tied with our ability to coexist with the natural world. For Beatley, a world expert on city-nature relations, this means reorganizing cities to satisfy our needs for clean, healthy, safe places to live while balancing the environmental impacts created in the process with the planet's capacity for renewal.[37] The solution, or part of it, lies in what Beatley calls "green urbanism"—meshing urban development with environmental and social goals in a manner that unites rather than divides communities.

Green urbanism is a necessary evolution of cities, says Beatley. First, he points out that humans have become an urban species. Globally, more than 50 percent of us now live in cities, and that proportion is quickly growing. By 2050, according to the United Nations Department of Economic and Social Affairs, the number is expected to reach 68 percent.[38] In Canada, we have already blown past this figure, with more than a third of all Canadians living in the three cities of Montreal, Vancouver, and Toronto.[39] Forecasts show that by 2050, seven billion people, about the same as the global population today, will be living in cities.

This leads to Beatley's second point. He fears that if we continue to plan and build our cities as we are today, the environmental systems that support us will be fatally compromised. Historical problem-solving techniques won't be able to fix them. That's what makes green urbanism different. It takes a longer view and creates cities that don't outpace nature's ability to sustain them.

Green urbanism is based on a number of design principles and goals—some practical, some inspirational. One goal is to reduce the ecological footprint—a measurement of the amount of resources we consume and the rate at which we consume them. Reducing consumption and being more efficient with resources helps reduce our ecological footprint. Footprint analysis is used to compare the consequences of certain choices, such as commuting by car or rail.

Another goal is to live within the limits of local resources. For example, in Calgary the availability of water will eventually limit our ability to develop. By 2036 the daily licence capacity will not be able to supply projected summertime daily peak usage.[40] At current flow rates, our rivers can support annual withdrawals for up to three million people, a population the city is expected to reach by 2076. What then? If the predictions of global warming (hotter, dryer weather) are fulfilled, we may breach those limits much sooner.

Green urbanism recognizes that cities, though human-made, function like living organisms and play an important role in the global ecology. City planners who practice green urbanism look to nature for inspiration in developing ways to manage our impacts. For example, nothing in nature is wasted. One organism's waste is another's breakfast: when the mountain ash sheds its leaves, it provides a feast for hundreds of micro-organisms whose own waste, in turn, provides food for plants. Green cities use this principle to find creative ways of organizing urban living while reducing environmental impacts.

These principles and goals point to a strong ethical component in green urbanism. Acknowledging our connections with the natural world, including other people, forces us to shed our urban cocoon—to stand up and take shared responsibility for a greater common good.

Green urbanism takes different forms in different places. Every place has its own challenges, and each one is shaped by a unique blend of geographic, cultural, political, and economic factors influencing the development of local institutions and processes. No one place is doing everything right, but Timothy Beatley affirms "the primacy of place in any program of green urbanism."[41] He maintains that if we focused on what is being done right in other places, North American cities, which are much less advanced in many ways, would probably move closer to green urbanism.

One place to see how these things can come together is Freiburg, Germany, a mid-sized city of 220,000 nestled along the western flank of the Black Forest. Under the leadership of world-renowned urban planner Wulf Daseking, Freiburg has become a model for twenty-first–century green urban development.

In an interview we conducted with Daseking in 2013, he began not with the expected overview of Freiburg's impressive environmental and social accomplishments but with a world tour of favelas, barrios, and slums—from Rio to Manila to Mumbai. "We are all connected to each other and to the environment," he began, affirming the principles of green urbanism.[42]

Freiburg's accomplishments are impressive. Long before the term *ecological footprint* was invented, the Academy of Urbanism's *Freiburg Charter* was already being used to develop a long-term plan to reduce the city's crippling fossil-fuel dependence.[43] Freiburg followed two related strategies. The first encouraged the development of solar power, both as an alternative energy source and as the focus of a new industry. Governments of all levels provided incentives to help the new industry along, from guaranteeing minimum prices for green energy to developing programs that helped businesses and homeowners convert. A solar research institute opened in 1981, which in turn attracted to Freiburg a cluster of private corporations, government agencies, and national and international sustainability organizations, all focused on solar power. Today, the city is festooned with solar panels—on homes, government facilities, and businesses.

The second strategy was to radically reformulate the goals of town planning. Instead of building more car-dependent suburbs, the city invested heavily to create a high-quality transportation network consisting of trams, buses, bikes, and foot traffic. New residential development, both in suburbs and the inner city, was designed so that residents could get along without cars if they so desired. Trams linking new neighbourhoods were up and running even as the first residents were moving in.

Daseking admits the new system isn't cheap. "We pay high taxes but we don't mind," he said. "We get good value for our money and at the same time we take responsibility to help preserve the environment." But Freiburg's success wasn't simply based on technology. Crucially, local government, in its role as master planner, facilitated collaboration between developers and residents in the creation of new neighbourhoods. This process transformed development goals from focusing on maximizing profit, based on the ideology of competition, to maximizing the well-being of residents.

At every stage of the process—beginning with the initial design and not ending until the final nail was pounded in—citizens were consulted, progress was assessed, and sustainability goals were scrutinized. From the largest vision to the smallest detail, ordinary people discarded their indifference and claimed responsibility for planning their city. Herein lies the secret and the hope of green urbanism.

The Freiburg model is not without its problems—affordability is an issue and suburban growth in Freiburg suffers from some of the same issues as we find in other cities. But the city is certainly an early adopter in the quest for more sustainable cities.

Many other places are equally innovative. For example, in the early 1970s, Curitiba, Brazil, a city similar in size to Calgary, was on the same auto-dependent track as we are. Inspired by a visionary group of architects, planners, and engineers, the city made a radical shift and created one of the most successful examples of green urbanism.[44] Since the 1970s, Curitiba has re-established natural drainage systems in parks to manage flooding. Some 1.5 million trees have been planted, and quality green space has increased fivefold. A large flock of sheep maintains city grasslands.

In the social realm, Curitiba has a comprehensive recycling program that involves citizens in poor neighbourhoods who can exchange what they call "trash-that-is-not-trash" for bus vouchers, theatre tickets, food, and school supplies. Downtown, the main car corridor was transformed into a thriving pedestrian street with many shops and services, similar to Calgary's Stephen Avenue mall. Curitiba's flagship achievement is its low-cost transit system that carries over two million passengers a day. From 1974 to 2000, Curitiba's population doubled, yet car usage declined 30 percent. Since 2000, the system seems to have deteriorated to some extent, resulting in a return to cars for some Curitibans, but commentators still rank Curitiba as an eco-city success story and as having set the bar for other cities, such as Bogotá, to aspire to.[45]

Another example of green urbanism is Växjö, a city of ninety-four thousand in southern Sweden that began a trek toward carbon neutrality in the late 1990s. Their idea was to use waste from the local timber industry to power a high-efficiency incinerator to generate electricity and create enough heat to meet most of the city's needs—all with no new carbon emissions. Following nature's example of using waste from one process to power another, Växjö's experience shows how major environmental milestones can be achieved without sacrificing quality of life.[46]

In Helsinki, Finland, a winter city, what was once Europe's biggest glass and ceramics manufacturing complex has been transformed into a green community called Arabianranta. Home to ten thousand residents, the new urban village contains a cluster of small- and medium-sized creative arts businesses employing around five thousand people, as well as a university campus for six thousand students. Following the city's master plan, a diverse group of interests including city social housing, not-for-profit groups representing seniors and the disabled, students, and private firms developed their own properties. Architectural competitions were held for every individual land parcel. High-quality green spaces and community gardens are around every corner, and 10 percent of the building budget has been ear-marked for public art. Arabianranta is serviced by an innovative high-speed communications network and owns and operates a high-efficiency district heating network that distributes heat to homes and businesses, negating their need to install a furnace. The community borders a protected wetland and is connected to central Helsinki by a dedicated cycle route. As well, two tramlines service the community.[47]

What about back home in Calgary? Although we hear about climate change, biodiversity loss, peak oil, threatened fisheries, looming water shortages, and so on, most of us have little personal sense of the enormity of their effects. It's even harder here because our prosperity has bankrolled an especially comfortable refuge to nestle in. Although innovative and creative schemes are blooming in Calgary—such as East Village, The Bridges, and Currie Barracks—most have been isolated initiatives rather than the result of coordinated action.

But with a supportive mayor and council, a Municipal Development Plan that points in the right direction, and citizen groups such as Sustainable Calgary, Calgary Climate Hub, and Calgary Alliance for the Common Good that have already made the commitment to reconnect with nature and people, perhaps things are turning around.

In the end, Calgary may do the right thing. The question is, Will nature force us to change or will we find a way to come together and change ourselves before it does?

NOTES

1   City of Calgary, *Investing in Mobility: Transportation Infrastructure Investment Plan* (Calgary: City of Calgary, 2014).

2   City of Calgary, *Keystone Hills Area Structure Plan* (Calgary: City of Calgary, 2012), https://www.calgary.ca/pda/pd/current-studies-and-ongoing-activities/keystone-hills. html.

3   UN Environment, *Global Environment Outlook 6: Healthy Planet, Healthy People* (Nairobi: United Nations Environment Programme, 2019).

4   City of Calgary, *Keystone Hills Area Structure Plan: Ecological Footprint*, report to Calgary Planning Commission, CPC212-041, Attachment 3, Appendix II, 12 April 2012.

5   Andrew Sudamant et al., *The Economics of Low Carbon Development* (Calgary: City of Calgary, 2019), https://climate.leeds.ac.uk/wp-content/uploads/2018/03/Calgary-Exec-Sum-draft-4_Web.pdf; City of Calgary, *Keystone Hills Area Structure Plan: Ecological Footprint*, 1.

6   City of Calgary, *Municipal Development Plan* (Calgary: City of Calgary, 2009), 2–3, https://www.calgary.ca/pda/pd/municipal-development-plan/municipal-development-plan-mdp.html.

7   Ian Janssen, "Health Care Costs of Physical Inactivity in Canadian Adults," *Applied Physiology, Nutrition, and Metabolism* 37, no. 4 (June 2012): 803–6.

8   City of Calgary, *Resilient Calgary* (Calgary: City of Calgary, 2019), https://www.calgary.ca/cs/calgary-resilience.html.

9   City of Calgary, *Transit Oriented Development: Policy Guidelines* (Calgary: City of Calgary, 2005), https://www.calgary.ca/pda/pd/current-studies-and-ongoing-activities/transit-oriented-development-tod.html.

10   City of Calgary, *Hillhurst Sunnyside Area Redevelopment Plan* (Calgary: City of Calgary, 2018), https://d3aencwbm6zmht.cloudfront.net/asset/399111/hillhurst-sunnyside-arp.pdf.

11   O2 Planning and Design, *Bow to Bluff Urban Design Framework* (Calgary: Bow to Bluff, 2011), https://www.cip-icu.ca/Files/Awards/Planning-Excellence/2013-16-Bow-to-Bluff-FULL-PLAN.aspx.

12   David Owen, *Green Metropolis: Why Living Smaller, Living Closer, and Driving Less Are the Keys to Sustainability* (New York: Riverhead Books, 2009), 1–36.

13   "COVID-19 Coronavirus Pandemic: Reported Case of Death by Country, Territory or Conveyance," *Worldometer*, 2020, https://www.worldometers.info/coronavirus/.

14   IBI Group, *The Implications of Alternative Growth Patterns on Infrastructure Costs* (Calgary: City of Calgary, 9 April 2009), http://www.reconnectingamerica.org/assets/Uploads/planitcalgarycoststudyanalysisaprilthird.pdf.

15   Noel Keough, Bob Morrison, and Celia Lee, *State of Our City 2020: An Urgent Call for a Just Transition* (Calgary: Sustainable Calgary Society, 2020), 49, http://www.sustainablecalgary.org/publications; UN Department of Economics and Social Affairs, *United Nations Demographic Yearbook 2015* (New York: United Nations, 2016), https://unstats.un.org/unsd/demographic-social/products/dyb/dybsets/2015.pdf.

16   "An Evening with Jan Gehl at the Calgary Public Library," *Canadian Architect*, 2 April 2011, https://www.canadianarchitect.com/an-evening-with-jan-gehl-at-the-calgary-public-library/.

17   Jan Gehl, *Cities for People* (Washington, DC: Island Press, 2010), 68.

18   Max Foran, *Expansive Discourses: Urban Sprawl in Calgary, 1945–78* (Athabasca, AB: Athabasca University Press, 2009).

19   Richard Knabb, Jamie Rhome, and Daniel Brown, *Tropical Cyclone Report: Hurricane Katrina 23–30 August 2005* (Miami: National Hurricane Center, 20 December 2005), https://www.nhc.noaa.gov/data/tcr/AL122005_Katrina.pdf.

20   Jarvis Deberry, "Today's a Day to Remember Those Killed by Hurricanes Katrina and Maria," *New Orleans Advocate*, 29 August 2018, https://www.nola.com/opinions/article_cb104aaa-aadf-5e90-b3a1-1413c51f85e2.html.

21 Adam Vincanne et al., "Aging Disaster: Mortality, Vulnerability, and Long-Term Recovery among Katrina Survivors," *Medical Anthropology* 30, no. 2 (May 2011): 247–70.

22 "Cuban Hurricane Preparation Offers Lessons in Organization," *Los Angeles Times*, 10 September 2005, https://www.latimes.com/archives/la-xpm-2005-sep-10-na-cuba10-story.html.

23 "Day 9: Tuesday, September 6," *PBS Frontline*, "14 Days: A Timeline," 22 November 2005, https://www.pbs.org/wgbh/pages/frontline/storm/etc/cron.html.

24 For Cuba's approach to disaster planning, see Martha Thompson, *Lessons in Risk Reduction from Cuba*, "Case Studies 2007," *UN-Habitat*, 2007, https://mirror.unhabitat.org/content.asp?typeid=19&catid=555&cid=5403.

25 Victoria Stilwell and Wei Lu, "The 10 Most Unequal Big Cities in America," *Bloomberg*, 10 November 2015, https://www.bloomberg.com/news/articles/2015-11-10/the-10-most-unequal-big-cities-in-america.

26 Ellyn Kail, "Photos of the New Orleans Neighborhood That Disappeared," *Feature Shoot*, 27 January 2017, https://www.featureshoot.com/2017/01/photos-new-orleans-neighborhood-disappeared/.

27 Richard Wilkinson and Kate Pickett, *The Spirit Level: Why Greater Equality Makes Societies Stronger* (London: Bloomsbury, 2009).

28 Peter Newman, Timothy Beatley, and Heather Boyer, *Resilient Cities: Responding to Peak Oil and Climate Change* (Washington, DC: Island Press, 2009).

29 Douglas Kelbaugh, *The Urban Fix: Resilient Cities in the War against Climate Change, Heat Islands and Overpopulation* (New York: Routledge, 2019).

30 Newman, Beatley, and Boyer, *Resilient Cities*, 7.

31 In the early 2000s, Albertans averaged 1,667 litres per person annually. Alberta Transportation, *Fuel Use Relative to Population: A Provincial Analysis* (Edmonton: Government of Alberta, n.d.).

32 "World Vehicles in Use, by Country, Region, and Type, 2005–2015," *International Organization of Motor Vehicle Manufacturers (OICA)*, accessed 31 August 2020, http://www.oica.net/category/vehicles-in-use/.

33 Keough, Morrison, and Lee, *State of Our City 2020*, 50.

34 City of Calgary, *Changing Travel Behaviour in the Calgary Region*, Travel Behaviour Report Series: Vol. 1, Table 5, 20 (Calgary: City of Calgary, June 2013), https://www.calgary.ca/Transportation/TP/Documents/forecasting/Changing%20Travel%20Behaviour%20in%20the%20Calgary%20Region_v1_forWeb_2013-06-04.pdf?noredirect=1.

35 Kasparas Adomaitis, "Top Developed World Cities with Low Reliance on Car-Based Mobility," *Euromonitor International*, 31 August 2015, https://blog.euromonitor.com/top-developed-world-cities-with-low-reliance-on-car-based-mobility/.

36 City of Calgary, *Resilient Calgary*.

37   Timothy Beatley, *Green Urbanism Down Under*, with Peter Newman (Washington, DC: Island Press, 2008), and *Green Urbanism: Learning from European Cities* (Washington, DC: Island Press, 2000), https://www.academia.edu/10399646/Green_Urbanism_Learning_From_European_Cities.

38   "68% of the World Population Projected to Live in Urban Areas by 2050, Says UN," *UN Department of Economic and Social Affairs*, 16 May 2018, https://www.un.org/development/desa/en/news/population/2018-revision-of-world-urbanization-prospects.html.

39   Statistics Canada, "Canada's Population Estimates: Subprovincial Areas, July 1, 2019," *Statistics Canada*, released 13 February 2020, https://www150.statcan.gc.ca/n1/daily-quotidien/200213/dq200213a-eng.htm.

40   Meghan Potkins, "Growth, Climate Change Could Push Calgary's Water Intake to the Limit by 2036," *Calgary Herald*, 14 May 2019, https://calgaryherald.com/news/local-news/calgary-could-reach-daily-water-licence-limit-by-2036.

41   Beatley, *Green Urbanism Down Under*, 236.

42   Wulf Daseking, personal communication, Freiburg, Germany, 17 June 2013.

43   Wulf Daseking, Babette Köhler, and Götz Kemnitz, *Freiburg Charter: Requirements on Urban Development and Planning for the Future* (Freiburg: Academy of Urbanism and City of Freiburg, 2012), http://www.wulf-daseking.de/files/8214/0110/4795/Charta_Freiburg_2012en.pdf.

44   Clara Irazabal, *City Making and Urban Governance in the Americas: Curitiba and Portland* (London: Routledge, 2017).

45   David Adler, "Stories of Cities #37: How Radical Ideas Turned Curitiba into Brazil's 'Green Capital,'" *The Guardian*, 6 May 2016, https://www.theguardian.com/cities/2016/may/06/story-of-cities-37-mayor-jaime-lerner-curitiba-brazil-green-capital-global-icon.

46   "Växjö: The Sustainable City Frontrunner," *Nordregio*, 29 June 2018, https://nordregio.org/sustainable_cities/europes-greenest-city-vaxjo/.

47   Jonna Kangasoja and Harry Schulman, eds., *Arabianranta: Rethinking Urban Living* (Helsinki: City of Helsinki Urban Facts, 2007).

Further Reading

Flint, Anthony. *Wrestling with Moses: How Jane Jacobs Took on New York's Master Builder and Transformed the American City.* New York: Random House, 2011.

Krier, Leon. "The Future of Cities: The Absurdity of Modernism." Nikos Salingaros: Interview with Leon Krier. *Planetizen*, 5 November 2001. https://www.planetizen.com/node/32.

Works Cited

"68% of the World Population Projected to Live in Urban Areas by 2050, Says UN." *UN Department of Economic and Social Affairs*, 16 May 2018. https://www.un.org/development/desa/en/news/population/2018-revision-of-world-urbanization-prospects.html.

Adler, David. "Stories of Cities #37: How Radical Ideas Turned Curitiba into Brazil's 'Green Capital.'" *The Guardian*, 6 May 2016. https://www.theguardian.com/cities/2016/may/06/story-of-cities-37-mayor-jaime-lerner-curitiba-brazil-green-capital-global-icon.

Adomaitis, Kasparas. "Top Developed World Cities with Low Reliance on Car-Based Mobility." *Euromonitor International*, 31 August 2015. https://blog.euromonitor.com/top-developed-world-cities-with-low-reliance-on-car-based-mobility/.

Alberta Transportation. *Fuel Use Relative to Population: A Provincial Analysis*. Edmonton: Government of Alberta, n.d.

Beatley, Timothy. *Green Urbanism Down Under*. With Peter Newman. Washington, DC: Island Press, 2008.

———. *Green Urbanism: Learning from European Cities*. Washington, DC: Island Press, 2000. https://www.academia.edu/10399646/Green_Urbanism_Learning_From_European_Cities.

City of Calgary. *Changing Travel Behaviour in the Calgary Region*. Travel Behaviour Report Series: Vol. 1. Calgary: City of Calgary, June 2013. https://www.calgary.ca/Transportation/TP/Documents/forecasting/Changing%20Travel%20Behaviour%20in%20the%20Calgary%20Region_v1_forWeb_2013-06-04.pdf?noredirect=1.

———. *Hillhurst Sunnyside Area Redevelopment Plan*. Calgary: City of Calgary, 2018. https://d3aencwbm6zmht.cloudfront.net/asset/399111/hillhurst-sunnyside-arp.pdf.

———. *Investing in Mobility: Transportation Infrastructure Investment Plan*. Calgary: City of Calgary, 2014.

———. *Keystone Hills Area Structure Plan*. Calgary: City of Calgary, 2012. https://www.calgary.ca/pda/pd/current-studies-and-ongoing-activities/keystone-hills.html.

———. *Keystone Hills Area Structure Plan: Ecological Footprint*. Report to Calgary Planning Commission. CPC212-041, Attachment 3, Appendix II, 12 April 2012.

———. *Municipal Development Plan*. Calgary: City of Calgary, 2009. https://www.calgary.ca/pda/pd/municipal-development-plan/municipal-development-plan-mdp.html.

———. *Resilient Calgary*. Calgary: City of Calgary, 2019. https://www.calgary.ca/cs/calgary-resilience.html.

———. *Transit Oriented Development: Policy Guidelines*. Calgary: City of Calgary, 2005. https://www.calgary.ca/pda/pd/current-studies-and-ongoing-activities/transit-oriented-development-tod.html.

"COVID-19 Coronavirus Pandemic: Reported Case of Death by Country, Territory or Conveyance." *Worldometer*, 2020. https://www.worldometers.info/coronavirus/.

"Cuban Hurricane Preparation Offers Lessons in Organization." *Los Angeles Times*, 10 September 2005. https://www.latimes.com/archives/la-xpm-2005-sep-10-na-cuba10-story.html.

Daseking, Wulf, Babette Köhler, and Götz Kemnitz. *Freiburg Charter: Requirements on Urban Development and Planning for the Future*. Freiburg: Academy of Urbanism and City of Freiburg, 2012. http://www.wulf-daseking.de/files/8214/0110/4795/Charta_Freiburg_2012en.pdf.

"Day 9: Tuesday, September 6." *PBS Frontline*, "14 Days: A Timeline," 22 November 2005. https://www.pbs.org/wgbh/pages/frontline/storm/etc/cron.html.

Deberry, Jarvis. "Today's a Day to Remember Those Killed by Hurricanes Katrina and Maria." *New Orleans Advocate*, 29 August 2018. https://www.nola.com/opinions/article_cb104aaa-aadf-5e90-b3a1-1413c51f85e2.html.

"An Evening with Jan Gehl at the Calgary Public Library." *Canadian Architect*, 2 April 2011. https://www.canadianarchitect.com/an-evening-with-jan-gehl-at-the-calgary-public-library/.

Foran, Max. *Expansive Discourses: Urban Sprawl in Calgary, 1945–78*. Athabasca, AB: Athabasca University Press, 2009.

Gehl, Jan. *Cities for People*. Washington, DC: Island Press, 2010.

IBI Group. *The Implications of Alternative Growth Patterns on Infrastructure Costs*. Calgary: City of Calgary, 9 April 2009. http://www.reconnectingamerica.org/assets/Uploads/planitcalgarycoststudyanalysisaprilthird.pdf.

Irazabal, Clara. *City Making and Urban Governance in the Americas: Curitiba and Portland*. London: Routledge, 2017.

Janssen, Ian. "Health Care Costs of Physical Inactivity in Canadian Adults." *Applied Physiology, Nutrition, and Metabolism* 37, no. 4 (June 2012): 803–6.

Kail, Ellyn. "Photos of the New Orleans Neighborhood That Disappeared." *Feature Shoot*, 27 January 2017. https://www.featureshoot.com/2017/01/photos-new-orleans-neighborhood-disappeared/.

Kangasoja, Jonna, and Harry Schulman, eds. *Arabianranta: Rethinking Urban Living*. Helsinki: City of Helsinki Urban Facts, 2007.

Kelbaugh, Douglas. *The Urban Fix: Resilient Cities in the War against Climate Change, Heat Islands and Overpopulation*. New York: Routledge, 2019.

Keough, Noel, Bob Morrison, and Celia Lee. *State of Our City 2020: An Urgent Call for a Just Transition*. Calgary: Sustainable Calgary Society, 2020. http://www.sustainablecalgary.org/publications.

Knabb, Richard, Jamie Rhome, and Daniel Brown. *Tropical Cyclone Report: Hurricane Katrina 23–30 August 2005*. Miami: National Hurricane Center, 20 December 2005. https://www.nhc.noaa.gov/data/tcr/AL122005_Katrina.pdf.

Newman, Peter, Timothy Beatley, and Heather Boyer. *Resilient Cities: Responding to Peak Oil and Climate Change.* Washington, DC: Island Press, 2009.

O2 Planning and Design. *Bow to Bluff Urban Design Framework.* Calgary: Bow to Bluff, 2011. https://www.cip-icu.ca/Files/Awards/Planning-Excellence/2013-16-Bow-to-Bluff-FULL-PLAN.aspx.

Owen, David. *Green Metropolis: Why Living Smaller, Living Closer, and Driving Less Are the Keys to Sustainability.* New York: Riverhead Books, 2010.

Potkins, Meghan. "Growth, Climate Change Could Push Calgary's Water Intake to the Limit by 2036." *Calgary Herald,* 14 May 2019. https://calgaryherald.com/news/local-news/calgary-could-reach-daily-water-licence-limit-by-2036.

Statistics Canada. "Canada's Population Estimates: Subprovincial Areas, July 1, 2019." *Statistics Canada,* released 13 February 2020. https://www150.statcan.gc.ca/n1/daily-quotidien/200213/dq200213a-eng.htm.

Stilwell, Victoria, and Wei Lu. "The 10 Most Unequal Big Cities in America." *Bloomberg,* 10 November 2015. https://www.bloomberg.com/news/articles/2015-11-10/the-10-most-unequal-big-cities-in-america.

Sudamant, Andrew, Matt Tierney, Eduard Cubi, Effie Papargyropoulou, Andy Gouldson, and Joule Bergerson. *The Economics of Low Carbon Development.* Calgary: City of Calgary, 2019. https://climate.leeds.ac.uk/wp-content/uploads/2018/03/Calgary-Exec-Sum-draft-4_Web.pdf.

Thompson, Martha. *Lessons in Risk Reduction from Cuba.* "Case Studies 2007." *UN-Habitat,* 2007. https://mirror.unhabitat.org/content.asp?typeid=19&catid=555&cid=5403.

UN Department of Economics and Social Affairs. *United Nations Demographic Yearbook 2015.* New York: United Nations, 2016. https://unstats.un.org/unsd/demographic-social/products/dyb/dybsets/2015.pdf.

UN Environment. *Global Environmental Outlook 6: Healthy Planet, Healthy People.* Nairobi: United Nations Environment Programme, 2019.

"Växjö: The Sustainable City Frontrunner." *Nordregio,* 29 June 2018. https://nordregio.org/sustainable_cities/europes-greenest-city-vaxjo/.

Vincanne, Adam, Sharon Kaufman, Taslim van Hattum, and Sandra Moody. "Aging Disaster: Mortality, Vulnerability, and Long-Term Recovery among Katrina Survivors." *Medical Anthropology* 30, no. 2 (May 2011): 247–70.

Wilkinson, Richard, and Kate Pickett. *The Spirit Level: Why Greater Equality Makes Societies Stronger.* London: Bloomsbury, 2009.

"World Vehicles in Use, by Country, Region, and Type, 2005–2015." *International Organization of Motor Vehicle Manufacturers (OICA).* Accessed 31 August 2020. http://www.oica.net/category/vehicles-in-use/.

Where Do We Grow from Here?

Getting growth right will be crucial to global sustainability in this urban age. The essays in this chapter explore several of the key issues associated with urban growth in North America. Suburban development, usually endowed with the characteristics of sprawl, continues to dominate growth in Calgary. In this chapter, we highlight some of the causes and consequences of the inexorable expansion of Calgary into surrounding farmland. We also discuss the related phenomenon of big box retail and examine its real costs.

This chapter brings to light issues of urban governance. What is evident in many of the essays is that decisions on growth go beyond city government. Regional highways, the protection of farmland, education infrastructure, and the global ecological implications of city planning decisions demonstrate the need to bring more than just the narrow interests and jurisdictions of city governments to urban design and growth.

Calgary is a perfect example of another phenomenon of outward expansion, which some have called "school sprawl." As we grow ever outwards, new families move to new suburbs; suburban schools become larger, capturing economies of scale in light of ever-tighter education budgets; and inner city schools empty out as families in established neighbourhoods mature. As a result, more kids are bused to school in Calgary, and scarce education dollars are diverted from the classroom to the bus fleet.

One instrument for sustainable urban growth is the urban growth boundary (UGB). The essay "No Limits, No More" takes up this planning tool. We examine the most well-known and successful UGB in Portland, Oregon. The essay describes the features of a successful UGB and examines its potential for Calgary and region.

These essays also highlight the political dimensions of urban growth. We revisit a particularly high-profile battle between Calgary's mayor and a prominent homebuilder. At stake is who gets to decide how our city grows. Should urban growth be left to the market? What responsibilities do our elected representatives have in the process? What roles do professional planners play? And most importantly, what role do citizens have in ensuring that growth is for the common good?

Finally, "Lessons from the Left Coast" features Vancouver, considered to be one of the best examples of modern urban sustainability. The essay offers examples not only of what Vancouver has got right, but how it got it right. It didn't just happen. Many dedicated citizens, planners, politicians, and developers made it happen.

A PRICEY RIDE TO SCHOOL: THE HIDDEN COSTS OF SUBURBAN SPRAWL

In the fall of 2019, the Calgary Board of Education made two significant yet contradictory announcements. The first was that cutbacks caused by budget shortfalls would result in the loss of four hundred teaching positions, among other losses.[1] The second—a proposed hike in school busing fees, forecast to increase the cost to families by 60 percent—was voted down by the Board.[2]

The province made it clear that there would be no new funding to cover budget shortfalls, so money once used for silly things like hiring teachers and ensuring adequate classroom resources was instead being diverted to pay for rising transportation costs. What a cruel irony.

A 2017 Brookings Institute study surveyed the issue of busing in American cities and estimated that delaying school start times by an hour would result in a lifetime earnings bump of $17,500 per student through better academic performance.[3] Reducing busing times would accomplish the same thing by allowing those perennially sleep-deprived teenaged students to sleep longer. Research published in the journal *Sleep Health* reported that later school start times resulted in improved attendance and graduation rates.[4] A 2009 study in the journal *Preventive Medicine* found that in Toronto, "between 1986 and 2006, walking mode share for trips to school declined (53.0%–42.5% for 11–13 year olds, 38.6%–30.7% for 14–15 year olds)."[5] Over roughly the same period, overweight and obesity became an increasingly critical issue for youth across Canada.[6] Creating communities where kids can safely walk to school provides the opportunity for a daily dose of exercise and goes a long way to promoting health and fitness.

Many suburban families—already stressed by the effects of rising energy prices, which in turn increase the costs of almost everything, from fuel to food to manufactured goods—are reaching their limits, and all families that are confronted with busing fees of any size lose. This is because the "fee" is not a fee at all: it's a targeted, regressive education tax penalizing families with kids in the system, with the poorest paying proportionally the most.

There are other, less obvious costs of excessive school busing. Getting 34,500 kids to and from school at the busiest times of the day adds considerable congestion to already crowded city streets. Counterproductive is a polite way to describe it. There are many culprits responsible for this backwards state of affairs, but at its heart, it's not a funding problem—it's a sprawl problem. Rising transportation costs, including school buses, are a byproduct of the way we have built the city—spread over the prairie like jam on toast. As the distance between where children live and where they go to school increases, so does the cost of getting them there.

School sprawl comes with other associated problems. In 2004 the Calgary Board of Education (CBE) created a firestorm by threatening to close seven inner city schools—a perennial problem in sprawling cities.[7] The issue is in part a numbers game. The CBE had to show appropriate levels of occupancy in a school district in order to have new school construction approved, so closing inner city schools where occupancy was less than 100 percent allowed them to reach those district occupancy targets. Many young families move to sprawling suburbs without schools, so we spend millions of dollars closing perfectly good schools and opening up new ones. In many of these communities, kids are bused for years and graduate by the time a promised school is actually built. After the school goes up, chaos ensues, as the inner city schools that were accommodating the bused students become "ghost towns," as one parent described the situation.[8]

In the CBE's 2019 Shaping the Future of High School survey of parents, staff, and community members, the principle "Allow students to attend school as close to home as possible" was rated highest among principles that should guide the Board's planning process. In that same survey, "proximity to home" was rated second only to "academics" when respondents were asked to rank factors affecting choice of high school.[9]

We tend to buy into the myth that suburbs provide affordable housing. But it only seems that way because many of the costs—school bus fees being only one example—are subsidized by taxpayers. Now that these costs can no longer be contained, another strand in that myth is unraveling.

BIG BOX BOONDOGGLE: WHY SMALL AND LOCAL IS BEAUTIFUL

In July 2012 City Council took a bold and unexpected decision to turn down an application from WinSport Canada to redesignate land uses at Canada Olympic Park.[10] The redesignation would have opened the door for Winsport to sell land for auto-dependent, big box commercial and retail development requiring the construction of an eight-lane interchange. Faced with objections from residents of Bowness and Montgomery about the effects of the development on traffic and on local businesses, and in deference to the Municipal Development Plan's goal of creating a more compact city, the application was rejected. Unfortunately, Trinity Hills Group came back to Council with a similar proposal, and in 2015 the development was approved.[11] It is now moving ahead, with a massive expansion of the Trans-Canada Highway already complete and the soon-to-be completed west section of the Ring Road ready to bring shoppers from the entire region to its doorsteps.

City Council's original rejection of Trinity Hills and big box shopping was well considered. In 2008 the City commissioned a comprehensive study of the thirty million–plus square feet of retail in Calgary and the surrounding region. The study noted that Calgary has more large-scale auto-oriented retail than most jurisdictions. These include "super-regional centres" like Chinook Centre and Sunridge Mall, "power centres" like Deerfoot Meadows and Country Hills, and "factory outlets" like Deerfoot Mall. The study also found that Calgary is actually deficient in community and neighbourhood retail.[12]

The study noted that peripheral commercial developments like the CrossIron Mills megamall are oversized but are opportunistically located to attract car-driving shoppers from the entire region. In the discussion of what elements of urban form best support high-quality retail, diversity of housing choice, walkability, and compact development all made the list. Most critical were accessible and convenient transportation networks and the co-location of shopping, residential, recreation, and jobs (often referred to as mixed-use development). The recommended strategy was to focus on smaller-scale retail inside the city.

While big box has its challenges, it also delivers jobs, economic development, and, most important, consumer choice—right? Well, not according to Stacy Mitchell of the American Independent Business Alliance and author of *Big Box Swindle: The True Cost of Mega-Retailers and the Fight for America's Independent Businesses*. Mitchell makes a strong case for the corrosive effects of big box retail. She argues that "mega-retailers impose a variety of hidden costs on society and contribute far less to our economic well-being than they take away."[13] Case in point—the development of retail and commercial space at COP will require at least $110 million of investment in road upgrades and interchanges.[14]

Mitchell goes on to argue that local business is a vital ingredient in the fabric of community life and that local business owners are more financially and personally invested in their communities. Unlike big box retailers, they have nowhere else to go. Their kids go to local schools, are taken care of at local hospitals, and swim at local pools, so they are more supportive of taxation that helps to fund these amenities. In fact, small business has been found to contribute twice as much per employee to charitable organizations as large businesses. Mitchell cites research showing that more local business ownership brings lower property crime and that citizens who live in communities better served by local businesses are more civically engaged, volunteer more, vote in greater numbers, and drive less.

The Institute for Local Self-Reliance, a research and policy non-profit based in Minneapolis, has done its homework on big box retail. A study in Austin, Texas, found that spending $100 at a big box bookstore generates $13 of local economic activity, while spending the same amount at a local bookstore generates $45.[15] A Loyola University study found that within a four-mile radius of a new Wal-Mart store in Chicago, one quarter of previously existing businesses closed.[16] A 2013 study by Civic Economics found that in British Columbia, every $1 million in sales by independent retail stores generates $450,000 in local economic activity, compared to just $170,000 for chain stores. The same study estimates that a 10 percent shift from chain stores to independents would create thirty-one thousand jobs in BC.[17]

All too often, the result of big box retail development is displacement of local jobs, depressed wages and benefits in the retail sector, reduced local tax revenues, and increased costs for social programs that low-wage workers rely on to make ends meet. Why? Because local retailers buy more from local producers; they buy local services like accounting and legal services, and they do not have the overhead of employees based in distant head offices. More money stays put.

A city requires only so much retail, the North American average being about twenty-five to thirty square feet per capita. More big box retail means less local retail. Big box at Canada Olympic Park will probably mean that the communities of Montgomery and Bowness will face an uphill battle to attract and grow local business and build vibrant main streets.

Absentee landlords have little understanding of, or allegiance to, our community as anything other than a source of revenue. The growth of on-line shopping is an even more disturbing trend for local businesses and for retail workers, with Amazon seemingly intent on monopolizing the global retail market. To the extent that the profit motive drives them to provide good service, that's great—but local businesses offer that and much more.

In the end, we exercise our own choices about where to shop. Will those choices be based solely on the sticker price, or will we make decisions (with our dollars and our votes) in support of healthy, vibrant, and resilient local and regional communities and economies?

FISCAL CLIFF: CALGARY'S GROWTH MANAGEMENT STRATEGY UNDER SIEGE

It's March 2020, and former councilor Brian Pincott is speaking to *The Sprawl*, an online journalism project. Approving fourteen new communities in Calgary, he says, "was as close to throwing out the Municipal Development Plan as you could get," and abolishing the Growth Management Overlay (GMO), an administration mechanism put in place to determine the long-term costs of proposed greenfield community developments, "takes us back to before the 2009 Plan It and a developer free-for-all."[18]

To understand how we got to this point, we have to go back to 2012, just three years into Plan It, when this proposed plan, designed to avoid a fiscal cliff brought on by a tsunami of infrastructure spending and maintenance that will bury us if we continue business as usual, was under siege.

On 3 December 2012, in a legislative showdown to determine if we would pull up short of the cliff or continue galloping toward it, City Council considered a proposal put forth by developers to neuter the City's growth management strategy. As a result of this meeting, Council agreed to create a pilot project for developer-funded area structure plans (ASPs), with Cornerstone ASP, in Calgary's far northeast, being the first guinea pig. In retrospect, this may have been the first successful gambit to neuter Plan It.

You could argue that this story began decades ago. In the 1950s, the City of Calgary essentially handed the responsibility for residential planning to the private development industry. Since that time, developers have delivered the suburban, sprawling, car-worshipping, and fiscally unsustainable city we have today. There have been attempts to turn the tide, most notably in the 1980s, when city planners presented a new vision of a more sustainable, walkable city that would tame the automobile. That didn't work out so well for many of the planners. They were unceremoniously run out of town by then-mayor Ralph Klein, and a chill settled over city planning for years.

It wasn't until January 2005 that Calgary began to recover from that trauma, when, under the leadership of councilors such as Joe Ceci, the City embarked on unprecedented citizen engagement to chart a new course. That effort culminated in 2006 at the World Urban Forum in Vancouver, where then-mayor David Bronconnier unveiled the imagineCalgary hundred-year vision.[19]

Eighteen thousand Calgarians had a hand in crafting that vision. The citizen panel that led the process included Naheed Nenshi and Brian Pincott—who later became mayor and councilor, respectively—as well as the CEOs of United Way and Glenbow Museum. In July 2006, at a special hearing of City Council, dozens of organizations presented letters of support for the imagineCalgary document, including Sustainable Calgary, Calgary Economic Development, and the Calgary Region Homebuilders Association.

Between 2007 and 2009, with the participation of thousands of citizens and the unanimous endorsement of Council, a sixty-year road map on how to achieve the imagineCalgary vision was developed and given legal weight in the Municipal Development Plan (MDP) and the Calgary Transportation Plan (collectively known as Plan It). Change is sometimes excruciatingly slow, but the planning process plods along. In December 2011, Council endorsed the continued development of a growth management strategy that would give teeth to the MDP.

The strategy established criteria, embodied in the GMO, for deciding where new residential development should occur. The point of the strategy is to encourage growth in places where providing infrastructure—transit, roads, water and sewer, and emergency services—is least costly. In the old system, we said yes to developments with little concern for the long-term cost to taxpayers or for the impending fiscal cliff. The growth management strategy, the MDP, and imagineCalgary represent the long road to fiscal prudence and sustainability for our city. The problem is that the road to fiscal prudence diverges from that of profit maximization for the development industry, and they were not amused. The industry refused to endorse the imagineCalgary vision in 2006; they challenged the MDP process every step of the way and, in the final analysis, diluted the plan during a closed-door eleventh-hour deal with then-mayor Bronconnier. In the winter of 2011, they were successful in lobbying Council to institute a 50 percent taxpayer subsidy of infrastructure costs for greenfield suburban development—over $80,000 per hectare—rather than absorbing all the costs themselves.[20]

The December 2012 proposal from developers to pay the cost of drawing up ASPs resulted in the aforementioned Cornerstone ASP pilot project. ASPs are the first of a series of statutory planning stages that culminate in the building of a new community. It sounds like a generous offer, but the industry's motivation was anything but altruistic. The existence of an ASP allows the developer to move forward to a stage of the development process where they are in the driver's seat. In effect, developers wanted to position themselves, with ASP in hand, to jump the land development–priorities queue that the growth management strategy would establish.

It is sad but true that over the last decade of a renaissance in city planning, the development industry has been consistently obstructionist. They appear offended by the notion of citizens having a place at the table when decisions are being made about the design of the neighbourhoods and communities where we will live and raise our families. They have profited handsomely from the back-room, closed-door development process, and they are loath to see it change.

Mayor Nenshi was elected in 2010 on a promise of more openness at City Hall. Over the last decade, thousands of citizens have responded, in good faith, to the City's invitation to participate in various planning processes. But the system still seems to be rigged in favour of developers. Many of the implementation decisions for the MDP have been made around an exclusive table featuring administration and developers, who constitute the City's Developer Advisory Committee.

We suggest that to balance the playing field, councilors need a gentle reminder about who they work for as they consider these crucial decisions. We place our trust in them to represent the common good rather than cater to a small but powerful private interest group.

NO LIMITS, NO MORE: IT'S TIME FOR AN URBAN GROWTH BOUNDARY

Calgary is losing valuable farmland at an astonishing rate. We need to draw a line around the city and say no to urban development beyond it. We can't afford any more sprawling, auto-dependent suburbs. We used to grow food in the Cranston, Tuscany, Taradale, and Coventry Hills neighbourhoods.

Rural sprawl is out, too—no more developments like Springbank, Heritage Pointe, or Bearspaw, where cattle once pastured or wildlife teemed. And certainly no more environmentally disastrous developments like CrossIron Mills, where an authentic rural community once prospered.

It's called an urban growth boundary (UGB), and many cities have one. Vancouver has its "green zone" and Toronto its "green belt." Ottawa has had a protected zone circling the city since the 1950s (thanks to the federal government). UGBs protect agricultural and natural lands from development by strictly limiting the permissible land uses outside it, where development such as residential suburbs, commercial and shopping districts, and industrial parks are forbidden.

The most famous and most studied UGB surrounds Portland, Oregon. Portland's UGB was created in 1972 as part of state legislation designed to inhibit rapidly accelerating urban encroachment on fertile, working agricultural lands. UGBs now surround not only Portland, but every major urban place in the state.

The Portland UGB is not an iron curtain. It includes a twenty-year supply of undeveloped land to satisfy natural growth pressures. The boundary can be extended when overall urban densities achieve target thresholds that support more compact forms of growth—like dense transit networks and walkable neighbourhoods. But in Oregon, extending the UGB is the last option, not the first.

UGBs are controversial and provoke intense emotions. They are opposed by a coalition of urban growth proponents—developers, home-builders, road-builders, and, not least, land and property speculators—as well as by owners of rural land eager to cash in on the urban bonanza. One claim of the growth coalition is that UGBs artificially restrict land supplies, causing unnatural price increases. This, in turn, limits growth proponents' ability to offer so-called affordable housing on the city's fringes. For them, the UGB is a pointless government intrusion on the free market. In Calgary, they say, a glance eastward, to the seemingly endless prairie, is all that is needed to confirm the "common sense" observation that there's plenty of land for both development and agriculture.

Another assertion, often accompanied by threats to leave town, is that UGBs are ineffective because when prices go up in the city, development, and the economic activity it generates, moves away. Restricting land supplies in Calgary just means higher growth rates—and more business—elsewhere.

But as appealing and persuasive as these arguments seem, they lack substance. In response to the contention that UGBs cause unwarranted increases in land prices, research from Portland State University, published in 2006, shows that in Oregon, land values inside and outside UGBs increased at about the same rate.[21] The same research found that, for comparable uses, land prices inside Oregon grew at about the same rate as in other states during the same period. Contrary to the free-market criticism, UGBs do not stifle growth; they establish sensible rules for locating it.

As for the claim that there's lots of land available for growth—well, this is an example of what Paul Krugman, a Nobel economist and influential *New York Times* columnist, calls a "zombie lie": no matter how many times you try to kill it, it refuses to die. The story, endlessly repeated by development lobbyists at public hearings, is that Canada is big—about nine million square kilometres. Of all that land, only 0.5 percent is urbanized.

Conclusion: There is no need for growth boundaries or density targets. It's mind-boggling.

Only 5 percent of Canada's land base is capable of producing food, and only a small fraction of that is rated Class 1 (the best agricultural soils). For geological, historical, and geographical reasons, many Canadian cities, including Calgary and Edmonton, sit smack in the middle of Class 1 farmland.

A 2014 study by the Canadian Forest Service reported that between 1988 and 2010, urban and suburban land use increased from 2.5 percent to 6.6 percent in the Edmonton-Calgary region, with 60 percent of the expansion occurring on agricultural land, of which two-thirds was highly suitable for farming.[22] The rate of loss over the period was accelerating. The report found that up to two thousand square kilometres of agricultural land could be lost between 2010 and 2036. We're relentlessly expanding into the last of the best land we have.

And the threat of leaving town is hooey. UGBs are effective because they work at a regional scale. If Calgary alone were to draw a line, the leaving-town argument might hold water. But if Airdrie, Cochrane, Okotoks, Strathmore, and the other small towns in the region also had UGBs, the threat would be empty.

Evidence shows that the primary purpose of UGBs—directing urban development away from precious farmland—has been successful in other cities. We need one. Our sustainability could depend on it.

PRIDE AND PREJUDICE—OR WHY DEVELOPERS AND BUILDERS WANT TO CONTROL CITY HALL

In spring 2013, with the municipal election heating up, we caught a rare glimpse into Calgary's development industry when excerpts of an audio-tape of the CEO of a major homebuilder in our city were broadcast. The CEO was advising fellow development industry members on which city councilors should be supported and which should be opposed for re-election.[23] Leaving aside the sordid aspects of this affair, the episode sheds light on some fundamental issues about how we govern and grow our city.

Three aspects of this unfortunate incident are particularly informative—the single-minded self-interest of the development industry, the presumed infallibility of the market (when it is convenient), and the shorts-in-a-knot bluster at having citizens sit at a table that industry insiders always thought was reserved solely for them and their buddies. The not-so-subtle message from the CEO was that the mayor and councilors have no business meddling in the workings of the all-knowing market. After all, they are merely the citizens' elected representatives, charged with steering our city toward the common good. How dare they think they have the right to create policy to that end!

Even more galling, how dare they invite citizens to roll up their sleeves and take an active part in shaping Calgary! Development industry players will have none of that. They are perfectly capable of deciding how our city grows, thank you very much. Never mind that as they make decisions about where Calgary should grow, they oblige the City to raise and spend tax dollars to provide the pipes, the police, the firefighters, and the freeways that give value to their investments.

Most insidious perhaps, this CEO's actions imply a cornerstone of market thinking that has found its way into democratic deliberation—the virtue of self-interest. Instead of an election being an opportunity for citizens to debate, argue, educate themselves, and come to consensus about what is best for our city, market thinking suggests that we all just show up at the polls, vote in our isolated self-interest, and the common good emerges, as if by magic, from the ballot box.

Then there is the matter of whether these free market defenders actually believe what they are saying. One of the most vexing things for the industry is City Council's slow but steady moves to eliminate the handsome subsidies developers have long enjoyed. The City of Calgary's 2009 cost-of-growth study makes it abundantly clear that for decades, the development industry has been enriched by billions of dollars that help make it oh so profitable.[24]

The market will decide. Really! Then why does the industry find itself in the uncomfortable position of having to defend its plan to build homes on land it purchased a generation ago? Most of those who buy a home in suburban developments were either yet to be born, still in diapers, or not living in the city, the province, or even the country when that land was purchased and developers began the process of making sure it would be where Calgary families would live. The industry shapes the market at least as much as it responds to it. The market is a valuable tool when deployed effectively, but it is no substitute for critical thinking, moral judgement, and democratic deliberation. We need look no further than the tragic 2012 garment industry fires in Bangladesh to see where unchecked market self-interest leads.

Those involved in the development industry claim they should be making the decisions because they are taking the risks when they plan communities and build homes. Fair enough, but as homeowners, we have plenty of skin in the game, too. We live our lives and raise families in these homes and neighbourhoods.

Industry players claim to be the experts. Unquestionably, they possess unique skills and expertise. But they are not public finance economists or public health experts; they have no special expertise in what constitutes quality of life or how to build social capital, or in the environmental effects of alternative ways of building homes, neighbourhoods, and cities. Every person who volunteers for soccer, participates in the river clean-up, sits on the board of a community association or arts agency, or volunteers with the United Way is a builder of this city. Sadly, the industry is loath to make room at the table for any of this expertise.

To claim that City Council is seeking to shut the industry out of City Hall is absurd. Homebuilders and developers will be busy for decades to come designing neighbourhoods and constructing homes in suburban communities already approved by the City. What Council and administration have been doing since the inauguration of imagineCalgary is making room at the table for diverse voices to be heard and, in the process, enabling more transparent, well-considered decisions about the future of our city.

Developers and builders should swallow their misplaced pride, put aside their prejudices, and make room at the table for the rest of us.

LESSONS FROM THE LEFT COAST

From a restaurant deck overlooking English Bay, it is hard to imagine a more liveable city than Vancouver. In the words of Captain Vancouver in 1792, "to describe the beauty of this region will be a very grateful task to the pen of a skilful panegyrist."[25] Beyond the city's spectacular natural endowments, those who eventually settled Vancouver have a long history of getting the big moves right.

In their book *City Making in Paradise: Nine Decisions That Saved Vancouver*, former mayor and provincial premier Mike Harcourt and city planner Ken Cameron provide an account of those big moves.[26] In 1949, two years after a historic flood that devastated the Fraser Valley, visionary pioneer planners gave birth to the Lower Mainland Regional Planning Board—later succeeded by the Metro Vancouver Regional District. From its inception, the Planning Board envisioned a regional land use pattern; started the vital process of getting neighbouring cities, towns, and rural municipalities talking to each other; and embedded city planning in its ecological context.

In Calgary, legislated regional planning dates to the establishment of the Planning Commission in the 1950s. The Klein government disbanded the legislated commission in 1995. Four years later, cities, towns, and rural municipalities established a voluntary Calgary Regional Partnership. It, too, disbanded following the reinstatement of legislated regional planning by the Notley government in 2018. That same year, the Calgary Metropolitan Region (CMR) Board was established. Made up of elected officials from the CMR's ten member municipalities, its ability to shape development patterns will be vital for the success of our region.

A second critical moment for Vancouver was in the fall of 1968, when ordinary citizens of the working-class inner city neighbourhood of Strathcona joined a battle to save their community from an elevated freeway. At the time, this sort of "urban renewal" was conventional practice, but it would have destroyed Chinatown and Gastown, which today are among downtown Vancouver's gems. Against all odds, community action was successful, and together with academics, planning and architecture students, and activist professionals—like the young lawyer Mike Harcourt—the action spawned a political movement that has shaped Vancouver for three decades.

A third "big move" took place in 1973, when the BC provincial government tabled legislation to create the Agricultural Land Reserve (ALR). Less than 1 percent of BC's land is Class 1 Arable, and by 1973, 20 percent of agricultural land in the Lower Fraser Valley had been gobbled up by sprawl. Today, cities everywhere recognize the critical need to protect and nurture urban agriculture. Some version of an ALR or urban growth boundary would curb sprawl and respond to the growing citizen and consumer call for local food production in and around Calgary.

There is no better example of the promise of sustainable city living than Granville Island and the greater area of False Creek. The district is at the heart of forty kilometres of what is essentially a car-free, pedestrian- and bike-oriented thoroughfare (including the twenty-eight–kilometre Seawall) where you can find all of life's necessities and amenities and where the otherwise ubiquitous and imposing urban accessory—the automobile—is absent or marginalized, taking a back seat to non-motorized transport. Granville Island itself is the most convincing argument against the modern segregated planning model where homes, jobs, shops, and services are rigorously partitioned so that movement between them literally defines car dependence. Where else can you find heavy industry, arts production and retail, tourism, markets, shops, educational institutions, high-end condo living, and affordable housing co-operatives co-existing in what Harcourt and Cameron call "a gem of urbanity in harmony with its local context"?[27] Granville Island is proof that the new wisdom of mixed land use is not only possible but desirable and, we would argue, urgently needed in Calgary.

In 2011 Vancouver's mayor Gregor Robertson cut the ribbon on the city's newly refurbished and extended system of pedestrian and bike thoroughfares. By 2019 the bike infrastructure had expanded beyond the expectations of many Vancouverites—the progam was a resounding success.[28] Who didn't marvel at the throngs of Lower Mainlanders who took over the streets of Vancouver during the Olympics and the Stanley Cup playoffs, as they do in lesser numbers on most summer evenings? Vancouver's aggressive bike planning strategy makes room for cyclists on dedicated lanes throughout the downtown and on some of the major arteries into the city—imagine dedicated bicycle lanes the length of Memorial Drive, Bow Trail, and 9th Avenue, and you get the idea.

We know Vancouver is not actually paradise. It has its own problems—unaffordable real estate, gang violence, homelessness, and a certain Left Coast smugness, perhaps—not to mention the odd riot in the streets when Stanley Cup fortunes falter. But Calgarians shouldn't let that get in the way of learning a thing or two from Vancouver's many successes.

The lessons for Calgary? The market has a role to play in making a city great, but only under the guidance of a collective vision. And we have a great start! We're back on the road to regional planning: imagineCalgary and Plan It together provide a collective vision for the future, and we've begun to move on a cycling strategy, the Step Forward pedestrian strategy, and the Calgary Eats! food system action plan.[29] But grit and determination and the ability to work together as a community will be required to build on this foundation. Most importantly, Vancouver shows us how average citizens, students, academics, and dedicated public servants can make a real difference. Activism is not a dirty word but a badge of honour.

NOTES

1   Dean Bennet, "Alberta Finance Minister Says No Money Available for Teacher Salary Increases," *Edmonton Journal*, 4 March 2020, https://edmontonjournal.com/news/local-news/alberta-finance-minister-says-no-money-available-for-teacher-salary-increases.

2   Sarah Reiger, "CBE Retroactively Scraps Fee-Free Busing, Calgary Transit Rebate for 2019–20 School Year," *CBC News*, 10 December 2019, https://www.cbc.ca/news/canada/calgary/cbe-bus-costs-1.5391732.

3   Marco Hafner, Martin Stepanek, and Wendy Troxel, *Later School Start Times in the US: An Economic Analysis* (Cambridge, UK: Rand Corporation, 2017), https://www.rand.org/content/dam/rand/pubs/research_reports/RR2100/RR2109/RAND_RR2109.pdf.

4   Pamela Malaspina McKeever and Linda Clark, "Delayed High School Start Times Later Than 8:30 a.m. and Impact on Graduation Rates and Attendance Rates," *Sleep Health* 3, no. 2 (2017): 119–25.

5   Ron Buliung, Raktim Mitra, and Guy Faulkner, "Active School Transportation in the Greater Toronto Area, Canada: An Exploration of Trends in Space and Time (1986–2006)", *Preventive Medicine* 48, no. 6 (2009): 507–12.

6   Noel Keough, Bob Morrison, and Celia Lee, *State of Our City 2020: An Urgent Call for a Just Transition* (Calgary: Sustainable Calgary Society, 2020), 54, http://www.sustainablecalgary.org/publications.

7   "2 Schools on Closure List, 5 Saved," *Calgary Herald*, 21 January 2004, https://www.cbc.ca/news/canada/calgary/2-schools-on-closure-list-5-saved-1.498204.

8   Eva Ferguson, "Parents Worry As New S.E. High School Fills Up, Turning Beaverbrook into a 'Ghost Town,'" *Calgary Herald*, 24 January 2019, https://calgaryherald.com/news/local-news/suburban-high-schools-overflow-as-inner-city-buildings-start-to-empty.

9   CBE Communication and Engagement Services, *Shaping the Future of High School Spring Survey, 2019* (Calgary: Calgary Board of Education, 2019), https://www.cbe.ab.ca/get-involved/public-engagement/Documents/01082019-full-survey-report-public.pdf.

10 Jason Markusoff, "WinSport 'Extremely Disappointed' in Council's Rejection of Plan to Sell Land," *Calgary Herald*, 31 July 2012, http://www.calgaryherald.com/news/calgary/winsport+extremely+disappointed+council+rejection+plan+sell+land/7020115/story.html.

11 "Paskapoo Slopes Development Plan Approved by City Council," *CBC News*, 27 July 2015, https://www.cbc.ca/news/canada/calgary/paskapoo-slopes-development-plan-approved-by-city-council-1.3169706.

12 Global Retail Strategies Inc., *Recommended Directions for City-Wide Commercial/Retail Policy (Macro/Micro Final Report)* (Calgary: City of Calgary, December 2008), amended 5 March 2009.

13 Stacy Mitchell, *Big-Box Swindle: The True Cost of Mega-Retailers and the Fight for America's Independent Businesses* (Boston: Beacon Press, 2007), xii.

14 I (Keough) was present at the meeting of City Council on 30 July 2012 when this number was presented to Council verbally during debate over the Winsport expansion proposal.

15 Stacy Mitchell, "Local Stores Create Triple the Economic Activity of Chains," *Institute for Local Self-Reliance*, 1 February 2003, https://ilsr.org/local-stores-create-triple-economic-activity-chains/.

16 Julie Davis et al., *The Impact of an Urban Wal-Mart Store on Area Businesses: An Evaluation of One Chicago Neighborhood's Experience* (Chicago: Loyola University, Center for Urban Research and Learning, December 2009), https://ecommons.luc.edu/cgi/viewcontent.cgi?article=1002&context=curl_pubs.

17 CUPE-BC and Civic Economics, *Independent BC: Small Business and the British Columbia Economy* (Chicago: Civic Economics, February 2013), https://ccednet-rcdec.ca/sites/ccednet-rcdec.ca/files/ccednet/pdfs/independant_bc_small_and_the_british_colombia_economy.pdf.

18 Jeremy Klaszus, "Sprawlcast: Plan It Calgary, 10 Years Later," *The Sprawl,* 6 February 2020, https://www.sprawlcalgary.com/sprawlcast-plan-it.

19 imagineCalgary, "imagineCalgary Plan for Long Range Urban Sustainability" (Calgary: City of Calgary, September 2007), https://www.calgary.ca/pda/pd/office-of-sustainability/imaginecalgary.html.

20 "Calgary Developers Lose 'Sprawl Subsidy' on Water, Road Costs," *CBC News*, 11 January 2016, https://www.cbc.ca/news/canada/calgary/developer-levy-increase-city-council-1.3399577.

21 Myung-jin Jun, "The Effects of Portland's Urban Growth Boundary on Housing Prices," *Journal of the American Planning Association* 72, no. 2 (2006): 239–43.

22 Federico Martellozzo et al., "Urbanization and the Loss of Prime Farmland: A Case Study in the Calgary-Edmonton Corridor of Alberta," *Regional Environmental Change* 15 (2015): 881–93.

23 Doug Vaessen and Lisa Geddes, "Mayor Calls for Investigation of Civic Election Campaign Contributions," *Global News*, 23 April 2013, https://globalnews.ca/news/504916/mayor-calls-for-investigation-of-civic-election-campaign-contributions/.

24   IBI Group, *The Implications of Alternative Growth Patterns on Infrastructure Costs* (Calgary: City of Calgary, April 2009), http://www.reconnectingamerica.org/assets/Uploads/planitcalgarycoststudyanalysisaprilthird.pdf.

25   Quoted in M. B. Synge, *A Book of Discovery: The History of the World's Exploration, from the Earliest Times to the Finding of the South Pole* (London: T. C. and E. C. Jack, 1912), released 20 October 2007, Project Gutenberg, https://archive.org/stream/abookofdiscovery23107gut/pg23107.txt.

26   Mike Harcourt and Ken Cameron, *City Making in Paradise: Nine Decisions That Saved Vancouver,* with Sean Rossiter (Vancouver: Douglas and McIntyre, 2007).

27   Harcourt and Cameron, *City Making in Paradise,* 9.

28   Gordon McIntyre, "Ten Years of Bike Lanes in Vancouver: Life Goes On, Chaos Averted," *Vancouver Sun,* 16 July 2019, https://vancouversun.com/news/local-news/ten-years-of-bike-lanes-in-vancouver-life-goes-on-chaos-averted.

29   City of Calgary, *Cycling Strategy* (Calgary: City of Calgary, June 2011), https://www.calgary.ca/transportation/tp/cycling/cycling-strategy/cycling-strategy.html; Calgary Food Committee and Serecon Management Consulting Inc., *Calgary Eats! A Food System Assessment and Action Plan for Calgary* (Calgary: City of Calgary, May 2012), https://www.calgary.ca/ca/cmo/calgary-food-system-assessment-and-action-plan.html; Calgary Transportation Department, *Step Forward: A Strategic Plan for Improving Walking in Calgary* (Calgary: City of Calgary, August 2016), https://www.calgary.ca/pedestrianstrategy.

Further Reading

Blais, Pamela. *Perverse Cities: Hidden Subsidies, Wonky Policy, and Urban Sprawl.* Vancouver: University of British Columbia Press, 2010.

Bruegmann, Robert. *Sprawl: A Compact History.* Chicago: University of Chicago Press, 2005.

Flyvbjerg, Bent. *Rationality and Power: Democracy in Practice.* Chicago: University of Chicago Press, 1998.

Works Cited

"2 Schools on Closure List, 5 Saved." *CBC News,* 21 January 2004. https://www.cbc.ca/news/canada/calgary/2-schools-on-closure-list-5-saved-1.498204.

Bennet, Dean. "Alberta Finance Minister Says No Money Available for Teacher Salary Increases." *Edmonton Journal,* 4 March 2020. https://edmontonjournal.com/news/local-news/alberta-finance-minister-says-no-money-available-for-teacher-salary-increases.

Buliung, Ron, Raktim Mitra, and Guy Faulkner. "Active School Transportation in the Greater Toronto Area, Canada: An Exploration of Trends in Space and Time (1986–2006)." *Preventive Medicine* 48, no. 6 (2009): 507–12.

"Calgary Developers Lose 'Sprawl Subsidy' on Water, Road Costs." *CBC News*, 11 January 2016. https://www.cbc.ca/news/canada/calgary/developer-levy-increase-city-council-1.3399577.

Calgary Food Committee and Serecon Management Consulting Inc. *Calgary Eats! A Food System Assessment and Action Plan for Calgary*. Calgary: City of Calgary, May 2012. https://www.calgary.ca/ca/cmo/calgary-food-system-assessment-and-action-plan.html.

Calgary Transportation Department. *Step Forward: A Strategic Plan for Improving Walking in Calgary*. Calgary: City of Calgary, August 2016. https://www.calgary.ca/pedestrianstrategy.

CBE Communication and Engagement Services. *Shaping the Future of High School Spring Survey, 2019*. Calgary: Calgary Board of Education, 2019. https://www.cbe.ab.ca/get-involved/public-engagement/Documents/01082019-full-survey-report-public.pdf.

City of Calgary. *Cycling Strategy*. Calgary: City of Calgary, June 2011. https://www.calgary.ca/transportation/tp/cycling/cycling-strategy/cycling-strategy.html.

CUPE-BC and Civic Economics. *Independent BC: Small Business and the British Columbia Economy*. Chicago: Civic Economics, February 2013. https://ccednet-rcdec.ca/sites/ccednet-rcdec.ca/files/ccednet/pdfs/independant_bc_small_and_the_british_colombia_economy.pdf.

Davis, Julie, David Merriman, Lucia Samayoa, and Brian Flanagan. *The Impact of an Urban Wal-Mart Store on Area Businesses: An Evaluation of One Chicago Neighborhood's Experience*. Chicago: Loyola University, Center for Urban Research and Learning, December 2009. https://ecommons.luc.edu/cgi/viewcontent.cgi?article=1002&context=curl_pubs.

Ferguson, Eva. "Parents Worry As New S.E. High School Fills Up, Turning Beaverbrook into a 'Ghost Town.'" *Calgary Herald*, 24 January 2019. https://calgaryherald.com/news/local-news/suburban-high-schools-overflow-as-inner-city-buildings-start-to-empty.

Global Retail Strategies Inc. *Recommended Direction for City-Wide Commercial/Retail Policy (Macro/Micro Final Report)*. Calgary: City of Calgary, December 2008. Amended 5 March 2009. https://kempton.files.wordpress.com/2009/03/commercial_study_final_macro_section.pdf.

Hafner, Marco, Martin Stepanek, and Wendy Troxel. *Later School Start Times in the US: An Economic Analysis*. Cambridge, UK: Rand Corporation, 2017. https://www.rand.org/content/dam/rand/pubs/research_reports/RR2100/RR2109/RAND_RR2109.pdf.

Harcourt, Mike, and Ken Cameron. *City Making in Paradise: Nine Decisions That Saved Vancouver*. With Sean Rossiter. Vancouver: Douglas and McIntyre, 2007.

IBI Group. *The Implications of Alternative Growth Patterns on Infrastructure Costs*. Calgary: City of Calgary, April 2009. http://www.reconnectingamerica.org/assets/Uploads/planitcalgarycoststudyanalysisaprilthird.pdf.

imagineCalgary. "imagineCalgary Plan for Long Range Urban Sustainability." Calgary: City of Calgary, September 2007. https://www.calgary.ca/pda/pd/office-of-sustainability/imaginecalgary.html.

Jun, Myung-jin. "The Effects of Portland's Urban Growth Boundary on Housing Prices." *Journal of the American Planning Association* 72, no. 2 (2006): 239–43.

Klaszus, Jeremy. "Sprawlcast: Plan It Calgary, 10 Years Later." *The Sprawl*, 6 February 2020. https://www.sprawlcalgary.com/sprawlcast-plan-it.

Markusoff, Jason. "WinSport 'Extremely Disappointed' in Council's Rejection of Plan to Sell Land." *Calgary Herald*, 31 July 2012. http://www.calgaryherald.com/news/calgary/winsport +extremely+disappointed+council +rejection+plan+ sell+land/7020115/story.html.

Martellozzo, Federico, Navin Ramankutty, Ron Hall, David T. Price, Brett Purdy, and Mark A. Friedl. "Urbanization and the Loss of Prime Farmland: A Case Study in the Calgary-Edmonton Corridor of Alberta." *Regional Environmental Change* 15 (2015): 881–93.

McIntyre, Gordon. "Ten Years of Bike Lanes in Vancouver: Life Goes On, Chaos Averted." *Vancouver Sun*, 16 July 2019. https://vancouversun.com/news/local-news/ten-years-of-bike-lanes-in-vancouver-life-goes-on-chaos-averted.

McKeever, Pamela Malaspina, and Linda Clark. "Delayed High School Start Times Later Than 8:30 a.m. and Impact on Graduation Rates and Attendance Rates." *Sleep Health* 3, no. 2 (2017): 119–25.

Mitchell, Stacy. *Big-Box Swindle: The True Cost of Mega-Retailers and the Fight for America's Independent Businesses.* Boston: Beacon Press, 2007.

———. "Local Stores Create Triple the Economic Activity of Chains." *Institute for Local Self-Reliance*, 1 February 2003. https://ilsr.org/local-stores-create-triple-economic-activity-chains/.

"Paskapoo Slopes Development Plan Approved by City Council." *CBC News,* 27 July 2015. https://www.cbc.ca/news/canada/calgary/paskapoo-slopes-development-plan-approved-by-city-council-1.3169706.

Reiger, Sarah. "CBE Retroactively Scraps Fee-Free Busing, Calgary Transit Rebate for 2019–20 School Year." *CBC News*, 10 December 2019. https://www.cbc.ca/news/canada/calgary/cbe-bus-costs-1.5391732.

Synge, M. B. *A Book of Discovery: The History of the World's Exploration, from the Earliest Times to the Finding of the South Pole.* London: T. C. and E. C. Jack, 1912. Released 20 October 2007, Project Gutenberg. https://archive.org/stream/abookofdiscovery23107gut/pg23107.txt.

Vaessen, Doug, and Lisa Geddes. "Mayor Calls for Investigation of Civic Election Campaign Contributions." *Global News*, 23 April 2013. https://globalnews.ca/news/504916/mayor-calls-for-investigation-of-civic-election-campaign-contributions/.

Sustainable Mobility: Bikes, Trams, and (Fewer) Automobiles

In most cities, nothing eats up more of the municipal budget than transportation. The movement of goods and people in cities is also one of the largest contributors to greenhouse gas emissions. In this chapter, the essays focus on sustainable alternatives to the automobile-dependent transportation systems entrenched in most of the world's cities. We also tackle the issue of CO_2-intensive air travel. The essays highlight the benefits of rail-based mass transit—in particular, tramlines—and present an overview of cities where rail-based transit thrives.

In this chapter, we introduce the concept of "induced demand" to explain the futility of the road engineers' conventional recommendation to build our way out of congestion. We put the issue of urban transportation in the context of resilience, arguing that a resilient city is one where rail-based mass transit is the go-to option and the private automobile is optional. We compare the social, economic, and ecological benefits of light rail transit versus tramlines.

We are particularly excited about the possibilities of trams, usually called streetcars in North America. In Calgary, trams were part of our heritage until the 1950s, when the cult of the automobile took hold across North America, streetcar systems were dismantled, and an unprecedented amount of public money was poured into automobile infrastructure in what influential urban planner Brent Toderian calls the "largest and most damaging social engineering experiment in history."[1] In fact, only very recently did the kilometres of light rail transit (LRT) surpass the historical extent of Calgary's streetcar network.

In this chapter, we take a look at some of the largest and most successful tram systems in the world today. Some of these, like the one in Melbourne, are long-established and have been modernized; others, like those in Portland and Seattle, are new and thriving. We also present a set of criteria for a good rail-based mass transit system and propose five tramline routes that make sense for Calgary. In the essay "In Praise of the Bicycle," we argue that this simple device may just hold the key to tackling the climate emergency while enhancing quality of life.

We end the chapter with a stroll through the heart of St. John's, Newfoundland, in the essay "Everything Old Is New Again." One of the most picturesque cities in North America, St. John's also lays claim to being the oldest—and that is the key to lessons it has to offer. St. John's is a city that was born and matured before the invention of the automobile—and before the advent of the professional planner. It has been designed for humans, not the automobile. Pre-auto cities like St. John's remind us how to build the urban environment for humans rather than machines.

TRAMS: THE MISSING LINK IN CALGARY'S TRANSPORTATION SYSTEM

Among the stories we tell about ourselves in Calgary is a tale of desperate love—for our cars. Calgarians are having a mass *affaire de coeur* with their four-fendered darlings. Our automotive passions run so deep, we consider life without cars to be utterly inconceivable. It's a story repeated worldwide, from Paris to Portland. Everyone everywhere, apparently, loves their cars above all else. But it's a myth. We know this because wherever high-quality, convenient, and speedy alternatives have been built, people readily abandon their clunkers and take to the rails, to bikes, and to their feet. Some places have actually ripped out highways only to discover they are not missed.

Myths persist because they contain elements of truth. At this point, no comprehensive transit alternatives exist for most Calgarians, and until they do, myth and fact are hard to separate. As it is, our city's system discourages more transit use.

At first glance, Calgary's LRT system, locally referred to as the C-train, seems to be one of the most successful on the continent. In January 2019, for example, Calgarians took 6.96 million trips on the C-train.[2] Only Guadelajara, Mexico, has more riders.[3] This is not an anomaly—Calgary has topped ridership lists for years.[4] But this success is not because we love our transit system. It is, at least in part, because City policy limits downtown parking but has not made the offsetting investment to increase access and usability for those needing alternatives. Many transit users feel herded to the C-train.

Even if downtown parking were unlimited and cheap, the road network already runs at capacity and there are no plans—and no room—for new expressways into downtown. Imagine if tens of thousands more people drove to the city centre each day. In contrast, what if tens of thousands of additional people had to (or wanted to) use public transportation as their first choice? This scenario was briefly foreshadowed when gas prices spiked in 2008. It was bad. So bad that in the morning rush, people travelling north would first take southbound trains to stations closer to the end of the line, just to get a spot on a northbound train.

Despite its apparent success, our transit system lacks diversity. We've streamlined the city for convenient driving, making more sustainable transit forms difficult to implement effectively. And Calgary isn't alone. Planners everywhere are contending with the same issues and battling the same myths. Many cities have responded by introducing, or reintroducing, the humble tram, also known in North America as the streetcar. All over the world, trams are being recognized as an essential ingredient of resilient urban transit networks.

Why trams? In their ongoing research into the effectiveness of different transportation modes, University of British Columbia planning professor Patrick Condon and his colleagues have concluded that trams have multiple benefits for cities interested in planning for resilience and sustainability.[5] Because trams and LRT cars are electric, they produce no carbon emissions or smog: they are better than buses for the environment and for our health. Lifetime maintenance and repair costs for trams rank lowest among the public transport alternatives. Although the initial capital investment is higher than for buses, trams have lower lifetime operating costs. Trams have lower capacity than LRT, but many more miles of track can be built for the same cost, because trams don't require special segregated infrastructure—you can step right from the curb onto the tram.

Overall, compared to other transit modes, both trams and LRT are greener, leaner, and cheaper. The key point, however, is that trams, unlike LRT or buses, play a significant role in fostering community and social resilience. Think of Calgary's best streets, such as 9th Avenue SE in Inglewood or 17 Avenue SW in the Beltline, and ask how they got that way. Would it be a surprise to find out that all of them evolved as tram streets? Trams evoke a sense of permanence and confidence in a way that bus routes do not, which in turn encourages social and financial investment along tramlines. Wherever trams have been built, commerce and social vitality have blossomed. Other forms of transit, like buses and LRT, simply can't compete.

Trams also add versatility. During rush hour, they service local commuters, decreasing the load on the rest of the public transport system overloaded with long distance commuters travelling between downtown and the suburbs. During the rest of the day, trams link neighbourhoods and communities in a predictable and trustworthy way, which inspires confidence and boosts ridership. Trams play a role in a complete transit network that neither LRT nor buses can.

Trams provide new options and ways to think about urban resilience and sustainability. Calgary was a tram city once. It needs to be one again. That's no myth.

LOVING TRANSIT: IF YOU BUILD IT (RIGHT), THEY WILL COME

In 1962 Anthony Downs, formerly a senior fellow at the prestigious Brookings Institution in Washington, DC, wrote an influential book entitled *Stuck in Traffic: Coping with Peak-Hour Traffic Congestion*.[6] Downs draws on the concept of "induced demand" to explain why building new roads does not relieve traffic congestion. In simple terms, providing more of something can lead to increased consumption. With new roads, this has the counter-intuitive effect of making traffic worse than it was before the roads were built. The 2020 report *Generated Traffic and Induced Travel*, produced by the Victoria Transport Policy Institute, confirms the dynamic of induced demand.[7]

Here's how it works. Building new roads creates what Downs calls "triple convergence." First, they entice drivers—who, because of congestion, had given up rush-hour driving—back to old habits. Second, drivers using alternate routes are drawn to the new, faster roads. And third, new roads lure both old and new users away from public transit. So not only do new roads not relieve traffic congestion; they create a feedback loop that draws money away from the one kind of investment that does—public transit. More road users means fewer transit users, which creates the temptation to reduce transit investment even further. What's worse is that this downward spiral fosters, even promotes, the fiction that money spent on public transit is a "subsidy" to those too poor to drive, as though carlessness is a disease searching for a cure.

"So what?" say free-marketers. "People make a rational choice to use their cars." Right? Wrong! The truth is we lack true choice. How can a threadbare transit system compete with a lavishly endowed road network on even terms? It can't. In fact, according to the City of Calgary's *2017*

Infrastructure Status Report, our city, historically, has spent more than five times as much on roads as on transit.[8]

But an efficient, well-appointed, properly planned transit network providing convenience, reliability, and an extended roster of destinations certainly could compete with roads and vehicles. In such a system, the lack of garage-to-garage convenience is offset by high user satisfaction rates and significant long-term savings to the city and to individuals.

Here are five suggestions for building a transit system that breeds enough confidence and loyalty to compete with cars.

1. *Provide seamless, city-wide connectivity.* The ability to get to (almost) anywhere from (almost) anywhere in a city is a hallmark of a great transit system. If people can't get to where they need to be, they won't use transit, no matter how user-friendly it is. Currently, Calgary's system focuses primarily on the downtown, leaving many major destinations difficult to reach via transit (Mount Royal University and the airport, for example). And because everything passes through the city's core, quadrant-to-quadrant connectivity is, at best, poor. Streetcars (trams) are an ideal means to supply such connectivity.

2. *Make ticketing friendlier.* Many cities have convenient swipe cards that can be recharged electronically. Others have cell phone apps for ticket payment. We do it for parking—why not for transit? Offer a variety of ticket packages to make the system more convenient for casual users, families, and tourists. Melbourne, for example, has a five-day pass, among many other options. Reducing prices on weekends builds ridership during non-peak periods. Very low prices for neighbourhood travel (one or two stops) bring more customers to local businesses. And why not ensure that ticket machines give change?

3. *Integrate the system.* Everything possible should be done to encourage ease of transfer between transportation modes. If transit can't be the whole trip, it can be part of it. We pay attention to the walkshed perimeter around train stations,

but what about bikesheds? In his 2017 PhD dissertation, Jason Ponto shows that most of Calgary could be served by investing in high-quality bike infrastructure within a ten-minute ride of train stations.[9] Provide secure bike parking, too—lots of it. And find more ways to have bike-friendly buses and trains.

4. *Get the language right.* Urban transit is a necessary and vital component of sustainable world-class cities, not a charity. Removing the word *subsidy* from the transit conversation and replacing it with the word *investment* would be a good start.

5. *Make transit free and implement user fees (e.g., tolls) for use of highways.* The city of Tallin, Estonia, did just that in 2013, with modest results for increased ridership but more significant results in terms of numbers of people in low-income neighbourhoods taking transit.[10] In 2018 the chair of the LA Metro Board called for free transit by 2028, funded by toll roads, and in 2020 Luxembourg became the first country to institute free transit.[11]

In building our transit system, the principle of induced demand should be applied in reverse: relieve congestion not with new roads but by building a transit system people love.

LOOKING AHEAD TO THE PAST: A TALE OF THREE TRAM CITIES

Prior to the Second World War, trams—also called streetcars—were the mainstay of public transportation systems in cities around the world. And for good reason: trams provided reliable, predictable, accessible, human-scaled transportation serving the needs of working folk and the wealthy alike. Savvy investors, entrepreneurs, and property developers quickly realized the profit potential along tramlines, and businesses that provided service and value to local communities were soon flourishing. This powerful mixture of social and economic energy fuelled the emergence of the streets that have become some of our best-loved places.

Calgary once had an extensive tram network. The first tracks were laid in the early 1900s, and at its height in 1945, the system had fifteen routes serving all parts of the city, including Parkdale, Hillhurst, Kensington, Rosedale, Capitol Hill, Tuxedo, Riverside (Bridgeland), Inglewood, Ogden, Manchester, Elbow Park, South Calgary (Marda), and Killarney. Calgary's tram network was dismantled in 1950, when the private automobile was taking over as the city's dominant transportation choice. Although the trams were replaced, first with electric trolleys and later with diesel buses, their place-making power could not be replicated.

Portland, Oregon, is also a city with tram origins dating back more than a century. Following the war, Portland, like most North American cities, tore out its tram network and began building roads and expressways. And as elsewhere, Portland's core soon deteriorated as wealth, jobs, and commerce migrated to the suburbs.

In contrast to almost everywhere, however, Portland began reinvesting in public transit early on. By the early 1970s, three proposed freeways had been successfully resisted through public opposition. Another, Harbor Drive, was actually ripped out and converted to a riverfront park. The money originally intended for freeways was instead invested in a light rail system similar to Calgary's LRT. Yet development in the core lagged. As if finally realizing the place-making power of trams, the city reimagined a downtown line in the early 1990s, and in 2001 Portland's downtown streetcar, the first to be built anywhere in North America in almost a century, was inaugurated.

The results have been spectacular. Portland's Pearl District, once a deteriorating downtown industrial and warehouse zone, has been transformed into a flourishing mixed residential and commercial inner city neighbourhood. Because trams provide certainty, investors responded by sinking $3.5 billion in private money along the line.[12] Now, instead of underused buildings and fearful streets, the area is festooned with parks, stores, restaurants, funky boutiques, food kiosks, museums, theatres, microbreweries, hotels, and one of the nation's liveliest coffee cultures. Oh—and people. Young and old, singles and families—people are reclaiming the inner city.[13]

Melbourne, Australia, is another city with a tram heritage akin to ours, but unlike Calgary and Portland, trams were never abandoned there. Today, Melbourne has the largest tram system in the world and, because of it, some of the best streets in the world.[14] Chapel Street in south Melbourne is a four-kilometre collage of shops, markets, restaurants, and entertainment that is adjacent to nearby high-density neighbourhoods. Here is persuasive evidence of the place-shaping power of trams. Small shops catering to local needs are interspersed with boutiques to provide a high-quality pedestrian realm. Pubs and eateries with abundant indoor-outdoor seating thrive year-round. Recent high-rise development is offset from the street, which retains the streetscape's original character and charm.

This is a tale of three cities. Melbourne embraced and maintained its tram identity. Portland lost it, but then reclaimed it. And in Calgary, trams are not even part of the conversation. This needs to change.

Apart from the social, economic, and environmental benefits of trams, perhaps the most compelling reason why we need them back is that they are a truly effective counterforce to urban sprawl. Calgary has the right idea by wanting to increase density around LRT stations, but the strategy as currently conceived does precious little to contain Calgary's relentless outward ooze. Sustainable Calgary's affordable living research found that trams can be a strong economic development attractor. They are more permanent than bus routes, so decisions about where to live, work, and go to school can be made based on the existence of a tramline. The tracks provide a legible, visual representation of the routes for tram users, and the technology for running trams on renewable electricity is proven in Calgary.[15]

A truly effective transit strategy makes the whole city transit-oriented, not just selected, ultra–high-density nodes. Only trams can make that happen. Unlike the standard LRT redevelopment model, which clusters high-density, high-rise living immediately adjacent to stations, tram-inspired transit-oriented design has a much gentler effect on local communities because the density is absorbed horizontally along corridors rather than vertically in towers. Progressive changes to zoning bylaws would permit mixed uses and moderate intensity near the line while ensuring that adjacent neighbourhoods remain intact.

If this strategy were implemented, a significant proportion of Calgary's future growth would be absorbed within its existing footprint, to the benefit of our health, our wealth, and the environment. The really great news is that having once been a tram city, Calgary's street pattern for trams is already in place. It will take enlightened citizens to demand it, and fearless leaders at City Hall to make it happen. Melbourne and Portland have harnessed the power of trams to shape their cities for the better. We should too.

IN PRAISE OF THE BICYCLE: PEDALLING TO THE RESCUE IN THE CLIMATE EMERGENCY

Has there ever been a more perfect and joyous transportation technology than the bicycle? "Silent, swift, translucent; they barely stirred the air," writes Pablo Neruda in his poem "Ode to Bicycles."[16] I've been a bike commuter in Calgary for over thirty-five years. The popularity of cycling has transformed over that time. My bike commute remains the most enjoyable part of my day, and apparently, I am not alone in this experience. A 2017 study by Dr. Yingling Fan of the University of Minnesota's Humphrey School of Public Policy found bicycling to be the happiest mode of transportation.[17] As we focus our attention on the climate emergency, the humble bicycle just might be the gateway to a sustainable future.

Calgary has made positive but plodding progress on active transportation—using one's own power to get from A to B. In 2011 the City introduced its cycling strategy.[18] In 2016 the City finally released *Step Forward*, its pedestrian strategy, which was recognized internationally in 2017 with a Best Project Award by the Institute of Transportation Engineers, based in Washington, DC.[19] But as with so many planning policies, the challenge has been putting policy into action.

The downtown cycle track network was a godsend for cyclists. The trip through downtown was no longer a stressful exercise of hyper-vigilance for cyclists as they tried to safely navigate downtown auto and bus traffic, sharing lanes where car drivers treated them as illegal impediments to their efficient navigation of the city. But the political capital expended in the debate and defense of the meagre $10 million spent on the modest 5.5 kilometres of cycle track was epic and exhausting, while hundreds of millions of dollars in road construction is routinely rubber-stamped by City Council with hardly a word spoken.

In 2020 we find ourselves in the midst of a global pandemic. In Calgary, we now see first-hand how active transportation infrastructure has become indispensable to a resilient city. Of all transportation modes, only active transport modes have seen an increase this year, and cycle shops are finding it hard to keep bikes in stock. They've seen sales go through the roof as many Calgarians are discovering the joy of cycling for the first time.

The trend is happening worldwide. Paris has just re-elected its progressive mayor, Anne Hidalgo, who has inspired the imaginations of urbanists around the world with her intention to make Paris a "ville de quartre-heure"—a fifteen-minute city, where everything residents need is a walk or bike ride away. The core of the plan is making all streets bike-friendly by 2024.[20] Indeed, Paris has been transformed this year, with hundreds of streets converted to bike lanes as a response to the pandemic. Paris, the ultimate global city of the past three hundred years, is set once again to transform the nature of cities with this bold initiative.

Paris seems intent on eclipsing Amsterdam and Copenhagen as Europe's most bike-friendly city. In 2016 Copenhagen achieved a milestone—there were more bike trips counted in Copenhagen's city centre than car trips.[21] In 1970 car trips had outnumbered bike trips 3.5 to 1. By 2018, an impressive 49 percent of all trips were by bicycle.[22] How did the citizens of Copenhagen make it happen? They elected a lord-mayor who dedicated himself to making Copenhagen a bike city, and the national government invested heavily in bike infrastructure. With the Cykelslangen (the Snake Bridge), the Inderhavnsbroen (the Kissing Bridge), and the Superkilen, Copenhagen now has some of the most beautiful and functional bike infrastructure in the world. Copenhagen officials have a goal to make the city centre car-free by 2025. A November 2016 article in *The Guardian* reported that the cost of twelve years (2004 to 2016) of creating bike infrastructure in Copenhagen was half that of constructing just one single vehicle bypass to the north of the city.[23] And as if that were not enough, this transformation has made Copenhagen one of the most rapidly decarbonizing cities in the world, with a 42 percent reduction in emissions from 2005 to 2019.[24]

In Amsterdam, a city long synonymous with the bicycle, over half of all city-centre trips are by bicycle. In the Dutch city of Groningen, the number is over 60 percent.[25] The first image of the city as you emerge from Amsterdam's central train station is a sea of parked bicycles and an impressive bikes-only roadway. London's bicycle use may catch up to these cities. With newly instituted policies to reduce air pollution and congestion, Transport for London reported in 2016 that bike commuters were expected to outnumber car commuters in the heart of the city by 2018.[26] And in fact, *WIRED* online magazine reported in 2018 that "during the morning rush in the City of London the most popular vehicle is now the bicycle."[27] Oslo, Norway, has a goal to make its city centre car-free and is investing much of its oil-generated wealth in new bike superhighways.[28] In response to the pandemic, Barcelona has added twenty-five kilometres of cycle lanes and continues to transform the core of its neighbourhood superblocks into car-free zones.[29]

Tune in to any debate at City Hall these days and you are sure to hear councilors of all political stripes lamenting the cost of running our city. Likewise, Albertans are more conscious than ever of our own bank accounts, and our provincial government makes no bones about the need to tighten our belts in what will undoubtedly be a long road to weaning ourselves off fossil fuel–generated wealth and balancing the books. Well, bicycles to the rescue! A Vancouver study from 2015 compared various transportation options using a full-cost accounting methodology.[30] A car commute was calculated to cost $2.78 per kilometre to society and $6.47 in personal costs. Biking was calculated to incur $3.70 per kilometre in personal costs and to actually deliver 75 cents in societal savings for every kilometre pedalled. Much of the savings from biking and walking are in avoided health care costs. For example, one UK study reported in the *British Medical Journal* in 2017 estimated that a regular bike commute cut the risk of cancer by 45 percent and of heart disease by 46 percent.[31]

ActiveCITY has just launched its *Playbook 2030*, a core element of its diversification strategy.[32] The *Playbook* is designed to make Calgary North America's most active city by 2030. Bikes, bike infrastructure, and bike riders will be indispensable in that quest.

So whether it is saving the planet, saving your money, or safeguarding your health, the bicycle is the answer. As Sherlock Holmes author Sir Arthur Conan Doyle once wrote, "When the spirits are low, when the day appears dark, when work becomes monotonous, when hope hardly seems worth having, just mount a bicycle and go out for a spin."[33]

EVERYTHING OLD IS NEW AGAIN: THE RIGHT STUFF ON THE EAST COAST

In the 1998 National Film Board of Canada documentary *Rain, Drizzle and Fog*, director Rosemary House profiles a series of St. John's artists, including Mary Walsh (*This Hour Has 22 Minutes*), in an exploration of the attachment to place that St. John's exerts, despite the oppressive dominance of various forms of moisture.[34] On a typical summer day, even during a particularly nasty bout of this meteorological affliction, St. John's remains one of the most walkable cities in North America.

Many characteristics make the city walkable, but one prominent feature is the fact that it is old enough—some claim it is the oldest city in North America—to have been built long before the invention of the automobile. As a result, it was designed with humans in mind, not the machines that transport them. Though St. John's and most other city districts of pre-auto vintage—Boston, New York, Montreal, Quebec City—have adapted to the automobile, the basic geometry remains human scale. These cities provide comfortable human habitat.

Google Maps provides a clear image of what is different about these pre-car cities—whether it is St John's or Boston, or the pre-car centres of London, Paris, or Rome, or for that matter informal settlements in the exploding cities of developing countries, where a car is still out of reach for most people. The block pattern of these cities is more organic, probably the result of pedestrian preferences rather than master planning, and the block sizes are much smaller. These places developed organically, without the guiding hand of city planners and with their own pedestrian logic.

In *The Oldest City: The Story of St. John's, Newfoundland*, Paul O'Neill recounts a British Navy lieutenant's description of St John's: "The Capital of Newfoundland consists of one very narrow street extending entirely along one side of the port."[35] Water Street was the centre of commerce for fish merchants in the heyday of the North Atlantic fishery and remains so today, with offshore oil now the economic driver. The two winding lanes of this still very narrow street are lined with small businesses and a dominant street profile of three to four storeys.

Some of these businesses, like the family-owned O'Brien's Music Store, are entering their eighth decade. The family still lives above the store—an example of mixed-use development before the term was ever coined. Water Street boasts bustling pedestrian traffic night and day and an acceptance of what in other cities might be derisively referred to as "jaywalking." Even today on Water Street, nothing moves much faster than your average human on foot.

Another unique feature of St. John's is its walking lanes. Starting from Water Street, they wind their way up from the harbour, providing a variety of experiences for the meandering tourist and safe, quiet routes for people travelling through the inner city. McMurdo's Lane is home to The Duke of Duckworth, the favourite watering hole of Jake Doyle (the loveable detective of *The Republic of Doyle*).[36] Solomon's Lane is home to the heart of traditional Irish and folk culture in St. John's, The Ship Inn. A few blocks further on is Willicott's Lane, a residential thoroughfare with a long history. It originally housed fifteen hundred residents in two hundred squalid buildings under the thumb of a slum landlord. It burned to the ground twice in the great fires that hit St. John's in the 1800s and is today a pleasant haven where city-centre homes open onto quiet, clean lanes too narrow for cars.

Of course, not all is rosy in St John's. Car-oriented high-rise development threatens the sense of place that allows residents to make their peace with the inclement North Atlantic weather. Metro St. John's has a growing sprawl problem to rival much larger cities. Even this old-city treasure finds it hard to resist the conventional development logic that defines North America. Roads, interchanges, big box malls are springing up at record pace. The west end of Water Street has been all but given over to the automobile, with an access freeway slicing into the downtown.

Calgary, like St. John's, was originally a walking city, and some remnants of that history can still be found along 17th Avenue and in Mission, Kensington, Inglewood, and a few other places. But in contrast to St. John's, which had almost five centuries to mature as a walking city, Calgary's experience lasted less than a generation. Already by 1910, just twenty-five years after Calgary's incorporation, the car was making an impact on city design. But we can and should learn from earlier eras. Calgary's laneways are an untapped resource, and City Council has begun exploring options like making laneway houses "allowable" rather than "discretionary" in city bylaws. In places like the downtown, East Village, and Manchester, we have a golden opportunity to once again put people first in city design.

Strolling along Water Street on a summer evening, with the fog horn at Fort Amherst, the entrance to St. John's harbour, sounding in the distance, it is not hard to see how very old cities like St John's offer clues to modern city design—liveability, walkability, and an appealing sense of place. In city building today, everything old is new again.

NOTES

1   Brent Toderian (@BrentToderian), Twitter post, 4 September 2019, https://twitter.com/ BrentToderian/status/1169307159491801088.

2   "Transit Yearly Ridership," *City of Calgary*, 2020, https://data.calgary.ca/ Transportation-Transit/Yearly-Ridership-current-year-is-year-to-date-/n9it-gzsq.

3   Numbers for US and Canadian cities can be found at "Public Transportation Ridership Report: Fourth Quarter 2018," *American Public Transportation Association*, 12 April 2019, https://www.apta.com/wp-content/uploads/2018-Q4-Ridership-APTA-3.pdf. For Guadalajara ridership, see "Guadalajara Light Rail System," *Railway Technology*, accessed 31 August 2020, https://www.railway-technology.com/projects/guadalajara-light-rail-system/.

4   Duncan W. Allen and Timothy H. White, "North American Light-Rail Transit Ridership and Operating Costs: A Basis for Comparison," in *Seventh National Conference on Light-Rail Transit* 2:27–35, Conference Proceedings 8, Baltimore, Maryland, 12–15 November 1995 (Washington, DC: National Academy Press, 1997), http://onlinepubs.trb.org/Onlinepubs/conf/1995/cp8/cp8v2-003.pdf.

5   Patrick Condon, Sigrid Gruenberger, and Marta Klaptocz, *The Case for the Tram: Learning from Portland*, Foundational Research Bulletin No. 6 (Vancouver: University of British Columbia, Design Centre for Sustainability, May 2008), http://www.sxd.sala.ubc.ca/8_research/sxd_FRB06_tram.pdf.

6   Anthony Downs, "The Law of Peak-Hour Expressway Congestion," *Traffic Quarterly* 16, no. 3 (1962): 393–409, https://hdl.handle.net/2027/ucl.$b3477?urlappend=%3Bseq=457.

7   Todd Litman, *Generated Traffic and Induced Travel: Implications for Transport Planning* (Victoria, BC: Victoria Transport Policy Institute, July 2020), https://www.vtpi.org/gentraf.pdf.

8   City of Calgary, *2017 Infrastructure Status Report* (Calgary: City of Calgary, 2017), 36.

9   Jason Ponto, "Cycling through Intersections: Regimes of Velomobility in Calgary and Amsterdam" (PhD diss., University of Calgary, 2017), http://hdl.handle.net/11023/3760.

10   Alex Gray, "Estonia Is Making Public Transport Free," *World Economic Forum*, 1 June 2018, https://www.weforum.org/agenda/2018/06/estonia-is-making-public-transport-free/.

11   Elijah Chiland, "Metro CEO Supports Congestion Pricing, Free Fares on Public Transit," *CURBED Los Angeles*, 6 December 2018, https://la.curbed.com/2018/12/6/18129258/congestion-pricing-free-fares-metro-los-angeles; Andrea Lo, "Luxembourg Makes All Public Transit Free," *CNN*, 1 March 2020, https://www.cnn.com/travel/article/luxembourg-free-public-transport/index.html.

12   E. D. Hovee and Company, *Streetcar-Development Linkage: The Portland Streetcar Loop*, prepared for City of Portland Office of Transportation, February 2008, http://www.reconnectingamerica.org/assets/Hovee-Report-Eastside-2008.pdf.

13   Rhonda Bell, "Understanding Streetcar Costs, Funding, Operations and Partnerships," *Metro Magazine*, 2 August 2017, https://www.metro-magazine.com/10002957/understanding-streetcar-costs-funding-operations-and-partnerships.

14   "Tram and Light Rail Transit Systems," *Wikipedia*, last edited 28 October 2020, https://en.wikipedia.org/wiki/Tram_and_light_rail_transit_systems.

15   Noel Keough, *Action Research on Transportation Housing Affordability: Final Report to Canada Mortgage and Housing Corporation*, CR File No. 6585-K090 (Ottawa: CMHC, 2011), 9, https://static1.squarespace.com/static/5ab716b9ee1759b04ca2703e/t/5ee006 3c22b445748442fe51/1591739967822/Housing%2BTransport+Affordable+Living+-+FinalReport.pdf.

16   Pablo Neruda and Ilan Stavans, eds., *All the Odes: A Bilingual Edition* (New York: Farrar, Strauss and Giroux, 2017).

17   Jing Zhu and Yingling Fan, "Daily Travel Behavior and Emotional Well-Being: A Comprehensive Assessment of Travel-Related Emotions and the Associated Trip and Personal Factors," in *Happy Cities: Role of Transportation* (Minneapolis: University of Minnesota, 2017), https://conservancy.umn.edu/handle/11299/185433.

18   City of Calgary, *Cycling Strategy* (Calgary: City of Calgary, June 2011), https://www.calgary.ca/transportation/tp/cycling/cycling-strategy/cycling-strategy.html.

19   City of Calgary, *Step Forward: A Strategic Plan for Improving Walking in Calgary* (Calgary: City of Calgary, August 2016), https://www.calgary.ca/transportation/tp/planning/calgary-transportation-plan/pedestrian-strategy.html?redirect=/pedestrianstrategy; "Calgary Wins International Award for Pedestrian Strategy," *Canadian Consulting Engineer*, 14 September 2017, https://www.canadianconsultingengineer.com/transportation/calgary-wins-international-award-pedestrian-strategy/1003406086/.

20   Kim Willsher, "Paris Mayor Unveils '15-Minute City' Plan in Re-Election Campaign," *The Guardian*, 7 February 2020, https://www.theguardian.com/world/2020/feb/07/paris-mayor-unveils-15-minute-city-plan-in-re-election-campaign.

21   Athlyn Cathcart-Keays, "Two-Wheel Takeover: Bikes Outnumber Cars for the First Time in Copenhagen," *The Guardian*, 30 November 2016, https://www.theguardian.com/cities/2016/nov/30/cycling-revolution-bikes-outnumber-cars-first-time-copenhagen-denmark.

22   Philippe Descamps, "Copenhagen, Cycle City," *Le Monde diplomatique*, March 2020, https://mondediplo.com/2020/03/13copenhagen-bikes.

23   Cathcart-Keays, "Two-Wheel Takeover."

24   "What's Copenhagen's Magic Formula to Reduce CO_2 Levels?" *Euronews*, 10 October 2019, https://www.euronews.com/2019/10/10/what-s-copenhagen-s-magic-formula-to-reduce-co2-levels.

25   Renate van der Zee, "How Amsterdam Became the Bicycle Capital of the World," *The Guardian*, 5 May 2015, https://www.theguardian.com/cities/2015/may/05/amsterdam-bicycle-capital-world-transport-cycling-kindermoord.

26   "London Bike Commuters Will Outnumber Cars by 2018," *The Energy Mix*, 9 May 2016, https://theenergymix.com/2016/05/09/london-bike-commuters-will-outnumber-cars-by-2018/.

27   Richard Priday, "London's Cycling Boom Is Slowing. And It's Still Mostly White Men," *WIRED*, 21 March 2018, https://www.wired.co.uk/article/cycling-london-city-centre-bikes-cycle-superhighway.

28   Adele Peters, "What Happened When Oslo Decided to Make Its Downtown Basically Car-Free?" *Fast Company*, 24 January 2019, https://www.fastcompany.com/90294948/what-happened-when-oslo-decided-to-make-its-downtown-basically-car-free; Feargus O'Sullivan, "Norway Will Spend Almost $1 Billion on New Bike Highways," *Bloomberg CityLab*, 3 March 2016, https://www.bloomberg.com/news/articles/2016-03-03/norway-s-national-transit-plan-will-spend-almost-1-billion-on-new-bike-highways.

29   Laura Millan Lombrana, "An Urban Planner's Trick to Making Bikeable Cities," *Bloomberg News*, 5 August 2020, https://www.bloomberg.com/news/articles/2020-08-05/an-urban-planner-s-trick-to-making-bike-able-cities, and Marta Bausells, "Superblocks to the Rescue: Barcelona's Plan to Give Streets Back to Residents," *The Guardian*, 17 May 2016, https://www.theguardian.com/cities/2016/may/17/superblocks-rescue-barcelona-spain-plan-give-streets-back-residents.

30   Tanvi Misra, "The Social Costs of Driving in Vancouver in 1 Chart," *Bloomberg CityLab*, 7 April 2015, https://www.bloomberg.com/news/articles/2015-04-07/an-interactive-tool-measures-the-social-costs-of-driving-and-transit-in-vancouver.

31   Carlos A. Celis-Morales et al., "Association between Active Commuting and Incident Cardiovascular Disease, Cancer, and Mortality: Prospective Cohort Study," *British Medical Journal* 357 (April 2017).

32   ActiveCITY Collective, *Playbook 2030: A Guide to Building Canada's Most Liveable Region* (Calgary: ActiveCITY Collective, 2020), https://static1.squarespace.com/static/5a668a99bce1765a27495af0/t/5fc14fdf4e98326c024109a0/1606504451803/Playbook+2030+FINAL-compressed.pdf.

33   Arthur Conan Doyle, "Cycling Notes," *Scientific American*, 18 January 1896, http://wheelbike.blogspot.com/2011/04/sir-arthur-conan-doyle-on-benefits-of.html.

34   Rosemary House, dir., *Rain, Drizzle and Fog* (Ottawa: National Film Board, 1998), https://www.nfb.ca/film/rain_drizzle_and_fog/.

35   Paul O'Neill, *The Oldest City: The Story of St. John's, Newfoundland* (Boulder, CO: Boulder, 2003), 621.

36   *The Republic of Doyle* (Toronto: Canadian Broadcasting Corporation, 2014), https://www.imdb.com/title/tt1297754/.

Further Reading

Condon, Patrick. *Seven Rules for Sustainable Communities: Design Strategies for a Post-Carbon World*. Washington, DC: Island Press, 2010.

Works Cited

ActiveCITY Collective. *Playbook 2030: A Guide to Building Canada's Most Liveable Region*. Calgary: ActiveCITY Collective, 2020. https://static1.squarespace.com/static/5a668a99bce1765a27495af0/t/5fc14fdf4e98326c024109a0/1606504451803/Playbook+2030+FINAL-compressed.pdf.

Allen, Duncan W., and Timothy H. White. "North American Light-Rail Transit Ridership and Operating Costs: A Basis for Comparison." In *Seventh National Conference on Light-Rail Transit* 2:27–35. Conference Proceedings 8. Baltimore, Maryland, 12–15 November 1995. Washington, DC: National Academy Press, 1997. http://onlinepubs.trb.org/Onlinepubs/conf/1995/cp8/cp8v2-003.pdf.

Bausells, Marta. "Superblocks to the Rescue: Barcelona's Plan to Give Streets Back to Residents." *The Guardian*, 17 May 2016. https://www.theguardian.com/cities/2016/may/17/superblocks-rescue-barcelona-spain-plan-give-streets-back-residents.

Bell, Rhonda. "Understanding Streetcar Costs, Funding, Operations and Partnerships." *Metro Magazine*, 2 August 2017. https://www.metro-magazine.com/10002957/understanding-streetcar-costs-funding-operations-and-partnerships.

"Calgary Wins International Award for Pedestrian Strategy." *Canadian Consulting Engineer*, 14 September 2017. https://www.canadianconsultingengineer.com/transportation/calgary-wins-international-award-pedestrian-strategy/1003406086/.

Cathcart-Keays, Athlyn. "Two-Wheel Takeover: Bikes Outnumber Cars for the First Time in Copenhagen." *The Guardian*, 30 November 2016. https://www.theguardian.com/cities/2016/nov/30/cycling-revolution-bikes-outnumber-cars-first-time-copenhagen-denmark.

Celis-Morales, Carlos A., Donald M. Lyall, Paul Welsh, Jana Anderson, Lewis Steell, Yibing Guo, Reno Maldonado et al. "Association between Active Commuting and Incident Cardiovascular Disease, Cancer, and Mortality: Prospective Cohort Study." *British Medical Journal* 357 (April 2017).

Chiland, Elijah. "Metro CEO Supports Congestion Pricing, Free Fares on Public Transit." *CURBED Los Angeles,* 6 December 2018. https://la.curbed.com/2018/12/6/18129258/congestion-pricing-free-fares-metro-los-angeles.

City of Calgary. *2017 Infrastructure Status Report.* Calgary: City of Calgary, 2017.

———. *Cycling Strategy.* Calgary: City of Calgary, June 2011. https://www.calgary.ca/transportation/tp/cycling/cycling-strategy/cycling-strategy.html.

———. *Step Forward: A Strategic Plan for Improving Walking in Calgary.* Calgary: City of Calgary, August 2016. https://www.calgary.ca/transportation/tp/planning/calgary-transportation-plan/pedestrian-strategy.html?redirect=/pedestrianstrategy.

Conan Doyle, Arthur. "Cycling Notes." *Scientific American,* 18 January 1896. http://wheelbike.blogspot.com/2011/04/sir-arthur-conan-doyle-on-benefits-of.html.

Condon, Patrick M., Sigrid Gruenberger, and Marta Klaptocz. *The Case for the Tram: Learning from Portland.* Foundational Research Bulletin No. 6. Vancouver: University of British Columbia, Design Centre for Sustainability, May 2008. http://www.sxd.sala.ubc.ca/8_research/sxd_FRB06_tram.pdf.

Descamps, Philippe. "Copenhagen, Cycle City." *Le Monde diplomatique,* March 2020. https://mondediplo.com/2020/03/13copenhagen-bikes.

Downs, Anthony. "The Law of Peak-Hour Expressway Congestion." *Traffic Quarterly* 16, no. 3 (1962): 393–409. https://hdl.handle.net/2027/ucl.$b3477?urlappend=%3Bseq=457.

E. D. Hovee and Company. *Streetcar-Development Linkage: The Portland Streetcar Loop.* Prepared for City of Portland Office of Transportation, February 2008. http://www.reconnectingamerica.org/assets/Hovee-Report-Eastside-2008.pdf.

Gray, Alex. "Estonia Is Making Public Transport Free." *World Economic Forum,* 1 June 2018. https://www.weforum.org/agenda/2018/06/estonia-is-making-public-transport-free/.

"Guadelajara Light Rail System." *Railway Technology.* Accessed 31 August 2020. https://www.railway-technology.com/projects/guadalajara-light-rail-system/.

House, Rosemary, dir. *Rain, Drizzle, and Fog.* Ottawa: National Film Board, 1998. https://www.nfb.ca/film/rain_drizzle_and_fog/.

Keough, Noel. *Action Research on Transportation Housing Affordability: Final Report to Canada Mortgage and Housing Corporation.* CR File No. 6585-K090. Ottawa: CMHC, 2011. https://static1.squarespace.com/static/5ab716b9ee1759b04ca2703e/t/5ee0063c22b445748442fe51/1591739967822/Housing%2BTransport+Affordable+Living+-+FinalReport.pdf.

Litman, Todd. *Generated Traffic and Induced Travel: Implications for Transport Planning.* Victoria, BC: Victoria Transport Policy Institute, July 2020. https://www.vtpi.org/gentraf.pdf.

Lo, Andrea. "Luxembourg Makes All Public Transit Free." *CNN*, 1 March 2020. https://www.cnn.com/travel/article/luxembourg-free-public-transport/index.html.

Lombrana, Laura Millan. "An Urban Planner's Trick to Making Bikeable Cities." *Bloomberg News*, 5 August 2020. https://www.bloomberg.com/news/articles/2020-08-05/an-urban-planner-s-trick-to-making-bike-able-cities.

"London Bike Commuters Will Outnumber Cars by 2018." *The Energy Mix*, 9 May 2016. https://theenergymix.com/2016/05/09/london-bike-commuters-will-outnumber-cars-by-2018/.

Misra, Tanvi. "The Social Costs of Driving in Vancouver in 1 Chart." *Bloomberg CityLab*, 7 April 2015. https://www.bloomberg.com/news/articles/2015-04-07/an-interactive-tool-measures-the-social-costs-of-driving-and-transit-in-vancouver.

Neruda, Pablo, and Ilan Stavans, eds. *All the Odes: A Bilingual Edition*. New York: Farrar, Strauss and Giroux, 2017.

O'Neill, Paul. *The Oldest City: The Story of St. John's, Newfoundland*. Boulder, CO: Boulder, 2013.

O'Sullivan, Feargus. "Norway Will Spend Almost $1 Billion on New Bike Highways." *Bloomberg CityLab*, 3 March 2016. https://www.bloomberg.com/news/articles/2016-03-03/norway-s-national-transit-plan-will-spend-almost-1-billion-on-new-bike-highways.

Peters, Adele. "What Happened When Oslo Decided to Make Its Downtown Basically Car-Free?" *Fast Company*, 24 January 2019. https://www.fastcompany.com/90294948/what-happened-when-oslo-decided-to-make-its-downtown-basically-car-free.

Ponto, Jason. "Cycling through Intersections: Regimes of Velomobility in Calgary and Amsterdam." PhD diss., University of Calgary, 2017. http://hdl.handle.net/11023/3760.

Priday, Richard. "London's Cycling Boom Is Slowing. And It's Still Mostly White Men." *WIRED*, 21 March 2018. https://www.wired.co.uk/article/cycling-london-city-centre-bikes-cycle-superhighway.

"Public Transportation Ridership Report: Fourth Quarter 2018." *American Public Transportation Association*, 12 April 2019. https://www.apta.com/wp-content/uploads/2018-Q4-Ridership-APTA-3.pdf.

The Republic of Doyle. Toronto: Canadian Broadcasting Corporation, 2014. https://www.imdb.com/title/tt1297754/.

"Tram and Light Rail Transit Systems." *Wikipedia*. Last edited 28 October 2020. https://en.wikipedia.org/wiki/Tram_and_light_rail_transit_systems.

"Transit Yearly Ridership." *City of Calgary*, 2020. https://data.calgary.ca/Transportation-Transit/Yearly-Ridership-current-year-is-year-to-date-/n9it-gzsq.

Van der Zee, Renate. "How Amsterdam Became the Bicycle Capital of the World." *The Guardian*, 5 May 2015. https://www.theguardian.com/cities/2015/may/05/amsterdam-bicycle-capital-world-transport-cycling-kindermoord.

"What's Copenhagen's Magic Formula to Reduce CO_2 Levels?" *Euronews*, 10 October 2019. https://www.euronews.com/2019/10/10/what-s-copenhagen-s-magic-formula-to-reduce-co2-levels.

Willsher, Kim. "Paris Mayor Unveils '15-Minute City' Plan in Re-Election Campaign." *The Guardian*, 7 February 2020. https://www.theguardian.com/world/2020/feb/07/paris-mayor-unveils-15-minute-city-plan-in-re-election-campaign.

Zhu, Jing, and Yingling Fan. "Daily Travel Behavior and Emotional Well-Being: A Comprehensive Assessment of Travel-Related Emotions and the Associated Trip and Personal Factors." In *Happy Cities: Role of Transportation*. Minneapolis: University of Minnesota, 2017. https://conservancy.umn.edu/handle/11299/185433.

Peak Auto: A Tragedy in the Making

For the average city-dweller, it is hard to imagine life, and cities, without cars. Yet most people don't bother to tally the amount of money they spend on their cars—purchase, insurance, fuel, maintenance, parking, repair. In this chapter, we delve into the costs of cars—not just the economic ones but also the social, ecological, and health costs. Not many people realize that the effects of automobile accidents rival those of the most dreaded diseases on the planet, or that the parking stall that comes with your average condominium purchase adds $20,000 to $50,000 to the condo price.

In "Ring Road Rethink," we consider an alternative to Calgary's Ring Road—a ring rail LRT system—and we crunch the numbers for this alternative. In the essay on auto dependence, we do the same for the private household cost of ownership. We also look at the "opportunity cost" of spending on a vehicle—what could a household spend that money on instead?

Perhaps even Henry Ford could not have dreamed of the impact of the automobile when he conceived of the first assembly line production of the Model T. The automobile is probably the single most material- and energy-intensive technology ever devised: estimates put the global population of automobiles at about 1.4 billion in 2020.[1] Consumer activist Ralph Nader, whose advocacy work we discuss in this chapter, describes the situation as the "automobile tragedy."

The dominance of and dependence on the automobile is the single biggest contributor to the sprawl we see in cities around the world. In the postwar period, we have re-engineered our cities as car habitat and systematically dismantled human habitat. We have come to accept this state of affairs, and most citizens, and even policy-makers, find it hard to imagine how it could be any different. For the most part, urban designers feel obliged to continue to make room for cars and rarely propose urban landscapes without them. Without even noticing it, we have turned our cities and our streets into industrial landscapes that are so unregulated they would never pass muster in any industrial workplace.

But there are alternatives, and this chapter introduces some of them. Cities like Freiburg, Germany, have built neighbourhoods where the automobile is optional, and the proposed community of Merwede, Netherlands, whose design is now under review by Utrecht residents, will be virtually car-free.[2] Even in Calgary, developers have begun to build condominiums with zero parking, and co-operative and private car-share systems are popping up in cities around the world.

AUTO DEPENDENCE: THE NUMBERS DON'T ADD UP

Since at least the year 2000, there have been heated intergovernmental debates about provincial infrastructure money for roads and transit. When gas prices spike and construction season for road building goes into high gear as summer approaches, road rage is sure to follow. A 2015 survey by State Farm Canada found that one in three Canadians suffers from road rage every month.[3] Here in Calgary, a road-building crewman was shot in a road rage incident in summer 2019.[4] And yet our love affair with our automobiles continues.

Or does it? I recently facilitated a workshop in Calgary in which I asked participants to group themselves according to their dominant form of transportation in the city. Not surprisingly, the largest group consisted of those dependent on the car. But when I asked people to identify, given the choice, their preferred mode of travel, there was a significant migration from the car cluster to the walking and bicycling group. So I decided to do a little number crunching.

How do the real costs of the automobile and public transit compare? I realized that the debate is unhelpfully clouded by the artificial separation of private and public spending—after all, whether private or public, it all comes from the pockets of the same citizens. Car ownership and operation, conservatively estimated, costs approximately $12,000 annually.[5] Given the 2019 vehicle ownership rate in Calgary of 740 vehicles per 1,000 people, there are approximately 890,000 registered automobiles in Calgary.[6] That adds up to an annual private contribution to our transportation system—the rolling stock for all those roads—of a whopping $10 billion! That's $10 billion every year—forever! Compare this to the 2019–22 average annual operation and capital budget for transportation in Calgary of approximately $1.14 billion.[7] Put another way, imagine if tomorrow the entire transportation system, private automobiles included, were nationalized and run by the state. To fund the transportation system, each of our municipal tax bills would increase by roughly $8,300 per capita. Suddenly, the several billion dollars in infrastructure costs to build a world-class transit system doesn't look so bad.

Then I got to thinking about the opportunity costs of the automobile. My wife and I sat down recently and calculated the savings we have realized by being car-free for twenty years. Assuming a conservative average cost of car ownership of $6,000 annually over that period, we have saved almost $120,000—that's a lot of RRSPs or a big down payment on our child's post-secondary education. Or consider housing. Right now in Calgary the purchase of a new condo could include up to $50,000 just for the purchase of your underground parking stall—that could be the difference between a condo you can afford and the condo you really want, in the community you would like to call home. Add to that the potential additional mortgage qualification if you hadn't just taken out that $30,000 car loan.

A little number crunching and suddenly that automobile in the driveway is looking a little less shiny and appealing, and a world-class accessible public transit system is worth a second look.

THE LIFE AND TIMES OF THE DEADLY AMERICAN AUTOMOBILE

Every year, the revved-up extravaganza known as the North American International Car Show takes over Detroit. There are the usual attractions—concept cars of the future, the latest hybrids, hype around the dawn of the era of electric cars, and of course, the holy grail of the autonomous vehicle. Meanwhile, in 2020 the median price of private automobiles purchased in Canada is just over $40,000.[8] Inescapably, the backdrop to the whole event is the continuing decay of Detroit—the city that cars built—a portent perhaps of the fate of the automobile itself.

More than fifty years ago, automobile safety crusader Ralph Nader delivered a wake-up call to the auto industry. In *Unsafe at Any Speed: The Designed-In Dangers of the American Automobile*, he wrote that "the automobile has brought death, injury, and the most inestimable sorrow and deprivation to millions of people."[9]

Even Nader probably didn't know the half of it. One of the most devastating effects of what he called the "mechanical or biological hazard" has been the destruction of the walkable human-scale city.[10] Observed from space, a North American city could be mistaken as the habitat of a single dominant species—the car. Suburbia was built for cars, where people seem to be an afterthought. As we recreate more walkable compact cities, we are starting to realize that cars do not fit well in a city designed for people. The biggest beef against more compact development? Too much traffic and not enough parking!

One of the most intractable and urgent problems we face is reducing transportation-based carbon emissions. According to the World Bank's *Global Burden of Disease* report, in 2015 five to ten thousand deaths in Canada were attributable to PM2.5 (fine inhalable particles) and ground level ozone.[11] A report by the International Institute for Sustainable

Development found that pollution in Canada was costing Canadians, conservatively, $42.3 billion annually.[12]

For poor people, a car is an unaffordable albatross. A single parent in Calgary holding down two minimum-wage jobs and obliged to own a beater of an automobile could be one flat tire away from homelessness. We work up to three months of the year just to pay for our cars. In *Energy and Equity*, renowned polymath and polemicist Ivan Illich famously calculated that we could walk everywhere we wanted to go in the time we work to pay for our vehicles.[13]

It used to be that car boosters could counter every argument against car ownership by saying that sales keep going up. That's no longer a slam dunk. Researchers at the University of Michigan Transportation Research Institute found that in the US, 69 percent of nineteen-year-olds had a driver's licence in 2014, compared to 87 percent in 1983.[14] In 2017 in the US, twenty-one- to thirty-four-year-olds purchased only 10 percent of the new cars sold, down from a peak of 38 percent in 1985.[15] Recent data suggests a bit of a rebound in vehicle ownership in Canada, with aging millennials purchasing family-friendly used cars.[16] But as we move into the 2020s, car ownership is being challenged. Numerous community-based and corporate car-share systems have come into operation in North America, and even bike-share and scooter systems are taking some of the mobility market.

In September 2012, *The Atlantic* reported that the puzzle now bewildering every automaker is how to sell cars to millennials, who seem to care much less about car ownership than their parents did.[17] In 2015 a *Washington Post* writer decried "America's once magical—now mundane—love affair with cars."[18] Ford's 2020 Trendbook has locked into millennials and Gen Zers, with promises that Ford's products can increase trust and alleviate loneliness: "At Ford, we think of the automobile as a gathering place—one of the last strongholds of uninterrupted conversations and bonding."[19] Certainly, Tesla has caught the imagination of millennials: Elon Musk surely dreams of a Tesla in every garage.

Knowing the reality of the carnage and ecological destruction caused by cars, it is almost criminal that car companies should be training their high-powered selling machines to seduce young people into buying a product they've decided they don't need. In a sane world, society would take the opportunity that this trend away from vehicle ownership provides to confront climate change by retooling the automobile sector's industrial might to manufacture solar panels, wind turbines, bicycles, and streetcars.

In *Clean Disruption of Energy and Transportation*, author Tony Seba makes the case that car ownership will soon be a thing of the past, purely for economic reasons.[20] He cites the confluence of five disruptions—cheap solar energy, cheap batteries, cheap electric vehicles, share-economy business models, and computing power enabling artificial intelligence and autonomous vehicles. Seba argues that electric car costs will soon be competitive with internal-combustion vehicles and that electric cars will last four to five times longer, largely because they have a fraction of the moving parts. Solar energy and battery technology will make electricity cheaper than gasoline, he says, and the expanded lifetimes of vehicles will make fleets rather than individual ownership more attractive. So with a fraction of the number of cars in a city, citizens will get the same level of convenient service.

But this argument contains some flaws. Will people accept driverless vehicles on our roads? Even though cars are parked 90 percent of the time, we usually need them all at once during rush hour. And finally, with cheaper auto mobility, supply and demand suggests we might see more auto trips, not fewer. Imagine Mom, Dad, and two kids ordering up four autonomous vehicles every morning to get to work and school. There is still uncertainty in the rosy economic projections of autonomous electric vehicles. But that does not mean car companies will not continue to try to sell as many units as possible.

Ironically, although initially cars allowed people to put some distance between their homes and the polluting factories where they worked, they have turned the entire modern city into a dangerous industrial landscape. In Calgary, over a ten-year period ending in 2014, there were 3,834 pedestrians involved in collisions, with ninety-five fatalities.[21] A 2018 OECD report by the Road Traffic Data and Analysis Group found that although road fatalities dropped 15 percent in Canada from 2010 to 2016, pedestrian deaths increased 10 percent over that same period.[22] Worldwide, cars kill an astounding 1.3 million people every year. Twenty-six percent of deaths (338,000 people) are pedestrians and cyclists. Over fifty million people sustain injuries.[23] These numbers rival deaths from HIV/AIDS, tuberculosis, and diarrhoeal diseases.[24] In a study published in *The Lancet,* the researchers estimate that in 2015, seventy million disability-adjusted life years were lost worldwide due to injuries sustained from car accidents.[25] According to Transport Canada, collisions cost about 2.2 percent of our nation's GDP.[26]

Yet with the bare minimum of training, we license almost anybody over fourteen years of age to drive these hulking machines on streets and in neighbourhoods at upwards of eighty kilometres per hour, living in fear of letting our children out the door unattended.

In August 2012, *Globe and Mail* writer Eric Reguly referred to cars as "unaffordable burdens."[27] They are indeed unaffordable and undoubtedly a burden, at any price. Automobiles kill and maim. They are a poverty trap and the death knell for convivial and vibrant city life. Sadly, we remain largely oblivious to what Nader called this "automobile tragedy."[28] Automobiles are arguably the most wasteful and inefficient mode of travel devised by industrial humans.

THE ROAD LESS TRAVELLED: LIFE BEYOND THE PRIVATE AUTOMOBILE

Marshall McLuhan once wrote, "The car has become an article of dress without which we feel uncertain, unclad, and incomplete in the urban compound."[29] This certainly seems true in Calgary, which is perennially at the bottom of the walkability heap, according to Walk Score.[30] In 2020 Calgary had a Walk Score of 48 compared to 78 for Vancouver, 71 for Toronto, and 70 for Montreal. Even our rival city to the north, Edmonton, scored 51. Isn't it time we had a serious conversation about this urban wardrobe malfunction?

Oh, but Calgarians love their cars, we are told—just as the Irish like their drink and Americans their guns. Even if there is some truth to these overblown stereotypes, are the Irish, Americans, and we Calgarians fated to live this way forever, no matter the consequences? For most people, cities without the private automobile are unimaginable. This deficit of imagination has everything to do with entrenched behaviour, misplaced desire, ignorance of the alternatives, and lack of political leadership.

As we saw in the essay "Auto Dependence," collectively, Calgarians spend about $10 billion annually to own, operate, and maintain our cars—about $12,000 per vehicle, based on Statistics Canada surveys.[31] If you could invest that $12,000 a year at 5 percent (a pretty modest return) over a forty-year working life, you could be sitting on a nest egg of $1.6 million.

Half of all Calgary households own more than one car.[32] If, over a ten-year period, we were able to reduce the current car fleet of 850,000 vehicles by one-quarter and put the savings toward public transit, we could fund a Green Line every two years—that's forty-five new kilometres of LRT. Or perhaps we could follow the lead of cities around the world and reintroduce streetcars. Currently, Melbourne (with 250 km of tramlines), Moscow (208 km), St. Petersburg (205 km), and Cologne (198 km) are best-in-class when it comes to trams.[33] At the cost of between $30 and $50 million per kilometre, we could build fifty to eighty-five kilometres of streetcar network every year.[34] We'd boast the best streetcar system in the world and run it on wind energy, to boot—just like our LRT!

Already, there are strong market trends away from private car ownership. One of the most promising transition strategies is car sharing. A University of California Berkeley study in 2015 found that car-share systems remove seven to eleven cars from the road for every car shared, reduce car ownership, and significantly reduce greenhouse gas emissions and vehicle kilometres travelled.[35]

Calgary's car-share co-op was around for over ten years, growing modestly in that time and providing a viable alternative for inner city residents until the well-capitalized Car2Go arrived on the scene. Sadly, for reasons Car2Go (now called Share Now) has not made entirely clear, the company is closing all of its North American operations, including Calgary.[36] Though Car2Go Calgary grew rapidly after its arrival in 2012, it quickly hit a ceiling, with low-density suburban Calgary deemed unprofitable for the system.[37] But it seems the notion of car sharing is not going away. In September 2020, Montreal-based Communauto set up shop in Calgary.[38]

In 2013 Avis purchased the car-share service Zipcar for $490 million.[39] As of spring 2020, Zipcar had grown to over a million members with twelve thousand vehicles in more than five hundred cities (including Toronto) and five hundred college campuses across nine countries.[40] In

2010 Zipcar founder Robin Chase added a twist to the business model. Through Buzzcar, you can rent out your own vehicle when you are not using it. Why waste money on more cars when there is an astounding amount of unused capacity in the existing fleet? Buzzcar (Boston) was swallowed by Drivy (France), which was swallowed by Getaround (San Francisco), which boasts more than five million users in three hundred US and European cities.[41]

In Freiburg, Germany, a city some consider a contender for the most sustainable city in the world, many of the local streets in the community of Vauban are reserved for walking, biking, and playing. Cars are parked on the edge of the community in a parkade that is only entered for occasional delivery and pickup. You buy your home, and then, only if you need one, you buy a parking stall. At the urging of the City of Calgary and the local community, some Calgary developers are adapting this strategy and offering condos that don't come with a parking stall—a potential saving for prospective buyers of tens of thousands of dollars.

One simple principle should guide residential growth in our city. Do not approve a new community unless we can be certain that people living in that community have a reasonable option to live car-free if they so choose. The money we spend on cars represents a staggering amount of our life energy invested in a seductive but ultimately wasteful and destructive technology. Are we really prepared to say it's the best we can do? Let's hope that "somewhere ages and ages hence," as Robert Frost famously penned, we will look back and think, "Two roads diverged in a wood, and I— /I took the one less traveled by / And that has made all the difference."

THE WINDING ROAD TO THE AIRPORT TUNNEL: A CASE OF THE TAIL WAGGING THE DOG

In 2011 the Calgary Airport Authority (CAA) decided that the city needed a $2.5 billion airport expansion, including the longest runway in North America. City officials were adamant about building new infrastructure to accommodate a tunnel under the new runway connecting northeast and northwest quadrants of the city, so Calgarians were asked to fork over $295 million. (The ultimate construction bill was closer to $414 million.)[42] But the tunnel, and the debate about whether it should be built, was not the real story. The bigger questions were, Do we really need the runway, and is it prudent to plan for ever-growing air travel in a climate-constrained world?

Prior to CAA's pitch, the City had just released a fine piece of work called *Options for Reducing GHG Emissions in Calgary*.[43] The report charted a course for an 80 percent reduction in greenhouse gas (GHG) emissions over the next forty years. Achieving these targets would have allowed us to meet our international commitments on climate change, including the Kyoto Protocol and the City's Climate Change Accord, the latter being an undertaking with the World Energy Cities Partnership (energycities. org), which is a fifteen-city agreement to support these cities' local energy sectors. As importantly, implementing the City's 2011 report would meet the commitments made to the citizens of Calgary through the imagine-Calgary and Plan It Calgary processes, both of which were designed to create a sustainable future.

Does the Airport Authority have either a stand on reducing emissions or a long-term strategy for this? Both seem to be missing in action. Meeting the City's politically ambitious, though ecologically conservative, GHG targets will require all hands on deck, yet the new runway, officially opened in June 2014, will result in more, not less, GHG emissions. The words "climate change" are nowhere to be found in the *YYC Strategic Operating Plan 2009–2013*, in which the expansion was pitched.[44] Where you *could* find reference to climate change was at the approach to the tunnel under the runway, on a giant billboard paid for by the Orwellianesque Friends of Science climate deniers.[45]

Despite the tobacco company–styled propaganda machine launched against climate change science, the opinion polls of the time showed that 80 percent of Canadians believed the science showing that GHG emissions are greatly damaging our environment.[46] Building North America's longest runway and enabling the growth of GHG emissions flies in the face of the evidence and will make it more difficult to meet Canadians' demands to address climate change.

The CAA's argument runs something like this: we need bigger runways for bigger airplanes so that we can take longer trips to more destinations. But in his 2006 book *Heat: How to Stop the Planet from Burning*, journalist George Monbiot demonstrates that one long airplane trip expends all of a

Calgarian's yearly GHG allowance (assuming we are to meet the City's 80 percent target) with no room left for your car, the heating and electricity for your home, or those fresh fruits and veggies shipped from all over the planet.[47] Aviation's share of GHG emissions may be relatively small, but it is growing faster than any other sector. A successful climate change strategy will require all sectors to be in reduction mode.

Economically, the larger picture is about the twentieth century's mantra of accelerating economic growth, based on the delusion that it can go on forever with a planning model that starts with the assumption that the future will be just like the past. We disagree! The future is likely to be radically different from the past. In the twenty-first century, there's a new reality—peak oil, peak water, peak food, and, yes, peak air travel. The era of exponential growth is flatlining.

Just before the airport tunnel debate began, economist Jeff Rubin wrote, in *Why Your World Is About to Get a Whole Lot Smaller*, "We are now living in a world of triple digit oil prices. The massive changes this will compel won't be limited to regime change in the Middle East."[48] We have found no evidence that YYC planners have taken any of this information into account in the assessment of the financial risk of its $2.5 billion expansion. In the summer of 2020, in the midst of the worst downturn in air travel in history, triggered by the global pandemic, the Airport Authority is left wondering how it will even service its massive debt premised on growth forever.[49] And with the climate change emergency growing more critical by the day, the relatively short-term pandemic crisis may not be the Airport Authority's biggest problem. The endgame of the discussions of sustainability—the necessary social, political, and cultural change—is the difficult part.

In Monbiot's blunt assessment, "Long-distance travel, high speed and the curtailment of climate change are not compatible. If you fly, you destroy other people's lives."[50] We're guilty too, having logged more than our share of air miles over the past twenty years. But collectively, we need to find a substitute for the adventure, pleasure, and sense of freedom that makes air travel so seductive.

The Calgary Airport Authority operates on behalf of the citizens of Alberta and is governed by the Airport Authority Act. Yet this quasi-governmental authority, not beholden to voters, remained aloof in this debate and did not present its proposal for public scrutiny. It's a case of the tail wagging the dog, with Calgarians left to deal with the aftermath of higher taxes and higher airport fees.

YYC is a great operation managed by competent professionals. But the runway expansion was a bad idea underpinned by faulty assumptions. We didn't need the runway because, in the long run, it made the city less sustainable and less resilient and diverted funds from other, better uses. If a modern passenger jet had operated with the same faulty radar as the CAA seems to have, it would never be cleared for takeoff.

RING ROAD RETHINK: FINDING OPPORTUNITY IN CRISIS

Back in January 2015, in the face of $40/barrel Western Canada Select and with predictions that this would be the new normal, perhaps for years, Alberta premier Jim Prentice warned that provincial finances were in the worst shape they had been in for twenty-five or even fifty years. We all know what happened next. The rapidly deteriorating provincial finances cost Prentice his job, and the first social democratic government in Alberta's history came to power with the promise of a new day.

Much did change during Premier Rachel Notley's four years in power. But some things did not. Facing a massive deficit, one of the first moves by the new government was to confirm $3 billion in funding to complete Calgary's and Edmonton's ring roads.[51] An ill-conceived, fifty-year-old, dated dream of a ring road megaproject is now moving toward completion. You might say, "Battle lost, move on." But the thinking that brought us the Ring Road remains, and transportation engineers will already be preparing for the next big road project.

When Calgary's Ring Road was conceived over half a century ago, driving was in its heyday.[52] In the US, the massive taxpayer-funded interstate highway system—the largest construction project in human history at the time—had set the stage for happy motoring and the love affair with the automobile. Rail-based transportation systems were being decommissioned and starved of funds. Infrastructure czar Robert Moses was boasting of taking a meat cleaver to beautiful old New York neighbourhoods, and North Americans were getting their first taste of suburban sprawl.

Calgary came of age in this period of urban planning. Over time, our industrial, economic, and urban planning systems were retooled to facilitate the efficient production of an urban landscape based on suburban sprawl. City building was locked into this particular energy-intensive development path. Developers, auto manufacturers, and oil companies struck a gusher of profit.

Today, we have a very different conception of good urban design, thanks to visionaries like former City of Vancouver planning director Larry Beasley, Danish architect Jan Gehl, and Jane Jacobs, who took on Robert Moses in New York. Walkability, public transit, and liveable communities is where it's at—except in Alberta Transportation's world, it would seem.

Still, the Ring Road was justified merely because it has been on the books for fifty years, so—damn it! We're going to get it done. In an October 2013 press release, then-premier Alison Redford claimed that the project would "dramatically improve traffic flows in, through and around Calgary and the surrounding region. . . . It will improve our quality of life, allowing us to spend less time stuck in traffic, and more time with our loved ones."[53]

The balance of evidence suggests that none of Redford's claims are true. A 2002 California study by Robert Cervero and Mark Hansen found an unequivocal relationship between road supply and road demand.[54] Why? Suburban development induces the purchase of more cars, resulting in more driving and more congestion, and traffic engineers prescribe more roads as the solution. But there is an alternative to building more roads to solve the problem. According to research by the Victoria Transport Policy Institute, "congested roads cause people to defer trips that are not urgent, choose alternative destinations and modes, and forego avoidable trips."[55]

Studies have found that new roads bring some initial economic benefit, but this dissipates over time. In contrast, investing in transit brings small initial gains that continue to multiply over time, as a 2019 article in the journal *Sustainability* demonstrates.[56] So for residents of Cranston or Tuscany, their smooth Ring Road ride may disappear in a few years as the highway invites more suburban development. It's a vicious cycle: more roads beget more low-density suburbs, which beget more roads.

It is difficult to find definitive information on the cost of the Ring Road. From information I have been able to piece together about the

Calgary Ring Road and the Anthony Henday Highway in Edmonton, a conservatively low estimate would be $50 million per kilometre, giving the one-hundred kilometre Calgary Ring Road a price tag of $5 billion.[57]

A rough calculation of the land area devoted to the Ring Road yields thirty-six hundred hectares. At the density of a community like Sunnyside, you could put 140,000 people in that space. Imagine if our governments had had some vision to really prioritize transit. Imagine a ring rail LRT for roughly the same cost of $5 billion. With the LRT, the right of way would be prime transit-oriented development land worth approximately $1 billion and capable of accommodating not only a major piece of transportation infrastructure but also $20 to $25 billion in mixed-use development.

Water under the bridge, you might say. Well, yes for the Ring Road, but do we want to throw good money after bad? There is a gathering storm for the oil patch, with ever more volatile booms and busts and the dark cloud of climate change looming. Research in the journal *Nature* proposes that to control climate change, Alberta will have to keep 85 percent of its reserves in the ground.[58]

The times, they are a-changin'. With the demise of the Notley government in 2019, the Conservatives may again have a lock on Alberta politics, but their bluster belies their impotence in the face of global change. At some point, we have to bite the bullet and start building the smart, compact, low-carbon Calgary of tomorrow rather than the fossil-fuelled, high-maintenance, Cadillac city of the past.[59]

NOTES

1   Andrew Chesterton, "How Many Cars Are There in the World?" *Carsguide*, 6 August 2018, https://www.carsguide.com.au/car-advice/how-many-cars-are-there-in-the-world-70629.

2   Marcos Martínez, "Merwede's Future: 12,000 Residents and Zero Parking Spaces," *Ferrovial* (blog), 19 October 2020, https://blog.ferrovial.com/en/2020/10/merwedes-future-12000-residents-and-zero-parking-spaces/.

3   Melissa Gilligan, "1 in 3 Canadians Suffer from Road Rage Each Month: Survey," *Global News*, 14 July 2015, https://globalnews.ca/news/2109293/1-in-3-canadians-suffer-from-road-rage-each-month-survey/.

4   Carolyn Kury de Castillo, "Construction Worker Shot in Suspected Road Rage Case in Calgary," *Global News*, 1 July 2019, https://globalnews.ca/news/5449633/construction-worker-shot-calgary-road-rage/.

5   Erica Alini, "Own a Car? You Won't Believe How Much That's Costing You Every Year," *Global News,* 9 November 2017, https://globalnews.ca/news/3832649/car-ownership-costs-public-transit-canada/.

6   Noel Keough, Bob Morrison, and Celia Lee, *State of Our City 2020: An Urgent Call for a Just Transition* (Calgary: Sustainable Calgary Society, 2020), 50, http://www.sustainablecalgary.org/publications.

7   City of Calgary, *One Calgary: 2019–2022 Service Plans and Budgets* (Calgary: City of Calgary), accessed 11 November 2020, https://www.calgary.ca/cfod/finance/plans-budgets-and-financial-reports/plans-and-budget-2019-2022/service-plans-and-budgets.html.

8   "February 2020 Price Index Results Released," *AutoTrader*, 5 March 2020, https://www.autotrader.ca/newsfeatures/20200305/february-2020-price-index-results-released.

9   Ralph Nader, *Unsafe at Any Speed: The Designed-In Dangers of the American Automobile* (Boston: Knightsbridge, 1991), vii.

10   Nader, *Unsafe at Any Speed*, ix.

11   International Institute for Sustainable Development, *Costs of Pollution in Canada: Measuring the Impacts on Families, Businesses and Governments* (Winnipeg: IISD, 2017), 26, https://www.iisd.org/system/files/publications/costs-of-pollution-in-canada.pdf.

12   International Institute for Sustainable Development, *Costs of Pollution in Canada: Measuring the Impacts on Families, Businesses and Governments* (Winnipeg: IISD, 2017), vii, https://www.iisd.org/system/files/publications/costs-of-pollution-in-canada.pdf.

13   Ivan Illich, *Energy and Equity* (London: Marion Boyers, 2000), 15–23.

14   Julie Beck, "The Decline of the Driver's License," *The Atlantic*, 22 January 2016, https://www.theatlantic.com/technology/archive/2016/01/the-decline-of-the-drivers-license/425169/.

15   "Vehicle Buyers in the United States in 2017, by Age Group," *Statista*, accessed 21 August 2020, https://www.statista.com/statistics/987393/age-distribution-of-vehicle-buyers-united-states/.

16   "When Buying Cars, Millennials Choose Used and Practical over New and Flashy," *Financial Post*, 21 September 2015, https://financialpost.com/personal-finance/young-money/when-buying-cars-millennials-choose-used-and-practical-over-new-and-flashy.

17   Derek Thompson and Jordan Weissmann, "The Cheapest Generation: Why Millennials Aren't Buying Cars or Houses, and What That Means for the Economy," *The Atlantic*, September 2012, https://www.theatlantic.com/magazine/archive/2012/09/the-cheapest-generation/309060/.

18   Marc Fisher, "Cruising toward Oblivion," *Washington Post,* 2 September 2015, https://www.washingtonpost.com/sf/style/2015/09/02/americas-fading-car-culture/.

19   Ford Motor Company, "Looking Further with Ford: 2020 Trends," accessed 3 September 2020, https://media.ford.com/content/dam/fordmedia/North%20America/US/2019/12/11/2020-Ford-Trends.pdf.

20   Tony Seba, *Clean Disruption of Energy and Transportation: How Silicon Valley Is Making Oil, Nuclear, Natural Gas, and Coal Obsolete* (Silicon Valley, CA: Clean Planet Ventures, 2014), https://tonyseba.com/wp-content/uploads/2014/05/book-cover-Clean-Disruption.pdf.

21   Trevor Scott Howell and Annalise Klingbeil, "Data Reveals Pedestrian Danger: One Hit Per Day, and Most Had the Right of Way," *Calgary Herald,* 19 February 2016, https://calgaryherald.com/news/local-news/oh-no-not-again-city-data-shows-one-pedestrian-collision-a-day-most-had-right-of-way-20-hit-and-run.

22   Alicja Siekierska, "Canada among Only Seven Countries to See Rise in Pedestrian Deaths, OECD Study Reveals," *Financial Post,* 25 May 2018, https://financialpost.com/transportation/canada-among-only-seven-countries-to-see-rise-in-pedestrian-deaths-oecd-study-finds.

23   World Health Organization (WHO), *Global Status Report on Road Safety 2018* (Geneva: WHO, 2018), 3, 10, ix, https://www.who.int/violence_injury_prevention/road_safety_status/2018/en/.

24   WHO, *Global Status Report on Road Safety 2018*, 5.

25   Simiao Chen et al., "The Global Macroeconomic Burden of Road Injuries: Estimates and Projections for 166 Countries," *Lancet Planet Health* 3 (2019): e396, https://www.thelancet.com/action/showPdf?pii=S2542-5196%2819%2930170-6.

26   Organisation for Economic Co-operation and Development, *Road Safety Annual Report 2019: Canada* (Geneva: OECD International Transport Forum, 2019), 7, https://www.itf-oecd.org/sites/default/files/canada-road-safety.pdf.

27   Eric Reguly, "Is the Car Dead?" *Globe and Mail,* 30 August 2012, https://www.theglobeandmail.com/report-on-business/rob-magazine/is-the-car-dead/article4510125/.

28   Nader, *Unsafe at Any Speed,* ix.

29   Marshall McLuhan, *Understanding Media: The Extensions of Man,* with new introduction by Lewis H. Lapham (1964; repr., Cambridge, MA: MIT Press, 1994), 217.

30   "Cities and Neighbourhoods," *Walk Score,* 2020, https://www.walkscore.com/cities-and-neighborhoods/.

31   Alini, "Own a Car?"

32   City of Calgary, *Changing Travel Behaviour in the Calgary Region*, Travel Behaviour Report Series: Vol. 1 (Calgary: City of Calgary, June 2013), https://www.calgary.ca/Transportation/TP/Documents/forecasting/Changing Travel Behaviour in the Calgary Region_v1_forWeb_2013-06-04.pdf?noredirect=1.

33   "Tram and Light Rail Transit Systems," *Wikipedia*, last edited 28 October 2020, https://
      en.wikipedia.org/wiki/Tram_and_light_rail_transit_systems.

34   Rhonda Bell, "Understanding Streetcar Costs, Funding, Operations and Partnerships,"
      Metro Magazine, 2 August 2017, https://www.metro-magazine.com/10002957/
      understanding-streetcar-costs-funding-operations-and-partnerships.

35   Elliot Martin and Susan Shaheen, "Impacts of Car2Go on Vehicle Ownership, Modal
      Shift, Vehicle Miles Traveled, and Greenhouse Gas Emission: An Analysis of Five
      North American Cities," Working Paper, Transportation Sustainability Research
      Center, University of California Berkeley, 12 July 2016, https://tsrc.berkeley.edu/
      publications/impacts-car2go-vehicle-ownership-modal-shift-vehicle-miles-traveled-
      and-greenhouse-gas.

36   "Car2Go to Shut Down in Montreal—And across North America," *CBC News*, 18
      December 2019, https://www.cbc.ca/news/canada/montreal/car2go-montreal-north-
      america-1.5401130.

37   Alanna Smith, "Car2Go Can't Make It Go in Calgary, Pulling out of 'Highly Volatile'
      Market," *Calgary Herald*, 27 September 2019, https://calgaryherald.com/news/local-
      news/car2go-leaving-calgary-in-light-of-highly-volatile-transportation-market-
      limited-success.

38   "Car-Sharing Rolls Back into Calgary as Communauto Offers 150 Vehicles in Some
      Inner City Neighbourhoods," *CBC News*, 26 August 2020, https://www.cbc.ca/news/
      canada/calgary/calgary-car-share-return-negotiations-fleet-1.5701573.

39   John Kell, "Avis to Buy Car-Sharing Service Zipcar," *Wall Street Journal*, 2 January
      2013, https://www.wsj.com/articles/SB10001424127887324374004578217121433322386.

40   "Zipcar Overview," *Zipcar*, 2021, https://www.zipcar.com/press/overview.

41   Getaround, "Getaround Becomes Global Carsharing Leader with $300 Million
      Acquisition of European Platform Drivy," press release, 24 April 2019, https://www.
      getaround.com/media/public/press/Getaround_Announces_300M_Acquisition_of_
      European_Platform_Drivy.pdf.

42   Jason Markusoff, "By the Numbers: What You Need to Know about the Airport
      Tunnel," *Calgary Herald*, 22 May 2014, https://calgaryherald.com/news/local-news/by-
      the-numbers-what-you-need-to-know-about-the-airport-tunnel.

43   Jesse Row et al., *Options for Reducing GHG Emissions in Calgary: Research Report*
      (Calgary: City of Calgary, February 2011), https://www.pembina.org/reports/calgary-
      ghg-main-report.pdf.

44   Calgary Airport Authority, *YYC Strategic Operating Plan 2009–2013* (Calgary: CAA,
      November 2008), https://www.yyc.com/portals/0/15_2009031710575YYCStratPlan[1].
      pdf.

45   A picture of the billboard features prominently in Charles Mandel, "Canadian Climate
      Denial Group, Friends of Science, Named as Creditor in Coal Giant's Bankruptcy
      Files," *National Observer*, 20 June 2016, https://thenarwhal.ca/canadian-climate-denial-
      group-friends-science-named-creditor-coal-giant-s-bankruptcy-files/.

46   Erick Lachapelle, Christopher Borick, and Barry G. Rabe, *Key Findings Report for the 2013 Canada–US Comparative Climate Opinion Survey* (Ottawa: Canada 2020), 3.

47   George Monbiot, *Heat: How to Stop the Planet from Burning* (San Francisco: South End, 2009), 170–88.

48   Jeff Rubin, "Why Saudi Arabia Can No Longer Temper Oil Prices," *Globe and Mail*, 23 February 2011, https://www.theglobeandmail.com/report-on-business/industry-news/energy-and-resources/why-saudi-arabia-can-no-longer-temper-oil-prices/article623163/.

49   Sarah Reiger, "Calgary's Airport Faces $67M Deficit This Year," *CBC News*, 7 July 2020, https://www.cbc.ca/news/canada/calgary/calgary-airport-1.5641441.

50   Monbiot, *Heat*, 188.

51   James Wood, "Alberta Government Commits to West Leg of Calgary's Ring Road," *Edmonton Journal*, 5 July 2015, https://edmontonjournal.com/news/politics/ndp-government-commits-to-west-leg-of-ring-road/wcm/cf3fce83-6e09-4a0d-992f-346808286719.

52   Jesse Salus, "The Origins of the Southwest Ring Road," *The History of a Road* (blog), 5 March 2016, https://calgaryringroad.wordpress.com/2016/03/05/the-origins-of-the-southwest-ring-road/.

53   Alberta Transportation press release, quoted in "Calgary Ring Road Deal Good for All," *NationTalk,* 25 October 2015, https://nationtalk.ca/story/calgary-ring-road-deal-good-for-all.

54   Robert Cervero and Mark Hansen, "Induced Travel Demand and Induced Road Investment: A Simultaneous Equation Analysis," *Journal of Transport Economics and Policy* 36, no. 3 (2002): 469–90, https://www.jstor.org/stable/20053915.

55   Todd Litman, *Generated Traffic and Induced Travel: Implications for Transport Planning* (Victoria, BC: Victoria Transport Policy Institute, July 2020), https://www.vtpi.org/gentraf.pdf.

56   Assel Nugmanova et al., "Effectiveness of Ring Roads in Reducing Traffic Congestion in Cities for Long Run: Big Almaty Ring Road Case Study," *Sustainability* 11, no. 18 (2019): 4973.

57   "Calgary Ring Road: Overview," *Government of Alberta*, 2020, https://www.alberta.ca/calgary-ring-road-overview.aspx. For more information on costs and history of the ring road, see Jesse Salus, *The History of a Road*, https://calgaryringroad.wordpress.com.

58   Christophe McGlade and Paul Ekins, "The Geographical Distribution of Fossil Fuels Unused When Limiting Global Warming to 2°C," *Nature* 517 (2015): 187–90.

59   I thought it might be useful to make transparent the logic of my calculations on which this article was based. These figures are, of course, based on very rough, back-of-the-napkin kinds of calculations, but they do serve the purpose of demonstrating how we could develop our city in a more sustainable manner—that there are viable alternatives to business as usual.

The most recent data available from City of Calgary documents estimates the cost of the remaining west and southwest portions of the Ring Road at approximately $5 billion. A CBC report put the cost of the SE leg at $770 million and that of the NE leg at $930 million. The NW leg was estimated to have cost $485 million. Total cost estimate: $7.2 billion. With each leg of the Ring Road having exceeded initial estimates, we could expect the same for the SW and NW legs, so I used a round figure of $8 billion. (It should be noted that these costs include over $50 million annually for thirty years for maintenance.)

The Government of Alberta allocated $2.9 billion for the final portions of Edmonton's Anthony Henday Drive (27 km) and the Calgary Ring Road (31 km). That's an average of $50 million per kilometre.

The SW LRT cost about $1 billion for eight kilometres, or about $125 million/kilometre. That's a Cadillac version of an LRT line built into established parts of the city—so, very expensive. Estimates of LRT costs range from $25 to $160 million per kilometre. I estimated a Ring Road LRT in the right of way to cost about 65 percent, per kilometre, of the SW LRT, so a 100 kilometre LRT line would cost roughly $8.25 billion.

The Sunnyside density (3,850 people/km²) is calculated from the City of Calgary's 2014 Census and Google Maps. The City of Calgary's "Snapshots" report on growth puts the housing density for Sunnyside at 40 units/hectare.

The Ring Road will be just over one hundred kilometres when complete. From Google Maps, I estimated the right of way of the Ring Road to be, on average, about 300 metres. At intersections, that width expands to between 650 and 800 metres. With the dozens of intersections, about 15 percent of the Ring Road is intersections. So 15 kilometres at 700 metres and 85 kilometres at 300 metres = 36 km² = 3,600 hectares. If the Ring Road right of way were developed at the density of Sunnyside: 36 km² at a density of 3,850 people per km² = 140,000 people. That's probably about five or six years of growth for our city.

To estimate the potential value of the land, I did a search and found a twenty-acre piece of property for sale at the intersection of Airport Trail and Stoney Trail for $110,000/ acres or $275,000 per hectare. So $275,000 x 3,600 ha = $990 million, or approximately $1 billion.

If the Ring Road right of way were developed like Sunnyside with similar property values, and persons per household (2,413 households in Sunnyside, from the 2014 Calgary Census), 90,000 households (averaging $700,000/unit) of housing stock would be worth about $60 billion.

If the right of way were developed at the density of Sunnyside (3,850 people/km²) with persons per unit at the city average (2.4 persons/unit based on the data in "Snapshot"), that would result in approximately 60,000 units. If units are valued at the Calgary average (house: $466,000; condo: $287,000, based on Calgary Real Estate Board numbers) and assuming half the households are houses and half are condos (making the average price of a unit $376,000), then 60,000 units x $376,000/unit = $23 billion in home values. This would probably be a conservative estimate for the right of way, as it does not include commercial development.

Further Reading

Bohm, Steffen, Campbell Jones, Chris Land, and Matthew Paterson, eds. *Against Automobility*. Oxford: Blackwell, 2006.

Crawford, J. H. *Carfree Cities*. Utrecht, Netherlands: International Books, 2002.

Dennis, Kingsley, and John Urry. *After the Car*. Cambridge, UK: Polity, 2009.

Works Cited

Alini, Erica. "Own a Car? You Won't Believe How Much That's Costing You Every Year." *Global News*, 9 November 2017. https://globalnews.ca/news/3832649/car-ownership-costs-public-transit-canada/.

Beck, Julie. "The Decline of the Driver's License." *The Atlantic*, 22 January 2016. https://www.theatlantic.com/technology/archive/2016/01/the-decline-of-the-drivers-license/425169/.

Bell, Rhonda. "Understanding Streetcar Costs, Funding, Operations and Partnerships." *Metro Magazine,* 2 August 2017. https://www.metro-magazine.com/10002957/understanding-streetcar-costs-funding-operations-and-partnerships.

Calgary Airport Authority. *YYC Strategic Operating Plan 2009–2013*. Calgary: CAA, November 2008. https://www.yyc.com/portals/0/15_2009031710575YYC StratPlan[1].pdf.

"Calgary Ring Road Deal Good for All." *NationTalk,* 25 October 2015. https://nationtalk.ca/story/calgary-ring-road-deal-good-for-all.

"Calgary Ring Road: Overview." *Government of Alberta*, 2020. https://www.alberta.ca/calgary-ring-road-overview.aspx.

"Car2Go to Shut Down in Montreal—And across North America." *CBC News*, 18 December 2019. https://www.cbc.ca/news/canada/montreal/car2go-montreal-north-america-1.5401130.

"Car-Sharing Rolls Back into Calgary as Communauto Offers 150 Vehicles in Some Inner City Neighbourhoods." *CBC News*, 26 August 2020. https://www.cbc.ca/news/canada/calgary/calgary-car-share-return-negotiations-fleet-1.5701573.

Cervero, Robert, and Mark Hansen. "Induced Travel Demand and Induced Road Investment: A Simultaneous Equation Analysis." *Journal of Transport Economics and Policy* 36, no. 3 (2002): 469–90. https://www.jstor.org/stable/20053915.

Chen, Simiao, Michael Kuhn, Klaus Prettner, and David E. Bloom. "The Global Macroeconomic Burden of Road Injuries: Estimates and Projections for 166 Countries." *Lancet Planet Health* 3 (2019): e390–98. https://www.thelancet.com/action/showPdf?pii=S2542-5196%2819%2930170-6.

Chesterton, Andrew. "How Many Cars Are There in the World?" *Carsguide*, 6 August 2018. https://www.carsguide.com.au/car-advice/how-many-cars-are-there-in-the-world-70629.

"Cities and Neighbourhoods." *Walk Score*, 2020. https://www.walkscore.com/cities-and-neighborhoods/.

City of Calgary. *Changing Travel Behaviour in the Calgary Region*. Travel Behaviour Report Series: Vol. 1. Calgary: City of Calgary, June 2013. https://www.calgary.ca/Transportation/TP/Documents/forecasting/Changing%20Travel%20Behaviour%20in%20the%20Calgary%20Region_v1_forWeb_2013-06-04.pdf?noredirect=1.

———. *One Calgary: 2019–2022 Service Plans and Budgets*. Calgary: City of Calgary. Accessed 11 November 2020. https://www.calgary.ca/cfod/finance/plans-budgets-and-financial-reports/plans-and-budget-2019-2022/service-plans-and-budgets.html.

"February 2020 Price Index Results Released." *AutoTrader*, 5 March 2020. https://www.autotrader.ca/newsfeatures/20200305/february-2020-price-index-results-released.

Fisher, Marc. "Cruising toward Oblivion." *Washington Post,* 2 September 2015. https://www.washingtonpost.com/sf/style/2015/09/02/americas-fading-car-culture/.

Ford Motor Company. "Looking Further with Ford: 2020 Trends." Accessed 3 September 2020. https://media.ford.com/content/dam/fordmedia/North%20America/US/2019/12/11/2020-Ford-Trends.pdf.

Getaround. "Getaround Becomes Global Carsharing Leader with $300 Million Acquisition of European Platform Drivy." Press release, 24 April 2019. https://www.getaround.com/media/public/press/Getaround_Announces_300M_Acquisition_of_European_Platform_Drivy.pdf.

Gilligan, Melissa. "1 in 3 Canadians Suffer from Road Rage Each Month: Survey." *Global News*, 14 July 2015. https://globalnews.ca/news/2109293/1-in-3-canadians-suffer-from-road-rage-each-month-survey/.

Howell, Trevor Scott, and Annalise Klingbeil. "Data Reveals Pedestrian Danger: One Hit Per Day, and Most Had the Right of Way." *Calgary Herald*, 19 February 2016. https://calgaryherald.com/news/local-news/oh-no-not-again-city-data-shows-one-pedestrian-collision-a-day-most-had-right-of-way-20-hit-and-run.

Illich, Ivan. *Energy and Equity*. London: Marion Boyers, 2000.

International Institute for Sustainable Development. *Costs of Pollution in Canada: Measuring the Impacts on Families, Businesses and Governments*. Winnipeg: IISD, 2017. https://www.iisd.org/story/costs-of-pollution-in-canada/.

Kell, John. "Avis to Buy Car-Sharing Service Zipcar." *Wall Street Journal*, 2 January 2013. https://www.wsj.com/articles/SB10001424127887324374004578217121433322386.

Keough, Noel, Bob Morrison, and Celia Lee. *State of Our City 2020: An Urgent Call for a Just Transition*. Calgary: Sustainable Calgary Society, 2020. http://www.sustainablecalgary.org/publications.

Kury de Castillo, Carolyn. "Construction Worker Shot in Suspected Road Rage Case in Calgary." *Global News*, 1 July 2019. https://globalnews.ca/news/5449633/construction-worker-shot-calgary-road-rage/.

Lachapelle, Erick, Christopher Borick, and Barry G. Rabe. *Key Findings Report for the 2013 Canada–US Comparative Climate Opinion Survey*. Ottawa: Canada 2020.

Litman, Todd. *Generated Traffic and Induced Travel: Implications for Transport Planning.* Victoria, BC: Victoria Transport Policy Institute, July 2020. https://www.vtpi.org/gentraf.pdf.

Mandel, Charles. "Canadian Climate Denial Group, Friends of Science, Named as Creditor in Coal Giant's Bankruptcy Files." *National Observer*, 20 June 2016. https://thenarwhal.ca/canadian-climate-denial-group-friends-science-named-creditor-coal-giant-s-bankruptcy-files/.

Markusoff, Jason. "By the Numbers: What You Need to Know about the Airport Tunnel." *Calgary Herald,* 22 May 2014. https://calgaryherald.com/news/local-news/by-the-numbers-what-you-need-to-know-about-the-airport-tunnel.

Martin, Elliot, and Susan Shaheen. "Impacts of Car2Go on Vehicle Ownership, Modal Shift, Vehicle Miles Traveled, and Greenhouse Gas Emission: An Analysis of Five North American Cities." Working Paper, Transportation Sustainability Research Center, University of California Berkeley, 12 July 2016. https://tsrc.berkeley.edu/publications/impacts-car2go-vehicle-ownership-modal-shift-vehicle-miles-traveled-and-greenhouse-gas.

Martínez, Marcos. "Merwede's Future: 12,000 Residents and Zero Parking Spaces." *Ferrovial* (blog), 19 October 2020. https://blog.ferrovial.com/en/2020/10/merwedes-future-12000-residents-and-zero-parking-spaces/.

McGlade, Christophe, and Paul Ekins. "The Geographical Distribution of Fossil Fuels Unused When Limiting Global Warming to 2°C." *Nature* 517 (2015): 187–90.

McLuhan, Marshall. *Understanding Media: The Extensions of Man.* With new introduction by Lewis H. Lapham. Cambridge, MA: MIT Press, 1994. First published 1964, McGraw-Hill (New York).

Monbiot, George. *Heat: How to Stop the Planet from Burning.* San Francisco: South End, 2009.

Nader, Ralph. *Unsafe at Any Speed: The Designed-In Dangers of the American Automobile.* Boston: Knightsbridge, 1991.

Nugmanova, Assel, Wulf-Holger Arndt, Md Aslam Hossain, and Jong Ryeol Kim. "Effectiveness of Ring Roads in Reducing Traffic Congestion in Cities for Long Run: Big Almaty Ring Road Case Study." *Sustainability* 11, no. 18 (2019): 4973.

Organisation for Economic Co-operation and Development. *Road Safety Annual Report 2019: Canada*. Geneva: OECD International Transport Forum, 2019. https://www.itf-oecd.org/sites/default/files/canada-road-safety.pdf.

Reguly, Eric. "Is the Car Dead?" *Globe and Mail*, 30 August 2012. https://www.theglobeandmail.com/report-on-business/rob-magazine/is-the-car-dead/article4510125/.

Reiger, Sarah. "Calgary's Airport Faces $67M Deficit This Year." *CBC News*, 7 July 2020. https://www.cbc.ca/news/canada/calgary/calgary-airport-1.5641441.

Row, Jesse, Erin Welk, Nathan Lemphers, and Paul Cobb. *Options for Reducing GHG Emissions in Calgary: Research Report*. Calgary: City of Calgary, February 2011. https://www.pembina.org/reports/calgary-ghg-main-report.pdf.

Rubin, Jeff. "Why Saudi Arabia Can No Longer Temper Oil Prices." *Globe and Mail*, 23 February 2011. https://www.theglobeandmail.com/report-on-business/industry-news/energy-and-resources/why-saudi-arabia-can-no-longer-temper-oil-prices/article623163/.

Salus, Jesse. "The Origins of the Southwest Ring Road." *The History of a Road* (blog), 5 March 2016. https://calgaryringroad.wordpress.com/2016/03/05/the-origins-of-the-southwest-ring-road/.

Seba, Tony. *Clean Disruption of Energy and Transportation: How Silicon Valley Is Making Oil, Nuclear, Natural Gas, and Coal Obsolete*. Silicon Valley, CA: Clean Planet Ventures, 2014. https://tonyseba.com/wp-content/uploads/2014/05/book-cover-Clean-Disruption.pdf.

Siekierska, Alicja. "Canada among Only Seven Countries to See Rise in Pedestrian Deaths, OECD Study Reveals." *Financial Post*, 25 May 2018. https://financialpost.com/transportation/canada-among-only-seven-countries-to-see-rise-in-pedestrian-deaths-oecd-study-finds.

Smith, Alanna. "Car2Go Can't Make It Go in Calgary, Pulling out of 'Highly Volatile' Market." *Calgary Herald*, 27 September 2019. https://calgaryherald.com/news/local-news/car2go-leaving-calgary-in-light-of-highly-volatile-transportation-market-limited-success.

Thompson, Derek, and Jordan Weissmann. "The Cheapest Generation: Why Millennials Aren't Buying Cars or Houses, and What That Means for the Economy." *The Atlantic*, September 2012. https://www.theatlantic.com/magazine/archive/2012/09/the-cheapest-generation/309060/.

"Tram and Light Rail Transit Systems." *Wikipedia*. Last edited 28 October 2020. https://en.wikipedia.org/wiki/Tram_and_light_rail_transit_systems.

"Vehicle Buyers in the United States in 2017, by Age Group." *Statista*. Accessed 21 August 2020. https://www.statista.com/statistics/987393/age-distribution-of-vehicle-buyers-united-states/.

"When Buying Cars, Millennials Choose Used and Practical over New and Flashy." *Financial Post*, 21 September 2015. https://financialpost.com/personal-finance/young-money/when-buying-cars-millennials-choose-used-and-practical-over-new-and-flashy.

Wood, James. "Alberta Government Commits to West Leg of Calgary's Ring Road." *Edmonton Journal*, 5 July 2015. https://edmontonjournal.com/news/politics/ndp-government-commits-to-west-leg-of-ring-road/wcm/cf3fce83-6e09-4a0d-992f-346808286719.

World Health Organization. *Global Status Report on Road Safety 2018*. Geneva: WHO, 2018. https://www.who.int/violence_injury_prevention/road_safety_status/2018/en/.

"Zipcar Overview." *Zipcar*, 2021. https://www.zipcar.com/press/overview.

A Culture of Sustainability

In this chapter, we present an eclectic set of essays that leverage seeming-ly modest issues to invite us to think more deeply about cultural beliefs and attitudes in relation to sustainability. In 1958 Raymond Williams wrote his classic *Culture and Society*. In it, he famously defined culture as "a whole way of life" and as having to do with the arts and learning.[1] Williams argued that culture is not, or should not be, an elitist pursuit and that, at that time, culture was being used as a means of "perpetuating and shoring up social inequality." He proposed, alternatively, that the "cultural worth of all human activity is socially equalizing."[2]

French anthropologist Pierre Bourdieu contributed to the cultural debate with his influential concept of "habitus"—the physical embodiment of our cultural capital, such as ways of carrying our bodies, the clothes we wear, the products we consume, our tastes and credentials. Our habitus defines who we are and can foster inclusivity or exclusivity.[3]

Williams' work preceded the contemporary debates about sustainability, of course, but his ideas are still important for our understanding of a culture of sustainability. Culture is the matrix of norms and meaning within which politics, economics, and technological change are immersed. Broad access to cultural institutions and to the process of cultural production is essential to sustainability. In this chapter, we exam both the exclusive and inclusive tendencies in culture, both its conservatism and its change-compelling nature.

In the first essay, we write in defense of Calgary's Peace Bridge. What does the bridge, and the debate that it sparked, say about creating a walkable city? Does a city just serve a utilitarian purpose, or do we aspire to a vibrant city that values beauty and that brings people out to recreate and celebrate in public spaces?

In "I and We," we take on the "me first" posture that our neoliberal free market economic model promotes, but we do so with a discussion not of economics but of culture. The big question we ask is, What kind of society promotes sustainability? Is it the "I" culture made famous by arch-conservative author Ayn Rand and encapsulated in Margaret Thatcher's infamous statement "There is no such thing as society"? Or is it a "we" culture, where citizens recognize their interdependence and act in the spirit of compassion and good will toward neighbours?

In a sustainable society, all citizens should have the right and the means to education and the information they need to participate fully in the life of their community. In this chapter, we argue for the unique role that libraries play in making that possible.

The chapter also includes an essay on dandelions. It may seem a trivial issue with respect to sustainability, but it does open a window for us to reflect on how we orient ourselves culturally toward the wider community of life. Surprisingly, dandelions, by their very ubiquity and familiarity in our lives, offer a chance to reflect on bigger questions.

GIVE PEACE A CHANCE

Probably no piece of Calgary's infrastructure has generated as much press per dollar of spending as the Peace Bridge. Despite the furor, for its utility and its aesthetic quality, it was money well spent. It has, in fact, become an iconic symbol of Calgary, constantly drawing tourists and Calgarians alike to its unique beauty and functionality.

There was much gnashing of teeth about the price tag, but $25 million, it turns out, is not out of line with similar footbridge projects.[4] The Peace Bridge cost about $30,000 per metre. The Fort Edmonton Bridge and Winnipeg's Esplanade Riel Bridge were built for about $34,000 and $50,000 per metre, respectively.[5]

Another bone of contention was the sole sourcing of the design to Spanish starchitect Santiago Calatrava. This bridge had some unique and demanding design considerations—no suspended overhead towers, to avoid conflict with the heliport; no mid-river piers, for environmental reasons; and of course, the aesthetic "wow factor." For his structural engineering expertise, design reputation, and proven ability to deliver the goods, the invitation to Calatrava was prudent public policy.

Still others complained that we didn't need another bridge. With the Peace Bridge, we now have nine bridges within five kilometres. In Florence, Italy, the famous Ponte Vecchio sits in the middle of eight bridges in a 4.4 kilometre stretch. In our opinion, Calgary's pedestrian network across the Bow River could use yet another bridge connecting the north shore with what will eventually be a densely populated West Village. The combined cost of three existing footbridges—the Elbow River Traverse (at the confluence of the Bow and Elbow rivers), the Peace Bridge, and the George C. King bridge to St. Patrick's Island (known as the Skipping Stone Bridge)—plus a future fourth bridge at West Village is less than the price of one suburban vehicle interchange.

Early on, the media decided that the Peace Bridge was a bad news story. Look back at the headlines. Phrases like "Celebrate Government Waste," "Notorious Peace Bridge," "Controversial Piece of Infrastructure," "Plagued by Further Delay," and "Cost Overruns" peppered the coverage.

It is instructive to look at Calgary's rival city, Edmonton, and its iconic Fort Edmonton footbridge. The cost was slightly higher. It, too, suffered delays due to technical problems. In the case of the Peace Bridge, it was faulty welds. In Edmonton, technical delays occurred with the main suspension cable. But a quick Internet search suggests that cost and delays did not result in an avalanche of mean-spirited negative press in Edmonton. Quite the opposite, in fact. One headline carried by the *Edmonton Journal* read "Has Edmonton Hit a Home Run with Its New Footbridge at Fort Edmonton Park?"[6] In this op-ed, the author wrote, "Some folks don't mind plain and ugly. But I mind. . . . Count me in as one taxpayer who is glad that our city council has decided to buck up and pay a bit more for design, to start creating public infrastructure that doesn't just serve us, it delights us."

So why heap so much scorn on the Peace Bridge? It seems that in Calgary, the default position is that any government spending is out of control, wasteful, and incompetent. Or perhaps it was simply another opportunity for the reactionary media to attack Druh Farrell, one of the city's most progressive councilors.

Immediately after the Peace Bridge opened, the construction of the Ring Road around Calgary began soaking up $4 to $5 billion in taxpayers' money, and Council reaffirmed its commitment to subsidize the suburban development industry to the tune of hundreds of millions of dollars annually with little or no sign of concern from mainstream media, the Canadian Taxpayers Federation, or supposedly tight-fisted taxpayer-avenging councilors.[7]

Through processes like imagineCalgary and Plan It Calgary, citizens have spoken loud and clear that they want a city where walking is safe, convenient, and pleasant. But you don't get a walkable city without building infrastructure for walkers. Compared to the spending on more roads for more cars, the health care costs of sedentary lifestyles, and the cost of injury and death due to automobile accidents, spending on pedestrian infrastructure is a bargain.

That brings us to our final point. There has been no more dogged and diligent champion of a walkable city than Councilor Farrell. Yet no other elected official received so much vitriol and nasty comment as she for her support of the Peace Bridge. Instead of throwing darts, we should be throwing a bouquet to Councilor Farrell for her diligence and determination to build a more sustainable and beautiful city.

Calgary will never be the great city it aspires to if, collectively, we cannot support bold and visionary local government efforts to create a sustainable, vibrant, and beautiful city. The Peace Bridge is a step in the right direction.

I AND WE: THE CASE FOR SOCIAL COHESION

In the climax of Ayn Rand's cult classic *The Fountainhead*, the hero, architect Howard Roark, dynamites a building of his own creation because its design had been subverted by a scheming partner.[8] Embodied in Roark, as well as other of Rand's literary characters, are the characteristics that inspired and reinforced the myth of the virtuous individual and the evils of "big" government. As Margaret Thatcher, a powerful devotee of the credo, infamously proclaimed in a 1982 interview with *Women's Own* magazine, "There is no such thing as society."[9]

Closer to home, the "rugged individual" was at the epicentre of Premier Ralph Klein's (1992–2006) revolution: the mythical westerner shaping the "Alberta Advantage" by virtue of his or her own will and effort to achieve wealth and prosperity. Those failing to take advantage of the Advantage, as Klein notoriously remonstrated time after time, had only themselves to blame.[10] Small government, "free" markets, low taxes, individual property rights, and low levels of social services are all policies stemming from Rand's self-adoring ideology. After an easing of the ideological rhetoric through four successive provincial governments, Premier Jason Kenney has turned the clock back once again.

Rand hated the word *we*, writing bluntly in *Anthem*, "It is the word by which the depraved steal the virtue of the good, by which the weak steal the might of the strong, by which the fools steal the wisdom of the sages. . . . I am done with the monster of 'We', the word of serfdom, of plunder, of misery, falsehood and shame." In its place, she saw "the face of god," a "god who will grant them [humans] joy and peace and pride. This god, this one word: 'I.'"[11]

Scary stuff!

As both the 2015 and 2019 provincial elections demonstrated, the starkest difference in values in our cities is between inner cities (we) and suburbs (I), particularly in Calgary and Edmonton and their metropolitan regions. For at least a decade, voting patterns have resulted in success for centre and left-of-centre MLAs and MPs in the inner city, with right-of-centre candidates achieving success in the suburbs. Philippe Fournier, founder of 338Canada.com, looked at this phenomenon ahead of the 2019 federal election. Using population density as a proxy for city centre districts, he found that the fifty-three densest electoral districts were all likely to vote either Liberal or NDP. In districts with densities above four thousand people per square kilometre, the Liberals led the Conservatives by a whopping 26 percent.[12] What accounts for this polarity?

Research by University of Toronto geographer Alan Walks confirms that this phenomenon—progressive inner city voting and conservative suburban voting—holds across Canada. As Walks delved into the reasons for this pattern, he found that suburban voters tend to believe that government is too big, taxes are too high, and the economy should be left to business. In broad strokes, suburbanites live a privatized, consumption-oriented lifestyle characterized by car-dominated transport, big box mall shopping, and the desire for private space in big suburban homes. They tend not to see a political dimension to that lifestyle; it is simply natural. Inner city dwellers, by contrast, seem to be much more deliberate in aligning their politics with their lifestyle and housing choices. They choose the inner city for its perceived sense of community, they support public transit, and they trade off larger homes and yards for easier access to public spaces like plazas, art galleries, museums, and theatres.[13]

Walks observed that these voting patterns began emerging in the early 1980s, coinciding precisely with the era in which Rand enthusiasts—including Margaret Thatcher, Ronald Reagan, Brian Mulroney, Alan Greenspan (a primary architect of the 2008 financial meltdown and once the world's most powerful central banker), Paul Wolfowitz, Dick Cheney, and others who drove America to war in Iraq—began retooling society toward Rand's vision.

Rand and her disciples made careers from demonizing "we," but logic and evidence tell us reality is different. As Canadians and Calgarians, our most successful endeavours—our legal, education, and health systems; our inherent inclination toward social justice and equality of opportunity; and, most dearly, our open form of democracy—all came about through people of vision in the service of a greater good. Our individual successes are, in large measure, a consequence of these community investments.

"We" is crucial because—as contemporary urban research, such as that reported in *All-In Cities* by PolicyLink, argues—the successful, sustainable urban places of the future will be those that best leverage the power of community to overcome mounting social and environmental challenges.[14] Wherever great urban developments are happening, you can be sure that behind them, there is a community of "we"—enlightened, engaged, and usually unselfish individuals.

The reasons inner city voters vote the way they do are complex and not necessarily tied to selflessness, but whatever the reason, they have it right and Rand had it wrong. There is a political sweet spot out there where "I" and "we" are not opposites. It's important that we find it, because in the end, "we" is much more resilient than "I."

LIBRARIES: WHAT ARE THEY GOOD FOR?

At times, our world seems headed for the new dark ages that urban sage Jane Jacobs warned about. Here at home, we are confronted with a variety of challenges—the erosion of our country's image as compassionate honest broker and environmental leader among the community of nations, economic uncertainty, growing inequality, half-hearted attention to reconciliation with First Nations, and the ethical challenge of tar sands development.[15]

In *Dark Age Ahead*, Jacobs identifies the public library as one of the indispensable assets of any community—as important as water and sewer systems, fire protection, and public health.[16] The public library, sometimes called "the people's university," plays an essential role in providing an inclusive place for citizens to engage in lifelong learning, ensuring that all have access to the information they need to participate in community life.

Calgary's new Central Library gives physical form to what is already one of the most successful public library systems in North America. It received more than fifty thousand visitors the first weekend it opened. From 1994 to 2009, total uses of the library system grew from 13.8 to 35.5 million. Between 2014 and 2017, the per capita use increased by 22 percent. Since 2013, the Calgary Public Library (CPL) has maintained an annual circulation of more than fifteen million items. It consistently has more visitors than the Stampede, Calgary Zoo, Heritage Park, Science Centre, recreation arenas, and all professional sporting events—combined![17]

The library is much more than a source of books, magazines, videos, and music. The CPL provides low-income Calgarians with tickets to arts and recreational opportunities, including dance, music, theatre, festivals, and rodeo. In 2009 over eleven thousand kids improved their reading skills through the library's Summer Reading Adventure. Between 2013 and 2019, the library hosted more than 170,000 participants in its programs.

Among the city's constellation of cultural institutions—to take nothing away from our thriving arts community—the library is uniquely important to Calgary's vitality and sustainability. In a city where economic inequalities dictate access to the benefits our city has to offer, the library is a pillar of social inclusion. In a world where the ability to purchase access to knowledge and even social connection defines our ability to participate in society, whether via university tuition or the latest technological gadgets, the library is almost alone in its promise of universal access. For example, according to the Program for the International Assessment of Adult Competencies, an international group that assesses access to the foundational information-processing skills required to participate in the social and economic life of advanced economies, 45 percent of adults in Alberta do not have the literacy skills to function effectively in society.[18] These functionally illiterate Albertans are far more likely to live in poor households, to have served jail terms, and to have misinterpreted medical instructions.[19] For Alberta to be at the forefront of realizing the dream of universal literacy, we need public libraries.

But as the new Central Library matures and the creative class rallies its support, we have to be vigilant to avoid potential dangers. Big shiny projects in the "cultural districts"—like libraries—are a centrepiece of "creative cities," but let's not make the mistake of assuming that creative cities are necessarily inclusive cities.[20]

Serendipitously, our new library is situated on the threshold of East Village. Its location is a symbolic opportunity for Calgarians to embrace the twin promise of a public library as both a celebration of the best of our culture and a symbol of a caring, inclusive society. East Village faces the challenge of reinvigorating itself without gentrifying and driving away "undesirables" to the point of making East Village and the Central Library an exclusive place enjoyed by the cultured classes but where the "uncultured" and the disenfranchised are alienated. If you have bad teeth, a tattered jacket, or Safeway bags holding your belongings, do you still feel comfortable stepping inside our new Central Library?

As Jacobs writes, community institutions like the public library encourage us to "deal civilly with people whose upbringing, cultures, and personalities are at odds with the traditions and customs of one's own nuclear family and [to] teach children to be both cosmopolitan and tolerant."[21]

It is hard to overstate the importance of a library. In 2002, after almost two thousand years, the world's most important library of the ancient world—the Great Library of Alexandria, in Egypt—was resurrected from the ashes and officially inaugurated as Bibliotheca Alexandrina. The Alexandria Declaration of 2004 recognized the new library's mission to advocate for reason over ideology, cultural expression over censorship, and social justice over oppression. The founding director of Bibliotheca Alexandrina spoke of it being "in the eye of the storm" of the Arab spring by fostering the "deep currents" of cultural change, and the emergence from a dark age of one of the world's great civilizations.[22]

In 2018 Calgary's Central Library was recognized by *Architectural Digest* as one of the nine most futuristic libraries in the world, along with the most recent addition to the world's great libraries—the Helsinki Central Library Oodi.[23] But beautiful design will only go so far. We need our new Central Library to foster compassion, wisdom, learning, understanding, and the deep currents of change that can create healthy and creative communities, a better Calgary, and a more just world! Calgary Public Library is on the right track with its 2019–22 *Strategic Plan*: "We engage in open, meaningful dialogue and deepen our understanding to inform Library practice and create an environment that is inclusive of all."[24]

ON DANDELIONS: SPEAKING TRUTH TO FLOWERS

Every spring, a yellow carpet covers the city, particularly infesting closely mown lawns and untended grassy or disturbed areas. And every year, about ten minutes after it appears, the squabble over toxic treatments to destroy it reignites. Alas, the poor dandelion. Has ever a more innocent, beneficial, and beautiful creation of nature been as embattled as this fecund little flower?

Officially, the province delisted the dandelion as a noxious weed in 2010, relieving local authorities from the obligation to keep it under complete control. The City has not sprayed for aesthetic purposes since 1995, and now only a small number of sites are treated with toxins—sites where dandelions are deemed out of control or where they present a danger (dandelion flowers make playing fields slipperier). However, obsessed lawnistas, who froth when waves of parachuting invaders waft over from a neighbouring cabbage patch, are under no such restrictions.

To our neatly manicured sensibilities, dandelions are weeds, perennially popping up where they're least desired. But the definition of "weed" is subjective. As one dandelion admirer put it, "If dandelions were hard to grow they would be welcome on any lawn."[25] Indeed, there are numerous benefits from this marvellous plant, named for the distinctive shape of its leaves (from the French *dent-de-lion*, 'tooth of the lion'). Dandelions have been gathered throughout human history, and the plant's medicinal properties documented since at least the tenth century.

Each part of the plant, from root to petal, is useful. Taken as tea, the roots treat kidney and liver complaints and act as a mild laxative. Ingested, they are highly nutritious, rich in Vitamins A, B, C, and D. Dried and roasted, they are used to brew a sort of coffee with a mild chicory flavour. The leaves, when young and tender, are delicious raw, and older leaves can be blanched like spinach or endives. When brewed, they are a powerful diuretic, and unlike conventional treatments, they do not leech potassium from the body. The latex in the stalks is effective in treating corns and warts. The flowers—aside from brightening our lives with their brilliantly jaunty yellow—can be boiled for tea and mixed with honey to treat coughs, or used as the essential ingredient in dandelion wine.[26]

The dandelion is one of the first spring sources of nectar for bumblebees and other pollinators. We hear ever more alarming news of the decline of pollinators. A 2020 article in the journal *Science* warns that population trends point to an extinction event for bumblebees.[27] We need to do all we can to ease the trauma that bees (and ultimately, we) are facing.

Strangely, despite their seeming abundance, dandelions are relatively lousy ecological competitors, thriving only in certain specialized habitats. Such sites are rare in nature, and as a result, dandelions do not normally overwhelm local ecosystems; they simply exist and compete as they are able. But in cities, dandelion habitat abounds. Why? It turns out that our preferred "weed"—lawn grass—is an even poorer competitor than dandelions. Extraordinary amounts of care and chemicals are required to keep this unnatural monoculture thriving. Ironically, short, neatly mown grass, particularly the clumpy varieties used on city land, provides the perfect niche for the dandelion's windborne seeds to settle and quickly establish. As we create something we love—neat grassy lawns—we also create ideal habitat for something we hate—dandelions. As the old comic-strip opossum Pogo astutely observed, "We have met the enemy and he is us."

A better approach to the dandelion is problem avoidance by design, a philosophy standing in stark contrast to the lazy we'll-deal-with-the-consequences-later approach that we're accustomed to. It's simple: the best way to deal with persistently vexing problems is to avoid them in the first place. Unfortunately, the penchant in our culture is for the opposite: wait until problems occur and then look for solutions. You don't have to ask which approach is more effective or which is costlier.

Spraying dandelions with toxic applications is a blunt and dangerous management practice. A comprehensive study by the Ontario College of Physicians, reported in 2005 in the *Canadian Journal of Public Health*, found, unsurprisingly, that "exposure to all commonly used pesticides" is associated with adverse health effects.[28] Though concentrations have been decreasing, more chemicals are sprayed in Calgary every year as the city spreads. In 2016, 0.23 kilograms per hectare of active ingredients were applied on public green spaces—the highest level since 2010.[29]

A better solution is to plant, wherever possible, hardy, locally adapted prairie species that work together to naturally resist the flowery yellow horde. There are trade-offs, to be sure. While it is shaggier than our groomed aesthetic demands, such urban landscaping strategies provide an array of benefits, including large cost savings due to decreased maintenance needs. For example, natural grass ecosystems need mowing only once a season, to prevent them from becoming fire hazards.

We are taking steps in the right direction. In 2016 Calgary hired private companies to deploy goat herds as natural weed control in Confluence Park in Calgary's northeast. In 2018 and 2020, the program was expanded, bringing goats to the inner city at McHugh Bluff in Sunnyside.[30] New Edinborough Park in Sunnyside was the first Calgary park to go pesticide-free after a strong advocacy campaign in the community. It has become one of the most popular spaces for pre-school play group meet-ups in the city. There are now five pesticide-free parks in Calgary.[31]

Dandelions are just the tip of the iceberg of ecological destruction. A 2019 study in the journal *Biological Conservation* reports that we are facing a worldwide decline in insects, the main cause being habitat loss by conversion to intensive agriculture and an additional driver being chemical use.[32] In September 2020, the UN Secretariat of the Convention on Biological Diversity reported that none of the targets set for biodiversity conservation in Aichi, Japan, in 2010 have been met, undermining efforts to address the climate emergency and attain the UN Sustainable Development Goals.[33]

Two oft-repeated principles of ecological sustainability are to promote and nurture diversity and to avoid introducing into the environment unnatural substances that nature is unable to assimilate. Lawns violate the first principle, and the use of pesticides to maintain them, the second. If the dandelion's tale were a fable, the moral would be this: if you don't want dandelions, don't create dandelion habitat. The safest and most cost-effective and ecologically defensible way to deal with dandelions is to nurture dandelion-resistant ecosystems.

NOTES

1   Raymond Williams, *Culture and Society: 1780–1950* (New York: Columbia University Press, 1983), 237.

2   Rodrigo, "What Does Raymond Williams Mean When He Describes Culture As Being 'a Whole Way of Life'?" *The WritePass Journal*, 21 November 2016, https://writepass. com/journal/2016/11/what-does-raymond-williams-mean-when-he-describes-culture-as-being-a-whole-way-of-life-what-are-the-merits-and-limitation-of-this-perspective/#_ftn10.

3   For more on the concept of "habitus," see Jean Hillier and Emma Rooksby, eds., *Habitus: A Sense of Place,* 2nd ed. (London: Routledge, 2005).

4   "Peace Bridge Builders Want More Money," *CBC News,* 13 March 2013, https://www.cbc.ca/news/canada/calgary/peace-bridge-builders-want-more-money-1.1392311.

5   "Fort Edmonton Footbridge and Trails Fact Sheet," *City of Edmonton,* accessed 3 September 2020, https://www.edmonton.ca/projects_plans/parks_recreation/fort-edmonton-footbridge-and-trails-fact-sheet.aspx; "Canadian Consulting Engineer Award of Excellence: Esplanade Riel," *Canadian Consulting Engineer,* 1 November 2014, https://www.canadianconsultingengineer.com/features/award-of-excellence-esplanade-riel/.

6   David Staples, "Has Edmonton Hit a Home Run with Its New Footbridge at Fort Edmonton Park?" *Edmonton Journal,* 16 August 2011, https://edmontonjournal.com/news/local-news/has-edmonton-hit-a-home-run-with-its-new-footbridge-at-fort-edmonton-park.

7   Morrison, Bob, "2012–2014 City Budget Submission by Governance, Finance, and Infrastructure Group," unpublished (Calgary: CivicCamp, 2012).

8   Ayn Rand, *The Fountainhead* (New York: Signet, 1952).

9   Brian Deer, "There Is No Such Thing As Society," *Brian Deer: Award-Winning Investigations,* accessed 6 February 2020, https://briandeer.com/social/thatcher-society.htm.

10   Frank Dabbs, "Ralph Klein's Real Legacy," *Alberta Views,* 1 September 2006, https://albertaviews.ca/ralph-kleins-real-legacy/.

11   Ayn Rand, *Anthem,* Part Eleven, Project Gutenberg, accessed 4 September 2020, first published 1938, https://www.gutenberg.org/files/1250/1250-h/1250-h.htm.

12   Philippe Fournier, "338Canada: The Urban-Rural Divide, Right along Party Lines," *Maclean's,* 29 September 2019, https://www.macleans.ca/politics/ottawa/338canada-the-urban-rural-divide-right-along-party-lines/.

13   R. Alan Walks, "The Causes of City-Suburban Political Polarization? A Canadian Case Study," *Annals of the Association of American Geographers* 96, no. 2 (2006): 390–414, https://www.jstor.org/stable/3694053.

14   Sarah Treuhaft, *All-In Cities: Building an Equitable Economy from the Ground Up* (Washington, DC: PolicyLink, 2016), https://www.policylink.org/aic-building-an-equitable-economy-from-the-ground-up.

15   Though the conventional description of this fossil fuel source is oil sands, I prefer to use the original term given the resource by industry and government. For a discussion of the politics of the use of the term, see Mike Gismondi and Debra Davidson, *Challenging Legitimacy at the Precipice of Energy Calamity* (New York: Springer, 2011), 27–28.

16   Jane Jacobs, *Dark Age Ahead* (Toronto: Vintage, 2005), 34–35.

17   Noel Keough, Bob Morrison, and Celia Lee, *State of Our City 2020: An Urgent Call for a Just Transition* (Calgary: Sustainable Calgary Society, 2020), 31, http://www.sustainablecalgary.org/publications.

18   Statistics Canada, "Literacy—Comparative Distributions of Proficiency Levels
      of Population Aged 16 and 65, Countries, Provinces and Territories," in *Skills in
      Canada: First Results from the Programme for the International Assessment of Adult
      Competencies,* chart 1.2, 17, Catalogue no. 89-555-X (Ottawa: Statistics Canada,
      2013), https://www150.statcan.gc.ca/n1/en/pub/89-555-x/89-555-x2013001-eng.
      pdf?st=gp3YoGfP. For more context on adult literacy in Calgary, see Keough, Lee, and
      Morrison, *State of Our City 2020.*

19   Canadian Association of Chiefs of Police, "The Link between Low Literacy and Crime."
      Literacy and Policing in Canada: Target Crime with Literacy, ch. 2, Fact Sheet 2 (Kanata,
      ON: CACP), accessed 5 January 2021, http://policeabc.ca/files/factsheets_englishPDFs/
      Ch02FactSheet02.pdf; ABC Life Literacy Canada, *What Is Life Literacy?* (Toronto: ABC
      Life Literacy Canada), accessed 5 January 2020, https://abclifeliteracy.ca/wp-content/
      uploads/2019/11/ABC-Life-Literacy.pdf.

20   For more on the concept of "cultural district," see "Natural Cultural Districts
      Exchange Toolkit," *Americans for the Arts,* accessed 4 January 2021, https://www.
      americansforthearts.org/by-program/reports-and-data/toolkits/national-cultural-
      districts-exchange-toolkit. As one example, planning is underway for Calgary's
      Rivers District: see "A Bold Vision for Calgary's Cultural and Entertainment District,"
      Calgary Municipal Land Corporation, 5 April 2018, https://www.calgarymlc.ca/news-
      full/2018/4/5/a-bold-vision-for-calgarys-cultural-and-entertainment-district.

      For a discussion of Florida's notion of "creative class" and his own critique of the
      concept, see "The 'Creative Class' Were Just the Rich All Along," *Long Reads,* accessed
      12 January 2021, https://longreads.com/2017/08/23/the-creative-class/.

21   Jacobs, *Dark Age Ahead,* 36.

22   Ismail Serageldin, "The Eye of the Storm: The Library of Alexandria and the
      Egyptian and Global Revolutions," in *Bibliotheca Alexandrina Annual Report,
      July 2010–June 2011* (Alexandria, Egypt: Bibliotheca Alexandrina, 2011), 137–46,
      https://www.bibalex.org/Attachments/Publications/Files/201208091245249995_
      AnnualReport20102011English982012small.pdf.

23   Julia Eskins and Karen Burshtein, "Step inside the World's 9 Most Futuristic Libraries,"
      Architectural Digest, 5 December 2018, https://www.architecturaldigest.com/story/
      futuristic-libraries.

24   Calgary Public Library, *Potential Realized: Calgary Public Library—Strategic Plan
      2019–2022* (Calgary: CPL, 2019), 2, https://calgarylibrary.ca/assets/PDFs/2020/2019-
      2022-strategic-plan-2020-initatives.pdf.

25   Andrew Mason, Twitter post, 27 April 2012, https://twitter.com/qikipedia/
      status/195787817627029504.

26   Dara Hourdajian. "Introduced Species Summary Project: Dandelion (*Taraxacum
      officinale*)," *Columbia University,* last edited 13 November 2006, http://www.columbia.
      edu/itc/cerc/danoff-burg/invasion_bio/inv_spp_summ/Taraxum_officinale.htm.

27   Peter Soroye, Tim Newbold, and Jeremy Kerr, "Climate Change Contributes to
      Widespread Declines among Bumble Bees across Continents," *Science* 367 (February
      2020): 685–88.

28   Neil Arya, "Pesticides and Human Health: Why Public Health Officials Should Support a Ban on Non-Essential Residential Use," *Canadian Journal of Public Health* 96 (2005): 89–92.

29   Keough, Morrison, and Lee, *State of Our City 2020,* 41.

30   Natalie Miller-Maleschuk, "Goats Return to Calgary Parks to Deal with Invasive Weeds," *CTV News*, 14 July 2020, https://calgary.ctvnews.ca/goats-return-to-calgary-parks-to-deal-with-invasive-weeds-1.5023865.

31   "Pesticide-Free Parks in Calgary," *City of Calgary,* 2020, https://www.calgary.ca/csps/parks/planning-and-operations/pest-management/pesticide-free-parks-in-calgary.html.

32   Francisco Sánchez-Bayo and Kris A. G. Wyckhuys, "Worldwide Decline of the Entomofauna: A Review of Its Drivers," *Biological Conservation* 232 (April 2019): 8–27.

33   UN Environment, *Global Biodiversity Outlook 5: Summary for Policymakers* (Montreal: Secretariat of the Convention on Biological Diversity, United Nations Environment Programme, 2020), https://www.cbd.int/gbo/gbo5/publication/gbo-5-spm-en.pdf.

Further Reading

Gardiner, Stephen M. *A Perfect Moral Storm: The Ethical Tragedy of Climate Change.* Oxford: Oxford University Press, 2011.

Monbiot, George. *Feral: Rewilding the Land, the Sea, and Human Life.* Chicago: University of Chicago Press, 2014.

Wohlleben, Peter. *The Hidden Life of Trees: What They Feel, How They Communicate.* Vancouver: Greystone Books, 2015.

Works Cited

ABC Life Literacy Canada. *What Is Life Literacy?* Toronto: ABC Life Literacy Canada. Accessed 5 January 2021. https://abclifeliteracy.ca/wp-content/uploads/2019/11/ABC-Life-Literacy.pdf.

Arya, Neil. "Pesticides and Human Health: Why Public Health Officials Should Support a Ban on Non-Essential Residential Use." *Canadian Journal of Public Health* 96 (2005): 89–92.

"A Bold Vision for Calgary's Cultural and Entertainment District." *Calgary Municipal Land Corporation,* 5 April 2018. https://www.calgarymlc.ca/news-full/2018/4/5/a-bold-vision-for-calgarys-cultural-and-entertainment-district.

Calgary Public Library. *Potential Realized: Calgary Public Library—Strategic Plan 2019–2022.* Calgary: CPL, 2019. https://calgarylibrary.ca/assets/PDFs/2020/2019-2022-strategic-plan-2020-initatives.pdf.

Canadian Association of Chiefs of Police. "The Link between Low Literacy and Crime." *Literacy and Policing in Canada: Target Crime with Literacy*, ch. 2, Fact Sheet 2. Kanata, ON: CACP. Accessed 5 January 2021. http://policeabc.ca/files/factsheets_englishPDFs/Ch02FactSheet02.pdf.

"Canadian Consulting Engineer Award of Excellence: Esplanade Riel." *Canadian Consulting Engineer,* 1 November 2014. https://www.canadianconsultingengineer.com/features/award-of-excellence-esplanade-riel/.

"The 'Creative Class' Were Just the Rich All Along." *Long Reads.* Accessed 12 January 2021. https://longreads.com/2017/08/23/the-creative-class/.

Dabbs, Frank. "Ralph Klein's Real Legacy." *Alberta Views*, 1 September 2006. https://albertaviews.ca/ralph-kleins-real-legacy/.

Deer, Brian. "There Is No Such Thing As Society." *Brian Deer: Award-Winning Investigations.* Accessed 6 February 2020. https://briandeer.com/social/thatcher-society.htm.

Eskins, Julia, and Karen Burshtein. "Step inside the World's 9 Most Futuristic Libraries." *Architectural Digest*, 5 December 2018. https://www.architecturaldigest.com/story/futuristic-libraries.

"Fort Edmonton Footbridge and Trails Fact Sheet." *City of Edmonton.* Accessed 3 September 2020. https://www.edmonton.ca/projects_plans/parks_recreation/fort-edmonton-footbridge-and-trails-fact-sheet.aspx.

Fournier, Philippe. "338Canada: The Urban-Rural Divide, Right along Party Lines." *Maclean's*, 29 September 2019. https://www.macleans.ca/politics/ottawa/338canada-the-urban-rural-divide-right-along-party-lines/.

Gismondi, Mike, and Debra Davidson. *Challenging Legitimacy at the Precipice of Energy Calamity*. New York: Springer, 2011.

Hillier, Jean, and Emma Rooksby, eds. *Habitus: A Sense of Place*. 2nd ed. London: Routledge, 2005.

Hourdajian, Dara. "Introduced Species Summary Project: Dandelion (*Taraxacum officinale*)." *Columbia University.* Last edited 13 November 2006. http://www.columbia.edu/itc/cerc/danoff-burg/invasion_bio/inv_spp_summ/Taraxum_officinale.htm.

Jacobs, Jane. *Dark Age Ahead*. Toronto: Vintage, 2005.

Keough, Noel, Bob Morrison, and Celia Lee. *State of Our City 2020: An Urgent Call for a Just Transition*. Calgary: Sustainable Calgary Society, 2020. http://www.sustainablecalgary.org/publications.

Miller-Maleschuk, Natalie. "Goats Return to Calgary Parks to Deal with Invasive Weeds." *CTV News*, 14 July 2020. https://calgary.ctvnews.ca/goats-return-to-calgary-parks-to-deal-with-invasive-weeds-1.5023865.

Morrison, Bob. "2012–2014 City Budget Submission by Governance, Finance, and Infrastructure Group." Unpublished. Calgary: CivicCamp, 2012.

"Natural Cultural Districts Exchange Toolkit." *Americans for the Arts*. Accessed 4 January 2021. https://www.americansforthearts.org/by-program/reports-and-data/toolkits/national-cultural-districts-exchange-toolkit.

"Peace Bridge Builders Want More Money." *CBC News*, 13 March 2013. https://www.cbc.ca/news/canada/calgary/peace-bridge-builders-want-more-money-1.1392311.

"Pesticide-Free Parks in Calgary." *City of Calgary*, 2020. https://www.calgary.ca/csps/parks/planning-and-operations/pest-management/pesticide-free-parks-in-calgary.html.

Rand, Ayn. *Anthem*. Project Gutenberg. First published 1938. https://www.gutenberg.org/files/1250/1250-h/1250-h.htm.

——. *The Fountainhead*. New York: Signet, 1952.

Rodrigo. "What Does Raymond Williams Mean When He Describes Culture As Being 'a Whole Way of Life'?" *The WritePass Journal*, 21 November 2016. https://writepass.com/journal/2016/11/what-does-raymond-williams-mean-when-he-describes-culture-as-being-a-whole-way-of-life-what-are-the-merits-and-limitation-of-this-perspective/#_ftn10.

Sánchez-Bayo, Francisco, and Kris A. G. Wyckhuys. "Worldwide Decline of the Entomofauna: A Review of Its Drivers." *Biological Conservation* 232 (April 2019): 8–27.

Serageldin, Ismail. "The Eye of the Storm: The Library of Alexandria and the Egyptian and Global Revolutions." In *Bibliotheca Alexandrina Annual Report, July 2010–June 2011*, 137–46. Alexandria, Egypt: Bibliotheca Alexandrina, 2011. https://www.bibalex.org/Attachments/Publications/Files/201208091245249995_AnnualReport20102011English982012small.pdf.

Soroye, Peter, Tim Newbold, and Jeremy Kerr. "Climate Change Contributes to Widespread Declines among Bumble Bees across Continents." *Science* 367 (February 2020): 685–88.

Staples, David. "Has Edmonton Hit a Home Run with Its New Footbridge at Fort Edmonton Park?" *Edmonton Journal*, 16 August 2011. https://edmontonjournal.com/news/local-news/has-edmonton-hit-a-home-run-with-its-new-footbridge-at-fort-edmonton-park.

Statistics Canada. "Literacy—Comparative Distributions of Proficiency Levels of Population Aged 16 and 65, Countries, Provinces and Territories." In *Skills in Canada: First Results from the Programme for the International Assessment of Adult Competencies*, chart 1.2, 17. Catalogue no. 89-555-X. Ottawa: Statistics Canada, 2013. https://www150.statcan.gc.ca/n1/pub/89-555-x/2013001/c-g/c-g1.2-eng.htm.

Treuhaft, Sarah. *All-In Cities: Building an Equitable Economy from the Ground Up*. Washington, DC: PolicyLink, 2016. https://www.policylink.org/aic-building-an-equitable-economy-from-the-ground-up.

UN Environment. *Global Biodiversity Outlook 5: Summary for Policymakers*. Montreal: Secretariat of the Convention on Biological Diversity, UN Environment Programme, 2020. https://www.cbd.int/gbo/gbo5/publication/gbo-5-spm-en.pdf.

Walks, R. Alan. "The Causes of City-Suburban Political Polarization? A Canadian Case Study." *Annals of the Association of American Geographers* 96, no. 2 (2006): 390–414.

Williams, Raymond. *Culture and Society: 1780–1950*. New York: Columbia University Press, 1983.

The Wheels Are Off the Growth Machine

At the core of our understanding of sustainability is the relationship between environment and economy. The Brundtland Commission's 1987 report, *Our Common Future*, proclaimed that sustainable development is about finding synergies between the two rather than seeing them as antagonistic. In this chapter, we focus on the economic pillar of sustainability.

We argue that the problem is the incompatibility not of economy and environment but of economic growth and human and ecological well-being. We make the case that economy, society, and environment are out of balance, with the economy taking up all the oxygen and depleting human and ecological well-being. To explain this state of affairs, we introduce the idea of multiple capitals—financial, natural, and social.

Economist Herman Daly's notion of uneconomic growth is a useful way to understand the problem of economic growth in a finite world. In addition to exploring Daly's ideas, we introduce Harvey Molotch's concept of the "growth machine," which is based on the alliance of economic and political forces, to understand what drives urban growth.

The essays in this chapter also present a critique of the resource-based Canadian economy—in particular, the fossil fuel–powered Calgary economy, which is based on the model of infinite growth powered by a finite energy resource. We discuss the implications of rapid growth in terms of the increase of corporate concentration of wealth and power and the growing income inequality.

We also present some viable alternatives. In one essay, we propose an economic development strategy for Calgary that does not rely on growth but does address key social and environmental challenges—affordable housing, zero waste, 100 percent renewable energy strategies, and the design and manufacture of human-powered transportation technologies. In "Minding Our Own Business," we introduce the concept of the solidarity economy, also called the social economy, and reveal Alberta's long tradition of this alternative way of organizing economic life.

ECONOMIC GROWTH IS NO LONGER DELIVERING THE GOODS

"Growth for the sake of growth doesn't interest me much." What's this—another wacky environmentalist spouting nonsense? No, actually it's former Suncor CEO Steve Williams, quoted in an October 2015 edition of the *Financial Post*.[1] While Mr. Williams was not really taking on the idea of growth, he did suggest that growth must have a purpose.

Two Canadian reports have converged on the question of growth and its purpose. Both present compelling evidence suggesting that in Canada, growth and well-being might be at odds. In 2016 the Canadian Index of Wellbeing (CIW) released its second report on sixty-four indicators of well-being.[2] The report includes measures of community vitality, health, education, leisure and culture, living standards, and the environment.

"The findings uncover some troubling truths about the connection between our economy and our wellbeing," said CIW's advisory board co-chair Roy Romanow.[3] From 1994 to 2014, Canada's economy, as measured by gross domestic product (GDP), grew by 38 percent, while improvements in Canadian well-being over the same seventeen-year period saw less than a 10 percent increase. In fact, over this period, Canadians' participation in arts, culture, and leisure activities actually decreased. So much for that promise of leisure way back in the 1960s that A. J. Veal explores in *Whatever Happened to the Leisure Society?*[4] Seems as though 1960s development advocate Walter Rostow's fifth stage of development, "mass consumerism," has found ways to commodify leisure to such an extent that we now have to work longer to afford the paraphernalia of leisure that then sits in the back of the garage because we have no leisure time.

In 2011 the CIW found that even "as the gap between Canadians at the top and those at the bottom continues to grow, . . . societies with greater inequality are shown to have worse health and wellbeing outcomes."[5] Since 2008, "even though the economy as measured by GDP is in slow recovery, the wellbeing of Canadians continues to decline."[6]

The CIW also reports that between 1994 and 2014, the health of our environment—as measured by indicators including energy consumption, greenhouse gas emissions, ecological footprint, ground level ozone, and available farmland—has deteriorated by 2.9 percent. As noted in a 2011 CIW document, "the environment domain speaks volumes about the tension between the relentless pursuit of economic growth and the finite reality of a planet experiencing massive climate change and dwindling natural resources."[7]

One of the most oft-repeated refrains in Canadian political debate is that health care is becoming a drain on the economy. It is hard not to conclude just the opposite—that the economy is making us (and the planet) sick. In the work of Linda Duxbury and Christopher Higgins, we find evidence for this idea. In their 2012 *Revisiting Life-Work Issues in Canada,* they report on two decades of research into work-life stress.[8] They found that since 1992, levels of stress for Canadian workers have gone up and life satisfaction has gone down. And no wonder! Over half of surveyed employees "take work home to complete outside regular hours."[9] Employees reported that work regularly interfered with family life and that "the increased availability of low-cost office technology has contributed to the decline in work-life balance by increasing expectations around work and making it possible for employees to work anytime and anywhere."[10] A 2018 study by Duxbury, Higgins, and Maggie Stevenson shows that overload at work, combined with family responsibilities, leads to higher levels of stress; not surprisingly, women more often feel these stresses.[11]

This state of affairs is self-defeating for the economy: Duxbury found work-life conflict to be associated with "higher absenteeism and lower productivity." Yet for all this effort by workers, "there has been little career mobility within Canadian firms over the past several years."[12]

The conventional storyline is that economic growth leads to greater leisure, a healthy environment, and increased well-being. The evidence from the last two decades tells a very different story. Strong economic growth has been coupled with stagnating well-being, longer hours of work, decreased leisure, less time with family, and a deteriorating environment. It appears, as ecological economist Herman Daly argues in *From Uneconomic Growth to a Steady-State Economy*, that we have entered an era of "uneconomic growth."[13]

We see lots of signs of uneconomic growth in Calgary, not all of them good. Anyone who commutes via the over-subscribed LRT has experienced the downside of growth. What about getting to the airport, or anywhere else on the Deerfoot during the ever-expanding rush hour? In 2019 City Council approved fourteen new suburban developments, in full knowledge of the fact that none of them will pay for themselves.[14] Against our better judgement, urban sprawl continues to eat up farmland. Yet our provincial government—through tar sands land-lease policies, low tax regimes, and deregulation—promotes economic growth without any objective assessment of its contribution to well-being.

Maybe Steve Williams was onto something without realizing it. The prescription for well-being in Calgary might just be to chill out. Apply the brakes to economic expansion, or at least stop stoking the fires of growth. As Janine Benyus, author of *Biomimicry: Innovation Inspired by Design*, so eloquently muses, "Restraint is not a popular notion in a society addicted to 'growing' the economy, but it is one of the most powerful practices we can adopt at this point in history."[15]

THE CURRENT CRISIS: IT'S MORE THAN THE ECONOMY

In *Growing Unequal?* the Organisation for Economic Co-operation and Development (OECD) reported that over a ten-year period in the first decade of the 2000s, the gap between rich and poor in Canada grew to one of the largest of any OECD country, and that by 2018 Canada ranked seventeenth out of thirty countries in terms of income equality.[16] This is not good for our social capital—the stock of assets we accumulate in society, in our communities, and in our public institutions. These assets include trust and good will, volunteer activity in our communities, effective governance, and our health care and education infrastructure. We draw on this social capital in times of need. It is indeed a crisis that during a decade of unprecedented economic wealth generation, most of these assets have declined. This loss of social capital contributes to a reduced capacity to act collectively when crises emerge.

For some time now, to fuel its insatiable appetite, our economy has been borrowing heavily against our natural and social capital stocks. Yet despite having recklessly converted critical social and natural capital into economic capital, the economy has tanked. The solution we are being offered? Keep feeding the beast.

We need a national and global debate that generates systemic and sustainable solutions to the current crisis. Sustainable development is about the realization that there are no independent economic, social, or environmental silos. Rather, these are deeply integrated and dynamic aspects of a whole system through which we secure well-being for ourselves and for future generations. We need a debate about the appropriate deployment of resources to shore up financial, natural, and social capital.

Restructuring in the face of the current crisis should include a national commitment to make the minimum wage a living wage and peg its movement to the cost of living. It is encouraging that in the face of the COVID-19 crisis, there is growing interest across the political spectrum for some form of basic minimum income.[17] Restructuring should also include a commitment to end homelessness. In 2017 the Trudeau government launched a national affordable housing strategy to replace the one the free marketeers dismantled during the years of Brian Mulroney's

Conservative government.[18] These policies alone would go a long way to shoring up our social capital.

During his tenure as prime minister, Stephen Harper was irresponsible in persuading Canadians that a carbon tax would be harmful. In fact, a carbon tax or a cap-and-trade mechanism would tackle climate change and replenish stocks of natural capital. The government of Justin Trudeau introduced a carbon tax, and the province of BC, in particular, has had significant success with its carbon tax.

The Alberta tar sands is the poster child of natural and social capital depletion. Its development devoured the windfall profits accumulated from the soaring oil prices of the decade prior to 2008. We need to hammer out a national consensus that allows us to divert a large portion of fossil fuel profits toward the development of a renewable energy economy. A companion policy would be the creation of a conversion economy in southern Ontario and Quebec, retooling the car industry to produce buses, LRT and tram cars, solar panels, and wind turbines. The manufacturing capacity of southern Ontario and Quebec could be transformed into a renewable energy manufacturing powerhouse to rival the German renewables industry—as it should have been after the crisis it faced in 2008. Precious years were lost.

Finally, a fundamental restructuring of our system of national accounts is long overdue. There is universal agreement that GDP was never up to the task of representing the well-being of nations. The rolling economic crises are opportunities to introduce a system of social, ecological, and economic accounts—the kind of work being pioneered through the University of Waterloo's Canadian Index of Wellbeing and by Prime Minister Jacinda Ardern's "well-being budget" for New Zealand—a global first.[19]

We face a triple threat of economic, social, and ecological crises triggered by economic hubris. This crisis can indeed be turned into an opportunity if we seize the day.

MINDING OUR OWN BUSINESS: CO-OPERATIVE SOLUTIONS TO A NEW ECONOMY

In its January 2020 publication *Fail Safe*, the Canadian Centre for Policy Alternatives reported that CEO compensation had reached an all-time high in Canada: in 2018 the one hundred most highly compensated CEOs in the country were paid, on average, 227 times the average Canadian salary.[20]

Economic inequality has been riding a bull market for twenty years. During that time, we have hardly made a dent in homelessness, and there is now a run on food banks. According to the provincial government's own statistics, we can't even find the funds to provide a poverty-line income for people with disabilities.[21]

In the midst of all of this, we are told there is no alternative—suck it up! Don't regulate, because the market frowns on such behaviour. Don't raise royalties, because oil companies will take their investment elsewhere. Living wage legislation will kill the economy. There is no choice but to let greed and competition lead us to the promised land of prosperity. This is a sad, morally dubious state of affairs.

Actually, there is an alternative—what Mike Lewis and Pat Conaty, in *The Resilience Imperative*, call the "solidarity economy."[22] Contrary to the laissez-faire myths we tell ourselves, it has deep roots in our agricultural community and is thriving in Alberta. It includes co-operatives, credit unions, and community-based social enterprises where the bottom line pays attention to social and environmental issues, not only the legally mandated corporate bottom line where nothing but shareholder financial return matters.

The solutions are all around us. Hands up if are you a member of a co-operative. Most people's first thought is that they are not, but then when you canvass people about membership in particular co-ops, people respond, "Oh yeah!" Perhaps the most established co-op in our city is the Calgary Co-op. With roots in the United Farmers of Alberta, it is one of Calgary's largest employers, with annual sales of over $1 billion and more than 440,000 consumer members. A relatively new kid on the block in the food sector, opened in 2004, is the Calgary Farmers' Market, with seventy-eight producer-members in 2020 (calgaryfarmersmarket.ca). Another new venture, opened in 2019, is The Allium, a locally owned vegetarian restaurant structured as a worker co-operative.

Mountain Equipment Co-op started selling climbing gear out of the back of a van fifty years ago. It now has over five million members, $462 million in sales and twenty-two stores nationwide. As the company's Facebook page explains, of "the six original members . . . none of them has extracted personal profit from the business, their original shares are still worth five dollars, no one has sued anyone else and they still get together for annual slide shows and potluck dinners" (23 March 2011).[23] Then there is banking: Alberta has a strong history of credit unions, one of the biggest being First Calgary, with more than 120,000 members and growing.

How about energy? There are thirty-eight rural electrification associations in Alberta and fifty-two gas co-ops—the largest rural gas co-op network in the world![24] Then there is the new energy retail upstart, Alberta Cooperative Energy—Alberta's first wholly member-owned retail electrical power co-op dedicated to providing Albertans with 100 percent renewable energy.

Many Calgarians will be familiar with the Sunnyhill Housing Co-op, a pillar of the inner city Sunnyside community. Housing co-ops provide affordable housing and nurturing communities in which to raise a family. There are twelve hundred homes in Calgary's fourteen housing co-ops— part of a network of twenty-two hundred housing co-ops across the country housing 250,000 Canadians.[25]

In *The Resilience Imperative*, Lewis and Conaty map out the solidarity economy and make the case for why and how to make it *the* new economy. Among the book's most important revelations is that a robust co-operative transition is happening around the world, with success stories like Quebec's Chantier de l'économie sociale (220,000 employees and $47.8 billion in sales), Spain's Mondragon Co-operative Corporation, and the Emilia-Romagna region in northern Italy, where 30 percent of GDP is generated by co-operatives.[26]

These organizations form a modest but growing network of socially and ecologically conscious, democratically governed (one member, one vote) enterprises in food, housing, energy, banking, transportation, and more. The solidarity economy may not be for everyone, but we are betting it is an attractive option for many. So if you are feeling less than satisfied with the direction in which the usual suspects are taking our economy, they're not the only game in town.

Back in 2012, the *Globe and Mail* ran an article celebrating the obscene salaries of Canadian CEOs, concluding with "Gentlemen, start your Ferraris."[27] Might we suggest that citizens ignite a different kind of revolution? Join a co-op; shop at a co-op; start a social enterprise; sell your car and take out a car-, bike-, or scooter-share membership. Help create a more just, fair, environmentally sustainable, resilient, and prosperous place for all Calgarians.

GROWING PAINS: ECONOMICALLY, THE END MAY BE NIGH

It could be the end of the world as we know it. The end of a world with economic growth, that is. That's what you're likely to think if you've been listening to the increasingly desperate chorus of world leaders who, if they agree on nothing else, speak as one on the global economic crisis: whatever the problem, growth is the answer.

So thoroughly have the world's economies become reliant on growth that should it disappear, economic and social chaos would be inevitable. Headlines are constantly warning of the disaster to ensue if growth slows—or, God forbid, stops. The January 2020 *Wall Street Journal* headline "Dow Drops 600 Points on Global Growth Concerns" is just one recent example.[28]

On the other hand, if you believe the thesis of Jeff Rubin's book *The End of Growth*, we had all better hope that someone out there has a Plan B. Part analysis, part warning, and part prescription, this second book by the former chief economist of CIBC World Markets portends a new global normal in which energy will be so costly that economic growth—a function of energy consumed—will end. It's not a supply problem, writes Rubin, contradicting the peak-oil theorists. Rather, "continually replacing cheap conventional crude with more expensive unconventional oil is shifting the industry's cost curve to a place our economies simply can't afford."[29]

Oil is the key, Rubin explains, because nothing can replace it as a transportation fuel, and transportation is the keystone of the global economy. Not only is oil itself easily transported and stored, but "most critically, it packs an unparalleled amount of energy into a tiny package."[30] So even as vast new reserves of methane are being discovered and solar and wind capacity steadily grows, none of these can yet replace oil (and its various byproducts like gasoline, diesel, and jet fuel) to move us and our cargo around the world. "The price of oil is the single most important ingredient in the outlook for the global economy," he writes. "Feed the world cheap oil and it will run like a charm. Send prices to unaffordable levels and the engine of growth will immediately seize up."[31]

Rubin's book is divided into two sections. In part one, he explains why the vitality of the global economy is so closely and deeply linked to oil prices and why, even as world events buffet oil prices up and down, the long-term trend for oil is irreversibly upward. Triple-digit oil prices are needed, he says, to make recovering it from increasingly harsh and isolated locations viable.

The end of growth is coming—we've known this since Malthus first predicted it at the end of the eighteenth century, when he argued that food production will never keep up with population growth.[32] It's only a matter of time. Rubin builds a convincing case to show that the critical variable, the one irreplaceable commodity whose scarcity will actually end growth, is oil. From plastics and pharmaceuticals to fertilizer and gasoline—oil is behind it all. Never before in history has one product been as essential to human well-being as oil is to ours.

But in part two, the wheels fall off as Rubin ponders the notion of a static economy. He draws on experiences from Denmark, Germany, and Japan as examples of adaptive strategies that countries have implemented to deal with high energy prices. Danes, for example, have been paying high energy taxes for years, drastically reducing per capita consumption while girding the economy and changing citizens' expectations. In Germany, employers, financed by government subsidies, have instituted Kurzarbeit (job sharing, literally 'short work') as a means of keeping more people employed.[33] The Japanese, meanwhile, have used drastic conservation measures to slash energy consumption since the nation's nuclear plants were taken offline in the aftermath of the 2011 tsunami and the Fukushima reactor meltdown.[34]

While admirable, if not inspiring, these strategies are simply inadequate to the task should growth "immediately seize up," as Rubin predicts.[35] Share jobs? How far can one car-manufacturing wage go when no one is buying cars? And with whom will all the former employees of the financial services, real estate, and stock market sectors share jobs as those growth-dependent industries shrivel to nothing? And what about the millions of newly unemployed Chinese and Indian factory workers whose livelihoods will vanish? Rubin's error is that he sees the post-growth economy as essentially the same as the growth economy, only smaller.

It's not that steady-state economics (which has been theorized for decades) couldn't work; the problem is that it is based on a set of principles emphasizing environmental limits that are fundamentally incompatible with those now in play. And there's no easy pathway from here to there. We are simply not equipped to not have growth. Fortunately, a fresh wave of economists is charting a smooth landing to a no-growth economy. Among the best is UK economist Peter Jackson, whose *Prosperity without Growth* lays out a new macro-economics for sustainability.[36] Other prominent advocates for this position include Greek economist Giorgos Kallis (co-editor of *DeGrowth*), an ecological economist from the Autonomous University of Barcelona; UK economist Kate Raworth (*Doughnut Economics*); and Peter Victor, professor emeritus from York University in Toronto and co-author, with Jackson, of "Towards an Ecological Macroeconomics."[37] All of these advocates argue that it is well-being rather than economic growth that should be the focus of our economies; that we need to implement policies such as basic minimum income; and that we need to shift from the production of stuff to the provision of services like health care and education, the pursuit of non-consumptive leisure pursuits, and the relocalization of production of the material goods we do in fact need.

There are silver linings, says Rubin. No growth means burning fewer fossil fuels, meaning lower carbon emissions, cleaner skies, and reduced danger from climate chaos. We'll have more leisure time and our attitude toward consumption will change. Maybe. But in the end, Rubin's analysis disregards the most important thing we can do: instead of waiting for the economy to slap us silly, we can act collectively to insist that governments and industry begin moving in a positive direction to avert or minimize the agony that the looming transition from growth to no growth, left to its own devices, will surely inflict.

THE GROWTH MACHINE: SECOND THOUGHTS ON CALGARY'S BOOMS AND BUSTS

For the first fifteen years of the new millennium, Calgary was growing—and fast! And the news coverage was triumphalist, "We're better than you are" kind of stuff. The 2015 to 2020 period tells a very different story. Now our own Premier Kenney portrays Alberta and its largest cities as basket cases in need of federal help or Confederation itself is in trouble.[38] The growth machine that was Calgary has stalled. But did it really deliver on its promises even in the good times?

Almost forty years ago, sociologist Harvey Molotch coined the phrase *growth machine* to describe what goes on in cities.[39] As Molotch explained it, developers, businessmen, and politicians literally treat a city as a giant machine designed to manufacture wealth and enhance their political and economic power, all the while extolling the supposed benefits of growth—improved quality of life and well-being for all citizens. Growth becomes a surrogate for all that is virtuous.

Alongside the triumphalist Calgary narrative, other realities tell a different story.

Exhibit 1: The number of homeless counted in 2018 is 6.5 times what it was in 1992, even though today's population is only about 57 percent greater. Yes, the count shows a decrease of 19 percent since 2008, but even that decrease is questionable given the move of the count from June to a bitterly cold January day.[40] In the wake of the 2008 meltdown, the Homeless Foundation was warning people not to come to Calgary if they did not have secure accommodation.

Exhibit 2: *Poverty Costs*, released by Vibrant Communities Calgary (VCC), revealed some startling statistics.[41] In 2012 almost 400,000 Albertans were living in poverty. Paradoxically, the biggest trend reversal in poverty statistics in Calgary occurred during the years of economic contraction: according to VCC's *Poverty in Calgary 2019*, from 2015 to 2017, the proportion of people living in poverty fell from 9.8 percent to 6.9 percent.[42] The report shows that even from a financial perspective, tolerating poverty is a bad idea. The cost to our economy in health care, crime, and lost economic productivity from the perpetuation of poverty in Alberta is $7 billion to $9.5 billion annually. In addition, despite having the highest average per capita income in Canada, Calgary's debt-to-income ratio is only marginally lower than the Canadian average.[43]

Exhibit 3: In his insightful 2012 book *Follow the Money*, Kevin Taft challenged the conventional wisdom of the time: that the Alberta boom was good for everyone and that public spending was out of control.[44] Taft shows us that the "stunning wealth" generated by Alberta's economy has been very unequally distributed. From 1989 to 2009, health, K-12 education, and post-secondary education spending had grown 28.6, 2.4, and 27.9 percent, respectively. Our collective nest egg, the Heritage Fund, was down 35 percent. Meanwhile, corporate profits were up a whopping 317 percent. With our provincial growth machine in high gear, we had seen, during those two decades, negligible or modest growth in public services, shocking shrinkage of our rainy day fund, and skyrocketing corporate profits.

Exhibit 4: Research in 2012 by CivicCamp's Governance, Finance, and Infrastructure Group showed that suburban sprawl would cost Calgary taxpayers roughly $400 million between 2011 and 2016: that is the difference between what developers pay and what it actually costs to service new subdivisions.[45] Figures released by the city in 2020 show that while current policy calls for developers to pay 100 percent of costs, between 2019 and 2022, greenfield development infrastructure will cost taxpayers almost $60 million.

Rapid population growth in our city certainly enriches developers and road builders, but it makes it even more difficult to curb sprawling suburban development. When a city grows as fast as Calgary is growing (426,000 new Calgarians from 2000 to 2019), it is much easier to plow under open farmland and throw up thousands of cookie-cutter homes than to accommodate newcomers on vacant lands inside the existing city footprint.[46] In Calgary, we do more of the former than anywhere else in Canada, and we have gotten pretty good at it. But in the long run, as the City's own 2009 report *Implications of Alternative Growth Patterns on Infrastructure Costs* makes clear, this kind of development offloads most of the costs onto future generations.[47]

Unfortunate circumstances, you say—but what control do we have over the global economy? As it turns out, quite a bit. Tar sands development has driven our growth, and not a drop of tar sands can be exploited without government offering a lease to allow it. But our government has been adamant that the market decides how fast we grow, and that model of growth has promoted growing poverty, a concentration of wealth among the very few, and a most unsustainable sprawling model of how our city grows.

So here's a proposal. A moratorium on tar sands development and coal mining until we can determine the full costs and benefits: Is growth (especially of the fossil fuel industry) improving our quality of life or making us worse off? The moratorium would include projects like expansion of the Trans Mountain Pipeline, the Teck Resources Frontier Project Tar Sands mine, and coal mining on Alberta's Eastern Slopes.[48] Maybe growth is not the future of our economy. Maybe in this post-carbon era, it is more important that we make sure our economy is fair rather than growing. Perhaps we can treat this current slow or no-growth state of our economy as an opportunity rather than a crisis.

We all know that at a personal level, decisions made in haste or with only short-term goals in mind are often bad decisions that we come to regret. The same goes for our economy—let's ease off on the gas pedal and get some breathing room for a sober second thought on the sustainability of growth.

BEYOND GROWTH: TIME FOR A RADICAL ECONOMIC DEVELOPMENT STRATEGY

In 2020 Calgary Economic Development launched its latest economic development strategy—*Calgary in the New Economy*.[49] The strategy's key pillars are talent, innovation, place, and business environment. The laudable goal is to wean the city off fossil fuel dependence, but the prime directive remains economic growth. There are abundant signals that it is time to forge a radically new pathway to prosperity.

Ecological economist Herman Daly argues that we are now in a full world—there is no more room for expansion without destroying the natural systems that underwrite the human economy.[50] In a world where resource consumption is maxed out, our economic development strategy should move beyond growth to a focus on well-being. In light of the breach of the 400 ppm threshold in atmospheric CO_2 concentration in

2017, we desperately need an economic development strategy that mounts a full assault on climate change with a long-term view to a post-carbon city.[51] Former CIBC World Markets chief economist Jeff Rubin argues convincingly in two recent books that in the new normal, our economies will have to be re-engineered to once again manufacture most of our stuff locally.[52] And finally, in a recent study, "Economics Versus Politics: Pitfalls of Economic Advice," two Harvard economists warn that "it is policies that economically strengthen already dominant groups, or weaken those that are acting as a counterbalance to them, that are especially likely to tilt the balance of political power further" and magnify economic inequality and democratic dysfunction.[53]

Given all of these converging analyses, it is time for a radical new strategic thrust in Calgary, one that transitions us to a no-growth world, gets serious about climate change, fosters greater economic equality, and is a catalyst for a post–fossil fuel future. Fortunately, there seems to be some appetite for such a departure at Calgary Economic Development.

We offer one way forward that draws from a report entitled *A Citizens' Agenda*, a Sustainable Calgary initiative undertaken with the participation of about one thousand Calgarians from all walks of life.[54] The initiative addressed the question, What are the most important policies that would make our city more healthy, caring, and vibrant? It recommended a dozen such policy priorities. Prominent among the recommendations was a call for sustainable economic diversification. Many of the remaining policy recommendations provided a framework for where to diversify.

In light of the fact that the lifestyle of the average Calgarian requires more resources than that of Canadians in any other city, *A Citizens' Agenda* calls for the creation of a zero-waste economy. Instead of sending millions of tonnes of material to landfills, we need to develop industries and industrial processes and districts with the mantra of "waste equals food"—that is, waste from one enterprise finds a home as the raw material for the next.

Homelessness is still a major scourge in our city. In partnership with the Calgary Homeless Foundation's *10 Year Plan to End Homelessness*, our economic development strategy could spur innovation in affordable housing, from the design of urban community land trusts to ultra–low-cost shelter, to laneway housing, to the evolution of planning and development processes that enable innovative community building approaches like Prairie Sky Cohousing to proliferate.[55]

Our economic development strategy should support the development of the most robust green building industry in the world demanding the highest standard—whether it be LEED platinum, Net Zero, Passivhaus, or the Living Building Challenge—for all new buildings.[56] With the expected doubling of our population in the next fifty years, Calgary would boast the greenest building stock on the planet.

Rather than competing in the race to attract the best and brightest to Calgary, why not put our resources toward improving the skills of people who already live here and making sure that every new immigrant is empowered to contribute the full potential of the skills he or she brings to our city? Driving a cab is an honourable profession, but trained medical doctors and engineers shouldn't be driving cabs for a living.

We buy and drive cars more than any other Canadians, and that represents money leaking out of our economy like fugitive methane emissions from a gas fracking operation. Calgary could become a design and manufacturing centre for cold climate commuter and cargo bikes. We could use our logistics know-how to design super-efficient car-share systems, reducing the number of cars in our city by 90 percent, according to a recent OECD study, and eliminating the need for every household to own and maintain its own car—or two, or three.[57]

The biggest opportunity for sustainable economic diversification is in the energy sector via the development of the vast solar and wind resources in southern Alberta. Calgary Economic Development could take up the challenge of charting the course to a fully renewable energy economy. An economy built for everyone, designed for the future and for a city that knows how much is enough—it's entirely within our grasp.

THE WEALTH OF OUR NATION

To paraphrase Adam Smith in *The Wealth of Nations*, where there is great concentration of wealth with the minority, there is poverty for the majority.[58] Recent research on Canadian corporate concentration shows that this is as true today as it was for Smith in 1776. This is not just a lamentable circumstance; it matters a whole lot for our well-being and sustainability.

To state the problem clearly—we are plagued by debilitating levels of poverty and a growing gap between the rich and the rest. In *State of Our City 2020*, Sustainable Calgary reports that in 2017 the ratio of Alberta's top 20 percent of earners to the bottom 20 percent was 26 to 1. That was down from 32 to 1 in 2016 but up from 25 to 1 in 2015. According to a report by the Professional Accountants of Canada, for the period 1982 to 2017, Calgary's after-tax inequality was four times higher than the national average, while Vancouver and Toronto followed closely behind. For after-tax income, Calgary is the most unequal city in the country. When it comes to the wealthiest 1 percent, Calgary is the most unequal city in both market income and after-tax income. The wealthiest 1 percent in our city take home two times the share of income as do the 1 percent in Toronto, Vancouver, and Montreal, and three times the share of income as the 1 percent in Edmonton.[59]

How did we come to this predicament? In *A Shrinking Universe*, Jordan Brennan provides some insight through an examination of the Canadian economy after the Second World War.[60] The period from 1945 to the mid-1970s was something of a golden age for Canada. Wages grew at over 3 percent annually, adjusted for inflation; much of our cherished social infrastructure, including universal health care, was put in place; and wealth was more equitably distributed than at any point before or since. Unionization reached its peak in this period, and Brennan makes the case that it was on the strength of the bargaining power of ordinary workers that all of this was made possible.

These gains have all been reversed since the mid-1970s, with the concentration of wealth now as great as it was in the 1920s. In explaining this reversal, Brennan paints a damning picture of greed and manipulation on the part of the Canadian corporate elite—the top sixty corporations listed on the Toronto Stock Exchange. In 2012 there was a total of 1.3 million registered corporations in Canada, but the TSX top sixty accounted for fully 60 percent of all corporate profit, up from 35 percent in 1961. The relative size of these sixty corporations had grown enormously since 1990, when they were six times the size of the average corporation. In 2012 that ratio was 23 to 1. In 1950 the top sixty earned 234 times as much as the rest. By 2007 that ratio was over 14,000 to 1. Yet the top ten's share of corporate revenue (as opposed to profit) grew only modestly, from 18 to

23 percent, over that period.[61] The largest corporations have used their economic clout and political influence to take a bigger cut, relative to their contribution, of the wealth Canadians collectively generate.

When we shift our gaze from corporations to individual income earners, we see a similar income inequality trend. Statistics Canada data for 2017 and 2020 show that the top 10 percent of income earners made over $96,000; the top 1 percent, over $236,000; the top 0.1 percent (28,000 Canadians), over $740,300; and the super-rich 0.01 percent earned at least $2.7 million. These are startling income inequities, but the most damning evidence to be found in these statistics is that the higher your income, the more your income grew—from 2.5 percent for the Canadian average, to 8.5 percent for the top 1 percent, to 17.2 percent for the top 0.1 percent.[62]

What does this have to do with corporate concentration? Brennan demonstrates that the income of the top 0.1 percent of Canadians and the profit of the sixty biggest corporations are, in statistical language, "tightly and positively correlated."[63]

Calgary has had its share of these mammoth corporations and of the super-rich. Sixteen of the top one hundred Canadian CEO incomes in 2010 were based in Calgary, with an average compensation of $8.8 million.[64] By 2018, nineteen of the top one hundred were in Calgary, and average compensation had risen to $9.8 million.[65]

This matters. We know from behavioural economics that people refuse to participate in obviously unjust economic relations. The extent of the corporate wealth grab is obviously unjust, and the relations that Canadians withdraw from (voter participation and efforts to address climate change, for example) constitute our social contract with each other and the world—the contract that enabled us to build the postwar golden-age in Canada that made us one of the most respected nations on earth. What's more, we know from the work of writers like Nobel Laureate Joseph Stiglitz that equity is arguably the most important predictor of well-being—even for the wealthiest among us.[66]

These are difficult things to talk about in Calgary. The corporate elite give generously. They volunteer their time to civic organizations like the United Way and the Homeless Foundation. These are worthy acts of charity. But this is not about charity; it's about social justice.

Corporate leaders and the 0.1 percent have forgotten the most elemental lessons of kindergarten—play fair and learn to share. And our city and our country are worse off for it.

NOTES

1   Claudia Cattaneo, "King of Pain: Steve Williams Seizes on Price Pangs to Prepare Suncor for Oilsands Dominance," *Financial Post*, 9 October 2015, https://financialpost.com/commodities/energy/king-of-pain-steve-williams-seizes-on-price-pangs-to-prepare-suncor-for-oilsands-dominance.

2   Canadian Index of Wellbeing, *How Are Canadians Really Doing? The 2016 CIW National Report* (Waterloo, ON: CIW and University of Waterloo, 2016), https://uwaterloo.ca/canadian-index-wellbeing/sites/ca.canadian-index-wellbeing/files/uploads/files/c011676-nationalreport-ciw_final-s.pdf.

3   Canadian Index of Wellbeing, "New Evidence Reveals Canadian Wellbeing on the Decline," press release, 23 October 2012, https://www.newswire.ca/news-releases/new-evidence-reveals-canadian-wellbeing-on-the-decline-511009361.html.

4   A. J. Veal, *Whatever Happened to the Leisure Society?* (New York: Routledge, 2018).

5   "About the Canadian Index of Wellbeing," *Canadian Index of Wellbeing*, accessed 25 November 2020, https://uwaterloo.ca/canadian-index-wellbeing/about-canadian-index-wellbeing.

6   CIW, *How Are Canadians Really Doing?* 10.

7   CIW, *How Are Canadians Really Doing?* 5.

8   Linda Duxbury and Christopher Higgins, *Revisiting Work-Life Issues in Canada: The 2012 National Study on Balancing Work and Caregiving in Canada,* Report 1 (Ottawa: Carleton University, 2012), https://newsroom.carleton.ca/wp-content/files/2012-National-Work-Long-Summary.pdf.

9   Duxbury and Higgins, *Revisiting Work-Life Issues in Canada,* 4.

10 Linda Duxbury, *Dealing with Work-Life Issues in the Workplace: Standing Still Is Not an Option*, 2004 Don Wood Lecture in Industrial Relations (Kingston, ON: Queen's University, Industrial Relations Centre, 2004), 11.

11 Linda Duxbury, Maggie Stevenson, and Christopher Higgins, "Too Much to Do, Too Little Time: Role Overload and Stress in a Multi-Role Environment," *International Journal of Stress Management* 25, no. 3 (2018): 250–66.

12 Carleton University, "Carleton Releases 2012 National Survey on Balancing Work and Caregiving in Canada: Linda Duxbury to Talk about Findings at Building Healthier Workplaces Conference," press release, 25 October 2012, https://newsroom.carleton.ca/archives/2012/10/25/carleton-releases-2012-national-study-on-balancing-work-and-

caregiving-in-canada-linda-duxbury-to-talk-about-findings-at-building-healthier-workplaces-conference/.

13   Herman Daly, *From Uneconomic Growth to a Steady-State Economy,* Advances in Ecological Economics Series (Cheltenham, UK: Edward Elgar, 2014).

14   Jeremy Klaszus, "Paying for It: Calgary's 14 New Communities: What Was City Council Thinking?" *The Sprawl,* 10 February 2020, https://www.sprawlcalgary.com/sprawlcast-calgarys-14-new-communities.

15   Janine Benyus, *Biomimicry: Innovation Inspired by Nature* (New York: William Morrow, 2002), 292.

16   Organisation for Economic Co-operation and Development, *Growing Unequal? Income Distribution and Poverty in OECD Countries* (Geneva: OECD, October 2008), 17–25, https://www.oecd.org/els/soc/growingunequalincomedistributionandpoverty inoecdcountries.htm.

17   Guy Standing, "Coronavirus Has Shown Us Why We Urgently Need to Make a Basic Income a Reality," *World Economic Forum,* 13 April 2020, https://www.weforum.org/agenda/2020/04/coronavirus-made-basic-income-vital/.

18   Peter Zimonjic, "Liberals Detail $40B for 10-Year National Housing Strategy, Introduce Canada Housing Benefit," *CBC News,* 22 November 2017, https://www.cbc.ca/news/politics/housing-national-benefit-1.4413615.

19   Emma Charlton, "New Zealand Has Unveiled Its First 'Well-Being' Budget," *World Economic Forum,* 30 May 2019, https://www.weforum.org/agenda/2019/05/new-zealand-is-publishing-its-first-well-being-budget/.

20   David Macdonald, *Fail Safe: CEO Compensation in Canada* (Ottawa: Canadian Centre for Policy Alternatives, January 2020), 4, https://www.policyalternatives.ca/sites/default/files/uploads/publications/National%20Office/2020/01/Fail%20Safe.pdf.

21   Noel Keough, Bob Morrison, and Celia Lee, *State of Our City 2020: An Urgent Call for a Just Transition* (Calgary: Sustainable Calgary Society, 2020), 56, http://www.sustainablecalgary.org/publications.

22   Mike Lewis and Pat Conaty, *The Resilience Imperative: Cooperative Transitions to the Steady-State Economy* (Gabriola Island, BC: New Society, 2012).

23   Sadly, in the fall of 2020, MEC filed for bankruptcy and was bought by a California investment firm, with no consultation with MEC's members. Michael Parent, "What the MEC Sale Might Really Be About," *The Tyee,* 6 October 2020, https://thetyee.ca/Analysis/2020/10/06/What-MEC-Sale-Is-Really-About/.

24   Toma and Bouma Management Consultants, *Alberta REA Strategic Review: Rural Economic Impacts,* prepared for Alberta Rural Electrification Associations, January 2013, https://ccrnrcrc.files.wordpress.com/2014/05/rea-report-f-2.pdf; *Federation of Alberta Gas Coops,* accessed 4 September 20, https://www.fedgas.com/about.

25   *Southern Alberta Cooperative Housing Association,* accessed 4 September 2020, http://www.sacha-coop.ca; *Cooperative Housing Federation of Canada,* accessed 4 September 2020, https://chfcanada.coop.

26   *Chantier de l'économie sociale*, accessed 4 September 2020, https://chantier.
     qc.ca/?lang=en. For an informative overview of Mondragon Cooperative, see Jill
     Bamburg, "Mondragon through a Critical Lens," *Employee Ownership News,* 3
     October 2017, https://medium.com/fifty-by-fifty/mondragon-through-a-critical-
     lens-b29de8c6049. See also "The Italian Region Where 30% of GDP Comes from
     Cooperatives," *Apolitical*, 8 January 2018, https://apolitical.co/en/solution_article/
     italian-region-30-gdp-comes-cooperatives.

27   Nathan Vanderklippe, "Bonuses Soar in the Oil Patch 'Bubble,'" *Globe and Mail*, 1 May
     2012, https://www.theglobeandmail.com/report-on-business/streetwise/bonuses-soar-
     in-oil-patch-bubble/article4103979/.

28   Gunjan Banerji, "Dow Drops 600 Points on Global Growth Concerns," *Wall Street
     Journal*, 31 January 2020, https://www.wsj.com/articles/global-stocks-drift-lower-on-
     economic-growth-concerns-11580466790.

29   Jeff Rubin, *The End of Growth* (Toronto: Random House, 2012), 105.

30   Rubin, *End of Growth*, 36.

31   Rubin, *End of Growth*, 36.

32   Thomas Malthus, *An Essay on the Principle of Population, As It Affects the Future
     Improvement of Society, with Remarks on the Speculations of Mr. Godwin, M. Condorcet,
     and Other Writers*, anonymously published, London, 1798.

33   "Kurzarbeit: Germany's Short-Time Work Benefit," *IMF News*, 15 June 2020, https://
     www.imf.org/en/News/Articles/2020/06/11/na061120-kurzarbeit-germanys-short-
     time-work-benefit.

34   Mark Golden, "Sacrifice and Luck Help Japan Survive without Nuclear Power, Stanford
     Visiting Scholar Says," *Stanford University News*, 4 January 2013, https://news.stanford.
     edu/news/2013/january/japan-nuclear-power-010413.html.

35   Rubin, *End of Growth*, 36.

36   Tim Jackson, *Prosperity without Growth: Economics for a Finite Planet* (New York:
     Routledge, 2009).

37   Giacomo D'Alisa, Federico Demaria, and Giorgos Kallis, eds., *Degrowth: A Vocabulary
     for a New Era* (New York: Routledge, 2014); Kate Raworth, *Doughnut Economics: 7
     Ways to Think Like a 21st Century Economist* (Vermont: Chelsea Green, 2017); Peter
     Victor and Tim Jackson, "Towards an Ecological Macroeconomics," prepared for INET
     Annual Plenary Conference "Paradigm Lost: Rethinking Economics and Politics,"
     Berlin, April 2012, https://www.ineteconomics.org/uploads/papers/victor-peter-berlin-
     paper-draft-w-Tim-Jackson.pdf.

38   Justin Giovannetti, "Kenney Seeks Nearly $1.7-Billion from Ottawa after Collapse in
     Alberta Oil Prices," *Globe and Mail*, 13 November 2019, https://www.theglobeandmail.
     com/canada/alberta/article-alberta-premier-jason-kenney-seeks-nearly-17-billion-
     bailout-from/.

39   Harvey Molotch, "The City As a Growth Machine: Toward a Political Economy of
     Place," *American Journal of Sociology* 82, no. 2 (1976): 309–32.

40   Keough, Morrison, and Lee, *State of Our City 2020*, 20.

41   C. A. Hudson, *Poverty Costs 2.0: Investing in Albertans* (Calgary: Vibrant Communities Calgary and Action to End Poverty in Alberta, 2013), http://vibrantcalgary.com/wp-content/uploads/2016/06/PCosts_2_Investing_In_Albertans_web.pdf.

42   Vibrant Communities Calgary, *A Snapshot of Poverty in Calgary 2019* (Calgary: VCC, August 2019), http://enoughforall.ca/wp-content/uploads/2019/08/A-Snapshot-of-poverty-in-Calgary-in-2019.pdf.

43   "Household Debt-to-Income Ratio Near Record High," *Canada Mortgage and Housing Corporation*, 13 December 2018, https://www.cmhc-schl.gc.ca/en/housing-observer-online/2018-housing-observer/household-debt-income-ratio-near-record-high.

44   Kevin Taft, *Follow the Money: Where Is Alberta's Wealth Going?* (Calgary: Detselig, 2012).

45   Bob Morrison, "2012–2014 City Budget Submission by Governance, Finance, and Infrastructure Group," unpublished (Calgary: CivicCamp, 2012).

46   "2019 Civic Census Results," *City of Calgary*, 2019, https://www.calgary.ca/ca/city-clerks/election-and-information-services/civic-census/censusresults.html.

47   IBI Group, *The Implications of Alternative Growth Patterns on Infrastructure Costs* (Calgary: City of Calgary, April 2009), http://www.reconnectingamerica.org/assets/Uploads/planitcalgarycoststudyanalysisaprilthird.pdf.

48   In February 2020, Teck Resources cancelled its Frontier Mines project. The Trans Mountain Pipeline is under construction, but its ultimate economic feasibility remains in question. For an analysis, see Tom Sanzillo and Kathy Hipple, "IEEFA Report: Additional $320 Million in Subsidies Used to Finance Trans Mountain Pipeline in First Half of 2019," press release, Institute for Energy Economics and Financial Analysis, Lakewood, ON, 19 November 2019, https://ieefa.org/ieefa-report-additional-320-million-in-subsidies-used-to-finance-trans-mountain-pipeline-in-first-half-of-2019/. On proposed coal mining along the Eastern Slopes, see Alberta Wilderness Association, "Continuing the Sacrifice of the Eastern Slopes to Old King Coal," press release, 4 December 2020, https://albertawilderness.ca/continuing-the-sacrifice-of-the-eastern-slopes-to-old-king-coal/.

49   Calgary Economic Development, *Calgary in the New Economy: The Economic Strategy for Calgary* (Calgary: CED, 2020), https://calgaryeconomicdevelopment.com/assets/Calgary-in-the-New-Economy/Calgary-in-the-New-Economy-Final.pdf.

50   Herman Daly, "Economics for a Full World," *Great Transition Initiative*, June 2015, http://www.greattransition.org/publication/economics-for-a-full-world.

51   Nicola Jones, "How the World Passed a Carbon Threshold and Why It Matters," *YaleEnvironment360*, 26 January 2017, Yale School of the Environment, https://e360.yale.edu/features/how-the-world-passed-a-carbon-threshold-400ppm-and-why-it-matters.

52   Jeff Rubin, *Why Your World Is About to Get a Whole Lot Smaller* (Toronto: Vintage, 2010); Rubin, *End of Growth*.

53   Daron Acemoglu and James A. Robinson, "Economics Versus Politics: Pitfalls of Policy Advice," NBER Working Paper 18921, National Bureau of Economic Research, Cambridge, MA, March 2013, 5.

54   Noel Keough, Maryam Nabavi, and Jeff Loomis, *A Citizens' Agenda: For a More Healthy, Caring and Vibrant Calgary* (Sustainable Calgary Society, 2005), https://static1.squarespace.com/static/5ab716b9ee1759b04ca2703e/t/5ee004c3984cb602a4c8a2c9/1591739598060/Citizens%27+Agenda+2006.pdf.

55   Calgary Homeless Foundation, *10 Year Plan to End Homelessness: 2008–2018*, January 2011 Update (Calgary: CHF, 2011), https://aventa.org/wp-content/uploads/2017/02/10-Year-Plan-Update.pdf.

56   These are four of the most common building efficiency standards in use today. "LEED Certification Process," *Canada Green Building Council,* accessed 5 September 2020, https://www.cagbc.org/CAGBC/Programs/LEED/LEED_Certification_Process.aspx; "What Is Net Zero?" *World Green Building Council,* 2016–20, https://www.worldgbc.org/advancing-net-zero/what-net-zero; "About Passive House," *Passive House Canada,* 2020, https://www.passivehousecanada.com/about-passive-house/; "Living Building Challenge 4.0 Basic," *International Living Future Institute,* 2020, https://living-future.org/lbc/basics4-0/.

57   International Transport Forum, *Urban Mobility System Upgrade: How Shared Self-Driving Cars Could Change City Traffic* (Paris: Organisation for Economic Co-operation and Development, 2015), https://www.itf-oecd.org/sites/default/files/docs/15cpb_self-drivingcars.pdf. For a short journalistic review of the full report, see David Roberts, "Shared Vehicles Could Make Our Cities Dramatically More Livable," *Vox,* 28 July 2016, https://www.vox.com/2016/7/28/12294214/shared-vehicles-livable-cities.

58   Adam Smith, *The Wealth of Nations* (London, 1776; New York: Bantam Dell, 2003), 338–39.

59   Keough, Morrison, and Lee, *State of Our City 2020,* 25.

60   Jordan Brennan, *A Shrinking Universe: How Concentrated Corporate Power Is Shaping Income Inequality in Canada* (Ottawa: Canadian Centre for Policy Alternatives, November 2012), https://www.policyalternatives.ca/sites/default/files/uploads/publications/National%20Office/2012/11/Shrinking_Universe_0.pdf.

61   Brennan, *Shrinking Universe,* 4, 19, 31.

62   Statistics Canada, "Table: 11-10-0055-01, High Income Tax Filers in Canada" (Ottawa: Statistics Canada, 2020), https://www150.statcan.gc.ca/t1/tbl1/en/tv.action?pid=1110005501; Nigel Wodrich and Aidan Worswick, *Estimating the Top Tail of the Family Wealth Distribution in Canada* (Ottawa: Office of the Parliamentary Budget Officer, 17 June 2020), https://www.pbo-dpb.gc.ca/web/default/files/Documents/Reports/RP-2021-007-S/RP-2021-007-S_en.pdf.

63   Brennan, *Shrinking Universe,* 12.

64   Hugh Mackenzie, *Canada's CEO Elite 100: The 0.01%* (Ottawa: Canadian Centre for Policy Alternatives, January 2012), https://www.policyalternatives.ca/sites/default/

files/uploads/publications/National%20Office/2012/01/Canadas%20CEO%20Elite%20 100FINAL.pdf.

65 Andy Holloway, "FP500: The Premier Ranking of Corporate Canada," *Financial Post*, 13 June 2019, https://financialpost.com/feature/fp500-the-premier-ranking-of-corporate-canada.

66 Joseph E. Stiglitz, *The Price of Inequality: How Today's Divided Society Endangers Our Future* (New York: W. W Norton, 2012).

Further Reading

Gismondi, Mike, Sean Connelly, Mary Beckie, and Mark Roseland. *Scaling Up: The Convergence of Social Economy and Sustainability.* Athabasca, AB: Athabasca University Press, 2016.

McNeill, J. R., and Peter Engelke. *The Great Acceleration: An Environmental History of the Anthropocene Since 1945.* Cambridge, MA: Harvard University Press, 2014.

Peredo, Ana Maria, and Murdith McLean. "Decommodification in Action: Common Property as Countermovement." *Organization* (July 2019): 1–23.

Post-Growth Institute. https://www.postgrowth.org.

Quarter, Jack, Laurie Mook, and Ann Armstrong. *Understanding the Social Economy: A Canadian Perspective.* 2nd ed. Toronto: University of Toronto Press, 2017.

Restakis, John. *Humanizing the Economy: Co-operatives in the Age of Capital.* Gabriola Island, BC: New Society, 2010.

Subhabrata, Bobby Banerjee, John M. Jermier, Ana Maria Peredo, Robert Perey, and André Reichel. "Special Issue: Theoretical Perspectives on Organizations and Organizing in a Post-Growth Era." *Organization* (2020): 1–21.

Works Cited

"2019 Civic Census Results." *City of Calgary*, 2019. https://www.calgary.ca/ca/city-clerks/election-and-information-services/civic-census/censusresults.html.

"About Passive House." *Passive House Canada*, 2020. https://www.passivehousecanada.com/about-passive-house/.

"About the Canadian Index of Wellbeing." *Canadian Index of Wellbeing.* Accessed 25 November 2020. https://uwaterloo.ca/canadian-index-wellbeing/about-canadian-index-wellbeing.

Acemoglu, Daron, and James A. Robinson. "Economics Versus Politics: Pitfalls of Policy Advice." NBER Working Paper 18921. National Bureau of Economic Research, Cambridge, MA, March 2013.

Alberta Wilderness Association. "Continuing the Sacrifice of the Eastern Slopes to Old King Coal." Press release, 4 December 2020. https://albertawilderness.ca/continuing-the-sacrifice-of-the-eastern-slopes-to-old-king-coal/.

Bamburg, Jill. "Mondragon through a Critical Lens." *Employee Ownership News*, 3 October 2017. https://medium.com/fifty-by-fifty/mondragon-through-a-critical-lens-b29de8c6049.

Banerji, Gunjan. "Dow Drops 600 Points on Global Growth Concerns." *Wall Street Journal*, 31 January 2020. https://www.wsj.com/articles/global-stocks-drift-lower-on-economic-growth-concerns-11580466790.

Benyus, Janine. *Biomimicry: Innovation Inspired by Nature*. New York: William Morrow, 2002.

Brennan, Jordan. *A Shrinking Universe: How Concentrated Corporate Power Is Shaping Income Inequality in Canada*. Ottawa: Canadian Centre for Policy Alternatives, November 2012. https://www.policyalternatives.ca/sites/default/files/uploads/publications/National%20Office/2012/11/Shrinking_Universe_0.pdf.

Calgary Economic Development. *Calgary in the New Economy: The Economic Strategy for Calgary*. Calgary: CED, 2020. https://calgaryeconomicdevelopment.com/assets/Calgary-in-the-New-Economy/Calgary-in-the-New-Economy-Final.pdf.

Calgary Homeless Foundation. *10 Year Plan to End Homelessness: 2008–2018*. January 2011 Update. Calgary: CHF, 2011. https://aventa.org/wp-content/uploads/2017/02/10-Year-Plan-Update.pdf.

Canadian Index of Wellbeing. *How Are Canadians Really Doing? The 2016 CIW National Report*. Waterloo, ON: CIW and University of Waterloo, 2016. https://uwaterloo.ca/canadian-index-wellbeing/sites/ca.canadian-index-wellbeing/files/uploads/files/c011676-nationalreport-ciw_final-s.pdf.

———. "New Evidence Reveals Canadian Wellbeing on the Decline." Press release, 23 October 2012. https://www.newswire.ca/news-releases/new-evidence-reveals-canadian-wellbeing-on-the-decline-511009361.html.

Carleton University. "Carleton Releases 2012 National Survey on Balancing Work and Caregiving in Canada: Linda Duxbury to Talk about Findings at Building Healthier Workplaces Conference." Press release, 25 October 2012. https://newsroom.carleton.ca/archives/2012/10/25/carleton-releases-2012-national-study-on-balancing-work-and-caregiving-in-canada-linda-duxbury-to-talk-about-findings-at-building-healthier-workplaces-conference/.

Cattaneo, Claudia. "King of Pain: Steve Williams Seizes on Price Pangs to Prepare Suncor for Oilsands Dominance." *Financial Post*, 9 October 2015. https://financialpost.com/commodities/energy/king-of-pain-steve-williams-seizes-on-price-pangs-to-prepare-suncor-for-oilsands-dominance.

Charlton, Emma. "New Zealand Has Unveiled Its First 'Well-Being' Budget." *World Economic Forum*, 30 May 2019. https://www.weforum.org/agenda/2019/05/new-zealand-is-publishing-its-first-well-being-budget/.

D'Alisa, Giacomo, Federico Demaria, and Giorgos Kallis, eds. *Degrowth: A Vocabulary for a New Era*. New York: Routledge, 2014.

Daly, Herman. "Economics for a Full World." *Great Transition Initiative*, June 2015. http://www.greattransition.org/publication/economics-for-a-full-world.

———. *From Uneconomic Growth to a Steady-State Economy*. Advances in Ecological Economics Series. Cheltenham, UK: Edward Elgar, 2014.

Duxbury, Linda. *Dealing with Work-Life Issues in the Workplace: Standing Still Is Not an Option*. 2004 Don Wood Lecture in Industrial Relations. Kingston, ON: Queen's University, Industrial Relations Centre, 2004.

———, and Christopher Higgins. *Revisiting Work-Life Issues in Canada: The 2012 National Study on Balancing Work and Caregiving in Canada*. Report 1. Ottawa: Carleton University, 2012. https://newsroom.carleton.ca/wp-content/files/2012-National-Work-Long-Summary.pdf.

———, Maggie Stevenson, and Christopher Higgins. "Too Much to Do, Too Little Time: Role Overload and Stress in a Multi-Role Environment." *International Journal of Stress Management* 25, no. 3 (2018): 250–66.

Giovannetti, Justin. "Kenney Seeks Nearly $1.7-Billion from Ottawa after Collapse in Alberta Oil Prices." *Globe and Mail*, 13 November 2019. https://www.theglobeandmail.com/canada/alberta/article-alberta-premier-jason-kenney-seeks-nearly-17-billion-bailout-from/.

Golden, Mark. "Sacrifice and Luck Help Japan Survive without Nuclear Power, Stanford Visiting Scholar Says." *Stanford University News*, 4 January 2013. https://news.stanford.edu/news/2013/january/japan-nuclear-power-010413.html.

Holloway, Andy. "FP500: The Premier Ranking of Corporate Canada." *Financial Post*, 13 June 2019. https://financialpost.com/feature/fp500-the-premier-ranking-of-corporate-canada.

"Household Debt-to-Income Ratio Near Record High." *Canada Mortgage and Housing Corporation*, 13 December 2018. https://www.cmhc-schl.gc.ca/en/housing-observer-online/2018-housing-observer/household-debt-income-ratio-near-record-high.

Hudson, C. A. *Poverty Costs 2.0: Investing in Albertans*. Calgary: Vibrant Communities Calgary and Action to End Poverty in Alberta, 2013. http://vibrantcalgary.com/wp-content/uploads/2016/06/PCosts_2_Investing_In_Albertans_web.pdf.

IBI Group. *The Implications of Alternative Growth Patterns on Infrastructure Costs*. Calgary: City of Calgary, April 2009. http://www.reconnectingamerica.org/assets/Uploads/planitcalgarycoststudyanalysisaprilthird.pdf.

International Transport Forum. *Urban Mobility System Upgrade: How Shared Self-Driving Cars Could Change City Traffic*. Paris: Organisation for Economic Co-operation and Development, 2015. https://www.itf-oecd.org/sites/default/files/docs/15cpb_self-drivingcars.pdf.

"The Italian Region Where 30% of GDP Comes from Cooperatives." *Apolitical*, 8 January 2018. https://apolitical.co/en/solution_article/italian-region-30-gdp-comes-cooperatives.

Jackson, Tim. *Prosperity without Growth: Economics for a Finite Planet*. New York: Routledge, 2009.

Jones, Nicola. "How the World Passed a Carbon Threshold and Why It Matters." *YaleEnvironment360*, 26 January 2017. Yale School of the Environment. https://e360.yale.edu/features/how-the-world-passed-a-carbon-threshold-400ppm-and-why-it-matters.

Keough, Noel, Bob Morrison, and Celia Lee. *State of Our City 2020: An Urgent Call for a Just Transition*. Calgary: Sustainable Calgary Society, 2020. http://www.sustainablecalgary.org/publications.

Keough, Noel, Maryam Nabavi, and Jeff Loomis. *A Citizens' Agenda: For a More Healthy, Caring and Vibrant Calgary*. Calgary: Sustainable Calgary Society, 2005. https://static1.squarespace.com/static/5ab716b9ee1759b04ca2703e/t/5ee004c3984cb602a4c8a2c9/1591739598060/Citizens%27+Agenda+2006.pdf.

Klaszus, Jeremy. "Paying for It: Calgary's 14 New Communities: What Was City Council Thinking?" *The Sprawl*, 10 February 2020. https://www.sprawlcalgary.com/sprawlcast-calgarys-14-new-communities.

"Kurzarbeit: Germany's Short-Time Work Benefit." *IMF News*, 15 June 2020. https://www.imf.org/en/News/Articles/2020/06/11/na061120-kurzarbeit-germanys-short-time-work-benefit.

"LEED Certification Process." *Canada Green Building Council*. Accessed 5 September 2020. https://www.cagbc.org/CAGBC/Programs/LEED/LEED_Certification_Process.aspx.

Lewis, Mike, and Pat Conaty. *The Resilience Imperative: Cooperative Transitions to the Steady-State Economy*. Gabriola Island, BC: New Society, 2012.

"Living Building Challenge 4.0 Basic." *International Living Future Institute*, 2020. https://living-future.org/lbc/basics4-0/.

Macdonald, David. *Fail Safe: CEO Compensation in Canada*. Ottawa: Canadian Centre for Policy Alternatives, 2020. https://www.policyalternatives.ca/sites/default/files/uploads/publications/National%20Office/2020/01/Fail%20Safe.pdf.

Mackenzie, Hugh. *Canada's CEO Elite 100: The 0.01%*. Ottawa: Canadian Centre for Policy Alternatives, January 2012. https://www.policyalternatives.ca/sites/default/files/uploads/publications/National%20Office/2012/01/Canadas%20CEO%20Elite%20100FINAL.pdf.

Malthus, Thomas. *An Essay on the Principle of Population, As It Affects the Future Improvement of Society, with Remarks on the Speculations of Mr. Godwin, M. Condorcet, and Other Writers*. Anonymously published, London, 1798.

Molotch, Harvey. "The City As a Growth Machine: Toward a Political Economy of Place." *American Journal of Sociology* 82, no. 2 (1976): 309–32.

Morrison, Bob. "2012–2014 City Budget Submission by Governance, Finance, and Infrastructure Group." Unpublished. Calgary: CivicCamp, 2012.

Organisation for Economic Co-operation and Development. *Growing Unequal? Income Distribution and Poverty in OECD Countries.* Geneva: OECD, October 2008. https://www.oecd.org/els/soc/growingunequalincomedistributionandpovertyinoecdcountries.htm.

Parent, Michael. "What the MEC Sale Might Really Be About." *The Tyee,* 6 October 2020. https://thetyee.ca/Analysis/2020/10/06/What-MEC-Sale-Is-Really-About/.

Raworth, Kate. *Doughnut Economics: 7 Ways to Think Like a 21st Century Economist.* Vermont: Chelsea Green, 2017.

Roberts, David. "Shared Vehicles Could Make Our Cities Dramatically More Livable." *Vox,* 28 July 2016. https://www.vox.com/2016/7/28/12294214/shared-vehicles-livable-cities.

Rubin, Jeff. *The End of Growth.* Toronto: Random House, 2012.

———. *Why Your World Is About to Get a Whole Lot Smaller.* Toronto: Vintage, 2010.

Sanzillo, Tom, and Kathy Hipple. "IEEFA Report: Additional $320 Million in Subsidies Used to Finance Trans Mountain Pipeline in First Half of 2019." Press release, Institute for Energy Economics and Financial Analysis, Lakewood, ON, 19 November 2019. https://ieefa.org/ieefa-report-additional-320-million-in-subsidies-used-to-finance-trans-mountain-pipeline-in-first-half-of-2019/.

Smith, Adam. *The Wealth of Nations.* New York: Bantam Dell, 2003. First published 1776 by W. Strahan and T. Cadell (London).

Standing, Guy. "Coronavirus Has Shown Us Why We Urgently Need to Make a Basic Income a Reality." *World Economic Forum,* 13 April 2020. https://www.weforum.org/agenda/2020/04/coronavirus-made-basic-income-vital/.

Statistics Canada. "Table 11-10-0055-01, High Income Tax Filers in Canada." Ottawa: Statistics Canada, 2020. https://www150.statcan.gc.ca/t1/tbl1/en/tv.action?pid=1110005501.

Stiglitz, Joseph E. *The Price of Inequality: How Today's Divided Society Endangers Our Future.* New York: W. W Norton, 2012.

Taft, Kevin. *Follow the Money: Where Is Alberta's Wealth Going?* Calgary: Detselig, 2012.

Toma and Bouma Management Consultants. *Alberta REA Strategic Review: Rural Economic Impacts.* Prepared for Alberta Rural Electrification Associations, January 2013. https://ccrnrcrc.files.wordpress.com/2014/05/rea-report-f-2.pdf.

Vanderklippe, Nathan. "Bonuses Soar in the Oil Patch 'Bubble.'" *Globe and Mail,* 1 May 2012. https://www.theglobeandmail.com/report-on-business/streetwise/bonuses-soar-in-oil-patch-bubble/article4103979/.

Veal, A. J. *Whatever Happened to the Leisure Society?* New York: Routledge, 2018.

Vibrant Communities Calgary. *A Snapshot of Poverty in Calgary 2019.* Calgary: VCC, August 2019. http://enoughforall.ca/wp-content/uploads/2019/08/A-Snapshot-of-poverty-in-Calgary-in-2019.pdf.

Victor, Peter, and Tim Jackson. "Towards an Ecological Macroeconomics." Prepared for INET Annual Plenary Conference "Paradigm Lost: Rethinking Economics and Politics," Berlin, April 2012. https://www.ineteconomics.org/uploads/papers/victor-peter-berlin-paper-draft-w-Tim-Jackson.pdf.

"What Is Net Zero?" *World Green Building Council,* 2016–20. https://www.worldgbc.org/advancing-net-zero/what-net-zero.

Wodrich, Nigel, and Aidan Worswick. *Estimating the Top Tail of the Family Wealth Distribution in Canada.* Ottawa: Office of the Parliamentary Budget Officer, 17 June 2020. https://www.pbo-dpb.gc.ca/web/default/files/Documents/Reports/RP-2021-007-S/RP-2021-007-S_en.pdf.

Zimonjic, Peter. "Liberals Detail $40B for 10-Year National Housing Strategy, Introduce Canada Housing Benefit." *CBC News,* 22 November 2017. https://www.cbc.ca/news/politics/housing-national-benefit-1.4413615.

The Energy Question

We generally think of the flow of cheap (low-interest) money as the currency that drives our economy, but from a sustainability perspective, the vital currency is the flow of cheap energy. In this chapter, we explore the nexus of energy and sustainability with a particular focus on Alberta's fossil fuel economy.

We present a critical commentary on the politics and economics of pipeline projects like Keystone XL. We discuss what many people consider to be a squandering of the vast wealth that oil and gas has generated for Alberta, comparing our province to places like Norway, where government management of the economy is an accepted and successful strategy. While many of our political and business leaders gush over the vastness of the tar sands reserves, in this chapter we argue that in many ways, the renewable energy potential in Alberta is far greater. We also discuss the role that subsidizing the fossil fuel industry plays in delaying the energy transition.

We outline the logic and math behind the "stranded assets" argument. An article in the journal *Nature* argues that to stabilize below 400 ppm of CO_2 in the atmosphere and to stay below 2°C warming, Canada can only burn a mere 15 percent of tar sands reserves.[1] This is indeed an inconvenient truth for fossil fuel–dependent economies. In "Do the Math," we investigate the implications of the growing fossil fuel–divestment strategies around the world.

In the essay "King Coal and the Carbon Calamity," we take a look at the prospects of the phase-out of coal, the most damaging of fossil fuels, in Canada's most coal-dependent province. While Alberta has made great strides toward coal phase-out in electricity production, it has embarked on yet another project of coal mining. We also take up the question of the ethics of the energy transition. What responsibility do citizens of communities who have grown rich on the exploitation of fossil fuels have to ensure a rapid transition to a low-carbon energy future?

A caveat to the numbers we present: Climate change research and technological innovation is moving so fast that any analysis more than a few months old is bound to be out of date. As new climate change research emerges, we see that historical modelling has been consistently conservative in comparison to actual change. Likewise, the renewables revolution seems to be moving more rapidly than most historical predictions. At the core of the energy question with respect to sustainability is the faceoff between conventional economics, which tells us we must burn fossil fuels, and ecology, which says that to do this is to court disaster.

DIVERSITY IS THE KEY: CONFRONTING OUR ENERGY HABITS

In late October 1973, the first global "oil shock" was triggered when Arab members of OPEC boycotted sales to specific industrialized nations—including Canada—to try to coerce them into changing their foreign policies concerning the Arab-Israeli war then raging. Along with the embargo came a 25 percent cutback in production, which, within months, caused world oil prices to quadruple. The global economy descended into chaos.[2]

Experts warn that other oil shocks are inevitable, since wild price swings up or down are problematic.[3] But unlike in 1973, when the scarcity was artificially induced, in 2020 the increasing world demand, decreasing reserves, and poor prospects for large new discoveries mean that we can expect prices to rise in the long term.

This isn't an ideological statement. Given that reserves of liquid fossil fuels are finite and that a growing world population is stimulating accelerating demand, at some point the two streams must cross. Demand will exceed supply; the main question is when. Some think we will cross the threshold very soon—within a decade. Others believe there is more time, perhaps fifty or a hundred years. Still others believe it's already in the rearview mirror. In *The Citizen's Guide to Climate Success*, Mark Jaccard argues that it is a dangerous myth that there will be a peak-oil reckoning. Long before oil runs out, he contends, greenhouse gas levels and planetary heating will wreak havoc on civilization. He argues persuasively that we need to get on with economic diversification and the regulation of carbon.[4]

So if cheap energy is not in our future, why are we still building cities as though it is? Isolated, auto-dependent suburbs and the structures they contain are not only the costliest form of human habitation ever devised; to function properly, they demand significantly more energy per person than all other urban forms. In Calgary, virtually all our growth has been, and continues to be, planned for the suburbs.[5] Plan It (the city's blueprint for more sustainable development) notwithstanding, the suburban monoculture we're building not only lacks social resilience—it's energy-stupid.

It is possible that technology will save us. We may find inexhaustible supplies of non-polluting energy alternatives, along with the means to store and deliver them to consumers. We may find ways to capture the emissions from coal-fired plants to keep pollution out of our lungs and carbon out of the atmosphere. We may find a way to extract natural gas from shale formations without ruining our drinking water. We may find ways to safely use up or store nuclear waste and methods to finance new plants and protect them from terrorism. We may find ways to live on Mars.

We may indeed, but is the promise enough, as they say in poker, to be going "all in"? We're betting the farm on the suburban model with a hand that's not exactly a pair of aces. Diversity, in all kinds of systems (not just cities), provides multiple pathways to choose from as conditions change. This is why diverse systems are more adaptable to new or unanticipated conditions. Diverse systems enable learning and evolution; they provide options. Uniform systems underperform or, if things get really bad, collapse.

The value of diversity was the lesson of the 1973 oil shock. The countries with the least energy resilience fared worst and took the longest to recover. Having learned this lesson, places like Denmark, Germany, and the Netherlands, which were among the hardest hit in the 1973 shock, began taking diversity seriously. Apart from diversifying their energy sources, these countries also began making heavy, long-term investments to reduce their urban energy footprint. Yes, the Europeans have suburbs too, but they invested in urban mass-transit systems and insisted that energy conservation be a core principle of their urban design and building construction. Germany has been a leader in building design with the Passivhaus brand, and cities like Oslo, Helsinki, and Paris have aggressive plans to make downtowns car-free and to build bicycle roadways.

Things are oddly upside down in Alberta. When the world suffers high-energy costs, we prosper. This muddles our thinking, causing us to flout both sense and prudence in our city-building habits. That's not to say there aren't some great things happening in our city. Some new communities are being built with sustainability features—The Bridges, East Village, Currie Barracks—but most are on the city's fringes, where alternatives to fossil fuel–powered car dependence don't exist. The sad truth is, progressive development projects constitute only a tiny fraction of Calgary's total development.

What about the next oil shock? Where would our urban form leave us if energy prices quadrupled tomorrow? To paraphrase acerbic suburban critic James Kunstler, "up cul-de-sac creek in a concrete canoe" is where.[6]

We know what's coming. It may not happen suddenly like it did in 1973, but we know that in the long term, energy prices are only going higher. We also know that, beyond a certain energy price threshold, suburbs become dysfunctional. The math is simple, so why don't we get it?

They tell us it's the market speaking. If so, it's operating with imperfect information. Or maybe it's that we don't want to know. Our prosperity bubble shields us, or seems to, for the present, and that's all that matters. Inside the bubble, we can pretend that energy is not a problem—at least not our problem.

PIPEDREAM NIGHTMARE: A CRISIS ENTIRELY OF OUR OWN MAKING

Throughout the 2010s, Calgarians witnessed a raging battle over approval and construction of pipelines to get Alberta's tar sands product to market. Keystone XL is on life support, but its boosters still dream. The Gateway project through northern BC seems dead in the water, as does Energy East, with fierce opposition from communities and governments along both routes. Whether or not Trans Mountain Pipeline is ultimately built, it is difficult to see a scenario in which Alberta comes out a winner. If the pipelines go ahead, we go further down the road of dependence on one of the most expensive, ecologically damaging, high-risk megaprojects on earth. If it is halted, Albertans are left to pick up the pieces of an economic development strategy in disarray.

Back in 2013, Alberta's premier, Alison Redford, bemoaned the $6 billion bitumen bubble that was forcing us to sell our resource at an almost 40 percent discount.[7] Knowing there were no secure routes to international markets, Conservative governments continued to lease the land that supported the $165 billion invested in tar sands development from 2000 to 2013. Stuck with what could turn out to be the biggest white elephant in history, the Redford government suddenly discovered that we have limited possibilities to get this product to market! If the various provincial Conservative governments saw this coming, they were spectacularly negligent to let it happen. If they did not see it coming (hard to believe), then they were merely spectacularly incompetent.

In a 2012 speech delivered at the University of Calgary, Carl Pope, who was with Sierra Club USA for thirty years, warned that the tar sands–anchored economic strategy was based on a hope and prayer. For this to turn out well for Albertans, he said, seven different trends would all have to break our way. He warned us about all the things with which we now find ourselves besieged—public opinion on climate change, market access, and price fluctuations that create a constant flailing from profitable to not profitable.[8]

Prime Minister Harper's Conservatives were largely to blame for the firestorm that erupted south of the border over Keystone (and smolders to this day) and for the controversy in the west over Gateway. Think of it as bad karma. Abroad, Canada, the honest broker and global citizen, had morphed into an arrogant bully and environmental pariah leading the pack in Fossil of the Day awards at global climate change meetings. Former Green Party leader Elizabeth May accused the government not only of indifference but of "sabotage." According to May, "Canada continues to be a country that pushes other countries to do less. Our role is not just an embarrassment, it's reckless and brings our once good national reputation into disrepute."[9]

At the height of the Keystone debate, in January 2012, the Conservatives went into their trademark attack mode with an open letter to Canadians from Natural Resources Minister Joe Oliver, in which he warned of "environmental and other radical groups" whose goal was "to stop any major project no matter what the cost to Canadian families."[10]

Six months later, in June 2012, with NGOs and environmentalists on the defensive, the Conservatives, under cover of the 420-page omnibus budget Bill C-38, gutted a raft of federal laws, including the Canadian Environmental Assessment Act (CEAA) and Fisheries Act, and abolished the National Round Table on the Environment and the Economy. In March 2012, a few months before Bill C-38 was passed, the hardly radical Canadian Environmental Law Association released an assessment of the CEAA review on which the bill was based, writing that the review "to date has been ineffectual, unduly limited by arbitrary timing, and largely driven by ideology rather than rational, evidence-based analysis" and that the government's rewrite would "effectively eviscerate the CEAA."[11] In June, after the bill had been passed, Ed Whittingham, executive director of the environmental research group Pembina Institute, said, "The passing of this bill is a significant step backward and will result in unnecessary damage to Canada's land, freshwater, and fish habitat."[12]

In September 2012, the federal Conservatives softened already drafted coal plant emissions rules to allow Canada's oldest and dirtiest plants, and those to be built before 2015, to operate outside of the new regulations for forty-five years. In November 2012, the Conservatives' Bill C-45 targeted the Navigable Waters Act and the Hazardous Materials Review Act, removing protection from all but ninety-seven of Canada's thirty-two thousand lakes.

Perhaps the crowning achievement of this six-month legislative wrecking ball was the repeal of the Kyoto Protocol Implementation Act, included in Bill C-38.[13] Canada was the only country to do so at the time.[14]

The governing parties, both provincially and federally, have changed since 2012. The Trudeau Liberal government purchased Trans Mountain to keep it alive when market forces could not, and we are still figuring out how much that purchase actually cost. Related court challenges from First Nations across BC have still not played out. Meanwhile, in February 2020, incredibly, the Liberal government was on the verge of giving a green light to another massive and damaging open pit tar sands mine, the Frontier Project, when proponent Teck Resources withdrew the application. The Conservative provincial government remains in attack mode on anyone who dares express opposition to these projects, stirring dangerous nationalist furor if such projects are not approved.[15]

In Alberta, we have burned through most of our conventional oil reserves, and the Alberta Heritage Fund, created in 1976, sits at a paltry $16.3 billion in 2020. The source of the fund is drying up, and our provincial government is in a state of what the *Globe and Mail* called "political desperation" over this crisis of its own making.[16] Meanwhile, Norway, comparable in population and oil reserves to Alberta but with a hands-on economic development policy, ranks number one on the Human Development Index.[17] Its future is secure, with more than $1 trillion from oil royalties in its Sovereign Wealth Fund.[18] Norway's fund started at zero in 1996, when Alberta's Heritage Fund was at $12 billion. The State of Alaska Permanent Fund, also derived from oil royalties, started the same year as the Heritage Fund and, in November 2020, was valued at $69.7 billion.[19]

Norway and Alaska have used their oil and gas resource as a path to prosperity. Alberta has allowed the oil and gas industry to use our province as a fast lane to profit while rerouting its citizens onto a road to ruin. Calgarians, whether they work in oil and gas or not—perhaps more so if they do—should be mad as hell. And not at those who object to these recurring pipedream nightmares.

OSTRICH ALBERTA: OUR HEADS IN THE TAR SANDS

Back in 2012, we conducted a scan of climate change policies—humanity's most profound challenge—and of renewable energy—the world's fastest growing energy sector—to see where they fit into Alberta's 2012 provincial election platforms. The result: "Reader has finished searching the document; no matches were found."

Eight years later, a lot has changed. Climate change was actually a pivotal issue in the 2019 federal election. All parties proposed policies to tackle the issue. The Conservatives really had nothing to offer, the major initiative being to actually cut the carbon tax. The Liberals had lofty goals (net zero carbon by 2050, for example) but no credible plan to reach them in the face of expanding fossil fuel infrastructure like pipelines. The New Democrats had a more ambitious policy and firm opposition to new pipelines but were short on implementation. Only the Green Party platform could credibly claim to present policies that would actually meet our global commitments and respond to the scale of the climate change emergency. Provincially, the policy platforms of the four parties in the 2019 provincial election were similar to those of their federal counterparts, the most notable difference being the New Democrats, who were staunch supporters of the Trans Mountain Pipeline.

Defenders of current energy policy rightly point out that the 165.4 billion barrels of recoverable oil currently under Alberta is enormous—the third-largest recoverable reserve in the world.[20] But if we take our heads out of the sand for just a moment, we can see that even this impressive reserve pales in comparison to the carbon-free energy contained in the sunshine that bathes us and in the winds blowing through our hair day, after day, after day—forever.

We typically talk about energy in units of joules, megawatt hours, or barrels of oil. Let's start with barrels of oil. According to Sustainable Calgary's *State of Our City 2020*, Calgarians' total energy use—for heating and lighting our homes, driving our automobiles, and running our economy—is the equivalent of approximately seventy-eight barrels per person per year.[21] Imagine a family of three with their yearly stock of 234 barrels of oil in the back yard. That's a lot of energy. But when you crunch the numbers, you find that a typical twenty-five-foot infill lot in inner city Calgary has the equivalent of 240 barrels of oil in the form of solar energy raining down on it every year. At current efficiencies of 20 percent for solar panels, harvesting that energy alone would cover 20 percent of the heat, electric, and gasoline energy requirements of that same family.

That's pretty impressive. Now imagine how much energy falls on southern Alberta—let's say the land use districts of the South Saskatchewan and Red Deer Regions (104,000 km²). If you do the math, what you discover is that over a mere eleven months, those two districts receive the solar energy equivalent of the total recoverable tar sands oil. Not all of this energy will ever be harvested, of course, but according to Alberta Solar Energy Society, as of 2020, the projects that are completed, under construction, or in some stage of planning would deliver almost four thousand megawatts of solar energy—enough to power approximately 750,000 Alberta households.[22]

Wind energy, though not quite as plentiful, is also very impressive and, as of 2020, the cheapest source of electricity in Alberta. With wind turbines covering 10 percent of the South Saskatchewan Region and generating energy a modest 30 percent of the time, we could harvest the equivalent of the recoverable tar sand reserves in about eight years and a month. According to the Canadian Wind Energy Association, Alberta now has 1,685 megawatts of installed wind energy capacity across thirty-eight wind projects, enough to power more than 431,000 average homes for as little as 3.7 cents a kilowatt hour.[23]

Do we have the capacity to realize this energy bonanza right now? The answer is a resounding yes. Here's a perfect example close to home. The City of Calgary has saved millions of dollars in the last ten years by contracting with Enmax to run our LRT on wind energy generated in southern Alberta. In 2001 the City of Calgary contracted with Enmax for twenty-one thousand megawatt hours of wind power a year, and Enmax erected twelve wind turbines in southern Alberta to meet the contract.[24]

As for solar, in some parts of the world where it is really sunny and conventional energy is relatively expensive, solar is already the cheapest alternative. For years, residents of Freiburg, Germany, have been receiving cheques in the mail for the excess energy their solar panel-adorned

Passivhauses feed into the grid. A decade of government subsidies to pay above the market rate for non-carbon energy has helped bring solar energy almost to parity with conventional sources, and the German industrial powerhouse is poised to sell the world its twenty-first–century energy technology.[25]

The price of power generated from photovoltaic technology has fallen from about five dollars per kilowatt hour in 1978 to five cents today. Efficiency gains in the technology are a big part of the story. A typical solar panel in 2000 was 10 percent efficient. In 2020 efficiencies exceed 20 percent. And the main ingredient in the panels, silicon dioxide, is the second-most abundant element on earth.[26] The World Energy Outlook 2020 confirmed that "solar PV is consistently cheaper than new coal- or gasfired power plants in most countries, and solar projects now offer some of the lowest cost electricity ever seen."[27] Closer to home, the triumph of renewables is being heralded, with University of Calgary researchers reporting that "the era of cheap wind and solar has arrived."[28]

While we've been ploughing our windfall oil and gas profits back into the technology of yesterday, or giving it away as Ralph Bucks, as Alberta's premier Ralph Klein did in 2005, other countries have been developing the technology of tomorrow.[29] In 2019 the European Union installed more photovoltaic electric capacity than any other power source and more than double the 2018 number.[30] In 2018 China installed almost twenty-three gigawatts of wind energy—almost 50 percent of total global installation.[31] As these energy sources mature, will Europe and China still want to buy dirty oil? In February 2020, the announcement of an unprecedented $500 million in what will be Canada's largest solar energy project was almost invisible in the political discourse, smothered by the provincial government's shilling for the proposed Teck Resources Frontier Oil Sands mining operation.[32]

This generation has the potential to capitalize on the single biggest business opportunity in human history—the shift to a low-carbon economy. We have the opportunity to confront the biggest ethical challenge in the history of humanity—the irreversible altering of our climate to one that is hostile to human life. The challenge of converting but a fraction of that abundant clean energy into usable form is a challenge worthy of Albertans. But none of this will happen without bold and visionary public policy. In order to realize the potential for a renewable future, our political parties need to pull their heads out of the tar sands and let the sun shine in.

THE 400 PPM THRESHOLD BREACHED—AND THE TRAGIC IRONY OF OUR PETRO-STATE

How many times have you fretted over something for days, weeks, maybe years, finally got up the nerve to just do it, and in retrospect thought to yourself, "That wasn't so hard!" Sometimes, it's a relatively minor hurdle and other times, a significant life milestone. Then we chastise ourselves for dithering and procrastinating.

I'm afraid that someday soon, we may face the same regret over climate change. In May 2013 we reached an ominous milestone when, for the first time, the Mauna Loa atmospheric monitoring station registered over 400 ppm (parts per million) daily average CO_2 concentration, already far beyond what is generally considered the safe target of 350 ppm.[33] In June 2020, Mauna Loa registered 417 ppm. CO_2 concentrations have not been this high in over three million years![34]

Far from raising any doubt about human-caused climate change, each new research report demonstrates that our estimates of the rate of change have been much too conservative. The earth's temperature is rising, and impacts like arctic ice melt are happening at a rate beyond what the models predicted.

At the same time, we've been underestimating the pace of a very different trend. According to the International Energy Agency, since 1975, solar panel prices have been falling about 7 percent annually, from over US$100 per kilowatt of installed capacity to under US$2 in 2020.[35] The US National Renewable Energy Laboratory calculated that the cost of solar electric energy fell from about fifty cents a kilowatt hour in 2010 to between three and five cents in 2020.[36] By 2019, utility scale solar PV, the rooftop solar you see on buildings, was at the lowest cost to consumers of any electricity source in the US.[37] In 2019 solar energy contracts were being signed in Alberta for under five cents a kilowatt hour.[38]

As a result of this dramatic cost decrease, the world's installed capacity of solar energy has increased by 490 times from 2000 to 2019, with Canada's production increasing by 442 times in that period.[39] In Europe, as of 2018, 32.3 percent of electricity was supplied by renewables.[40] In a 2019 article in the *Globe and Mail*, writer Chris Turner did a ten-year retrospective on Germany's Energiewende—the name given to its renewable energy revolution.[41] He found it alive and well, with over 40 percent of electric energy now supplied by renewables, much of it owned by farmers and private citizens. The industry supports 340,000 jobs, five times more than are currently employed by coal. Ninety percent of Germans support the transition, with the Green Party harvesting the second-most votes in the recent European Parliament elections.

Bloomberg's 2019 *New Energy Outlook* reported that the cost of solar, wind, and battery storage had decreased 85, 49, and 85 percent, respectively, since 2010.[42] With these kinds of cost curves, estimates of the pace of investment in low-carbon renewable energy production continue to be revised upwards.

As we enter the third decade of the millennium, we seem to have reached the holy grail: solar technology has become not only the cleanest but also the cheapest energy on the planet. At this point, everything changes, because solar energy will flow to us as long as the sun shines, with a fraction of the carbon footprint of fossil fuels. We are starting to see significant movement in financial markets and among the world's largest private investor groups. Conservative economists like Mark Carney, former governor of the Bank of Canada and the Bank of England, no crazy environmentalist, warned in the December 2019 edition of *The Guardian* that climate change is "a tragedy on the horizon" and that assets in the fossil fuel sector "could end up 'worthless.'"[43]

But if current trends continue, the day we reach that threshold will be bittersweet. By that time, we will probably have crossed the point of no return for climate change, and we will be powerless to reverse it. Imagine arriving at that day with the realization that the transition to low-carbon energy would not have been that hard at all, but with the full knowledge of the grim future our children and grandchildren face because we could not find the wherewithal to make the transition just a little sooner and avoid the climate change point of no return.

We may, as a species, muddle along, adapt, and survive but in a diminished state, having created a much more hostile climate for our species and the many others with whom we share the planet. On that day, the likes of

David Suzuki, Al Gore, and NASA climatologist James Hansen will take no pleasure in being able to say "I told you so."

In 2015 a research report by Will Steffen and the Climate Council of Australia found that in order to avoid 2°C warming, the world can burn no more than 12 percent of remaining coal reserves, 48 percent of its gas reserves, and 35 percent of its oil reserves.[44] In that same year, the journal *Nature* published a paper arguing that between 2015 and 2050, Canada can burn only about 25 percent of its conventional oil reserves, 76 percent of its gas reserves, and 1 percent of its bitumen reserves if we want to avoid catastrophic climate change.[45] Conventional economics tells us we must burn tar sands oil. The earth's ecology tells us that to do so is to court disaster.

The challenge of climate change will require the equivalent of World War II mobilization or the postwar Marshall Plan for the reconstruction of Europe.[46] But wherever we sit in relation to the point of no return, it is never too late to act—and act we must. Having reaped the treasure of the fossil fuel age, Calgarians have the moral obligation to do so. It will wreak havoc on the economy for years, you say. But the trade-off is wreaking havoc on the planet for millennia. Calgary has the wealth, the creative energy, and the intellectual and social capital to lead the transition. We are one of the wealthiest places on the planet. It is not more wealth we need. It is a planet that our children can inhabit.

The Poppy Plaza in inner city Calgary commemorates the heroic and selfless acts that Calgarians of a previous generation made for our freedoms. This historic crossroads at which we currently find ourselves requires a very different but no less crucial heroism and selflessness from our generation. What stuff are we made of?

DO THE MATH: FOSSIL FUEL DIVESTMENT, STRANDED ASSETS, AND THE DAWN OF THE SOLAR AGE

In 2014 Alberta premier Jim Prentice voiced two truths that had been obvious for some time: environmental concerns threaten to cancel the oil patch's social licence to operate, and faltering oil prices wreak havoc with our provincial economy. Subsequent premiers Notley and Kenney have faced the same dilemma. But these mundane political talking points are being upstaged in a big way by two emerging phenomena. Fossil fuel divestment and the stranded asset trap could make for the economic version of one of those increasingly frequent superstorms, right in our back yard.

The divestment campaign has been gathering steam for some time. On more than five hundred campuses all around the globe, students are demanding that their universities divest of fossil fuels. Stanford University has decided to divest of coal and is considering other fossil fuels.[47] Three Quebec universities have pledged to divest from all fossil fuels (Laval, Université du Québec à Montréal, and Concordia).[48] University of British Columbia has announced its intention to partially divest, while McGill and University of Toronto continue to resist calls from student and faculty coalitions for divestment.[49]

Calls for divestment, like the anti-apartheid campaign in the 1980s, are founded on a moral argument. Campaigns such as these typically emerge out of faith communities and activist citizen groups. The World Council of Churches, representing 590 million people in 150 countries, announced its divestment plans in 2014.[50] The report *$11 Trillion and Counting*, detailing the state of the global divestment campaign, was released by 350.org in 2019.[51] In January 2020, New York mayor Bill de Blasio and London mayor Sadiq Khan called on all cities of the world to follow their lead and divest city pension funds from fossil fuels.[52]

As with the anti-apartheid movement of the 1980s, divestment campaigns, initially anchored in ethical concerns, have gained momentum through the economic logic of the market. Ethically motivated divestment creates the conditions for economically motivated investors who begin to see the economic risk of a morally tainted investment. The Rockefeller family, who for the past 150 years has made its fortune from oil, made headlines in 2016 by announcing its decision to divest of $860 million in fossil fuel assets.[53] In 2020, following a 2014 coal divestment decision, a Swedish pension fund, Första AP-fonden (AP1), announced its decision to divest of all fossil fuel investments due to "a substantial uncertainty for companies involved in coal, oil and natural gas activities." AP1's chair described the decision as being "in line with the Paris Agreement."[54]

The investment risk is summed up in the story of stranded assets and unburnable carbon being told by Carbon Tracker—a savvy group of investment professionals using their skills to confront climate change.

The story is based on the single climate change target for which we have achieved global consensus—beyond 2°C lies catastrophe.

Putting another 565 gigatonnes of CO_2 into the atmosphere gets us to 2°C. Burning all the declared reserves of the world's major oil companies would produce almost three thousand gigatonnes—five times the limit.[55] It's simple arithmetic: 80 percent of the assets of the global oil companies must stay in the ground. It's unburnable! Carbon Tracker's strategy is to disturb money managers with this simple truth.

In 2014 a Carbon Tracker press release warned that "investors in Canadian oil sands are at a heightened risk of companies wasting $271 billion of capital on projects in the next decade [including those of Suncor, CNRL, and Cenovus] that need high oil prices of more than $95 a barrel to give a decent return."[56] Between 2016 and 2018, over $78 billion was actually invested.[57] In its 2018 report *Mind the Gap*, Carbon Trackers warns of the growing risk of $1.6 trillion in investments in the sector, with $110 billion of future investments in Canada's tar sands highly exposed.[58] By 2019, the number of institutional investors divesting of fossil fuels had risen from 180, with assets of $5.2 billion in 2014, to 1,244, with assets of $14.61 trillion.[59]

As Alberta dithers, the world is transitioning to the solar economy. Albertans should be wary of the assurances we receive from our political and economic leaders. Case in point: Are assurances from industry leaders credible when up to 79 percent of the compensation packages of the largest oil and gas companies in Calgary are based on share value?[60] They have a considerable vested interest in distracting us from investment forecasts that put share values in question and that place the industry that floats our economy in peril.

The long reign of fossil fuels has left a quagmire of perverse subsidies that mask its real state of competitiveness. The International Energy Agency reported that in 2018 annual global fossil fuel subsidies had actually increased to a total of over $400 billion, 40 percent more than the entire investment in renewables.[61] Part of the problem, according to Carbon Trackers' accountability report is that "current financial reporting standards, stock market listing requirements, [and] industry reporting framework . . . do not alert investors to the risks of reserves associated with climate change."[62] But that is changing, and Albertans need to be listening.

I'm pretty sure that not even the staunchest supporters of the oil industry would claim that oil, coal, or gas (especially sour gas) are pleasant substances to work with. Most of the world is aching to get off fossil fuels. But we put up with them because of the service they provide—compact, inexpensive energy. As soon as consumers of energy see that there is an alternative that does not carry the health and environmental costs of fossil fuels, even if it entails a marginal cost, they will ditch fossil fuels in a heartbeat. It will be game over for those two thousand gigatonnes of stranded reserves. Albertans need to do the math.

KING COAL AND THE CARBON CALAMITY: TIME TO FACE OUR DIRTY LITTLE SECRETS

While tar sands production gets all the press, Albertans have another energy demon to face down. Our province is endowed—or cursed, depending on your perspective—with some of the biggest coal deposits in North America; it's one of the main reasons why we have enjoyed among the lowest electricity rates in the world. But as reports from the Pembina Institute have detailed, there are high costs for that cheap power.[63] It seems that for a long time, we were in the dark, at least figuratively, about this dirty little secret. Surveys have found that only one-third of Albertans realize that historically we generated almost 80 percent of our electricity from coal.[64]

In 2017 Alberta's four big coal power plants were among Canada's six largest greenhouse gas (GHG) emitters.[65] At forty-three megatonnes in 2017, GHGs generated from coal were second only to emissions from tar sands exploitation. We produce more GHGs per kilowatt hour of electricity than any other province—for example, about seven hundred times those of Quebec.[66] True, in part it is the hand we were dealt. Emissions from BC, Manitoba, Quebec, and Newfoundland's vast hydropower resources are a fraction of those emitted by coal burning. Yet other coal provinces are taking aggressive action. Ontario stopped producing electricity from coal in 2014.[67]

While Calgary-based TransAlta staked a claim as one of Canada's largest wind power generators, it was hard to avoid the conclusion that it was a laggard, not a leader, when it came to curbing GHG emissions from the burning of coal. Prior to the federal government's 2012 coal phase-out legislation, TransAlta's five largest Alberta facilities, generating about forty-one hundred megawatts, were all coal fired. Its eleven wind facilities were its smallest, generating about five hundred megawatts.[68] TransAlta's vice-president for Sustainable Development, Don Wharton, seemed to be arguing against a coal phase-out in 2013 when he said that "cutting out coal could lead to a 30 to 50 per cent jump in the price of electricity."[69] TransAlta was, at the time, not entirely forthcoming about its motives and actions. It claimed to be playing by the rules, yet with its industry partners, it actively sought to weaken them, resulting in a weakening of regulations on coal phase-outs.[70]

While we may have "cheap" electricity, that artificially low price (artificial because it externalizes the costs of climate change and public health) makes us energy hogs. The Pembina Institute referred to Alberta as Canada's energy-efficiency "laggard."[71] Why conserve when we pay so little? Until 2017, Alberta was the only province without a renewable electricity policy.[72] That changed in 2017 with the start-up of the highly successful Energy Efficiency Alberta (EEA) funding project, with lifetime energy bill savings of $806 million and a 6.8 million tonne reduction in GHG emissions in just two years.[73] Unfortunately, EEA did not fit with the pro–fossil fuel ideology of the new UCP government, and its programs were scrapped in October 2019.[74]

In the meantime, thanks to the tireless work of a grassroots coal phase-out campaign in Alberta, led by Dr. Joe Vipond of the Canadian Association of Physicians for the Environment (CAPE), Dr. David Layzel and Dr. Mishka Lysack at the University of Calgary, and former Calgary MLA Dr. David Swann, in November 2015, the provincial NDP government announced a plan to phase out coal-fired electricity generation by 2030.[75] As of 2019, coal was the fuel source for less than half of our electricity, down from three-quarters twenty years ago, and the coal phase-out was being heralded as a Canadian success story.[76] Job well done, but not the end of the story.

By 2018, coal exports from Alberta had rebounded to near record levels, with older mines like the Grand Cache Coal Mine recommissioned and new mines like the Vista Coal Mine near Hinton opening for business, with up to seven more in the works.[77] Albertans will surely benefit from the health impacts of reduced coal-burning, but Alberta coal will continue to put the world in climate peril, even after the 2030 coal phase-out. We are shuffling our coal production around like chairs on the deck of the Titanic. Alberta is in good company with China. China is aggressively moving to renewables, in large part to freshen the air in the capital, Beijing, while through its Belt and Road initiative, it uses its vast financial resources to finance coal-fired power-generation facilities around the world.[78]

The coal-fired electricity generation phase-out in Alberta shows that climate activism can work. The continued expansion of coal exports from Alberta shows that there is still work to be done. A good place to start is withdrawing coal's social licence to operate. It is time to end the reign of King Coal. Mark Jaccard, respected energy economist and former government advisor turned coal-train blockader, said that what propelled him into activism was the thought that decades down the road, we will be asked, "What did you do when there was still time to make a difference?"[79] It's a worthwhile question to ponder.

NOTES

1   Christophe McGlade and Paul Ekins, "The Geographical Distribution of Fossil Fuels Unused When Limiting Global Warming to 2° C," *Nature* 517 (2015): 187–90.

2   Daniel Yergin, *The Prize: The Epic Quest for Oil, Money and Power* (New York: Free Press, 2008).

3   Tim Gould and Neil Atkinson, "The Global Oil Industry Is Experiencing a Shock Like No Other in Its History," *International Energy Agency*, 1 April 2020, https://www.iea.org/articles/the-global-oil-industry-is-experiencing-shock-like-no-other-in-its-history.

4   Mark Jaccard, *The Citizen's Guide to Climate Success: Overcoming Myths That Hinder Progess* (Cambridge: Cambridge University Press, 2020).

5   City of Calgary, *Municipal Development Plan/Calgary Transportation Plan 2018 Monitoring Progress Report* (Calgary: City of Calgary, 2018), https://www.calgary.ca/pda/pd/municipal-development-plan/municipal-development-plan-and-calgary-transportation-plan-2018-monitoring-progress-report.html.

6   "We're literally stuck up a cul-de-sac in a cement SUV without a fill-up": James Howard Kunstler, quoted in Gregory Greene, dir., *The End of Suburbia: Oil Depletion and the Collapse of the American Dream* (Belleville, ON: Electric Wallpaper Co., 2004), 0:19.

7   Josh Wingrove, "'Bitumen Bubble' Means a Hard Reckoning for Alberta, Redford Warns," *Globe and Mail*, 24 January 2013, https://www.theglobeandmail.com/news/national/bitumen-bubble-means-a-hard-reckoning-for-alberta-redford-warns/article7833915/.

8   There appears to be no written record of this talk by Karl Pope at the University of Calgary. The authors were present at the event and wrote this commentary the following week for *Fast Forward Weekly*.

9   Max Paris, "Greens Leader Accuses Tories of Sabotaging Climate Talks," *CBC News*, 29 November 2012, https://www.cbc.ca/news/politics/greens-leader-accuses-tories-of-sabotaging-climate-talks-1.1130619.

10 Joe Oliver, "An Open Letter from Natural Resources Minister Joe Oliver," *Globe and Mail*, 9 January 2012, https://www.theglobeandmail.com/news/politics/an-open-letter-from-natural-resources-minister-joe-oliver/article4085663/.

11 Richard L. Lindgren, *Legal Analysis of the Report of the Standing Committee on Environment and Sustainable Development Regarding the* Canadian Environmental Assessment Act (Edmonton: Canadian Environmental Law Association, March 2012), https://cela.ca/wp-content/uploads/2019/07/826CELA-Analysis-CEAA-ReportMarch-2012.pdf.

12 Pembina Institute, "Pembina Reacts to Passage of Bill C-38," media release, 19 June 2012, https://www.pembina.org/media-release/2351.

13 "Canada Pulls Out of Kyoto Protocol," *CBC News*, 12 December 2011, https://www.cbc.ca/news/politics/canada-pulls-out-of-kyoto-protocol-1.999072; Green Party of Canada, "May Clarifies Deliberately Confusing Bill-C38," press release, 10 May 2012, https://www.greenparty.ca/en/media-release/2012-05-10/may-clarifies-deliberately-confusing-bill-c-38.

14 UN Framework Convention on Climate Change, *Canada's Withdrawal from the Kyoto Protocol and Its Effects on Canada's Reporting Obligations under the Protocol: Note by the Secretariat* (Bonn, Germany: UNFCCC Compliance Committee, August 2014), https://unfccc.int/files/kyoto_protocol/compliance/enforcement_branch/application/pdf/cc-eb-25-2014-2_canada_withdrawal_from_kp.pdf.

15 The federal Liberals, at long last, have begun to move, with a November 2020 announcement of a Climate Strategy, including a crucial decision to introduce a carbon tax.

16 Janet French, "Alberta's Heritage Savings Trust Fund Hits Lowest Value in Eight Years," *CBC News*, 13 July 2020, https://www.cbc.ca/news/canada/edmonton/alberta-s-heritage-savings-trust-fund-1.5648392; Paul Mason, "Alberta Is about to Learn How the Other Half Lives," *Globe and Mail*, 25 October 2019, https://www.theglobeandmail.com/canada/british-columbia/article-alberta-is-about-to-learn-how-the-other-half-lives/.

17 Pedro Conceição. *Beyond Income, Beyond Averages, Beyond Today: Inequalities in Human Development in the 21st Century*, Overview: Human Development Report 2019 (New York: United Nations Development Programme, 2019), http://hdr.undp.org/sites/default/files/hdr_2019_overview_-_english.pdf.

18   Reuters, "Norway Wealth Fund Hits Record 10 Trillion Kroner As Stocks Rise," *Al Jazeera*, 25 October 2019, https://www.aljazeera.com/ajimpact/norway-wealth-fund-hits-record-10-trillion-kroner-stocks-rise-191025095606511.html.

19   *Alaska Permanent Fund Corporation*, https://apfc.org.

20   "Oil Sands Fact and Statistics," *Government of Alberta*, 2020, https://www.alberta.ca/oil-sands-facts-and-statistics.aspx.

21   Noel Keough, Bob Morrison, and Celia Lee, *State of Our City 2020: An Urgent Call for a Just Transition* (Calgary: Sustainable Calgary Society, 2020), 51, http://www.sustainablecalgary.org/publications.

22   This information comes from a presentation on 11 February 2020 at the University of Calgary by Benjamin Thibeault, executive director of Solar Alberta (https://solaralberta.ca).

23   "Wind Markets: Wind Energy in Alberta," *Canadian Wind Energy Association*, accessed 6 September 2020, https://canwea.ca/wind-energy/alberta/; "Wind Facts: Affordable Power," *Canadian Wind Energy Association*, accessed 6 September 2020, https://canwea.ca/wind-facts/affordable-power/.

24   David Dodge and Duncan Kinney, "Calgary's Wind-Powered LRT an Incredibly Successful System: Nenshi," *Pembina Institute* (blog), 6 July 2015, https://www.pembina.org/blog/calgary-s-wind-powered-lrt-an-incredibly-successful-system-nenshi.

25   Anna Pegels, "Germany: The Energy Transition as a Green Industrial Development Agenda," in *Green Industrial Policy: Concept, Policies, Country Experiences*, ed. T. Altenburg and C. Assmann (Bonn, Germany: UN Environment; German Development Institute, 2017), 166–84, https://www.un-page.org/files/public/green_industrial_policy_book_aw_web.pdf.

26   Ajit Niranjan, "Falling Solar Panel Prices Spell Sunny Future for Clean Energy," *Deutche Welle*, 28 May 2020, https://www.dw.com/en/cheap-solar-energy-prices-explained/a-53590607.

27   "World Energy Outlook 2020," *International Energy Agency*, 2020, https://www.iea.org/reports/world-energy-outlook-2020.

28   Nick Schumacher et al., *Energy and Environmental Policy Trends* (Calgary: University of Calgary, 2020), https://www.policyschool.ca/wp-content/uploads/2020/11/Energy-Trends-Renewables-Nov.pdf.

29   Matthew Black, "'Ralph Bucks' 14 Years Later: Could the Prosperity Bonus Have Saved Alberta's Bottom Line?" *CTV News*, 14 January 2020, https://edmonton.ctvnews.ca/ralph-bucks-14-years-later-could-the-prosperity-bonus-have-saved-alberta-s-bottom-line-1.4767107.

30   Michael Schmela, "EU Market Outlook for Solar Power/2019–2023" (Brussels: SolarPower Europe, 2019), https://www.solarpowereurope.org/wp-content/uploads/2019/12/SolarPower-Europe_EU-Market-Outlook-for-Solar-Power-2019-2023_.pdf?cf_id=7181.

31   Heymi Bahar, "Solar PV: Tracking Report," *International Energy Agency*, June 2020, https://www.iea.org/reports/solar-pv.

32 Bill Kaufmann, "Vulcan Solar Farm—Canada's Largest—Receives Key $500-Million Investment," *Calgary Herald*, 4 February 2020, https://calgaryherald.com/business/local-business/greengate-secures-partner-to-finance-countrys-largest-solar-project.

33 Jessica Blunden, "2013 State of the Climate: Carbon Dioxide Tops 400 ppm," *National Oceanic and Atmospheric Association*, 13 July 2014, https://www.climate.gov/news-features/understanding-climate/2013-state-climate-carbon-dioxide-tops-400-ppm.

34 Trevor Nace, "Carbon Dioxide Levels Just Hit 417 ppm, Highest in Human History," *Forbes*, 1 June 2020, https://www.forbes.com/sites/trevornace/2020/06/10/carboN-dioxide-levels-just-hit-417ppm-highest-in-human-history/#5ee942ca229f.

35 "Evolution of Solar PV Module Cost by Data Source, 1970–2020," *International Energy Agency,* last updated 30 June 2020, https://www.iea.org/data-and-statistics/charts/evolution-of-solar-pv-module-cost-by-data-source-1970-2020.

36 Laura Vimmerstedt et al., *Annual Technology Baseline: The 2020 Electricity Update* (Golden, CO: National Renewable Energy Laboratory, July 2020), https://www.nrel.gov/docs/fy20osti/76814.pdf.

37 "Levelized Cost of Energy and Levelized Cost of Storage 2019," *Lazard*, 7 November 2019, https://www.lazard.com/perspective/lcoe2019.

38 This information comes from a presentation on 11 February 2020 at the University of Calgary by Benjamin Thibeault, executive director of Solar Alberta (https://solaralberta.ca).

39 "Global New Installed Solar PV Capacity from 2000 to 2019," *Statista*, 14 July 2020, https://www.statista.com/statistics/280200/global-new-installed-solar-pv-capacity/; C. Baldus-Jeurson, Y. Poissant, and Wes Johnston, *National Survey Report of PV Power Applications in Canada 2018* (Paris: International Energy Agency, 2018), https://iea-pvps.org/wp-content/uploads/2020/01/2019-223_RP-ANU_DER-PVNORD_CBaldus-Jeursen_YPoissant_EN.pdf.

40 Agora Energiewende and Sandbag, *The European Power Sector in 2018: Up-to-Date Analysis on the Electricity Transition* (Berlin, Germany: Agora Energiewende and Sandbag, January 2019), https://www.agora-energiewende.de/fileadmin2/Projekte/2018/EU-Jahresauswertung_2019/Agora-Energiewende_European-Power-Sector-2018_WEB.pdf.

41 Chris Turner, "The Greenprint: Checking on Germany's Transition to Renewable Energy," *Globe and Mail*, 1 June 2019, https://www.theglobeandmail.com/opinion/article-the-greenprint-checking-up-on-germanys-transition-to-renewable/.

42 Seb Henbest et al., *Bloomberg 2019 New Energy Outlook* (New York: Bloomberg New Energy Finance, 2019), https://about.bnef.com/new-energy-outlook/.

43 Andrew Sparrow, "Firms Must Justify Investment in Fossil Fuels, Warns Mark Carney," *The Guardian*, 30 December 2019, https://www.theguardian.com/business/2019/dec/30/firms-must-justify-investment-in-fossil-fuels-warns-mark-carney.

44 Will Steffen, *Unburnable Carbon: Why We Need to Leave Fossil Fuels in the Ground* (Potts Point, Australia: Climate Council of Australia, 2015), 5, https://www.climatecouncil.org.au/uploads/a904b54ce67740c4b4ee2753134154b0.pdf.

45   McGlade and Ekins, "Geographical Distribution of Fossil Fuels," 189–90.

46   "History of the Marshall Plan," *George C. Marshall Foundation*, accessed 6 September 2020, https://www.marshallfoundation.org/marshall/the-marshall-plan/history-marshall-plan/.

47   Zahra Hirji, "Stanford, Once Hailed for Divesting From Coal, Criticized for Not Going Further," *Inside Climate News*, 26 April 2016, https://insideclimatenews.org/news/26042016/stanford-divestment-coal-oil-gas-fossil-fuels-climate-change.

48   Ethan Cox, "Laval Becomes First University in Canada to Divest from Fossil Fuels," *Ricochet*, 15 February 2017, https://ricochet.media/en/1684/laval-becomes-first-university-in-canada-to-divest-from-fossil-fuels; "UQAM Halts Investment in Fossil Fuels," *CTV News*, 17 May 2019, https://montreal.ctvnews.ca/uqam-halts-investments-in-fossil-fuels-1.4426978; Canadian Press, "Concordia University Says It Will Divest Entirely from Coal, Oil and Gas by 2025," *CBC News*, 8 November 2019, https://www.cbc.ca/news/canada/montreal/concordia-divests-1.5353808.

49   "UBC Votes to Divest $380M from Fossil Fuels, but Students Demand More," *CBC News*, 24 November 2019, https://www.cbc.ca/news/canada/british-columbia/ubc-divestment-vote-1.5371719.

50   Adam Vaughan, "World Council of Churches Rules out Fossil Fuel Investments," *The Guardian*, 11 July 2014, https://www.theguardian.com/environment/2014/jul/11/world-council-of-churches-pulls-fossil-fuel-investments.

51   Yossi Cadan, Ahmed Mokgopo, and Clara Vondrich, *$11 Trillion and Counting* (Boston: 350.org, 2019), https://631nj1ki9k11gbkhx39b3qpz-wpengine.netdna-ssl.com/divestment/wp-content/uploads/sites/52/2019/09/FF_11Trillion-WEB.pdf.

52   Bill de Blasio and Sadiq Khan, "As New York and London Mayors, We Call on All Cities to Divest from Fossil Fuels," *The Guardian*, 10 September 2018, https://www.theguardian.com/commentisfree/2018/sep/10/london-new-york-cities-divest-fossil-fuels-bill-de-blasio-sadiq-khan.

53   John Schwartz, "Rockefellers, Heirs to an Oil Fortune, Will Divest Charity of Fossil Fuels," *New York Times*, 22 September 2014, https://www.nytimes.com/2014/09/22/us/heirs-to-an-oil-fortune-join-the-divestment-drive.html.

54   Anmar Frangoul, "Swedish Pension Fund with Billions of Assets under Management to Stop Fossil Fuel Investments," *CNBC*, 17 March 2020, https://www.cnbc.com/2020/03/17/swedish-pension-fund-to-stop-fossil-fuel-investments.html.

55   The Carbon Tracker math was popularized by an explosive article by Bill McKibben: "Global Warming's Terrifying New Math," *Rolling Stone*, 19 July 2012, https://www.rollingstone.com/politics/politics-news/global-warmings-terrifying-new-math-188550/.

56   Carbon Trackers, "Nine out of Ten Barrels in Undeveloped Oil Sands Projects at Risk from Eroding Oil Price," press release, 4 November 2014, https://carbontracker.org/nine-out-of-ten-barrels-in-undeveloped-oil-sands-projects-at-risk-from-eroding-oil-price/.

57   "Oil Sands Facts and Statistics."

58   Andrew Grant, *Mind the Gap: The $1.6 Trillion Investment Risk* (London: Carbon Trackers, 2018), https://carbontracker.org/reports/mind-the-gap/.

59   "Divestment: Overview," *Fossil Free,* accessed 6 September 2020, https://gofossilfree. org/divestment/commitments/.

60   David Macdonald, *Fail Safe: CEO Compensation in Canada* (Ottawa: Canadian Centre for Policy Alternatives, 2020), 4, https://www.policyalternatives.ca/sites/default/files/ uploads/publications/National%20Office/2020/01/Fail%20Safe.pdf.

61   Wataru Matsumura and Zakia Adam, "Fossil Fuel Consumption Subsidies Bounced Back Strongly in 2018," *International Energy Agency,* 13 June 2019, https://www.iea.org/ commentaries/fossil-fuel-consumption-subsidies-bounced-back-strongly-in-2018.

62   Carbon Trackers, "Accounting for Hidden Reserves," press release, 4 December 2013, https://carbontracker.org/accounting-for-hidden-reserves-press-release-2/.

63   Kristi Anderson et al., *A Costly Diagnosis: Subsidizing Coal Power with Albertans' Health,* prepared for Pembina Foundation for Environmental Research and Education by the Pembina Institute, Canadian Association of Physicians for the Environment, Asthma Society of Canada, and Lung Association, Alberta and Northwest Territories, March 2013.

64   Ian Hussey and Emma Jackson, *Alberta's Coal Phase-Out: A Just Transition?* (Edmonton: Parkland Institute), 1, https://d3n8a8pro7vhmx.cloudfront.net/ parklandinstitute/pages/1763/attachments/original/1574261140/coal_phaseout. pdf?1574261140.

65   Canada, *Greenhouse Gas Emissions from Large Facilities: Canadian Environmental Sustainability Indicators* (Ottawa: Environment Canada, 2018), https://www.canada. ca/content/dam/eccc/documents/pdf/cesindicators/greenhouse-gas-emissions-large- facilities/2020/greenhouse-gas-emissions-large-facilities-en.pdf.

66   Canada, *Greenhouse Gas Emissions: Canadian Environmental Sustainability Indicators,* 11 (fig. 7) (Ottawa: Environment and Climate Change Canada, 2020), https://www. canada.ca/content/dam/eccc/documents/pdf/cesindicators/ghg-emissions/2020/ greenhouse-gas-emissions-en.pdf.

67   "The End of Coal," *Government of Ontario,* accessed 6 September 2020, https://www. ontario.ca/page/end-coal.

68   The capacity in 2012 was based on our calculations, using the Transalta website, of all electricity generating stations at the time. Those data are no longer available online.

69   "Coal Plants Cost Alberta $300M in Health Costs: Report," *CBC News,* 26 March 2013, https://www.cbc.ca/news/canada/edmonton/coal-plants-cost-alberta-300m-in-health- costs-report-1.1326727.

70   Darcy Henton, "MSA Seeks Ban against Energy Traders in TransAlta Case," *Calgary Herald,* 3 January 2014, http://www.calgaryherald.com/business/ seeks+against+energy+traders+TransAlta+case/9565197/story.html.

71   "Improving Energy Efficiency in Alberta's Buildings," *Pembina Institute* (blog), 13 February 2013, https://www.pembina.org/blog/improving-energy-efficiency-alberta-s- buildings.

72   Pembina Institute, "Pembina Reacts to Energy Efficiency Alberta Announcement," media release, 27 October 2016, https://www.pembina.org/media-release/pembina-reacts-to-energy-efficiency-alberta-announcement.

73   Energy Efficiency Alberta, *2019–2020 Annual Report* (Calgary: Energy Efficiency Alberta, 2020), 2.

74   Amanda Stephenson, "Energy Efficiency Alberta Programs Scrapped by UCP," *Calgary Herald*, 31 October 2019, https://calgaryherald.com/business/local-business/energy-efficiency-alberta-programs-scrapped-by-ucp.

75   Darcy Henton and Chris Varcoe, "Alberta Launches $3-Billion Cimate Change Strategy with Carbon Tax," *Calgary Herald,* 23 November 2015, https://calgaryherald.com/news/politics/alberta-unveils-details-of-its-climate-plan. For more on the coal phase-out campaign, see Mishka Lysack, "Effective Policy Influencing and Environmental Advocacy: Health, Climate Change, and Phasing Out Coal," *International Social Work* 58, no. 3 (2015): 435–47.

76   Andrew Leach and Blake Shaffer, "Opinion: Alberta's Shift Away from Coal Power Is a Climate Action Success Story," *CBC News*, 15 October 2020, https://www.cbc.ca/news/canada/calgary/road-ahead-alberta-coal-power-electricity-decline-1.5761858.

77   Jim Bentein, "Alberta Coal Mining Activity Rebounds in 2018," *Canadian Mining Journal,* 1 April 2019, https://www.jwnenergy.com/article/2019/4/1/coal-mining-activity-alberta-rebounds-2018/.

78   Jonathan Watts, "Belt and Road Summit Puts Spotlight on Chinese Coal Funding," *The Guardian*, 25 April 2019, https://www.theguardian.com/world/2019/apr/25/belt-and-road-summit-puts-spotlight-on-chinese-coal-funding.

79   Mark Jaccard, "The Accidental Activist: How an Energy Economist and Former Government Advisor Found Himself Blocking a Coal Train," *The Walrus*, 13 April 2020, https://thewalrus.ca/the-accidental-activist/.

Further Reading

Jaccard, Mark. *The Citizen's Guide to Climate Success: Overcoming Myths That Hinder Progress.* Cambridge, UK: Cambridge University Press, 2020.

McKibben, Bill. *Oil and Honey: The Education of an Unlikely Activist.* New York: Henry Holt, 2013.

Nikiforuk, Andrew. *Slick Water: Fracking and One Insider's Stand against the World's Most Powerful Industry.* Vancouver: Greystone Books, 2015.

Smil, Vaclav. *Energy and Civilization: A History.* Cambridge, MA: MIT Press, 2018.

Turner, Chris. *The Patch: The People, Pipelines and Politics of the Oil Sands.* Toronto: Simon and Schuster, 2017.

Works Cited

Agora Energiewende and Sandbag. *The European Power Sector in 2018: Up-to-Date Analysis on the Electricity Transition*. Berlin, Germany: Agora Energiewende and Sandbag, January 2019. https://www.agora-energiewende.de/fileadmin2/ Projekte/2018/EU-Jahresauswertung_2019/Agora-Energiewende_European-Power-Sector-2018_WEB.pdf.

Anderson, Kristi, Tim Weis, Ben Thibault, Farrah Khan, Beth Nanni, and Noah Farber. *A Costly Diagnosis: Subsidizing Coal Power with Albertans' Health*. Prepared for Pembina Foundation for Environmental Research and Education by the Pembina Institute, Canadian Association of Physicians for the Environment, Asthma Society of Canada, and Lung Association, Alberta and Northwest Territories, March 2013.

Bahar, Heymi. "Solar PV: Tracking Report." *International Energy Agency*, June 2020. https://www.iea.org/reports/solar-pv.

Baldus-Jeurson, C., Y. Poissant, and Wes Johnston. *National Survey Report of PV Power Applications in Canada 2018*. Paris: International Energy Agency, 2018. https:// iea-pvps.org/wp-content/uploads/2020/01/2019-223_RP-ANU_DER-PVNORD_ CBaldus-Jeursen_YPoissant_EN.pdf.

Bentein, Jim. "Alberta Coal Mining Activity Rebounds in 2018." *Canadian Mining Journal*, 1 April 2019. https://www.jwnenergy.com/article/2019/4/1/coal-mining-activity-alberta-rebounds-2018/.

Black, Matthew. "'Ralph Bucks' 14 Years Later: Could the Prosperity Bonus Have Saved Alberta's Bottom Line?" *CTV News*, 14 January 2020. https://edmonton.ctvnews. ca/ralph-bucks-14-years-later-could-the-prosperity-bonus-have-saved-alberta-s-bottom-line-1.4767107.

Blunden, Jessica. "2013 State of the Climate: Carbon Dioxide Tops 400 ppm." *National Oceanic and Atmospheric Association*, 13 July 2014. https://www.climate.gov/news-features/understanding-climate/2013-state-climate-carbon-dioxide-tops-400-ppm.

Cadan, Yossi, Ahmed Mokgopo, and Clara Vondrich. *$11 Trillion and Counting*. Boston: 350.org, 2019. https://631nj1ki9k11gbkhx39b3qpz-wpengine.netdna-ssl.com/ divestment/wp-content/uploads/sites/52/2019/09/FF_11Trillion-WEB.pdf.

Canada. *Greenhouse Gas Emissions: Canadian Environmental Sustainability Indicators*. Ottawa: Environment and Climate Change Canada, 2020. https://www.canada.ca/ content/dam/eccc/documents/pdf/cesindicators/ghg-emissions/2020/greenhouse-gas-emissions-en.pdf.

———. *Greenhouse Gas Emissions from Large Facilities: Canadian Environmental Sustainability Indicators*. Ottawa: Environment Canada, 2018. https://www.canada. ca/content/dam/eccc/documents/pdf/cesindicators/greenhouse-gas-emissions-large-facilities/2020/greenhouse-gas-emissions-large-facilities-en.pdf.

"Canada Pulls Out of Kyoto Protocol." *CBC News*, 12 December 2011. https://www.cbc.ca/ news/politics/canada-pulls-out-of-kyoto-protocol-1.999072.

Canadian Press. "Concordia University Says It Will Divest Entirely from Coal, Oil and Gas by 2025." *CBC News*, 8 November 2019. https://www.cbc.ca/news/canada/montreal/concordia-divests-1.5353808.

Carbon Trackers. "Accounting for Hidden Reserves." Press release, 4 December 2013. https://carbontracker.org/accounting-for-hidden-reserves-press-release-2/.

———. "Nine out of Ten Barrels in Undeveloped Oil Sands Projects at Risk from Eroding Oil Price." Press release, 4 November 2014. https://carbontracker.org/nine-out-of-ten-barrels-in-undeveloped-oil-sands-projects-at-risk-from-eroding-oil-price/.

City of Calgary. *Municipal Development Plan/Calgary Transportation Plan 2018 Monitoring Progress Report*. Calgary: City of Calgary, 2018. https://www.calgary.ca/pda/pd/municipal-development-plan/municipal-development-plan-and-calgary-transportation-plan-2018-monitoring-progress-report.html.

"Coal Plants Cost Alberta $300M in Health Costs: Report." *CBC News*, 26 March 2013. https://www.cbc.ca/news/canada/edmonton/coal-plants-cost-alberta-300m-in-health-costs-report-1.1326727.

Conceição, Pedro. *Beyond Income, Beyond Averages, Beyond Today: Inequalities in Human Development in the 21st Century*. Overview: Human Development Report 2019. New York: United Nations Development Programme, 2019. http://hdr.undp.org/sites/default/files/hdr_2019_overview_-_english.pdf.

Cox, Ethan. "Laval Becomes First University in Canada to Divest from Fossil Fuels." *Ricochet*, 15 February 2017. https://ricochet.media/en/1684/laval-becomes-first-university-in-canada-to-divest-from-fossil-fuels.

De Blasio, Bill, and Sadiq Khan. "As New York and London Mayors, We Call on All Cities to Divest from Fossil Fuels." *The Guardian*, 10 September 2018. https://www.theguardian.com/commentisfree/2018/sep/10/london-new-york-cities-divest-fossil-fuels-bill-de-blasio-sadiq-khan.

"Divestment: Overview." *Fossil Free*. Accessed 6 September 2020. https://gofossilfree.org/divestment/commitments/.

Dodge, David, and Duncan Kinney. "Calgary's Wind-Powered LRT an Incredibly Successful System: Nenshi." *Pembina Institute* (blog), 6 July 2015. https://www.pembina.org/blog/calgary-s-wind-powered-lrt-an-incredibly-successful-system-nenshi.

"The End of Coal." *Government of Ontario*. Accessed 6 September 2020. https://www.ontario.ca/page/end-coal.

Energy Efficiency Alberta. *2019–2020 Annual Report*. Calgary: Energy Efficiency Alberta, 2020.

"Evolution of Solar PV Module Cost by Data Source, 1970–2020." *International Energy Agency*. Last updated 30 June 2020. https://www.iea.org/data-and-statistics/charts/evolution-of-solar-pv-module-cost-by-data-source-1970-2020.

Frangoul, Anmar. "Swedish Pension Fund with Billions of Assets under Management to Stop Fossil Fuel Investments." *CNBC*, 17 March 2020. https://www.cnbc.com/2020/03/17/swedish-pension-fund-to-stop-fossil-fuel-investments.html.

French, Janet. "Alberta's Heritage Savings Trust Fund Hits Lowest Value in Eight Years." *CBC News*, 13 July 2020. https://www.cbc.ca/news/canada/edmonton/alberta-s-heritage-savings-trust-fund-1.5648392.

"Global New Installed Solar PV Capacity from 2000 to 2019." *Statista*, 14 July 2020. https://www.statista.com/statistics/280200/global-new-installed-solar-pv-capacity/.

Gould, Tim, and Neil Atkinson. "The Global Oil Industry Is Experiencing a Shock Like No Other in Its History." *International Energy Agency*, 1 April 2020. https://www.iea.org/articles/the-global-oil-industry-is-experiencing-shock-like-no-other-in-its-history.

Grant, Andrew. *Mind the Gap: The $1.6 Trillion Investment Risk*. London: Carbon Trackers, 2018. https://carbontracker.org/reports/mind-the-gap/.

Green Party of Canada. "May Clarifies Deliberately Confusing Bill-C38." Press release, 10 May 2012. https://www.greenparty.ca/en/media-release/2012-05-10/may-clarifies-deliberately-confusing-bill-c-38.

Greene, Gregory, dir. *The End of Suburbia: Oil Depletion and the Collapse of the American Dream*. Belleville, ON: Electric Wallpaper Co., 2004.

Henbest, Seb, Matthias Kimmel, Jef Callens, Tifenn Brandily, Meredith Annex, Julia Attwood, Melina Bartels et al., *Bloomberg 2019 New Energy Outlook*. New York: Bloomberg New Energy Finance, 2019. https://about.bnef.com/new-energy-outlook/.

Henton, Darcy. "MSA Seeks Ban against Energy Traders in TransAlta Case." *Calgary Herald*, 3 January 2014. http://www.calgaryherald.com/business/seeks+against+energy+traders+TransAlta+case/9565197/story.html.

———, and Chris Varcoe. "Alberta Launches $3-Billion Cimate Change Strategy with Carbon Tax." *Calgary Herald*, 23 November 2015. https://calgaryherald.com/news/politics/alberta-unveils-details-of-its-climate-plan.

Hirji, Zahra. "Stanford, Once Hailed for Divesting from Coal, Criticized for Not Going Further." *Inside Climate News*, 26 April 2016. https://insideclimatenews.org/news/26042016/stanford-divestment-coal-oil-gas-fossil-fuels-climate-change.

"History of the Marshall Plan." *George C. Marshall Foundation*. Accessed 6 September 2020. https://www.marshallfoundation.org/marshall/the-marshall-plan/history-marshall-plan/.

"Improving Energy Efficiency in Alberta's Buildings." *Pembina Institute* (blog), 13 February 2013. https://www.pembina.org/blog/improving-energy-efficiency-alberta-s-buildings.

Jaccard, Mark. "The Accidental Activist: How an Energy Economist and Former Government Advisor Found Himself Blocking a Coal Train." *The Walrus*, 13 April 2020. https://thewalrus.ca/the-accidental-activist/.

———. *The Citizen's Guide to Climate Success: Overcoming Myths That Hinder Progress.* Cambridge: Cambridge University Press, 2020.

Kaufmann, Bill. "Vulcan Solar Farm—Canada's Largest—Receives Key $500-Million Investment." *Calgary Herald*, 4 February 2020. https://calgaryherald.com/business/local-business/greengate-secures-partner-to-finance-countrys-largest-solar-project.

Keough, Noel. *State of Our City Report 2011: Sustainability in a Generation.* Calgary: Sustainable Calgary Society, 2011. https://static1.squarespace.com/static/5ab716b9ee1759b04ca2703e/t/5bff5fd970a6ad4f2ff729e0/1543462882064/2011-SOOC-Report.pdf.

———, Bob Morrison, and Celia Lee. *State of Our City 2020: An Urgent Call for a Just Transition.* Calgary: Sustainable Calgary Society, 2020. http://www.sustainablecalgary.org/publications.

Leach, Andrew, and Blake Shaffer. "Opinion: Alberta's Shift Away from Coal Power Is a Climate Action Success Story." *CBC News*, 15 October 2020. https://www.cbc.ca/news/canada/calgary/road-ahead-alberta-coal-power-electricity-decline-1.5761858.

"Levelized Cost of Energy and Levelized Cost of Storage 2019." *Lazard*, 7 November 2019. https://www.lazard.com/perspective/lcoe2019.

Lindgren, Richard L. *Legal Analysis of the Report of the Standing Committee on Environment and Sustainable Development Regarding the* Canadian Environmental Assessment Act. Edmonton: Canadian Environmental Law Association, March 2012. https://cela.ca/wp-content/uploads/2019/07/826CELA-Analysis-CEAA-ReportMarch-2012.pdf.

Lysack, Mishka. "Effective Policy Influencing and Environmental Advocacy: Health, Climate Change, and Phasing Out Coal." *International Social Work* 58, no. 3 (2015): 435–47.

Macdonald, David. *Fail Safe: CEO Compensation in Canada.* Ottawa: Canadian Centre for Policy Alternatives, 2020. https://www.policyalternatives.ca/sites/default/files/uploads/publications/National%20Office/2020/01/Fail%20Safe.pdf.

Mason, Paul. "Alberta Is About to Learn How the Other Half Lives." *Globe and Mail*, 25 October 2019. https://www.theglobeandmail.com/canada/british-columbia/article-alberta-is-about-to-learn-how-the-other-half-lives/.

Matsumura, Wataru, and Zakia Adam. "Fossil Fuel Consumption Subsidies Bounced Back Strongly in 2018." *International Energy Agency*, 13 June 2019. https://www.iea.org/commentaries/fossil-fuel-consumption-subsidies-bounced-back-strongly-in-2018.

McGlade, Christophe, and Paul Ekins. "The Geographical Distribution of Fossil Fuels Unused When Limiting Global Warming to 2° C." *Nature* 517 (2015): 187–90.

McKibben, Bill. "Global Warming's Terrifying New Math." *Rolling Stone*, 19 July 2012. https://www.rollingstone.com/politics/politics-news/global-warmings-terrifying-new-math-188550/.

Nace, Trevor. "Carbon Dioxide Levels Just Hit 417 ppm, Highest in Human History." *Forbes*, 1 June 2020. https://www.forbes.com/sites/trevornace/2020/06/10/carbon-dioxide-levels-just-hit-417ppm-highest-in-human-history/#5ee942ca229f.

Niranjan, Ajit. "Falling Solar Panel Prices Spell Sunny Future for Clean Energy." *Deutsche Welle*, 28 May 2020. https://www.dw.com/en/cheap-solar-energy-prices-explained/a-53590607.

"Oil Sands Fact and Statistics." *Government of Alberta*, 2020. https://www.alberta.ca/oil-sands-facts-and-statistics.aspx.

Oliver, Joe. "An Open Letter from Natural Resources Minister Joe Oliver." *Globe and Mail*, 9 January 2012. https://www.theglobeandmail.com/news/politics/an-open-letter-from-natural-resources-minister-joe-oliver/article4085663/.

Paris, Max. "Greens Leader Accuses Tories of Sabotaging Climate Talks." *CBC News*, 29 November 2012. https://www.cbc.ca/news/politics/greens-leader-accuses-tories-of-sabotaging-climate-talks-1.1130619.

Pegels, Anna. "Germany: The Energy Transition as a Green Industrial Development Agenda." In *Green Industrial Policy: Concept, Policies, Country Experiences*, edited by T. Altenburg and C. Assmann, 166–84. Bonn, Germany: UN Environment; German Development Institute, 2017. https://www.un-page.org/files/public/green_industrial_policy_book_aw_web.pdf.

Pembina Institute. "Pembina Reacts to Energy Efficiency Alberta Announcement." Media release, 27 October 2016. https://www.pembina.org/media-release/pembina-reacts-to-energy-efficiency-alberta-announcement.

———. "Pembina Reacts to Passage of Bill C-38." Media release, 19 June 2012. https://www.pembina.org/media-release/2351.

Reuters. "Norway Wealth Fund Hits Record 10 Trillion Kroner As Stocks Rise." *Al Jazeera*, 25 October 2019. https://www.aljazeera.com/ajimpact/norway-wealth-fund-hits-record-10-trillion-kroner-stocks-rise-191025095606511.html.

Schmela, Michael. "EU Market Outlook for Solar Power/2019–2023." Brussels: SolarPower Europe, 2019. https://www.solarpowereurope.org/wp-content/uploads/2019/12/SolarPower-Europe_EU-Market-Outlook-for-Solar-Power-2019-2023_.pdf?cf_id=7181.

Schumacher, Nick, Victoria Goodday, Blake Shaffer, and Jennifer Winter. *Energy and Environmental Policy Trends*. Calgary: University of Calgary, 2020. https://www.policyschool.ca/wp-content/uploads/2020/11/Energy-Trends-Renewables-Nov.pdf.

Schwartz, John. "Rockefellers, Heirs to an Oil Fortune, Will Divest Charity of Fossil Fuels." *New York Times*, 22 September 2014. https://www.nytimes.com/2014/09/22/us/heirs-to-an-oil-fortune-join-the-divestment-drive.html.

Sparrow, Andrew. "Firms Must Justify Investment in Fossil Fuels, Warns Mark Carney." *The Guardian*, 30 December 2019. https://www.theguardian.com/business/2019/dec/30/firms-must-justify-investment-in-fossil-fuels-warns-mark-carney.

Steffen, Will. *Unburnable Carbon: Why We Need to Leave Fossil Fuels in the Ground*. Potts Point, Australia: Climate Council of Australia, 2015. https://www.climatecouncil.org.au/uploads/a904b54ce67740c4b4ee2753134154b0.pdf.

Stephenson, Amanda. "Energy Efficiency Alberta Programs Scrapped by UCP." *Calgary Herald*, 31 October 2019. https://calgaryherald.com/business/local-business/energy-efficiency-alberta-programs-scrapped-by-ucp.

Turner, Chris. "The Greenprint: Checking on Germany's Transition to Renewable Energy." *Globe and Mail*, 1 June 2019. https://www.theglobeandmail.com/opinion/article-the-greenprint-checking-up-on-germanys-transition-to-renewable/.

"UBC Votes to Divest $380M from Fossil Fuels, but Students Demand More." *CBC News*, 24 November 2019. https://www.cbc.ca/news/canada/british-columbia/ubc-divestment-vote-1.5371719.

UN Framework Convention on Climate Change. *Canada's Withdrawal from the Kyoto Protocol and Its Effects on Canada's Reporting Obligations under the Protocol: Note by the Secretariat*. Bonn, Germany: UNFCCC Compliance Committee, August 2014. https://unfccc.int/files/kyoto_protocol/compliance/enforcement_branch/application/pdf/cc-eb-25-2014-2_canada_withdrawal_from_kp.pdf.

"UQAM Halts Investment in Fossil Fuels." *CTV News*, 17 May 2019. https://montreal.ctvnews.ca/uqam-halts-investments-in-fossil-fuels-1.4426978.

Vaughan, Adam. "World Council of Churches Rules Out Fossil Fuel Investments." *The Guardian*, 11 July 2014. https://www.theguardian.com/environment/2014/jul/11/world-council-of-churches-pulls-fossil-fuel-investments.

Vimmerstedt, Laura, Sertaç Akar, Philipp Beiter, Wesley Cole, David Feldman, Parthiv Kurup, Ashwin Ramdas et al. *Annual Technology Baseline: The 2020 Electricity Update*. Golden, CO: National Renewable Energy Laboratory, July 2020. https://www.nrel.gov/docs/fy20osti/76814.pdf.

Watts, Jonathan. "Belt and Road Summit Puts Spotlight on Chinese Coal Funding." *The Guardian*, 25 April 2019. https://www.theguardian.com/world/2019/apr/25/belt-and-road-summit-puts-spotlight-on-chinese-coal-funding.

"Wind Facts: Affordable Power." *Canadian Wind Energy Association*. Accessed 6 September 2020. https://canwea.ca/wind-facts/affordable-power/.

"Wind Markets: Wind Energy in Alberta." *Canadian Wind Energy Association*. Accessed 6 September 2020. https://canwea.ca/wind-energy/alberta/.

Wingrove, Josh. "'Bitumen Bubble' Means a Hard Reckoning for Alberta, Redford Warns." *Globe and Mail*, 24 January 2013. https://www.theglobeandmail.com/news/national/bitumen-bubble-means-a-hard-reckoning-for-alberta-redford-warns/article7833915/.

"World Energy Outlook 2020." *International Energy Agency*, 2020. https://www.iea.org/reports/world-energy-outlook-2020.

Yergin, Daniel. *The Prize: The Epic Quest for Oil, Money and Power*. New York: Free Press, 2008.

Justice, Fairness, and Inclusion

"There is nothing so finely perceived and finely felt as injustice," declares Pip in Charles Dickens' *Great Expectations*. Like Pip, we all have a keen sense of fairness. Research shows that faced with an unfair situation, people will often make decisions against their own interests just to deny other individuals unjust rewards.[1]

Nobel economist Amartya Sen puts a finer point on injustice, arguing that leaders like Gandhi and Martin Luther King did not expect perfect justice—they were simply acting "to remove clear injustices."[2]

A sustainable society is a just society. Furthermore, the path to sustainability has to be seen to be just and fair, or people will not offer their support. In this chapter, we discuss, from several perspectives, some of the "clear injustices" in our city and how they relate to sustainability. Some of the essays address big questions, while others approach the topic from seemingly mundane local issues.

Secondary suites may not seem to be a crucial issue in the face of the vast sustainability challenges we face, but it is an example of the everyday small decisions we make that can either advance sustainability or impede it. The issue of secondary suites is only one aspect of the larger affordable housing issue. It touches not only on issues of diversity, fairness, and equity but also on the debates over urban sprawl, transportation, and car dependence.

Another essay delves into the idea of affordable living. Research pioneered in the United States and adapted to Calgary demonstrates the advantage of integrated thinking in urban planning. What if we considered housing and transportation policy together? What difference would it make to how we plan cities and to the decisions that households make about where to live?

A sustainable society nurtures economic, ecological, and cultural diversity. In this chapter, we reflect on the importance of recognizing, celebrating, and leveraging the diversity that the processes of globalization create. We examine research conducted by Sustainable Calgary on the amount of diversity in positions of power and influence in our city. The data suggest that in twenty years, there has been negligible movement on inclusion of women, visible minorities, or Indigenous people around the decision-making forums in our city.

We close the chapter with "How Much Is Enough?"—an essay on consumerism and its implications for our own well-being and that of our neighbours in the global village. We argue that to achieve sustainability, we need to resist the consumerist society and the advertising that invites us to partake in it and to consciously reflect on what lies beyond materialism.

HOME SUITE HOME: A PRIMER ON SECONDARY SUITES

Tens of thousands of Calgary households rent a secondary suite—most of them operating outside of the law.[3] Council has been divided on this issue for years. To paraphrase a former prime minister, does government have any business in the secondary suites of the city, or should this relationship be left to the discretion of consenting owners and renters?

There are well-worn claims for why secondary suites should not be permitted. Some say they bring unsavoury characters into the neighbourhood and lower property values. But a Canada Mortgage and Housing Corporation (CMHC) study found that most occupants of secondary suites share similar social values to those of the neighbourhood they rent in and are looking for quiet, family-oriented neighbourhoods.[4] The truth is, obnoxious, messy, loud neighbours can be either renters or owners and are found in every sort of housing—single family dwellings, condos, acreages, and, yes, secondary suites.

Overcrowding is another complaint levelled at secondary suites. "We'll be living like sardines!" people cry. Yet today, half as many people live in twice as much space as we did a generation ago—that's about one-quarter the density.[5] Surely the issue can't be too many people. Too many cars, perhaps? An Ontario study found parking to be the biggest concern with respect to secondary suites.[6] In fact, modest increases in density, coupled with smart transit investment, moves us toward fewer cars, not more. If the issue is too many cars, secondary suites are part of the solution.

One thing is for sure—Calgary has a chronic affordability problem. Remember the horrific situation in 2008 at the height of the economic boom? Rent increased 50 percent between 2005 and 2008—in extreme cases, more than doubling overnight.[7] By 2009, there were eighteen thousand fewer rental units than in the mid-1990s—mostly due to an aggressive apartment-to-condo conversion trend.[8] Rental affordability has eased in recent years, but still, in 2016 more than eighty-eight thousand households spent more than they should on housing, based on CMHC affordability criteria.[9] The number of Calgarians who have no roof over their heads or who are one paycheque away from homelessness has increased dramatically this past decade, and substantially more renters find themselves in this fix than do homeowners.[10] The bottom line is that Calgary needs more modestly priced rental accommodation, and secondary suites offer a flexible, affordable way to provide it. For example, a three-bedroom secondary suite rents for about the same price as a one-bedroom condo.

A survey of research on the topic published in a 2017 special issue of *Canadian Geographer* found that the stock of available secondary suites rises and falls in step with both house prices and rental housing availability.[11] It also found that secondary suites are particularly important for new immigrant families, whether they are tenants or landlords. A Calgary-based study suggests that, especially in areas with high percentages of new immigrants, the rationale for secondary suites has four distinct elements: the desire for proximity of generations with a level of autonomy, care provision, pooling of financial and human resources, and accommodation for visiting family and friends.[12] Another Calgary study suggested an element of NIMBYism in the resistance to secondary suites, and perhaps some zenophobia.[13]

A 2019 survey in Kamloops, BC, found that more than 75 percent of respondents agreed that secondary suites provide an affordable housing option, assist with mortgage payments, and allow families to stay together by housing young adult children or aging family members.[14] So with a strong secondary-suite policy in place, more Calgarians would get to join the ranks of homeownership, and renters would have more options in a more stable market. Secondary suites bolster that key ingredient of urban sustainability—resiliency!

But if we allow secondary suites in all communities, are we going to be inundated with renters and their cars? Hardly. In Canada's large cities, secondary suites make up about a quarter of all rental units.[15] Since Edmonton introduced its policy in 2000, the uptake has been quite modest, with fifty-five hundred legal secondary suites as of September 2020— about 3 percent of housing stock.[16] As of September 2020, there were just under thirty-six hundred legal secondary suites in Calgary, with inner city and northeast neighbourhoods being the most popular locations.[17] That's hardly a radical remake of Calgary neighbourhoods. The sky is not falling! In fact, the data suggest that most of the secondary suites we will ever see in the city already exist.

The Calgary Homeless Foundation (CHF) and the Chamber of Commerce are strong supporters of liberalized rules for secondary suites.

The CHF, through its 10 Year Plan (2008–18), hopes to provide "11,250 affordable and specialized units" and to work toward "increasing the supply of legal and safe secondary suites" over ten years as a contribution to ending homelessness in our city.[18] The Foundation proposes requiring that new developments have a percentage of housing that are ready for secondary suites.[19] The Chamber of Commerce proposes permitting the suites in every residential neighbourhood and housing type, with only the minimum of regulation needed to ensure safe operation and building code compliance.[20]

So the available research strongly supports the benefits of secondary suites, and respected local organizations have examined the issue and are advocating for a more liberal policy. The kicker is that Calgarians are out in front on this issue. A 2011 survey commissioned by the University of Calgary Students Union found that 74 percent of us support secondary suites in our own neighbourhood.[21] Almost half of us are not that concerned about parking issues. Even laneway housing—the most contentious form of secondary suite—was supported by 60 percent of respondents. A study by graduate students in the School of Architecture, Planning, and Landscape found that laneway housing could provide forty thousand new housing units in Calgary.[22]

A liberalized policy on this issue hits a sustainability sweet spot. Not only do secondary suites increase housing opportunities for Calgarians of modest means; they also help reduce sprawl and car-dependence by increasing the amount of affordable housing close to transit—all with a negligible impact on our lives.

Come on, Calgary. In ten years we'll look back at this and wonder what all the fuss was about.

AFFORDABLE LIVING: THE HOUSE HUNTER'S NEW MANTRA

In 2012 an interesting casting call for the show *Urban Suburban* appeared in local papers—HGTV was recruiting families who were home hunting but couldn't decide between the inner city and the suburbs.

Once upon a time, the rule of thumb was "drive 'til you qualify," meaning that the further afield from the inner city you go, the more the price of your dream home drops—or the bigger the house gets for the mortgage you qualified for. But research out of the US is challenging the "drive 'til you qualify" approach to house hunting. *Penny Wise Pound Fuelish*, a 2010 groundbreaking research report by the Center for Neighborhood Technology (CNT), argues that you ignore transportation cost implications of where you choose to live at your peril.[23]

The emerging wisdom is that rather than having a singular focus on affordable housing, the savvy buyer will look for affordable living. The CNT researchers found that the combined costs of transportation and housing in twenty-eight of the largest municipalities in the US consumed about 60 percent of household income, and that inner city living with good public transit is often easier on your pocketbook than suburban living. For example, living in more compact neighbourhoods resulted in annual combined transportation and housing cost savings of $1,830 in Minneapolis and $3,850 in Boston. The Housing and Transportation Affordability Index continues to track these data by neighbourhood across the United States.[24] A more recent report from CNT found that for those who do choose to locate in proximity to good transit, a home maintains its price more robustly than homes not in a transit shed.[25]

A research report by Sustainable Calgary, *Affordable Living: Housing +Transportation*, applies this approach to our city, and the results may surprise you.[26] In 2014, 29 percent of the average Canadian household's spending went to shelter, while 20 percent went to transportation.[27] When you add up all private transportation spending in Calgary, it works out to about $5.2 billion annually, with the overwhelming portion devoted to buying, operating, and maintaining our cars.[28] That's equivalent to about three southwest LRT lines plus one thousand kilometres of streetcars—all for what we spend in just one year on our cars!

Some of the implications of these numbers for choice and affordability are eye-popping. For example, if a family with an income of $80,000 could live without a car (or with one less car), and devote that savings to their mortgage, the number of Calgary communities where they could afford the average house price increases fourfold. With house prices flat and the average price of a car at record levels, the figures are probably even more impressive in 2020. The research is clear that more transit can increase housing choice and affordability for the average Calgary family.

The implications are even more dramatic for low-income Calgarians. Imagine a family with a meagre $20,000 income looking for a place to rent on an average day in 2009. Using the 32 percent affordability threshold, this family would need a place costing no more than $500/month.[29] But if they could devote $300 more to rent—the difference between what a family spends on a private car versus their costs for public transportation—such families would have ten times as many rental units to choose from, based on a survey of the city's most popular rental accommodation website (rentfaster.ca).

All fine and good, you say, but Calgary is a car-dependent city. Well, yes and no. Life in most Calgary communities is certainly hostage to the car. But as we shift to more residential construction in inner city neighbourhoods, and as transit investment increases, more people will have the option of going car free. A 2011 issue of the City's *Mobility Monitor* newsletter shows us where some of those communities are located.[30] Communities like Sunalta, Hillhurst, Sunnyside, and East Village score "excellent" because "most trips are convenient by transit," whereas anywhere south of Southwood scores "minimal," with the comment "It is possible to get on a bus." More investment in active transportation would also make communities less car dependent. Recent research at the University of Calgary suggests that rapid expansion of bicycling infrastructure could bring ten times as many Calgarians within the catchment zone of the existing LRT with relatively modest investment.[31]

A big piece of the puzzle here is information. If the City developed a reliable transportation-housing affordability index similar to the one developed by the CNT, mortgage lenders might be persuaded to offer "location efficient" mortgages that provide better terms for individuals living in prime transit accessible and walkable neighbourhoods.[32] This could guide families to neighbourhoods where transportation costs are lower, helping both lenders and borrowers make more prudent decisions.

Calgarians love their cars, or so we tell ourselves. We can't possibly change, right? And why should we? Because the downside is getting too big to ignore. Given a choice, maybe some of us can change. With or without location-efficient mortgages or improved transit service, these savings are real—today. So the next time you are in the market for a new home, think affordable living. It could mean substantially less time in congested traffic, more money in your wallet, and more time with your kids. The HGTV series might be stage managed, but the savings from reduced car dependence are real.

CULTURAL DIVERSITY, SOCIAL INCLUSION, AND SUSTAINABILITY: OPPORTUNITY KNOCKS

Cowboy imagery is an important part of Calgary's identity. We put it everywhere—the airport, Stephen Avenue, City Hall. But our true character is much different than the image we cultivate.

The 2009 election of Mayor Nenshi made the rest of the country, and not a few Calgarians, reconsider their impressions of our city. The mayor is perhaps the most visible manifestation of a dramatic change in the face of Calgary over the past twenty years. No less significant is the fact that his "colour purple" campaign struck gold at the end of a decidedly rainbow collective of supporters and campaign workers.

Taking advantage of the opportunities that Calgary's gender, ethnic, and cultural diversity provide could be the key to our sustainability. We can talk about diversity in various ways. Demographically speaking, Canadian cities are among the most diverse in the world. According to World Cities Culture Forum, at 47 percent in 2016, Toronto was just behind Miami as the North American city with the highest percentage of foreign-born residents.[33] Metro Vancouver was close, with 44 percent. In 2016, 29.4 percent of Calgarians were foreign born, making our city the third most ethnically diverse major city in Canada.[34] The Canadian Census also reports that 33.7 percent of Calgary's metro population comprises visible minorities—again, third in the country behind Toronto (51.4%) and Vancouver (48.9%).[35]

A truly good news story is how our diversity has helped define Calgary as a more vibrant, sophisticated, and welcoming city. This is especially visible in our arts and culture scene. Though it is still dominant, gone are the days when the Calgary Stampede was the only cultural game in town. Our city's cultural mosaic is multi-faceted and expanding. From imagineAsia, to GlobalFest, Sled Island, Afrikadey, and Carifest, the diversity of our city is finding its voice. No question, we are a diverse community, and increasingly, we celebrate that diversity through festivals of music, food, dance, and theatre.

But although the Canadian multicultural experiment is envied around the world, it is not without its failings. Evidence suggests that we don't practice inclusion or embrace diversity in the political and economic life of our city. Since 2001, Sustainable Calgary has been tracking the diversity of approximately 220 positions of power and influence in the city. The list includes elected politicians, from trustees to MPs; the boards of directors of the city's largest social development and private sector organizations; and media personalities. The survey asks, With respect to gender, visible minorities, and Aboriginal peoples, does the diversity within political and economic life represent the diversity of our city? Sadly, the answer is no.

As reported in *State of Our City 2020*, in 2018 women constituted 50 percent of Calgary's population; visible minorities, 36 percent; and Aboriginal people, 2.9 percent. Among the 218 positions of power and influence identified in the survey, 34 percent were women (the same as in 2001) and 12.4 percent were visible minorities. The group included just three Aboriginal people (1.4% of the total).

With 39 percent in the government and media, women were best represented in those sectors, followed by 36 percent in the not-for-profit sector. At 21 percent, visible minorities were best represented among our politicians. Of the five largest private sector employers surveyed, 23 percent of board members were women, 10 percent were visible minorities, and only 2.1 percent of the sample of forty-eight directorships were Aboriginal people.

Of course, Calgary is no more or less diversity-challenged than the rest of the country. Women make up 29 percent of our parliamentarians, ranking Canada sixty-fourth among nations of the world. In contrast, in countries such as Rwanda (63%), Cuba (53%), Sweden (47%), and Costa Rica (46%), women's representation among elected representatives parallels their percentage of the populace.[36] Canadian women fare no better at the Toronto Stock Exchange. Of those companies who self-reported in 2018, women held only 16.4 percent of board seats. Twenty-four percent of boards were all male, only 4.4 percent of companies had a female board chair, and only 52 percent of those reporting had a policy to increase female recruitment.[37]

Research has shown that embracing diversity builds social capital; improves the quality of political debate; and enhances our capacity to understand, communicate, and trade with the wider world. Research published in 2019 by Dr. Irene Herremans from the University of Calgary found that more gender-diverse boards delivered better environmental performance, especially in the high-impact resource industry.[38] The Maytree Foundation, an Ontario-based not-for-profit, reports that diverse boards make better decisions, provide greater legitimacy in the community, and are more in keeping with our representative democracy.[39]

The embrace of diversity also resonates with the latest business trend and social media buzz around the wisdom of the crowd. James Surowiecki makes the case in his 2005 book *The Wisdom of Crowds* that the crowd is talented, creative, and stunningly productive but that, crucially, wise crowds need a diversity of opinion.[40]

Collectively, Calgarians represent a wide range of life experience, world views, spiritual beliefs, and cultural knowledge—assets that we will need to create a competitive, resilient, and sustainable economy in the twenty-first century. Diversity is smart business strategy, provides equality of opportunity, and leads to better decisions. Valuing gender, ethnic, and cultural diversity makes us stronger.

We've come a long way and there is much to celebrate, but there's no room for complacency. Our future will be brighter if we honour, nurture, and leverage diversity in all its dimensions. Opportunity knocks.

HOW MUCH IS ENOUGH? BUY NOTHING DAY AN OPPORTUNITY FOR REFLECTION AND REDIRECTION

On November 1, no more than twelve hours after the Hallowe'en festivities, with bags of sugar-infused treats in the closet and never-to-be-worn-again costumes shoved into the garbage bin, shopping malls across the city roll out Christmas music, displays, and discounts. It used to be that we marked the passage of time by natural phenomena—the seasons, phases of the moon, bird migrations. Now we can set our calendars by the orgies of consumerism.

We don't wish to deprive our kids of the joys of trick or treating or the magic of Christmas morning. But we do want to take issue with the diminished and destructive vision of a hyper-consumerist culture that we adults offer them.

In 2020, August 22 marked what has come to be known as Earth Overshoot Day—in eight months, humanity exhausted the earth's resource budget for the year (overshootday.org). Because of COVID-related industrial shutdowns, work closures, and air travel groundings that gave non-human nature a temporary reprieve, this was actually better than in 2019, when the date was July 29. But the pandemic arrived in Canada too late to impact the country. On March 18, just as the first shutdowns were occurring, Canada arrived at its own overshoot date.[41]

Back in 1992, we made it all the way to October 22 before overshoot. We are now well into overdraft, maintaining our collective lifestyles by harvesting more fish than the sea can replenish, cutting trees faster than the forests can grow them, pumping more carbon into the skies than the earth can assimilate back into the biosphere.

While this is starting to cause noticeable discomfort in our country, it is unconscionable what it is doing to our neighbours in the global village. In September 2012, the Climate Vulnerable Forum and DARA, a non-profit committed to working for the well-being of the most vulnerable countries on the planet, released the *Climate Vulnerability Monitor: A Guide to the Cold Calculus of a Hot Planet*. In a plea to the most affluent countries, the report decries what it calls "fundamental injustices that simply cannot go unaddressed."[42]

Despite having contributed negligibly to climate change, the least developed countries—places like Gabon, Central Africa Republic, Mozambique, Somalia, Afghanistan, and Vanuatu—will suffer most. Over 90 percent of the mortality forecast to result from climate change and fossil fuel combustion will occur in developing countries. Working from 2010 data, the report estimates that 400,000 deaths every year are caused directly by climate change and another 4.5 million deaths annually are a result of our carbon-intensive economy, via hunger, malaria, meningitis, air pollution, and cancer associated with the burning of fossil fuels. Furthermore, the report estimates $700 billion in economic losses annually from climate change.[43] A 2019 paper in the *New England Journal of Medicine* estimates that between 314,000 and 736,000 deaths per year are caused by climate change.[44]

According to the *Climate Vulnerability Monitor* report, "while some countries are committed to change and making progress, there is still a lack of conviction among the governments of too many industrialized and developing nations."[45] Sadly, under the Harper government, our country became the poster child for the lack-of-conviction club.

In 2012 the *Global Environment Outlook (GEO) 5* found that growing population, glaring inequality, and a precarious environmental base were causes for profound concern.[46] The 2019 *GEO 6* report warned that the "overall environmental situation globally is deteriorating and the window for action is closing."[47] The frank assessment of the *GEO 5* report was that "globalization allows goods to be produced under circumstances that consumers would refuse to tolerate in their own community, and permits waste to be exported out of sight, enabling people to ignore both its magnitude and its impacts."[48]

The collective tragedy is that the evidence suggests that hyper-consumption, fueled by fossil fuel combustion and unsustainable resource extraction, is not even improving our own well-being—quite the opposite. While GDP in the US has tripled since 1950, measures of happiness have remained essentially unchanged.[49] In general, the research finds that at a given point in time, more wealthy people rate their happiness higher, but over time, increased wealth does not make individuals happier. According to the 2020 *World Happiness Report* and the *OECD Better Life Index*, the bottom line is that once the basics of life are taken care of, it is the quality of human relationships that determines happiness and life satisfaction, not material affluence.[50] Upon reflection, most people would acknowledge this to be true, which is why advertisers worldwide spend more than US$500 billion every year to convince us otherwise.[51]

So the lifestyle we sell to our kids and ourselves is making the earth uninhabitable, short-changing most people on the planet and all future generations, without any appreciable improvement in well-being, contentment, or happiness. While this realization is rather overwhelming, there is something small but meaningful that you can do to focus attention on hyper-consumption. Every year on Buy Nothing Day, you can "relax and do nothing for the economy and for yourself—at least for a single day."[52] On the last Friday in November—not coincidentally Black Friday, the annual orgy of consumerism in the US and, more recently, in Canada—take time out to think about how much is enough. Buying absolutely nothing would be a heroic act, but why not experiment? Refuse to even stroll in a shopping mall. Buy only locally grown food—say, within five hundred kilometres—from locally owned businesses (see belocal.org for inspiration). Sell your car and get healthy by walking or biking to work. Subscribe to bike-, scooter-, or car-share services. Talk to friends and neighbours about how to redirect your passion and energy toward life-affirming non-material pursuits.

And take consolation in the words of the late Kenyan Nobel Laureate Wangari Maathai: "There is a huge amount to be done if we are to reach a state of sustainability. Do not despair, do not be weighed down by it. All I ask of you is that you go home and do what you can."[53]

NOTES

1   See, for example, Amy R. Bland et al., "Cooperative Behavior in the Ultimatum Game and Prisoner's Dilemma Depends on Players' Contributions," *Frontiers in Psychology*, 16 June 2017, https://www.frontiersin.org/articles/10.3389/fpsyg.2017.01017/full.

2   Amartya Sen, *The Idea of Justice* (Cambridge, MA: Belknap Press, 2009), vii.

3   Jeff Doherty, "Secondary Suites: Can Calgary Put This Debate to Bed?" *Alberta Views*, 1 April 2016, https://albertaviews.ca/secondary-suites/.

4   Canada Mortgage and Housing Corporation, *Accessory Apartments: Characteristics, Issues and Opportunities,* Research and Development Highlights: Socio-Economic Series No. 3 (Ottawa: CMHC, October 1991).

5   For data on number of people per household, see Statistics Canada, *The Shift to Smaller Households over the Past Century,* Canadian Megatrends, Catalogue no. 11-630-X (Ottawa: Statistics Canada, 2017), https://www150.statcan.gc.ca/n1/en/pub/11-630-x/11-630-x2015008-eng.pdf?st=UY-2ok55. For data on size of homes, see Preet Banerjee, "Our Love Affair with Home Ownership Might Be Doomed," *Globe and Mail*, 18 January 2012, https://www.theglobeandmail.com/real-estate/mortgages-and-rates/our-love-affair-with-home-ownership-might-be-doomed/article4179012/, and Darrin Qualman, "Home Grown: 67 Years of US and Canadian House Size Data," *Darrin Qualman*, 8 May 2018, https://www.darrinqualman.com/house-size/.

6   Canada Mortgage and Housing Corporation, *Ontario Secondary Suite Research Study,* Research Insight (Ottawa: CMHC, May 2017), https://assets.cmhc-schl.gc.ca/sf/project/cmhc/pubsandreports/pdf/69095.pdf?rev=394642f2-9564-489e-8258-2fdc4bdc8446.

7   Pressreader, "Landlord Loopholes: Condo Conversion Rules Too Loose to Protect Renters," *Calgary Herald*, 24 January 2008, https://www.pressreader.com/canada/calgary-herald/20080124/281736970133548.

8   Susan Ruttan, "A Home for the Homeless," *Alberta Views*, 1 January 2011, https://albertaviews.ca/a-home-for-the-homeless/.

9   City of Calgary, *Foundations for Home: Calgary's Corporate Affordable Housing Strategy 2016–2025* (Calgary: City of Calgary, 2016), https://www.calgary.ca/cs/olsh/affordable-housing/affordable-housing.html. For more research on affordable housing, see City of Calgary, *Housing in Calgary: An Inventory of Housing Supply, 2015–2016* (Calgary: City of Calgary, Affordable Housing Division), accessed 14 November 2020, https://www.calgary.ca/cs/olsh/affordable-housing/learning-about-affordable-housing.html.

10   Murtaza Haider and Stephen Moranis, "Renters in Canada Are Three Times More Likely to Be in Need of Adequate Housing Than Owners," *Financial Post,* 13 October 2020, https://financialpost.com/real-estate/renters-in-canada-are-three-times-more-likely-to-be-in-need-of-adequate-housing-than-owners.

11   Richard Harris and Kathleen Kinsella, "Secondary Suites: A Survey of Evidence and Municipal Policy," *Canadian Geographer* 61, no. 4 (2017): 493–509.

12   Pernille Goodbrand, Tamara Humphreys, and Jyoti Gondek, "Relatives or Rentals? Secondary Suites through a Multi-Generational Family Lens," *Canadian Geographer* 61, no. 4 (2017): 525–39.

13   Kylee van der Poorten and Byron Miller, "Secondary Suites, Second-Class Citizens: The History and Geography of Calgary's Most Controversial Housing Policy," *Canadian Geographer* 61, no. 4 (2017): 564–78.

14   City of Kamloops, *Residential Suites Policy Update: Community Engagement Summary Report* (Kamloops, BC: City of Kamloops, March 2019), https://letstalk.kamloops.ca/7728/documents/15030.

15   Canada Mortgage and Housing Corporation, *The Secondary Rental Market in Canada: Estimated Size and Composition,* 2011 Census/National Household Survey Housing Series: Issue 11 (Ottawa: CMHC, April 2016), https://assets.cmhc-schl.gc.ca/sf/project/cmhc/pubsandreports/pdf/68565.pdf?rev=960c40f1-b6d7-4cf0-ae6a-a832159ee503.

16   "Secondary Suites (Completed Permits)," *City of Edmonton,* accessed 7 September 2020, https://data.edmonton.ca/Sustainable-Development/Secondary-Suites-Completed-Permits-/q3qs-7g3d.

17   "Registered Secondary Suites," *City of Calgary,* accessed 7 September 2020, https://secondarysuites.calgary.ca.

18   "Calgary's 10 Year Plan to End Homelessness 2008–2018," *Homeless Hub,* 2019, https://www.homelesshub.ca/resource/calgary's-10-year-plan-end-homelessness-2008-2018; Calgary Homeless Foundation, *10 Year Plan to End Homelessness: 2008–2018,* January 2011 Update (Calgary: CHF, 2011), 25, https://aventa.org/wp-content/uploads/2017/02/10-Year-Plan-Update.pdf.

19   Calgary Homeless Foundation, *10 Year Plan to End Homelessness.*

20   Trevor Scott Howell, "Update: Business Throw Backing behind Secondary Suites," *Calgary Herald,* 13 December 2014.

21 Zinc Research, *Calgary Secondary Suites Survey* (Calgary: Students Union, University of Calgary, 3 March 2011), https://www.yumpu.com/en/document/read/26865862/report-for-press-release-secondary-suites-students-union-.

22 Aaron Bombeck et al., *Laneway Housing in Calgary: A GIS Methodology for Site Suitability* (Calgary: University of Calgary, Faculty of Environmental Design, December 2016).

23 Center for Neighborhood Technology, *Penny Wise Pound Fuelish: New Measures of Housing and Transportation Affordability* (Chicago: CNT, 2010), https://www.cnt.org/sites/default/files/publications/CNT_pwpf.pdf.

24 "Housing + Transportation Index," *Center for Neighborhood Technology*, accessed 29 November 2020, https://htaindex.cnt.org.

25 Sophia Becker, Scott Bernstein, and Linda Young, *The New Real Estate Mantra: Location Near Public Transportation* (Chicago: Center for Neighborhood Technology, 2013), https://www.cnt.org/sites/default/files/publications/CNT_TheNewRealEstateMantra.pdf.

26 Noel Keough, *Action Research on Transportation Housing Affordability: Final Report to Canada Mortgage and Housing Corporation*, CR File No. 6585-K090 (Ottawa: CMHC, June 2011), https://static1.squarespace.com/static/5ab716b9ee1759b04ca2703e/t/5ee0063c22b445748442fe51/1591739967822/Housing%2BTransport+Affordable+Living+-+FinalReport.pdf.

27 "Survey of Household Spending, 2014," *Statistics Canada,* last modified 2017, https://www150.statcan.gc.ca/n1/daily-quotidien/160212/dq160212a-eng.htm.

28 Keough, *Action Research,* 7.

29 For the calculation of 32 percent, see Keough, *Action Research,* 9–10.

30 City of Calgary, "Walkable and Transit Friendly Communities in Calgary," *Mobility Monitor,* May 2011, 3, https://www.calgary.ca/transportation/tp/planning/transportation-data/transportation-monitoring-reports.html.

31 Jason Ponto, "Cycling through Intersections: Regimes of Velomobility in Calgary andAmsterdam" (PhD diss., University of Calgary, 2017), http://hdl.handle.net/11023/3760.

32 Bryan Jaskolka, "What Is a Location Efficient Mortgage?" *Canadian Mortgages Inc.*, 29 April 2013, https://canadianmortgagesinc.ca/2013/04/what-is-a-location-efficient-mortgage.html.

33 "Foreign Born Population %," *World Cities Culture Forum*, accessed 7 September 2020, http://www.worldcitiescultureforum.com/data/foreign-born-population.

34 "NHS Focus on Geography Series, 2016 Census," *Statistics Canada*, modified 18 July 2019, https://www12.statcan.gc.ca/census-recensement/2016/as-sa/fogs-spg/Facts-cma-eng.cfm?LANG=Eng&GK=CMA&GC=825&TOPIC=7; "Calgary Facts: Who Is a Calgarian?" *Life in Calgary*, accessed 27 November 2020, https://www.lifeincalgary.ca/moving/calgary-facts#demographics.

35   "Data Tables, 2016 Census," *Statistics Canada,* last modified 2019, https://www12.stat-can.gc.ca/census-recensement/2016/dp-pd/dt-td/Rp-eng.cfm?TABID=2&Lang=E&AP-ATH=3&DETAIL=0&DIM=0&FL=A&FREE=0&GC=0&GID=1341679&GK=0&GRP=1&PID=110531&PRID=10&PTYPE=109445&S=0&SHOWALL=0&SUB=0&Tempo-ral=2017&THEME=120&VID=0&VNAMEE=&VNAMEF=&D1=0&D2=0&D3=0&D4=0&D5=0&D6=0.

36   "Monthly Ranking of Women in National Parliaments," *Interparliamentary Union Parline,* 2020, https://data.ipu.org/women-ranking?month=8&year=2020.

37   Andrew MacDougall and John Valley, *2019 Diversity Disclosure Practices: Women in Leadership Roles at TSX-Listed Companies* (Toronto: Osler, Hoskin and Harcourt, 2019), https://www.osler.com/osler/media/Osler/reports/corporate-governance/2019-Diversity-Disclosure-Practices-Women-in-leadership-roles-at-TSX-listed-companies.pdf.

38   Irene Herremans and Jing Lu, "Board Gender Diversity and Environmental Performance: An Industries Perspective," *Business Strategy and the Environment* 28, no. 7 (2019): 1449–64.

39   Nancy Averill, *Diversity Matters: Changing the Face of Public Boards* (Toronto: Maytree Foundation, 2009).

40   James Surowiecki, *The Wisdom of Crowds* (New York: Anchor Books, 2005).

41   "Country Overshoot Days," *Earth Overshoot Day,* 2020, https://www.overshootday.org/newsroom/country-overshoot-days/.

42   DARA and Climate Vulnerable Forum, *A Guide to the Cold Calculus of a Hot Planet,* Climate Vulnerability Monitor, 2nd ed. (Madrid: Fundación DARA Internacional, 2012), 9, https://daraint.org/wp-content/uploads/2012/09/CVM2ndEd-FrontMatter.pdf.

43   DARA and Climate Vulnerable Forum, *Guide to the Cold Calculus of a Hot Planet,* 17–18.

44   Haines, Andy, and Kristie Ebi, "The Imperative for Climate Action to Protect Health," *New England Journal of Medicine* 380 (2019): 263–73.

45   DARA and Climate Vulnerable Forum, *Guide to the Cold Calculus of a Hot Planet,* 8.

46   UN Environment, *Global Environment Outlook 5: Environment for the Future We Want* (Nairobi: United Nations Environment Programme, 2012), https://wedocs.unep.org/bitstream/handle/20.500.11822/8021/GEO5_report_full_en.pdf?sequence=5&isAllowed=y.

47   UN Environment, *GEO-6 Key Messages* (Nairobi: UN Environment Programme, 2019), https://wedocs.unep.org/bitstream/handle/20.500.11822/28774/GEO6_keymessages_EN.pdf?sequence=1&isAllowed=y.

48   UN Environment, *Global Environment Outlook 5,* xviii.

49   Mark Anielski, *The Economics of Happiness: Building Genuine Wealth* (Gabriola Island, BC: New Society, 2007), 225.

50   John Helliwell et al., eds., *World Happiness Report 2020* (New York: Sustainable Development Solutions Network, 2020), https://happiness-report.s3.amazonaws.com/2020/WHR20.pdf; "OECD Better Life Index," *Organisation for Economic Co-operation and Development*, accessed 4 September 2020, http://www.oecdbetterlifeindex.org/#/11111111111.

51   "Global Advertising Revenue from 2012–2024," *Statista*, accessed 29 November 2020, https://www.statista.com/statistics/236943/global-advertising-spending/.

52   Meredith MacLeod, "Made-in-Canada Buy Nothing Day Takes Aim at Black Friday Consumer Excess," *CTV News*, 29 November 2019, https://www.ctvnews.ca/canada/made-in-canada-buy-nothing-day-takes-aim-at-black-friday-consumer-excess-1.4708081.

53   Quoted in UN Environment, *The GEO-5 Process: End Matter* (Nairobi: United Nations Environment Programme, 2012), https://issuu.com/christinadianparmionova/docs/geo5_endmatter.

Further Reading

Condon, Patrick. "Portland Just Showed Vancouver How to Fix Its Housing Crisis." *The Tyee*, 28 August 2020. https://thetyee.ca/Analysis/2020/08/28/Portland-Showed-Vancouver-Fix-Housing-Crisis/?fbclid=IwAR07mvtiPUA3B9oAQROtswmBhVUY2tlxWzG6a1Q-1SJaTVewPNGcUoZVkXc.

Dietz, Rob, and Dan O'Neill. *Enough Is Enough: Building a Sustainable Economy in a World of Finite Resources*. San Francisco: Brett-Koehler, 2013.

Lees, Loretta, Tom Slater, and Elvin Wyly. *Gentrification*. London: Routledge, 2007.

Shell, Ellen Ruppel. *Cheap: The High Cost of Discount Culture*. New York: Penguin, 2009.

Works Cited

Anielski, Mark. *The Economics of Happiness: Building Genuine Wealth*. Gabriola Island, BC: New Society, 2007.

Averill, Nancy. *Diversity Matters: Changing the Face of Public Boards*. Toronto: Maytree Foundation, 2009.

Banerjee, Preet. "Our Love Affair with Home Ownership Might Be Doomed." *Globe and Mail*, 18 January 2012. https://www.theglobeandmail.com/real-estate/mortgages-and-rates/our-love-affair-with-home-ownership-might-be-doomed/article4179012/.

Becker, Sophia, Scott Bernstein, and Linda Young. *The New Real Estate Mantra: Location Near Public Transportation*. Chicago: Center for Neighborhood Technology, 2013. https://www.cnt.org/sites/default/files/publications/CNT_TheNewRealEstateMantra.pdf.

Bland, Amy R., Jonathan P. Rosier, Mitul A. Mehta, Thea Schei, Barbara J. Sahakian, Trevor W. Robbins, and Rebecca Elliott. "Cooperative Behavior in the Ultimatum Game and Prisoner's Dilemma Depends on Players' Contributions." *Frontiers in Psychology*, 16 June 2017. https://www.frontiersin.org/articles/10.3389/fpsyg.2017.01017/full.

Bombeck, Aaron, Pat Dudar, Erica Hansen, Sarah Christensen, and Oghentega Odogu. *Laneway Housing in Calgary: A GIS Methodology for Site Suitability*. Calgary: University of Calgary, Faculty of Environmental Design, December 2016.

"Calgary Facts: Who Is a Calgarian?" *Life in Calgary*. Accessed 27 November 2020. https://www.lifeincalgary.ca/moving/calgary-facts#demographics.

Calgary Homeless Foundation. *10 Year Plan to End Homelessness: 2008–2018*. January 2011 Update. Calgary: CHF, 2011. https://aventa.org/wp-content/uploads/2017/02/10-Year-Plan-Update.pdf.

Canada Mortgage and Housing Corporation. *Accessory Apartments: Characteristics, Issues and Opportunities*. Research and Development Highlights: Socio-Economic Series No. 3. Ottawa: CMHC, October 1991.

———. *Ontario Secondary Suite Research Study*. Research Insight. Ottawa: CMHC, May 2017. https://assets.cmhc-schl.gc.ca/sf/project/cmhc/pubsandreports/pdf/69095.pdf?rev=394642f2-9564-489e-8258-2fdc4bdc8446.

———. *The Secondary Rental Market in Canada: Estimated Size and Composition*. 2011 Census/National Household Survey Housing Series: Issue 11. Ottawa: CMHC, April 2016. https://assets.cmhc-schl.gc.ca/sf/project/cmhc/pubsandreports/pdf/68565.pdf?rev=960c40f1-b6d7-4cf0-ae6a-a832159ee503.

Center for Neighborhood Technology. *Penny Wise Pound Fuelish: New Measures of Housing and Transportation Affordability*. Chicago: CNT, 2010. https://www.cnt.org/sites/default/files/publications/CNT_pwpf.pdf.

City of Calgary. *Foundations for Home: Calgary's Corporate Affordable Housing Strategy 2016–2025*. Calgary: City of Calgary, 2016. https://www.calgary.ca/cs/olsh/affordable-housing/affordable-housing.html.

———. *Housing in Calgary: An Inventory of Housing Supply, 2015–2016*. Calgary: City of Calgary, Affordable Housing Division. Accessed 14 November 2020. https://www.calgary.ca/cs/olsh/affordable-housing/learning-about-affordable-housing.html.

———. "Walkable and Transit Friendly Communities in Calgary." *Mobility Monitor*, May 2011. https://www.calgary.ca/transportation/tp/planning/transportation-data/transportation-monitoring-reports.html.

City of Kamloops. *Residential Suites Policy Update: Community Engagement Summary Report*. Kamloops, BC: City of Kamloops, March 2019. https://letstalk.kamloops.ca/7728/documents/15030.

"Country Overshoot Days." *Earth Overshoot Day*, 2020. https://www.overshootday.org/newsroom/country-overshoot-days/.

DARA and Climate Vulnerable Forum. *A Guide to the Cold Calculus of a Hot Planet.* Climate Vulnerability Monitor, 2nd ed. Madrid: Fundación DARA Internacional, 2012. https://daraint.org/wp-content/uploads/2012/09/CVM2ndEd-FrontMatter. pdf.

"Data Tables, 2016 Census." *Statistics Canada,* last modified 2019. https://www12.statcan. gc.ca/census-recensement/2016/dp-pd/dt-td/Rp-eng.cfm?TABID=2&Lang=E&AP-ATH=3&DETAIL=0&DIM=0&FL=A&FREE=0&GC=0&GID=1341679&GK=0 &GRP=1&PID=110531&PRID=10&PTYPE=109445&S=0&SHOWALL=0&SUB- =0&Temporal=2017&THEME=120&VID=0&VNAMEE=&VNAMEF=&D1=0&D 2=0&D3=0&D4=0&D5=0&D6=0.

Doherty, Jeff. "Secondary Suites: Can Calgary Put This Debate to Bed?" *Alberta Views,* 1 April 2016. https://albertaviews.ca/secondary-suites/.

"Foreign Born Population %." *World Cities Culture Forum.* Accessed 7 September 2020. http://www.worldcitiescultureforum.com/data/foreign-born-population.

"Global Advertising Revenue from 2012–2024." *Statista.* Accessed 29 November 2020. https://www.statista.com/statistics/236943/global-advertising-spending/.

Goodbrand, Pernille, Tamara Humphreys, and Jyoti Gondek. "Relatives or Rentals? Secondary Suites through a Multi-Generational Family Lens." *Canadian Geographer* 61, no. 4 (2017): 525–39.

Haider, Murtaza, and Stephen Moranis. "Renters in Canada Are Three Times More Likely to Be in Need of Adequate Housing Than Owners." *Financial Post,* 13 October 2020. https://financialpost.com/real-estate/renters-in-canada-are-three-times-more-likely-to-be-in-need-of-adequate-housing-than-owners.

Haines, Andy, and Kristie Ebi. "The Imperative for Climate Action to Protect Health." *New England Journal of Medicine* 380 (2019): 263–73.

Harris, Richard, and Kathleen Kinsella. "Secondary Suites: A Survey of Evidence and Municipal Policy." *Canadian Geographer* 61, no. 4 (2017): 493–509.

Helliwell, John, Richard Layard, Jeffrey D. Sachs, and Jan Emmanuel De Neve, eds. *World Happiness Report 2020.* New York: Sustainable Development Solutions Network, 2020. https://happiness-report.s3.amazonaws.com/2020/WHR20.pdf.

Herremans, Irene, and Jing Lu. "Board Gender Diversity and Environmental Performance: An Industries Perspective." *Business Strategy and the Environment* 28, no. 7 (2019): 1449–64.

"Housing + Transportation Index." *Center for Neighborhood Technology.* Accessed 29 November 2020. https://htaindex.cnt.org.

Howell, Trevor Scott. "Update: Business Throw Backing behind Secondary Suites." *Calgary Herald,* 13 December 2014.

Jaskolka, Bryan. "What Is a Location Efficient Mortgage?" *Canadian Mortgages Inc.,* 29 April 2013. https://canadianmortgagesinc.ca/2013/04/what-is-a-location-efficient-mortgage.html.

Keough, Noel. *Action Research on Transportation Housing Affordability: Final Report to Canada Mortgage and Housing Corporation*. CR File No. 6585-K090. Ottawa: CMHC, 2011. https://static1.squarespace.com/static/5ab716b9ee1759b04ca2703e/t/5ee0063c22b445748442fe51/1591739967822/Housing%2BTransport+Affordable+Living+-+FinalReport.pdf.

MacDougall, Andrew, and John Valley. *2019 Diversity Disclosure Practices: Women in Leadership Roles at TSX-Listed Companies*. Toronto: Osler, Hoskin and Harcourt, 2019. https://www.osler.com/osler/media/Osler/reports/corporate-governance/2019-Diversity-Disclosure-Practices-Women-in-leadership-roles-at-TSX-listed-companies.pdf.

MacLeod, Meredith. "Made-in-Canada Buy Nothing Day Takes Aim at Black Friday Consumer Excess." *CTV News*, 29 November 2019. https://www.ctvnews.ca/canada/made-in-canada-buy-nothing-day-takes-aim-at-black-friday-consumer-excess-1.4708081.

"Monthly Ranking of Women in National Parliaments." *Interparliamentary Union Parline*, 2020. https://data.ipu.org/women-ranking?month=8&year=2020.

"NHS Focus on Geography Series, 2016 Census." *Statistics Canada*, modified 18 July 2019. https://www12.statcan.gc.ca/census-recensement/2016/as-sa/fogs-spg/Facts-cma-eng.cfm?LANG=Eng&GK=CMA&GC=825&TOPIC=7.

"OECD Better Life Index." *Organisation for Economic Co-operation and Development*. Accessed 4 September 2020. http://www.oecdbetterlifeindex.org/#/11111111111.

Ponto, Jason. "Cycling through Intersections: Regimes of Velomobility in Calgary and Amsterdam." PhD diss., University of Calgary, 2017. http://hdl.handle.net/11023/3760.

Pressreader. "Landlord Loopholes: Condo Conversion Rules Too Loose to Protect Renters." *Calgary Herald*, 24 January 2008. https://www.pressreader.com/canada/calgary-herald/20080124/281736970133548.

Qualman, Darrin. "Home Grown: 67 Years of US and Canadian House Size Data." *Darrin Qualman*, 8 May 2018. https://www.darrinqualman.com/house-size/.

"Registered Secondary Suites." *City of Calgary*. Accessed 7 September 2020. https://secondarysuites.calgary.ca.

Ruttan, Susan. "A Home for the Homeless." *Alberta Views*, 1 January 2011. https://albertaviews.ca/a-home-for-the-homeless/.

"Secondary Suites (Completed Permits)." *City of Edmonton*. Accessed 7 September 2020. https://data.edmonton.ca/Sustainable-Development/Secondary-Suites-Completed-Permits-/q3qs-7g3d.

Sen, Amartya. *The Idea of Justice*. Cambridge, MA: Belknap Press, 2009.

Statistics Canada. *The Shift to Smaller Households over the Past Century*. Canadian Megatrends. Catalogue no. 11-630-X. Ottawa: Statistics Canada, 2017. https://www150.statcan.gc.ca/n1/en/pub/11-630-x/11-630-x2015008-eng.pdf?st=UY-2ok55.

Surowiecki, James. *The Wisdom of Crowds*. New York: Anchor Books, 2005.

"Survey of Household Spending, 2014." *Statistics Canada,* last modified 2017. https://www150.statcan.gc.ca/n1/daily-quotidien/160212/dq160212a-eng.htm.

UN Environment. *The GEO-5 Process: End Matter*. Nairobi: UN Environment Programme, 2012. https://issuu.com/christinadianparmionova/docs/geo5_endmatter.

———. *GEO-6 Key Messages*. Nairobi: UN Environment Programme, 2019. https://wedocs.unep.org/bitstream/handle/20.500.11822/28774/GEO6_keymessages_EN.pdf?sequence=1&isAllowed=y.

———. *Global Environmental Outlook 5: Environment for the Future We Want*. Nairobi: UN Environment Programme, 2012. https://sustainabledevelopment.un.org/index.php?page=view&type=400&nr=546&menu=35.

Van der Poorten, Kylee, and Byron Miller. "Secondary Suites, Second-Class Citizens: The History and Geography of Calgary's Most Controversial Housing Policy." *Canadian Geographer* 61, no. 4 (2017): 564–78.

Zinc Research. *Calgary Secondary Suites Survey*. Calgary: Students Union, University of Calgary, 3 March 2011. https://www.yumpu.com/en/document/read/26865862/report-for-press-release-secondary-suites-students-union-.

Governance: The Sine Qua Non of Sustainability

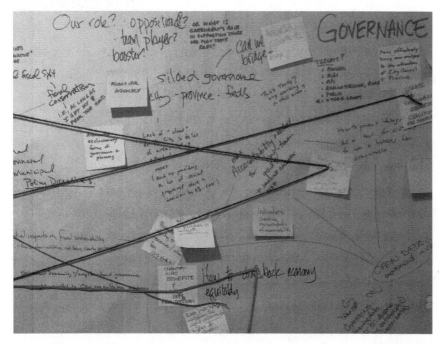

Governance is nothing more than how we organize society and how we make decisions. Good governance is about transparency, efficiency, effectiveness, meaningful participation, and, perhaps most importantly, fairness in *all* of our institutions—voluntary organizations, the media, the private sector, and the public sector.

In this chapter, we examine the notion of good governance with examples drawn from practical and philosophical debates at municipal, provincial, federal, and global scales. The opening essay reflects on social capital, trust, and basic knowledge of our rights and responsibilities as citizens—the lubricants of our democratic system. We present a summary of the five proposals for improved governance put forward by Sustainable Calgary.

In "Democracy on the Ropes," we look at the corrosive influence of money and corporate power in politics. Who pays for election campaigns? Who gets access to our political decision-makers? What are the implications of these questions of funding and access for our participation in elections and the level of trust in our systems of governance?

Can we learn from other places? Of course we can. In "The Gift That Keeps On Giving," we turn our attention to the Nordic countries. It turns out that these countries combine high levels of trust, economic equality, and social stability with highly competitive, sustainable, and innovative economies. The secret ingredient might just be good governance.

Other essays place the issue of governance at the heart of real-life decisions about whether and how cities and our province should grow and who bears the costs of growth. We make the case that the public good and private profit maximization are at odds with each other, and that strong governance must deliver good public policy for the common good. In "Silent Spring 2012," we discuss global governance and the implications for a sustainable future. In 1992, at the Rio Earth Summit, the world's governments agreed to make sustainability a priority. We discuss why we, as a global community, have faltered in honouring that commitment and what the implications are of the failure to do so.

BEYOND THE LAW OF THE JUNGLE: GOOD IDEAS FOR GOOD GOVERNANCE

Think about all the decisions that each of us must make when choosing among insurance, energy, cable, and phone companies and their plans. The game seems to be that if a company can pull the wool over your eyes, rip you off, or in any other way extract extra cash from your pocket—good for them, and too bad you were so gullible and naïve.

There is a variation on this theme in public life. We elect politicians who assure us of their honesty and their desire to serve us, their constituents, but we know that they must be watched diligently and are usually not to be trusted. If they do bad things—well, we elected them. While there may be a grain of truth in the statement that we get the government we deserve, accepting this simplistic notion feeds a pervasive and corrosive sentiment—a competitive, every man-for-himself, trust-nobody ethos that permeates our lives, both public and private.

Do we really want to live our lives that way, in a society where we have to be hyper-vigilant and where the less capable are at the mercy of snake oil salesmen and shell-game con artists? The capitalist modus operandi of self-interest above all else has infiltrated our lives to a very unhealthy degree, and we let politicians and salespeople off too easy when we acquiesce to this state of affairs. Businesses seem intent on creating not a menu of choices but a minefield of options designed to separate people from their hard-earned money. Grocery stores lure us in with bargains but place items with jacked-up prices at the checkouts. Mortgage insurance agreements fill pages with finely printed caveats to avoid paying out when hardship strikes.

Political parties game the system too. They master the strategy of boutique tax breaks and legislation whose sole aim is to gain the vote of some narrow but valuable constituency. Attack ads have become part of doing politics. Never mind debate on ideas—just rip your opponent's reputation to shreds with lies, innuendo, half-truths, and distortions. Even the line between legal and illegal gets not so delicately straddled with robocall tactics.[1] Government scientists and parliamentary auditors get muzzled when the truth is inconvenient.[2]

"It's just human nature," people often say. But this is not our nature: it is a behaviour that has been nurtured by a particular style of governance. So if we reject the law of the jungle, then how should we govern ourselves? In a 2014 workshop hosted by Sustainable Calgary, a group of citizens gave up a Saturday and took on the question of good governance and how we might measure it, and they actually seemed to have a lot of fun doing it. They came up with five good ideas for better governance.

1. *Improve the quality of electoral democracy.* Because many of us do not bother to vote, the outcomes of voting are seldom representative of popular sentiment. We are all familiar with dismal voter turnouts, but many people are discouraged by our

first-past-the-post system, by which a minority of votes typically results in a majority government, or we send a representative to Ottawa with the consent of as little as 10 percent of eligible voters, as happened in the 2014 Calgary Centre byelection.

2. *Provide the resources government needs to do what it does best.* Though it seems the Canadian Taxpayers Federation has never seen a problem a tax cut could not solve, a more pragmatic and effective approach would be to ensure that all levels of government get sufficient funds to carry out their responsibilities and that they distribute the resources we entrust them with in an equitable manner.

3. *Ensure that governance—whether in the public, private, or not-for-profit sector—is independent, transparent, and accountable.* Elections should not be won and lost based on who attracts the most money from anonymous economic interests promoting agendas. If organizations lobby governments, we should know who pays the bills for their activities. We should have access to records of the meetings between our elected representatives and those lobbyists. How our representatives vote should be made public. How and why decisions were taken should be more transparent and not locked in so-called cabinet confidence.

4. *Ensure that government prioritizes educating citizens about how government works.* Citizens should be given the opportunity for meaningful participation in the decisions that affect their lives beyond the important but limited act of voting. After all we are a democracy—which means "government by the people."

5. *Evaluate and report on the government's effectiveness.* Government strategies, policies, and plans should not be derailed by professional incompetence, short-term political manoeuvres, or interference from powerful economic interests.

It is not too much to expect honesty from our politicians. Nor should it be too much to expect businesspeople to deal ethically and in good faith.

Next time a sitting or aspiring politician comes looking for your vote, ask them what they will do to support these five pillars of good governance.

THE GIFT THAT KEEPS ON GIVING: LESSONS IN GOVERNANCE FROM THE NORDIC LIGHTS

Over the past decade, we have been exposed to a steady stream of issues related to governance—and election processes, in particular—that signals a crisis of governance, both in Calgary and more generally across the landscape of democracies the world over. Mayor Nenshi has been praised for his advocacy of stricter fundraising guidelines in municipal politics, and indeed, the rules were tightened up by the Notley government.[3] But fifteen months into the term of the Kenney government, we see the rules under the Elections Act being dismantled to allow money more influence in our electoral system.[4] A cloud hangs over the 2019 election of Premier Kenney, with allegations of illegal funding of party leadership campaigns under investigation. South of the border, democracy seems to be under siege on several fronts.

Governance is nothing more than how we organize ourselves and how we make decisions. What happens when good governance—transparent, efficient, and fair—goes bad? When promises are broken and secret deals are made? Citizens, having become cynical about our leaders and our institutions, don't bother to vote. People retreat from civic life and become more individualistic—if nobody is looking out for me, then I won't bother looking out for anyone else. We waste money on litigation and tie ourselves in legal knots rather than reap the abundant harvests borne of nurturing seeds of trust and reciprocity. The gun ownership nightmare in the US is an extreme outcome of the erosion of trust.

Still, there are good news stories. In Calgary, we have tended to look south for our inspiration, but what do the Nordic countries have to offer when it comes to good governance? A lot, it turns out. In 2009 the Organisation for Economic Co-operation and Development began reporting on a set of sustainable governance indicators (SGIs) for forty-one countries. To construct the SGI index, they asked questions like the following: Do tax policies realize the goals of equity, competitiveness, and the generation of sufficient public revenues? Are the media independent, and do they express a diversity of opinions? Is corruption prevented? Does government implement policy effectively?[5]

The SGI index includes thirty-three different measures, including electoral process, rule of law, civil rights, and economy. The Policy Performance sub-index uses sixteen measures to evaluate the capacity of government to formulate, coordinate, and implement economic, social, and environmental policy.[6] In 2020 Sweden, Finland, Norway, and Denmark took the top four spots in the Quality of Democracy sub-index and spots 2, 2, 6 and 1, respectively, in the Governance sub-index. Canada ranked eleventh in Quality of Democracy and seventh in Governance.[7]

In its special feature of January 2013, the free market standard-bearer *The Economist* asked, What's up with Nordic countries?[8] They found that these socialist nirvanas outperform most others in surprising categories. Most people are familiar with the notion that Nordic countries have more egalitarian societies, are quite liberal socially, and champion international justice. What people are less aware of is that in the midst of Europe's 2008–13 economic meltdown, Nordic countries were bastions of stability. They are also among the most competitive, transparent, fair-dealing, innovative, and creative countries in the world. *The Economist* calls them a "hothouse of entrepreneurship," one funky example being the wildly successful initiative at Helsinki's Aalto University called the Startup Sauna, a meeting place designed to support student-run startups and young entrepreneurs.[9]

Nordic countries seem to show a remarkably pragmatic approach to trying new approaches to public service delivery, from schools to health care. No doubt the openness to change and experimentation comes from high levels of that most precious and stable of currencies—trust.

Ultimately, good governance is a means to improved well-being. And as we see in Nordic countries, that's exactly where good governance leads. These countries are perennially at the top of the United Nations Development Programme's Human Development Index—Norway (1), Iceland (6), Sweden (8), Denmark (11), and Finland (12) all ranked above Canada (13).[10] In 2015 Nordic countries (Finland, Norway, Denmark, and Sweden) all ranked above Canada in the Gini Index of income equality.[11] The kicker is that—as Richard Wilkinson and Kate Pickett argue rigorously in their acclaimed 2010 bestseller, *The Spirit Level*—the most important factor in well-being is, in fact, equality.[12] The special focus on Nordic countries in the *2020 World Happiness Report* is consistent with this finding.[13]

Why are these countries more equal? How do they weather the foul economic winds sweeping across Europe? And how did this relatively small population huddled in the north of Europe manage to become leaders in innovation and creativity? The answer is that good governance—carefully constructed, nurtured, and sustained—gives birth to highly egalitarian, trusting, innovative, and economically successful societies. You might say it's the gift that keeps on giving.

Of particular relevance to Calgarians, the crowning achievement of all that good governance and its accoutrements is having some of the most sustainable cities in the world—Helsinki in Finland, Copenhagen in Denmark, and Stockholm and Malmo in Sweden.

As citizens of this great city, we have regular opportunities to engage in this conversation about good governance, a topic that is often considered mundane. It is a notion that will, we hope, continue to figure prominently in the campaigns of candidates, new and incumbent, across the political spectrum and at all levels of government. It is, in truth, far from mundane or of little consequence. There is nothing more central to the sustainability of our city and the future well-being of our children than good governance. As the celebrated 1970s ParticipAction campaign urged—just ask the average sixty-year-old Swede.[14]

SACRED TRUST: WITHOUT IT, WE'RE LOST

As we entered the 2020s, there was a lot of hand-wringing at Calgary's City Hall. In December 2019, the top civil servant, David Duckworth, was defending city spending in the face of calls by some councilors that spending was out of control and trust in government was broken.[15] In the early weeks of 2020, there were calls for resignation as another councilor was under siege for "misreporting" on expense claims.[16] Not to be outdone, the provincial government was under fire from multiple fronts, charged with having broken trust with teachers, people dependent on disability benefits, health care workers, and municipal governments.[17]

In this age of fake news, increasingly polarized political debate, the weaponization of social media, and an increasingly complex public discourse blending economics, politics, and science, trust has become a hot commodity. Many commentators have noted that in this political environment, most people are unable to discern the finer points of debate and default to a simple question—Who do I trust? Especially in leadership contests, pundits like to debate whether aspirants to political office are "trustworthy." But trustworthiness is not a characteristic like hair colour; trust has to be earned through deeds. Trust building is a long-term project, but trust breaking can happen in an instant.

It is therefore concerning to see the many signs of eroding trust across most institutions of governance at all political scales. We see evidence of this trend in a Statistics Canada census survey on confidence in Canadian institutions, in the City of Calgary's annual Citizen Satisfaction Surveys, and in the 2017 OECD report *Trust and Public Policy.*

In 2013, according to the Statistics Canada General Social Survey, only 43 percent of Calgarians had some or a great deal of confidence in the federal Parliament, and a mere 34 percent had confidence in major corporations. The highest levels of trust were reported for the school system (63%) and the police (81%). Calgarians reported having more confidence in institutions than the average of all cities across Canada, where levels of confidence in police, government, and corporations were 76, 39, and 30 percent, respectively. Levels of confidence in the police in Moncton, Oshawa, Guelph, and Abbotsford-Mission range from 86 percent to 82 percent. Residents of St. John's and Edmonton registered the most confidence in the school system (both at 66%). Only Toronto (45%) outperformed Calgary for confidence in Parliament. Hamiltonians reported the most confidence in corporations (38%), followed by Winnipeg and St. John's (36%). Victorians had the lowest confidence in corporations (26%), and Halifax had the lowest in Parliament (27%).[18]

These data highlight some serious problems when we examine how few people expressed "a great deal of confidence." Only 9 percent of Canadians had a great deal of confidence in the media, only 10 percent said that of Parliament, and only 6 percent expressed this about major corporations.[19] These findings have serious implications for our democracy and our economy—even more so since we have entered a period when some leaders seem to have decided that lying and deception are winning strategies. The combination of ownership concentration of social media, technological innovation, and polarization in society has undermined our willingness to trust our institutions and those who represent them.

When asked whether the City of Calgary practices open and accessible government, is working to improve citizens' input, and uses their input in decision-making, and whether citizens have meaningful input, roughly 60 to 80 percent of Calgarians said yes. But in all areas surveyed in the Citizen Satisfaction Surveys, the trend is negative, with the downward trend being most pronounced with respect to open and accessible government. Those who expressed trust in City Hall fell from 62 percent in 2017 to 52 percent in 2019, to 48 percent in fall 2020. Levels of distrust rose from 15 percent in 2017 to 21 percent in 2020.[20]

The 2017 OECD report *Trust and Public Policy* highlights a noticeable reduction in trust in government after the 2008 global economic crisis (from 2007 to 2015). The report states that "against a background of perceived inequalities in income and opportunities, high unemployment and job insecurity, resistance to globalisation and concern over global pressures such as migration and climate change, restoring this trust is essential."[21] Notably, Canadians express high levels of trust in comparison to most OECD countries, though Canada still lagged behind the Nordic countries.[22] This may be related to the relatively mild impact of the 2008 crisis on Canada. Canadians, for example, are almost as confident in banks as they are in the school system.[23]

In Canada, unlike most other countries, confidence in institutions was higher among immigrants than those born in Canada and even higher for recent immigrants. But trust is not uniform across demographic boundaries. Women and older Canadians express higher levels of confidence than men and younger Canadians. Aboriginal people are less confident in institutions than other Canadians. Canadians with higher incomes and higher levels of education express higher levels of confidence.[24]

Trust is a valuable and fragile currency that bolsters the social and economic health of a community. Trust builds social cohesion and social capital and is in turn strengthened by social capital. Without trust, information flow and communication are slowed and compromised, and policy reform in areas like fair taxation and climate change is made more difficult. Low levels of trust have economic costs—high transaction costs, higher legal fees, more complicated contracts, slower transactions, risk aversion for investors, and non-compliance with regulations. Low levels of trust translate into low voter turnouts and resistance to change. They also lead to alienation and reluctance to support social welfare programs.[25] Citizens expect institutions to be reliable, responsive, and efficient. They expect them to act with integrity, openness and transparency, and fairness. If institutions fail to deliver on these values, people will withdraw their support, and that is bad for everyone.

In *1984* George Orwell imagined an authoritarian regime with Big Brother obsessed with making sure people did not trust each other.[26] Margaret Atwood, in a 2017 interview in *The New Yorker*, remarked that in the US "you really don't trust your fellow-citizens very much," and her choice to situate the rise and fall of Gilead in the US was perhaps inspired by that observation.[27] Certainly, in the US of 2020, the president has done everything in his power to foment distrust of everything and everyone except himself—a dangerous game. When our leaders toy with trust, they play with fire.

DEMOCRACY ON THE ROPES: MONEY, ACCESS, AND THE PERVERSITY OF FIRST-PAST-THE-POST

In December 2012, Calgary City Council's Legislative Task Force debated rules for reporting gifts to the mayor and Council. We learned that though the mayor apparently has a stash of gifted coffee mugs and socks and has never received anything valued over about $100, he believes rules are required to "avoid the appearance of impropriety" in Council decision-making.[28]

The discussion about gifts and governance might seem rather mundane. But in that same week, Council's debate on a growth management motion initially drafted by the development industry provided a clear example of why good governance is critical to the future of our democracy.[29]

Climate change is another governance issue of municipal, provincial, and federal concern. Though the science and economics of climate change leave no doubt about the urgency of decisive action, and although polls consistently show that Canadians want to see real action, our government has dithered for forty years. The reasons for this are many, but chief among them is the sorry state of our governance. The makeup of Parliament does not represent Canadian opinion when our first-past-the-post system disproportionately awards seats to the dominant party, the fossil fuel industry lobby shapes provincial government policy, shadowy political campaign financing erodes democracy, and too many Canadians have given up on an unrepresentative electoral system.

In the 2012 Calgary Centre byelection, the self-identified "progressives" won over 60 percent of the vote. But with no progressive candidate having a decisive edge, the Conservatives, with 37 percent of a dismal voter turnout of 29.4 percent, won the right to represent Calgary Centre on the strength of the support of only 11 percent of eligible voters.[30] This is not an atypical result. In 2012 the Conservatives held a majority in Parliament, having gamed the system to win 54 percent of parliamentary seats while capturing only 38 percent of votes cast—and a mere 23 percent of eligible voters.[31]

If this were an anomaly, we might chalk it up to bad luck, but this happens regularly in federal and provincial elections. In British Columbia in 1996, the New Democrats actually lost the popular vote yet won a majority in the provincial legislature.[32] Even more incredibly, in New Brunswick in 1987, Frank McKenna's Liberals won 60 percent of the vote—and every seat![33]

In a report funded by the University of Calgary Institute for Advanced Policy Research, our city was found to have one of the most lax election campaign finance regimes in the country.[34] The development industry is a much more prominent campaign financier here than in, for example, Toronto. The lion's share of the industry's dollars go to incumbents, with the result that sitting councilors and mayors are less likely to be challenged and more likely to win than in the more balanced process in Toronto.

The Polaris Institute report *Big Oil's Oily Grasp* raised the veil on yet another governance issue—lobbying. Between 2008 and 2012, the country's largest oil and gas companies and industry associations registered 2,733 communications with federal bureaucrats and politicians. The Canadian Association of Petroleum Producers (CAPP) was responsible for 536 of those communications. Along with the Canadian Energy Pipeline Association, CAPP recorded 78 percent more communications than the two primary Canadian mining industry associations and 367 percent more than the two major automotive industry associations.[35] The report chronicled the extent of the revolving door between senior bureaucracies (including the National Energy Board), industry, Conservative party insiders, and the high-powered lobby groups that support the effort.

This rapid increase in oil and gas industry lobbying coincided with the gutting of the Fisheries Act, the rewriting of over seventy federal laws via Bill C-38, and a major multimedia public relations effort by both government and industry designed to counter increasing opposition to the tar sands. The fallout from all of this? Huge numbers of Canadians have given up on our electoral system. Calgary's municipal voter turnout has oscillated between a dismal 18 percent in 2004 to a barely respectable 58 percent in 2017.[36] Provincially, voting rates of 80+ percent in the 1930s have plummeted to as low as 40 percent in 2008, and they rarely top 60 percent.[37] Federally, in election after election, we struggle to hit the 70 percent mark, with a clear downward trend since the early 1960s.[38]

Governance is really about how we as a society make decisions. Good decision-making requires robust, fair, and transparent processes—and an engaged citizenry!

BOOMS, BUSTS, AND BUDGETS

In a June 2020 column, CBC journalist Drew Anderson asked the unthinkable: Should Calgary plan for contraction? Anderson proposed that "Calgary will either have to find a way to pay for a vision of growth, or to tactically shrink in a way that doesn't bring down the house in the process."[39] Joseph Arvai, professor of sustainable enterprise at Michigan University, had posed a similar dilemma in the *Globe and Mail* in 2013. Arvai wrote, "If the city stays on its current industrial and economic trajectory, Calgary's fate—like that of Detroit before it—will be sealed *when* (not if) a downward shift in demand for current, made-in-Alberta industrial products occurs."[40]

With those simple statements, one of the most enduring tales of our time lies exposed—that economic growth, the prime directive, is synonymous with prosperity and well-being for all. Certainly, almost every institution of our society subscribes to this growth myth, including City Council, the Chamber of Commerce, and Calgary Economic Development. In *The Rise of the Creative Class*, Richard Florida tell us it's all about attracting the best and the brightest, the creatives and investors, because therein lies the recipe for growth.[41]

One often-heard refrain at any hint of anti-growth sentiment focuses on its inevitability: What are you going to do, turn people back at the city gates? Well no, but let's be clear what has fuelled and sustained growth in Calgary. It's oil and gas. We have been the most single-industry–dependent city in Canada and perhaps North America. In 2018 almost 30 percent of our city's GDP and over 70 percent of our province's export earnings were generated from oil and gas.[42] For more than forty years, that industry manufactured jobs at an incredible rate. As many as forty thousand new Calgarians arrived annually to fill those jobs, and even now, with the highest unemployment in the country, Canadians are drawn to the lure of the next big boom.

Conventional wisdom has it that the pace of oil and gas development was dictated by the oil companies, their ability to attract capital investment and market forces as immutable as gravity. But wait a minute—resource management is a provincial responsibility in Canada. Almost all oil and gas development occurs on public land that the provincial government is solely responsible for leasing to industry. *It* is the gatekeeper! Yet in the magical belief that business and shareholder profit maximization is synonymous with the prosperity and well-being of all Albertans, that growth is good and more growth is better, our government signed that responsibility over to industry.

With such fabulous riches, our prosperity and well-being must surely have been off the charts. Not so! Between 2000 and 2014, Calgarians saw housing prices more than triple, homelessness increase almost tenfold, record per capita usage of food banks, a worsening daycare crisis, chronic shortages of hospital beds and classrooms, and the second-lowest minimum wage in the country—not to mention those rising taxes. In the slow-growth years of 2015–19, each of these indicators improved through sound government policy.[43]

Though Calgarians have spoken loudly and clearly against sprawl, when an economy is at full throttle, it is almost impossible for the inner city and other existing communities to absorb the annual pilgrimage of newcomers. The easy option is going for the short-term gain of sprawling car-dependent communities and the inevitable long-term pain of a serious fiscal liability of expensive-to-maintain urban infrastructure for those sprawling communities. In a 2014 interview with the *Calgary Herald*, the city's chief financial officer, Eric Sawyer, pointed out that rapid growth "drives us further into the hole."[44] And in *Better Not Bigger,* community planning consultant Eben Fodor makes a persuasive case for improving our communities by controlling urban sprawl.[45]

So why do we continue to ignore the elephant in the room—uneconomic growth?

American political scientist Clarence Stone coined the term "urban regimes" to describe how influential economic players create informal coalitions with each other and with local governments to spin a tale about the unassailable virtues of growth and shape cities into what sociologist Harvey Molotch called "growth machines."[46] If we imagine Calgary as a growth machine, it is not hard to identify who has their hands on the throttle—large suburban developers, homebuilders, and civil engineering firms. They have grown fabulously rich on the strength of Calgary's suburban sprawl. The end of growth would mean the end of their business model.

As long as personal consumption keeps going up, Calgarians are loath to question the logic of the growth machine. We still boast the highest GDP per capita in Canada, the highest incomes and highest consumer spending in all of Canada, and we are at or near the top of the heap globally.[47] We are arguably the most affluent society in the history of our species. But are we any happier and healthier than other Canadians? Atlantic Canadians have long reported greater levels of happiness than their wealthier neighbours, though there are signs that oil wealth is actually diminishing Newfoundlanders' sense of well-being.[48]

So what is our end game? At 4 percent growth, we will be twice as rich in eighteen years and four times as rich in thirty-six years. Our grandchildren can look ahead to ten thousand-square-foot homes, eight cars in the garage, a flat screen on every wall, a computer in every room—including all twelve bathrooms. Yes, it's absurd.

Perhaps before every year's budget deliberations, Council should convene a city-wide debate, with special invitations to all MLAs and MPs, on how much is enough.

SILENT SPRING 2012: SUSTAINABILITY VISION BETRAYED

Tragedy silently unfolded in Rio de Janeiro in the spring of 2012. Twenty years earlier, at a global summit held in the same Brazilian city, world leaders had agreed that economic justice and environmental stewardship were the twin challenges faced by humanity and that solving them did not have to be at the expense of a healthy economy. At Rio+20, they changed their minds. Economic growth was put back on its pedestal as the gold standard of global policy objectives, effectively abandoning twenty years of progress. Eight years later, in 2020, growth continues to be enshrined in documents like the UN's Sustainable Development Goals.[49]

This about-face came at a time when the diagnosis of the ongoing global crisis pointed toward the need for accelerated action on the sustainability vision first agreed to in Rio de Janeiro. What has been sold as an economic crisis is in fact an ongoing sustainability crisis, with social and ecological dimensions at its core. The social crisis is about the increasing gap between the rich and the rest. Since Rio 1992, the gap has grown to levels not seen since the lead-up to the Great Depression.

In *End This Depression Now*, Nobel economist Paul Krugman writes, "To understand the deeper reasons for our present crisis, in short, we need to talk about income inequality."[50] Krugman argues that inequality fuels bitter partisanship and has resulted in the hijacking of the political process by those with money who never hesitate to spend vast sums of it to get what they want.

Krugman's analysis confirms the ground-breaking research contained in Richard Wilkinson and Kate Pickett's *The Spirit Level: Why Greater Equality Makes Societies Stronger*.[51] Unequal societies suffer from higher rates of obesity, mental illness, and crime, and lower levels of trust, literacy, and social cohesion. Tragically, the lack of trust and social cohesion makes it much harder for societies to act on the economic and ecological crises.

There are many manifestations of the ecological crisis, but it is summed up in *Global Environmental Outlook 6*, released in 2019, where only fifteen of ninety-four environmental indicators were reported as having seen change in a positive direction. A UN press release announcing the report states that "damage to the planet is so dire that people's health will be increasingly threatened unless urgent action is taken." According to the executive director of UN Environment, "We are at a crossroads. Do we continue on our current path, which will lead to a bleak future for humankind, or do we pivot to a more sustainable development pathway? That is the choice our political leaders must make, now."[52]

The year 2012 also marked the twentieth anniversary of the decimation of the North Atlantic cod stock and the subsequent cod fishery moratorium in Newfoundland that threw sixty thousand rural Newfoundlanders out of work.[53] That ecological tragedy is a microcosm of the current global crisis—unsustainable economic growth drawing down the last of the planet's resources, bringing the earth's capacity to renew itself to the breaking point, and wreaking havoc on the economy. As ecological economist Herman Daly points out, we have crossed a threshold—growth is now *uneconomic*.[54]

Meanwhile, world leaders remain myopically fixated on growth. With growth flagging in 2012, the European Central Bank, the Bank of England, and the People's Bank of China took coordinated action to boost it.[55] Yet there was barely a whimper from these leaders about the unconscionable appropriation of wealth by the very few or the breaching of the limits of global ecosystems and the twin threats these pose to a truly sustainable economy. Tragically, it would appear that our leaders, while paying lip service to sustainability for thirty years, have understood nothing about the interrelationships between social, ecological, and economic systems or about limits to growth on a finite planet.

But why should Calgarians care? In 2012, seemingly impervious and oblivious to this unfolding tragedy, we celebrated one hundred years of the Calgary Stampede as we rode the Brahma bull of oil wealth with gusto. We were touted as a global energy superpower, and our material standard of living increased relentlessly.

As we enter the third decade of the twenty-first century, things look quite different. Yet our provincial government and our corporate leaders still seem singularly concerned with increasing the pace of economic growth—cut taxes for the rich, roll back regulation to allow more fossil fuel resource exploitation, leave ecological restoration for the next generation.[56] The cost of oil and gas well cleanup in Alberta stands at a staggering $58.7 billion, with no plan to fund it.[57]

Sadly, Canada was once considered one of the good guys and a key architect of the Rio Summit in 1992.[58] At the convening of Rio+20, we had become a pariah, slashing environmental legislation, actively undermining global environmental agreements, and twisting arms to persuade others to do the same.

Less than a year into his term and almost a decade after Rio+20, Premier Jason Kenney made it abundantly clear that his number one priority is a growing fossil fuel industry. If corporate taxes have to be slashed, environmental regulations gutted, social support programs and health and education funding eviscerated to make it happen, so be it.[59]

Sixty years after the launch of the modern environmental movement with the publication of Rachel Carson's *Silent Spring*, we find ourselves at a fork in the road. As Carson wrote, "We urgently need an end . . . to the sugar coating of unpalatable facts."[60] One such unsavoury fact is that our wealth is founded on a deeply unsustainable economic model.

We have a moral obligation to change the model and honour the definition of sustainable development agreed to at the 1992 Rio Earth Summit—to refuse to compromise future generations by our actions today. We have a historic opportunity to show international leadership. If we fail to take up the sustainability challenge, we will be a lesser city for it.

NOTES

1   Canadian Press, "Key Facts in Canada's Robocalls Controversy," *CBC News*, 14 August 2014, https://www.cbc.ca/news/politics/key-facts-in-canada-s-robocalls-controversy-1.2736659.

2   Brian Owens, "Half of Canada's Government Scientists Still Feel Muzzled," *Science Magazine*, 21 February 2018, https://www.sciencemag.org/news/2018/02/half-canada-s-government-scientists-still-feel-muzzled.

3   Naheed Nenshi, "Bad Optics: Alberta Confronts Its Wild West Municipal Election Campaign Funding Rules—the Laxest in the Country," *Alberta Views*, 1 April 2010,

https://albertaviews.ca/bad-optics/; Graham Thomson, "NDP Tightens Election Financing Rules, but Leaves Government a Loophole," *Calgary Herald*, 30 November 2016, https://calgaryherald.com/opinion/columnists/thomson-ndp-tightens-election-financing-rules-but-leaves-government-a-loophole.

4   Madeline Smith, "New Local Election Rules Would Let City Council Hopefuls Disclose Donors after Election Day," *Calgary Herald*, 25 June 2020, https://calgaryherald.com/news/politics/alberta-rolls-out-proposed-changes-to-municipal-election-funding-rules.

5   "About the SGI: Questionnaire," *Sustainable Governance Indicators*, 2020, https://www.sgi-network.org/2020/Questionnaire.

6   "About the SGI: Survey Structure," *Sustainable Governance Indicators*, 2020, https://www.sgi-network.org/2020/Survey_Structure.

7   "SGI 2020 Scores," at "Downloads SGI 2020," *Sustainable Governance Indicators*, 2020, https://www.sgi-network.org/2020/Downloads.

8   Astrid Gunnar, "The Secret of Their Success: The Nordic Countries Are Probably the Best-Governed in the World," *The Economist*, 31 January 2013, https://www.economist.com/special-report/2013/01/31/the-secret-of-their-success.

9   *Startup Sauna,* accessed 8 September 2020, http://startupsauna.com.

10   "2019 Human Development Index Ranking," *United Nations Development Programme: Human Development Reports*, 2019, http://hdr.undp.org/en/content/2019-human-development-index-ranking.

11   "Gini Index (World Bank Estimate)—Country Ranking," *IndexMundi,* accessed 21 August 2020, https://www.indexmundi.com/facts/indicators/SI.POV.GINI/rankings.

12   Richard Wilkinson and Kate Pickett, *The Spirit Level: Why Greater Equality Makes Societies Stronger* (London: Bloomsbury, 2009).

13   John Helliwell et al., eds., *World Happiness Report 2020,* 129–43 (New York: Sustainable Development Solutions Network, 2020), https://worldhappiness.report/ed/2020/#read.

14   Jean Marmoreo, "We're Still Not As Fit As Swedes, but We Shouldn't Stop Trying," *Globe and Mail*, 28 January 2015, https://www.theglobeandmail.com/opinion/were-still-not-as-fit-as-swedes-but-we-shouldnt-stop-trying/article22674881/.

15   "Public Trust and Spending Concerns on Agenda for Calgary Council Next Year," *CBC News*, 9 December 2019, https://www.cbc.ca/news/canada/calgary/public-trust-spending-calgary-council-strategy-1.5390001.

16   Madeline Smith and Jason Herring, "Magliocca's False Expenses Included Flight Upgrades, Hotel Stays, Meals and Booze: Report," *Calgary Herald*, 30 July 2020, https://calgaryherald.com/news/local-news/magliocca-expense-investigation-shows-years-of-problematic-spending-nenshi-says.

17   Don Braid, "UCP Cancels Doctor Pay Contract, Imposes Radical Change," *Calgary Herald*, 21 February 2020, https://calgaryherald.com/opinion/columnists/braid-ucp-cancels-doctor-pay-contract-imposes-radical-change.

18   Adam Cotter, *Public Confidence in Canadian Institutions,* Spotlight on Canadians: Results from the General Social Survey, Catalogue no. 89-652-X2015007 (Ottawa:

Statistics Canada, December 2015), Table 5, 22–23, https://www150.statcan.gc.ca/n1/en/pub/89-652-x/89-652-x2015007-eng.pdf?st=ZAcCmKdF.

19   Cotter, *Public Confidence in Canadian Institutions,* 5.

20   City of Calgary, *2019 Quality of Life and Citizen Satisfaction Survey* (Calgary: City of Calgary, 2019), 81, https://newsroom.calgary.ca/2019-citizen-satisfaction-survey-results/; City of Calgary, *Fall 2020 Quality of Life and Citizen Satisfaction Survey* (Calgary: City of Calgary, 2020), 16, 86, https://www.calgary.ca/cfod/csc/citizen-satisfaction.html?redirect=/citsat.

21   Organisation for Economic Co-operation and Development,*Trust and Public Policy: How Better Governance Can Help Rebuild Public Trust,* OECD Public Governance Reviews (Paris: OECD, March 2017), 3, http://www.oecd.org/corruption-integrity/reports/trust-and-public-policy-9789264268920-en.html.

22   OECD,*Trust and Public Policy*, 20.

23   Cotter, *Public Confidence in Canadian Institutions,* 5.

24   Cotter, *Public Confidence in Canadian Institutions,* 5–7.

25   Cotter, *Public Confidence in Canadian Institutions*, 4.

26   George Packer, "Doublethink Is Stronger Than Orwell Imagined: What 1984 Means Today," review of *The Ministry of Truth: The Biography of George Orwells's 1984,* by Dorian Lynskey, *The Atlantic,* July 2019, https://www.theatlantic.com/magazine/archive/2019/07/1984-george-orwell/590638/.

27   Rebecca Mead, "Margaret Atwood, the Prophet of Dystopia," *The New Yorker,* 10 April 2017, https://www.newyorker.com/magazine/2017/04/17/margaret-atwood-the-prophet-of-dystopia; Margaret Atwood, *The Handmaid's Tale* (Toronto: McClelland and Stewart, 1985).

28   Sherri Zickefoose, "Mayor Seeks Clarity on Gift Policy," *Calgary Herald*, 11 December 2012, https://www.pressreader.com/canada/calgary-herald/20121211/281878705685855.

29   "Confirmed Minutes 2012-10-15, Regular," available at "Council and Committee Meetings and Bylaws," *City of Calgary,* 2017, agenda item 8, https://publicaccess.calgary.ca/searchCCProc/index.htm.

30   "November 26, 2012 By-Elections, Poll-by-Poll Results, Alberta, Calgary Centre," *Elections Canada,* accessed 8 September 2020, https://www.elections.ca/res/rep/off/ovr_2012b/9635_e.html.

31   "Official Voting Results Forty-First General Election 2011," *Elections Canada*, accessed 8 September 2020, https://www.elections.ca/scripts/ovr2011/default.html.

32   Maryze Zeidler, "How the B.C. Election of '96 Changed Provincial Politics," *CBC News,* 29 April 2017, https://www.cbc.ca/news/canada/british-columbia/how-the-b-c-election-of-96-changed-provincial-politics-1.4089562.

33   Andrew Coyne, "New Brunswick Provides More Ammunition for Blowing Up First Past the Post," *National Post*, 27 September 2018, https://nationalpost.com/opinion/andrew-coyne-n-b-election-provides-still-more-reasons-for-blowing-up-first-past-the-post.

34   Sam Austin and Lisa Young, "Political Finance in City Elections: Toronto and Calgary Compared," paper prepared for presentation at the 2006 Annual Meeting of the Canadian Political Science Association, York University, 1–3 June 2006, https://www. cpsa-acsp.ca/papers-2006/Austin-Young.pdf. A similar analysis is found in a more recent article: Jack Lucas and Zack Taylor, "Political Science and City Elections: Local Campaign Finance," *University of Calgary, School of Public Policy*, 5 October 2017, https://www.policyschool.ca/political-science-city-elections-local-campaign-finance/.

35   Daniel Cayley-Daoust and Richard Girard, *Big Oil's Oily Grasp: The Making of Canada as a Petro-State and How Oil Money Is Corrupting Canadian Politics* (Ottawa: Polaris Institute, 2012), 3–4, https://www.polarisinstitute.org/big_oil_s_oily_grasp.

36   Jamie Komarnicki, "Voter Turnout Drops from Last Election," *Calgary Herald*, 22 October 2013, http://www.calgaryherald.com/news/ voter+turnout+drops+from+last+election/9064000/story.html; Michael Franklin, "Voter Turnout Highest in 40 Years in Calgary," *CTV News*, 17 October 2017, https:// calgary.ctvnews.ca/voter-turnout-highest-in-40-years-in-calgary-1.3636034.

37   Tony Seskus and Renata D'Aliesio, "Voter Turnout Lowest in Alberta's History," *Edmonton Journal*, 5 March 2008, https://edmontonjournal.com/news/voter-turnout-lowest-in-albertas-history.

38   "Voter Turnout at Federal Elections and Referendums 1867–2015," *Elections Canada*, last modified 12 May 2020, https://www.elections.ca/content. aspx?section=ele&dir=turn&document=index&lang=e.

39   Drew Anderson, "Calgary's Tough Choices: Gamble on Growth or Gamble on Retreat," *CBC News*, 12 June 2020, https://www.cbc.ca/news/canada/calgary/calgary-tough-choices-economy-growth-shrinkage-1.5609548.

40   Joe Arvai, 'This Canadian City Could Be the Next Detroit," *Globe and Mail*, 9 December 2013, https://www.theglobeandmail.com/opinion/this-canadian-city-could-be-the-next-detroit/article15820368/.

41   Richard Florida, *The Rise of the Creative Class: Revisited,* 10th anniversary ed. (Philadelphia: Basic Books, 2014).

42   Noel Keough, Bob Morrison, and Celia Lee, *State of Our City 2020: An Urgent Call for a Just Transition* (Calgary: Sustainable Calgary Society, 2020), 21, http://www.sustainablecalgary.org/publications.

43   Vibrant Communities Calgary, *A Snapshot of Poverty in Calgary 2019* (Calgary: VCC, August 2019), http://enoughforall.ca/wp-content/uploads/2019/08/A-Snapshot-of-poverty-in-Calgary-in-2019.pdf.

44   Jason Markusoff, "Calgary Tax Increases Not Enough to Cover Growth Costs, Council Told," *Calgary Herald,* 28 October 2014, https://calgaryherald.com/news/local-news/calgary-tax-increases-not-enough-to-cover-growth-costs-council-told.

45   Eben Fodor, *Better Not Bigger: How to Take Control of Urban Growth and Improve Your Community* (Gabriola Island, BC: New Society, 2007).

46   Harvey Molotch, "The City As a Growth Machine: Toward a Political Economy of Place," *American Journal of Sociology* 82, no. 2 (1976): 309–32.

47   Calgary Economic Development, *Economy* (Calgary: CED), accessed 4 January 2021, https://calgaryeconomicdevelopment.com/dmsdocument/87; Calgary Economic Development, *Fact Sheet: Calgary Wealth* (Calgary: CED, 2019), 5, https://calgaryeconomicdevelopment.com/research-and-reports/report-library/report-library/?q=FactSheet-Wealth-2018-Edition-2019-07.pdf&sort=LastChanged%20 DESC; "Household Spending, Canada, Regions and Provinces," *Statistics Canada,* last modified 3 January 2021, https://www150.statcan.gc.ca/t1/tbl1/en/cv.action?pid=1110022201.

48   Richard J. Needham, "The Happiest Canadians," *Maclean's*, 2 November 1964, https://archive.macleans.ca/article/1964/11/2/the-happiest-canadians; Ken MacQueen, "Canada's Most Dangerous Cities: Newfoundland's Other Boom," *MacLean's*, 15 December 2011, https://www.macleans.ca/news/canada/newfoundland-the-rocks-other-boom/.

49   "Sustainable Development Goals," *United Nations,* accessed 2 September 2020, https://sustainabledevelopment.un.org/?menu=1300.

50   Paul Krugman, *End This Depression Now* (New York: W. W. Norton, 2012), 70.

51   Wilkinson and Pickett, *Spirit Level.*

52   UN Environment, "Human Health in Dire Straits If Urgent Actions Are Not Made to Protect the Environment, Warns UN Landmark Report," press release, 13 March 2019, https://www.unenvironment.org/news-and-stories/press-release/human-health-dire-straits-if-urgent-actions-are-not-made-protect.

53   Michael Harris, *Lament for an Ocean: The Collapse of the Atlantic Cod Fishery* (Toronto: McClelland and Stewart, 2011).

54   Herman Daly, *From Uneconomic Growth to a Steady-State Economy,* Advances in Ecological Economics Series (Cheltenham, UK: Edward Elgar, 2014).

55   "Three Central Banks Take Action in Sign of Alarm," *Reuters,* 5 July 2012, https://ca.reuters.com/article/us-centralbanks-action/three-central-banks-take-action-in-sign-of-alarm-idUSBRE8640RN20120705.

56   Geoff Dembicki, "The Emperor Kenney's New Clothes," *The Tyee,* 24 April 2020, https://thetyee.ca/Analysis/2020/04/24/The-Emperor-Kenneys-New-Clothes/.

57   Michelle Bellefontaine, "$260B Liability Figure for Abandoned Energy Infrastructure an 'Error in Judgement': AER," *CBC News,* 1 November 2018, https://www.cbc.ca/news/canada/edmonton/alberta-energy-regulator-liability-figure-error-1.4888532.

58   Elizabeth May, "When Canada Led the Way: A Short History of Climate Change," *Policy Options*, 1 October 2006, https://policyoptions.irpp.org/magazines/climate-change/when-canada-led-the-way-a-short-history-of-climate-change/.

59   Dembicki, "Emperor Kenney's New Clothes."

60   Rachel Carson, *Silent Spring,* 40th anniversary ed. (1962; repr., New York: Houghton Mifflin, 2002), 13.

Further Reading

Hanson, Lorelei, ed. *Public Deliberation on Climate Change: Lessons from Alberta Climate Dialogue.* Athabasca, AB: Athabasca University Press, 2018.

Latour, Bruno. *Down to Earth: Politics in the New Climatic Regime.* Cambridge, UK: Polity, 2017.

Meslin, Dave. *Teardown: Building Democracy from the Ground Up.* Toronto: Penguin, 2019.

Monbiot, George. *Out of the Wreckage: A New Politics for an Age of Crisis.* London: Verso, 2017.

Works Cited

"2019 Human Development Index Ranking." *UN Development Programme: Human Development Reports*, 2019. http://hdr.undp.org/en/content/2019-human-development-index-ranking.

"About the SGI: Questionnaire." *Sustainable Governance Indicators*, 2020. https://www.sgi-network.org/2020/Questionnaire.

"About the SGI: Survey Structure." *Sustainable Governance Indicators*, 2020. https://www.sgi-network.org/2020/Survey_Structure.

Anderson, Drew. "Calgary's Tough Choices: Gamble on Growth or Gamble on Retreat." *CBC News*, 12 June 2020. https://www.cbc.ca/news/canada/calgary/calgary-tough-choices-economy-growth-shrinkage-1.5609548.

Arvai, Joe. "This Canadian City Could Be the Next Detroit." *Globe and Mail*, 9 December 2013. https://www.theglobeandmail.com/opinion/this-canadian-city-could-be-the-next-detroit/article15820368/.

Atwood, Margaret. *The Handmaid's Tale.* Toronto: McClelland and Stewart, 1985.

Austin, Sam, and Lisa Young. "Political Finance in City Elections: Toronto and Calgary Compared." Paper prepared for presentation at the 2006 Annual Meeting of the Canadian Political Science Association, York University, 1–3 June 2006. https://www.cpsa-acsp.ca/papers-2006/Austin-Young.pdf.

Bellefontaine, Michelle. "$260B Liability Figure for Abandoned Energy Infrastructure an 'Error in Judgement': AER." *CBC News*, 1 November 2018. https://www.cbc.ca/news/canada/edmonton/alberta-energy-regulator-liability-figure-error-1.4888532.

Braid, Don. "UCP Cancels Doctor Pay Contract, Imposes Radical Change." *Calgary Herald*, 21 February 2020. https://calgaryherald.com/opinion/columnists/braid-ucp-cancels-doctor-pay-contract-imposes-radical-change.

Calgary Economic Development. *Economy.* Calgary: CED. Accessed 4 January 2021. https://calgaryeconomicdevelopment.com/dmsdocument/87.

———. *Fact Sheet: Calgary Wealth.* Calgary: CED, 2019. https://calgaryeconomic development.com/research-and-reports/report-library/report-library/?q=FactSheet-Wealth-2018-Edition-2019-07.pdf&sort=LastChanged%20DESC.

Canadian Press. "Key Facts in Canada's Robocalls Controversy." *CBC News*, 14 August 2014. https://www.cbc.ca/news/politics/key-facts-in-canada-s-robocalls-controversy-1.2736659.

Carson, Rachel. *Silent Spring*. 40th anniversary ed. 1962. Reprint, New York: Houghton Mifflin, 2002.

Cayley-Daoust, Daniel, and Richard Girard. *Big Oil's Oily Grasp: The Making of Canada as a Petro-State and How Oil Money Is Corrupting Canadian Politics*. Ottawa: Polaris Institute, 2012. https://www.polarisinstitute.org/big_oil_s_oily_grasp.

City of Calgary. *2019 Quality of Life and Citizen Satisfaction Survey*. Calgary: City of Calgary, 2019. https://newsroom.calgary.ca/2019-citizen-satisfaction-survey-results/.

———. *Fall 2020 Quality of Life and Citizen Satisfaction Survey*. Calgary: City of Calgary, 2020. https://www.calgary.ca/cfod/csc/citizen-satisfaction.html?redirect=/citsat.

"Confirmed Minutes 2012-10-15, Regular." Available at "Council and Committee Meetings and Bylaws." *City of Calgary*, 2017. https://publicaccess.calgary.ca/searchCCProc/index.htm.

Cotter, Adam. *Public Confidence in Canadian Institutions*. Spotlight on Canadians: Results from the General Social Survey. Catalogue no. 89-652-X2015007. Ottawa: Statistics Canada, December 2015. https://www150.statcan.gc.ca/n1/en/pub/89-652-x/89-652-x2015007-eng.pdf?st=ZAcCmKdF.

Coyne, Andrew. "New Brunswick Provides More Ammunition for Blowing Up First Past the Post." *National Post*, 27 September 2018. https://nationalpost.com/opinion/andrew-coyne-n-b-election-provides-still-more-reasons-for-blowing-up-first-past-the-post.

Daly, Herman. *From Uneconomic Growth to a Steady-State Economy*. Advances in Ecological Economics Series. Cheltenham, UK: Edward Elgar, 2014.

Dembicki, Geoff. "The Emperor Kenney's New Clothes." *The Tyee*, 24 April 2020. https://thetyee.ca/Analysis/2020/04/24/The-Emperor-Kenneys-New-Clothes/.

Florida, Richard. *The Rise of the Creative Class: Revisited*. 10th anniversary ed. Philadelphia: Basic Books, 2014.

Fodor, Eben. *Better Not Bigger: How to Take Control of Urban Growth and Improve Your Community*. Gabriola Island, BC: New Society, 2007.

Franklin, Michael. "Voter Turnout Highest in 40 Years in Calgary." *CTV News*, 17 October 2017. https://calgary.ctvnews.ca/voter-turnout-highest-in-40-years-in-calgary-1.3636034.

"Gini Index (World Bank Estimate)—Country Ranking." *IndexMundi*. Accessed 21 August 2020. https://www.indexmundi.com/facts/indicators/SI.POV.GINI/rankings.

Gunnar, Astrid. "The Secret of Their Success: The Nordic Countries Are Probably the Best-Governed in the World." *The Economist*, 31 January 2013. https://www.economist.com/special-report/2013/01/31/the-secret-of-their-success.

Harris, Michael. *Lament for an Ocean: The Collapse of the Atlantic Cod Fishery.* Toronto: McClelland and Stewart, 2011.

Helliwell, John, Richard Layard, Jeffrey D. Sachs, and Jan Emmanuel De Neve, eds. *World Happiness Report 2020.* New York: Sustainable Development Solutions Network, 2020. https://happiness-report.s3.amazonaws.com/2020/WHR20.pdf.

"Household Spending, Canada, Regions and Provinces." *Statistics Canada,* last modified 3 January 2021. https://www150.statcan.gc.ca/t1/tbl1/en/cv.action?pid=1110022201.

Keough, Noel, Bob Morrison, and Celia Lee. *State of Our City 2020: An Urgent Call for a Just Transition.* Calgary: Sustainable Calgary Society, 2020. http://www.sustainablecalgary.org/publications.

Komarnicki, Jamie. "Voter Turnout Drops from Last Election." *Calgary Herald,* 22 October 2013. http://www.calgaryherald.com/news/voter+turnout+drops+-from+last+election/9064000/story.html.

Krugman, Paul. *End This Depression Now.* New York: W. W. Norton, 2012.

Lucas, Jack, and Zack Taylor. "Political Science and City Elections: Local Campaign Finance." *University of Calgary, School of Public Policy,* 5 October 2017. https://www.policyschool.ca/political-science-city-elections-local-campaign-finance/.

MacQueen, Ken. "Canada's Most Dangerous Cities: Newfoundland's Other Boom." *MacLean's,* 15 December 2011. https://www.macleans.ca/news/canada/newfoundland-the-rocks-other-boom/.

Markusoff, Jason. "Calgary Tax Increases Not Enough to Cover Growth Costs, Council Told." *Calgary Herald,* 28 October 2014. https://calgaryherald.com/news/local-news/calgary-tax-increases-not-enough-to-cover-growth-costs-council-told.

Marmoreo, Jean. "We're Still Not As Fit As Swedes, but We Shouldn't Stop Trying." *Globe and Mail,* 28 January 2015. https://www.theglobeandmail.com/opinion/were-still-not-as-fit-as-swedes-but-we-shouldnt-stop-trying/article22674881/.

May, Elizabeth. "When Canada Led the Way: A Short History of Climate Change." *Policy Options,* 1 October 2006. https://policyoptions.irpp.org/magazines/climate-change/when-canada-led-the-way-a-short-history-of-climate-change/.

Mead, Rebecca. "Margaret Atwood, the Prophet of Dystopia." *The New Yorker,* 10 April 2017. https://www.newyorker.com/magazine/2017/04/17/margaret-atwood-the-prophet-of-dystopia.

Molotch, Harvey. "The City As a Growth Machine: Toward a Political Economy of Place." *American Journal of Sociology* 82, no. 2 (1976): 309–32.

Needham, Richard J. "The Happiest Canadians." *Maclean's,* 2 November 1964. https://archive.macleans.ca/article/1964/11/2/the-happiest-canadians.

Nenshi, Naheed. "Bad Optics: Alberta Confronts Its Wild West Municipal Election Campaign Funding Rules—the Laxest in the Country." *Alberta Views,* 1 April 2010. https://albertaviews.ca/bad-optics/.

"November 26, 2012 By-Elections, Poll-by-Poll Results, Alberta, Calgary Centre." *Elections Canada*. Accessed 8 September 2020. https://www.elections.ca/res/rep/off/ ovr_2012b/9635_e.html.

"Official Voting Results Forty-First General Election 2011." *Elections Canada*. Accessed 8 September 2020. https://www.elections.ca/scripts/ovr2011/default.html.

Organisation for Economic Co-operation and Development. *Trust and Public Policy: How Better Governance Can Help Rebuild Public Trust*. OECD Public Governance Reviews. Paris: OECD, March 2017. http://www.oecd.org/corruption-integrity/ reports/trust-and-public-policy-9789264268920-en.html.

Owens, Brian. "Half of Canada's Government Scientists Still Feel Muzzled." *Science Magazine*, 21 February 2018. https://www.sciencemag.org/news/2018/02/half-canada-s-government-scientists-still-feel-muzzled.

Packer, George. "Doublethink Is Stronger Than Orwell Imagined: What 1984 Means Today." Review of *The Ministry of Truth: The Biography of George Orwells's 1984*, by Dorian Lynskey. *The Atlantic*, July 2019. https://www.theatlantic.com/magazine/ archive/2019/07/1984-george-orwell/590638/.

"Public Trust and Spending Concerns on Agenda for Calgary Council Next Year." *CBC News*, 9 December 2019. https://www.cbc.ca/news/canada/calgary/public-trust-spending-calgary-council-strategy-1.5390001.

Seskus, Tony, and Renata D'Aliesio. "Voter Turnout Lowest in Alberta's History." *Edmonton Journal*, 5 March 2008. https://edmontonjournal.com/news/voter-turnout-lowest-in-albertas-history.

"SGI 2020 Scores." At "Downloads SGI 2020," *Sustainable Governance Indicators*, 2020. https://www.sgi-network.org/2020/Downloads.

Smith, Madeline. "New Local Election Rules Would Let City Council Hopefuls Disclose Donors after Election Day." *Calgary Herald*, 25 June 2020. https://calgaryherald. com/news/politics/alberta-rolls-out-proposed-changes-to-municipal-election-funding-rules.

———, and Jason Herring. "Magliocca's False Expenses Included Flight Upgrades, Hotel Stays, Meals and Booze: Report." *Calgary Herald*, 30 July 2020. https:// calgaryherald.com/news/local-news/magliocca-expense-investigation-shows-years-of-problematic-spending-nenshi-says.

Startup Sauna. Accessed 8 September 2020. http://startupsauna.com.

"Sustainable Development Goals." *United Nations*. Accessed 2 September 2020. https:// sustainabledevelopment.un.org/?menu=1300.

Thomson, Graham. "NDP Tightens Election Financing Rules, but Leaves Government a Loophole." *Calgary Herald*, 30 November 2016. https://calgaryherald.com/ opinion/columnists/thomson-ndp-tightens-election-financing-rules-but-leaves-government-a-loophole.

"Three Central Banks Take Action in Sign of Alarm." *Reuters*, 5 July 2012. https://ca.reuters.com/article/us-centralbanks-action/three-central-banks-take-action-in-sign-of-alarm-idUSBRE8640RN20120705.

UN Environment. "Human Health in Dire Straits If Urgent Actions Are Not Made to Protect the Environment, Warns UN Landmark Report." Press release, 13 March 2019. https://www.unenvironment.org/news-and-stories/press-release/human-health-dire-straits-if-urgent-actions-are-not-made-protect.

Vibrant Communities Calgary. *A Snapshot of Poverty in Calgary 2019*. Calgary: VCC, August 2019. http://enoughforall.ca/wp-content/uploads/2019/08/A-Snapshot-of-poverty-in-Calgary-in-2019.pdf.

"Voter Turnout at Federal Elections and Referendums 1867–2015." *Elections Canada*, last modified 12 May 2020. https://www.elections.ca/content.aspx?section=ele&dir=turn&document=index&lang=e.

Wilkinson, Richard, and Kate Pickett. *The Spirit Level: Why Greater Equality Makes Societies Stronger*. London: Bloomsbury, 2009.

Zeidler, Maryze. "How the B.C. Election of '96 Changed Provincial Politics." *CBC News*, 29 April 2017. https://www.cbc.ca/news/canada/british-columbia/how-the-b-c-election-of-96-changed-provincial-politics-1.4089562.

Zickefoose, Sherri. "Mayor Seeks Clarity on Gift Policy." *Calgary Herald*, 11 December 2012. https://www.pressreader.com/canada/calgary-herald/20121211/281878705685855.

13

Our Petro-State at a Crossroads

In this final series of essays, we situate Calgary, Alberta, and Canada in the global community at a crossroads. The material wealth enjoyed by Calgarians is directly tied to the exploitation of abundant fossil fuels. But at every scale—local, national, global—we are seeing signs of cracks in the very foundations of our fossil-fueled civilization. In Calgary, the sand is shifting beneath our feet. In 2020 Calgarians are finding it hard to come to terms with the fact that being at the top of the heap economically, as they have grown accustomed to over the past thirty years, is no longer the natural order of things. The provincial government finds itself in the uncomfortable position of switching from its long-successful strategy of railing against interference from the federal government to demanding more from Ottawa as its economy stagnates.

In "Tax Is Not a Four-Letter Word," we challenge the notion that less tax is the best tax. We think of taxes as a collective pooling of resources to improve the common good. We argue that to finance the sustainability transition, we need a fair, sufficient, and sustainable tax regime. We draw on the work of Canadian financial writer Linda McQuaig to gain some insight into how our tax system came to be so dysfunctional.

After forty years of an oil boom and astounding amounts of wealth flowing from oil and gas, how has Alberta fallen so quickly into dire economic circumstances, with no nest egg to fuel the transition to a sustainable economy? We explore this question in "Where Has All the Money Gone?" and we compare Alberta's situation with that of Norway, an oil and gas powerhouse.

We live in a grotesquely unjust economic order. As world events unfold politically, economically, and ecologically, maintaining this unjust order is becoming untenable. In "Alberta's Inconvenient Truths," we offer an interpretation of Calgary's and Alberta's place in the world order. In "Sleepwalking into Crisis," we ask how we will respond as a nation: What stuff are we made of? In the final essay, we critically examine the role our capitalist economic system plays in all of this—and whether a sustainability transition requires a new economic operating system.

This final set of essays invites us to consider Sustainable Calgary's fifth principle: Sustainability cannot be achieved at the expense of our fellow citizens, whether they be our next-door neighbours or members of our shared global village.

TAX IS NOT A FOUR-LETTER WORD

On the eve of an election in 2015, on CBC Radio's *Alberta at Noon*, Alberta premier Jim Prentice was asked, "How can a provincial economy become so needy so quickly when you had so much money coming in?" The premier began his response with "In Alberta, we have had the most expensive public services of anywhere in Canada."[1] If the premier had been honest about the root of our budget problem, he would have responded by saying that Alberta has had the lowest corporate taxes and the most profitable corporations in all of Canada and that wealthy Albertans pay far less tax than other wealthy Canadians. Premier Kenney would be correct to say the same thing in 2020.

It is dishonest to suggest, as Premier Prentice did, that we are living beyond our means. Our system of taxation is grossly unfair and rewards the most affluent and politically powerful. That must change, and here is how it could be done.

1. Get rid of the (essentially) flat tax. Until 2016, Alberta was the only province with a true flat tax. Whether you made $20,000 or $20 million, you paid 10 percent provincial income tax. That was grossly unfair. In 2016 that changed for the top 8 to 10 percent of income earners, which was a good thing, but the other 90 percent still paid 10 percent. As of spring 2020, the poorest in Alberta pay the same tax as an individual making $130,000. In other provinces, rates begin to rise in the $30,000 to $50,000 income range. Nine of the other twelve provinces and territories have a lower rate of taxation for low-income earners than does Alberta.[2]

2. Introduce a graduated tax system with more brackets at the top. In 1972 the top combined federal and provincial personal tax rate was 70 per-cent; in 2020 it is 58.75 percent. Alberta's combined rate was 48 percent in 2020. Alberta's top income tax bracket kicks in at 43 percent higher (start-ing at $314,928) than the next highest, Ontario (starting at $220,000).[3]

Research in 2013 by Public Interest Alberta demonstrated that "a very modest progressive tax scheme of 13% over $100,000 and 15% over $150,000 and increasing the corporate tax rate from 10% to 12%" would bring in an additional $2 billion annually.[4] Bev Dahlby and Greg Flanagan argued in *Alberta Views* in May 2019 that if Alberta's tax regime mirrored that of the province with the next-lowest taxes, we could raise an addi-tional $11 billion. If we taxed like the highest-taxed province, we could raise an additional $21 billion.[5] Even Adam Smith noted, "It is not very unreasonable that the rich should contribute to the public expense not only in proportion to their revenue, but something more than in that proportion."[6]

3. Increase corporate taxation. Back in 1972, the top combined feder-al-provincial corporate tax was 46.5 percent.[7] Since 2000, the Canadian government has chopped the federal corporate tax rate from 28 percent

to 15 percent and boasts that this is the lowest rate in all of the G7 countries. In 2014 Alberta's corporate tax was 10 percent. The New Democrat government raised it to 12 percent in 2017, and now Premier Kenney has lowered it to 8 percent, the lowest in the country.[8] You begin to see why, in *Follow the Money*, Kevin Taft reported an explosion of corporate profits in Alberta.[9]

4. Treat all income equally—no special deals for capital gains and dividends. In Canada, if you work for your money, you pay a higher rate of taxation than if you let your money make money. In Alberta, we tax capital gains and dividends at half the rate that we tax working income. Alberta's rates are the second lowest in Canada, and Canada has the lowest capital gains tax in the G7.[10]

A 2000 CBC article underscores how unfair this is: "Government figures from 1997 indicate that 45 per cent of total capital gains tax breaks went to individuals earning more than a quarter of a million dollars a year. People in that tax bracket amount to less than one per cent of the population."[11]

5. Work with the international community to close down tax havens. In 2015 CBC reported that at HSBC alone, "the value of [tax haven] accounts tied to Canada is around $4 billion Canadian, spread across 1,859 people and companies."[12] According to Canadians for Tax Fairness, tax haven revenue loss in Canada is at least $8 billion annually.[13]

Though the Canadian government has feigned interest in controlling this criminal tax avoidance, financial writer Linda McQuaig argues that Canada's rules were so poorly designed, "they've actually opened the floodgates to . . . allowing multinational corporations to route their profits through the tax haven, thereby avoiding Canadian corporate tax."[14]

6. Persuade Ottawa to champion a financial transaction tax (also called a "Tobin tax," after the Nobel economist who first proposed the idea).[15] Much of the volatility in world markets that we see today is due to rampant and massive currency speculation rather than productive investment activity. It should come as no surprise that, as McQuaig writes, "with some of the world's leading governments finally on side [with the idea of a Tobin Tax], Ottawa is emerging as an obstacle."[16]

In that interview on *Alberta at Noon*, then premier Jim Prentice said, "I hope Albertans trust me." Premier Kenney seeks the same trust. As with Prentice, we should trust Kenney only if he comes clean on how an unfair tax system has imperilled our future and proposes a sustainable, sufficient, and fair system of taxation to secure it. As respected University of Calgary economist Trevor Tombe so bluntly stated in a 2018 report, "Alberta's fiscal policies are unsustainable."[17]

WHERE HAS ALL THE MONEY GONE? THE GREAT ALBERTA GIVEAWAY

Premier Kenney has been hard at work setting the stage for an eventual plan to deal with Western Canada Select oil being well south of US$40 a barrel (ranging from $29.06 to $34.69 in August 2020, according to oilprice. com). Lamentably, indications are that the same well-worn Conservative refrains are being rehearsed—we are all in this together, we are living beyond our means, we have a spending problem, public sector wages are out of line, and our social programs are unaffordable.

The evidence suggests that the premier is wrong on all counts. We do not have so much a spending problem as a revenue problem, and evidently, we are not all in this together. Some have done extremely well in the boom times, but many more are struggling to survive with what little trickles down. Public sector wages are what we might expect in the wealthiest economy in Canada.

By any measure, the wealth generated from oil and gas has been enormous. According to the Conference Board of Canada, in 2016 our per capita income was 14 percent larger than that of the United States and on par with that of Norway.[18]

In *Follow the Money*, Kevin Taft reported that between 1989 and 2008, Alberta's economy on a per capita basis (GDP) went from 27 percent to a whopping 84 percent larger than the rest of Canada, while provincial government spending was only slightly more per capita than the Canadian average.[19] Over that period, spending on health, education, housing, social services—what Taft calls human services—was never more than 10 percent above the Canadian average. In 2014–15 Alberta teachers were making 7 percent above the Canadian average. Statistics Canada data show that in 2018 total compensation (at the top of the salary scale) for teachers in Ontario was 3 percent more than for those in Alberta, while in BC, teacher compensation was 10 percent lower than in Alberta.[20]

In 2013 Alberta's GDP was 85 percent more than the rest of Canada, and in 2018 it was still 34 percent greater. Arguably, in comparison to our wealth, Alberta has been the most frugal public service spender of all provinces.

Then there is the sad story of the Alberta Heritage Trust Fund. Norway, Abu Dhabi, and Kuwait have amassed trust funds of $1,200, $697, and $592 billion (US dollars), respectively.[21] Alberta, at $13.6 billion, comes in just behind East Timor's $15.8 billion fund and is only slightly larger than when it was started in 1976![22]

So with such a record, you might ask, Where did all the money go?

There is certainly a case to be made that many Albertans have lived large. From 1989 to 2009, personal income was up a healthy 240 percent and is consistently 20 to 25 percent ahead of the Canadian average.[23] Many Albertans, especially those on the high side of the average income, have, knowingly or not, traded quality health, education, and social support for the less fortunate for big cars, big homes, big spending.

But to really answer the question, you need to examine corporate profits. According to Taft, from 1989 to 2009 corporate income per capita went up a staggering 340 percent.[24] Corporations were taking a much bigger chunk of a much bigger pie. It is not too strong a statement to suggest that we have been subjected to a government-enabled corporate fleecing!

So when Premier Prentice, quoted in the *Calgary Sun* in 2015, said that "everyone in the private sector is experiencing this," that "it comes down to wages" and "a lack of discipline," he was simply wrong.[25] By almost any comparison with other provinces and other nations, our taxes are too low and pander to corporations and the wealthy.

With this track record, it should come as no surprise that Alberta is the most inequitable province in the country. Between 2006 and 2012, the share of total income for the top 10 percent of earners in Canada actually decreased to 39.7 percent. In Alberta, in 2012 the share for the top 10 percent was not only the highest in the country at 50.4 percent, but it had increased since 2006.[26]

Alberta has the dubious distinction of having more unequal distribution of income than the United States.[27] In contrast, among OECD countries, Norway, our European energy-superpower cousin, is second only to Denmark in terms of income equality.[28]

What is the on-the-ground manifestation of unequal income distribution? According to Sustainable Calgary's *State of Our City 2020* report, more Calgarians than ever before are using food banks, a single parent of two has to work over fifty-five hours a week at minimum wage just to reach the poverty line, and the ratio of house price to income has ballooned since 2000.[29] We are not all in this together, Mr. Premier.

A fair, sufficient, and sustainable tax regime will get us a long way toward a solution to our predicament. In the words of economist Robert Reich, "Simple fairness requires three things: More tax brackets at the top, higher rates in each bracket, and the treatment of all sources of income (capital gains included) exactly the same."[30]

ALBERTA'S INCONVENIENT TRUTHS

Most Albertans have grown accustomed to the periodic boom and bust bravado from our government—from energy superpower spending with reckless abandon in the boom to belt-tightening, living beyond our means, and getting our house in order in the bust. I contend that our leaders have failed to recognize, or perhaps chosen to avoid, some inconvenient truths at the core of how we live in Alberta—our fossil fuel dependence, our addiction to stuff, the failed promise of economic growth, and our fundamentally dysfunctional and disenfranchising democracy.

The first inconvenient truth is that the fossil fuels that power Alberta's economy—the cornerstone of our way of life—are making our planet uninhabitable. The Oil and Gas Reliance Index developed by Sustainable Calgary suggests that we are as dependent on this resource as we have ever been.[31] If we stop or drastically reduce the exploitation of fossil fuels, the economy we've relied upon for the past fifty years withers. If we do not, then the climate sweet spot that has allowed our species to thrive on this planet disappears.

Inconvenient truth number two: If every person on the planet lived like the average Albertan, we would need at least four planets to provide the food, wood products, energy, and manufactured goods we consume annually.[32] Talk about living beyond our means! But have you ever heard a politician voice this dilemma? Some don't believe or understand it. Others are afraid that therein lies electoral suicide.

On a finite planet, there are direct connections among a number of uncomfortable realities: our voracious consumption of the earth's resources, the phenomenon of terrorism, our government's assertion that we need to send Canadians to die in places like Afghanistan and Iraq, and the barricades at Oka and the unceded lands of the Wet'suwet'en First Nation in northern BC.[33] To live as we do requires us not only to turn a blind eye but to actively maintain unjust relations with First Nations at home and to contribute and acquiesce to an oppressive world economic order.

It is an inconvenient truth that living as we do results in the degradation of human life support systems on a global scale—the continental shelf; coral reefs; temperate, tropical, and boreal forests; biodiversity; and fresh water. According to *National Geographic*, humans have accelerated species extinction to one thousand times natural historic rates.[34] The United Nations warns that almost every ecosystem type on the planet is in decline.[35]

I've seen the results of these inconvenient truths firsthand—in the near enslavement of the cotton pickers in Tajikistan and the sugar cane cutters in the Philippines. I've listened to the stories of Guatemalans exiled in Mexico, witnesses to the torture and brutal murder of their loved ones by CIA-trained death squads. I've witnessed the destruction of the mountain forests and coastal mangroves of the Philippines, the smoldering remains of southern Brazil's tropical forests to make way for soybean and cattle pasture, and the decimation of the northern cod stocks in my native Newfoundland. The irony is that those who berate us for living beyond our economic means remain silent in the face of the rampant destruction of the natural world that ultimately sustains any kind of human economy.

After decades of robust economic growth in Alberta, it is an inconvenient truth that most indices of inequality and of poverty have either stagnated or worsened. Homelessness has increased more than fivefold in the past twenty-five years, and the last time the minimum wage was sufficient to cover the most basic of needs for food and shelter in Calgary was 1978.[36] Based on income share for the top 1 percent, Calgary now stands as the most unequal jurisdiction in the country.[37] Yet political leaders lack the fortitude to acknowledge this inconvenient truth, even though research demonstrates clearly that beyond a rudimentary level of material wealth, it is a society's level of equality that is the most important indicator of well-being.[38]

Our leaders are unwilling to face the fact that our democracy has been tossed in a dumpster with barely a perceptible pulse. On average, over the past six elections, the governing party has won the support of barely 25 percent of eligible voters and only 50 percent of those who actually voted, yet has secured between 60 and 90 percent of the seats in the legislature.[39] We desperately need a system that encourages engagement and robust debate and delivers to the legislature a fair representation of Alberta's diverse political views.

Some may find these assertions provocative or unpalatable. Perhaps, but they are also true. We take pride in living in one of the best places on earth and thinking of ourselves as educated, entrepreneurial, worldly, straight-talkin' problem-solvers. If our political leaders won't do it, then who among us will speak these inconvenient truths?

SLEEPWALKING INTO CRISIS: HAS CANADA LOST ITS WAY?

Entering the third decade of the twenty-first century, it is hard not to be confused, overwhelmed, and depressed about the current state of the world. We hover on the brink of economic meltdown, social upheaval and war, and climate calamity, and we now find ourselves in the midst of a global pandemic. To some, these appear to be discrete events in a chaotic world. It would be wiser to view them through the lens of a key principle of sustainability—everything is connected.

Economically, the world is still reeling from the 2008 global meltdown. In *Capital in the Twenty-First Century*, economist Thomas Piketty's meticulous historical analysis suggests that at the heart of the matter is an economic system where gross inequality is not an anomaly of our time but a "structural feature" of capitalism.[40] Yet the business-as-usual mantra of less government and more unfettered market freedom still dominates policy, and obscene inequality lives on.

Having recently retreated from ten years of war in Afghanistan, which seems only to have spawned more violence, Canada embarked upon what could prove to be a longer and even more vicious war in the Middle East to confront ISIS. We find ourselves dangerously exposed to being drawn into the US's campaigns of military aggression in the Middle East.

Then there is the *UN Climate Change Annual Report 2019*, the latest in a long line of increasingly urgent warnings about the spectre of climate change. The world's leading scientists are now 95 percent certain that human activity has caused the largest buildup of greenhouse gases in the atmosphere in 800,000 years—propelling our planet toward changes where "a 1.5 °C increase in global average surface temperature is a limit beyond which climate change will have devastating consequences."[41] The UN report notes that poor countries contribute little to the problem but are especially vulnerable to its consequences.

Everything is connected. Our growth-at-all-costs economic system promotes greed and the relentless exploitation of earth's resources to exhaustion. It promotes a destructive winner-take-all competition locally and globally. Our addiction to oil compels us to violence in the Middle East like a junkie desperate for another fix. The burning of that same fuel threatens to make our planet uninhabitable. The violence we see exploding from Palestine to Pakistan results from generations of this grotesquely unjust economic relationship, and all attempts to confront it democratically and non-violently are met with indifference and violence.

At a time when we are in desperate need of principled diplomacy and moral leadership, the Trudeau government stalls on our commitments to the Paris Accord, and our official opposition seems more interested in picking sides, picking fights, and fanning the flames of violence—a dangerously ideological, simple-minded strategy likely to make things a whole lot worse.

There was a time when Canadian Prime Minister Lester B. Pearson won a Nobel Prize as the father of UN peacekeeping; when Canadian diplomats led the charge in organizing the Rio Earth Summit, where sustainable development became the mantra for our common future; when the well-being of Canadians was front and centre in economic policy, exemplified by Tommy Douglas' campaign for universal health care. The values that underlay these initiatives became synonymous with Canadian values.

In 2010 Ed Broadbent, one of the most respected statesmen of our era, warned of a coming barbarity on the heels of the unjust economic system.[42]

In *Dark Age Ahead*, the celebrated urban visionary Jane Jacobs warned of the dangers to civilization of environmental crisis, racism, and the growing gulf between rich and poor.[43] And in *War*, military historian Gwynne Dyer writes that since at least the mid-1800s, nations have subscribed to Carl von Clausewitz's dictum that "war is merely a continuation of policy by other means."[44] Dyer argues that we can no longer afford that kind of politics: "We have reached a point where our moral imagination must expand again to embrace the whole of mankind, or else we will perish."[45]

Ecological footprint analysis, created by Canadian ecologist William Rees, tells us that on a finite planet of almost eight billion, Canadians appropriate much more than our fair share of the earth in order to live as we do.[46] Our insatiable appetite for fully loaded pickups, supersized houses, sun-and-surf holidays, and endless consumer toys and trinkets is filled at the expense of the majority of our fellow human beings and most other gloriously diverse forms of life on earth.

We in the West consume more than the earth can bear, and we are destroying basic life support systems through the burning of fossil fuels. We routinely resort to violence to guarantee access to those resources, and we have been satisfied to allow the small minority to live in relative luxury while the vast majority live in dehumanizing poverty. None of this can be sustained ecologically, politically, or morally.

Christopher Clark, in *The Sleepwalkers: How Europe Went to War*, describes the protagonists of World War I as "watchful but unseeing, haunted by dreams, yet blind to the reality of the horror they were about to bring into the world."[47] His words could be a warning to the contemporary world as we stand at another crossroads in the history of our species.

CAPITALISM AND CLIMATE CHANGE: GOD BLESS US ONE AND ALL!

One of the most beloved stories of the Christmas season, *A Christmas Carol*, celebrates the redemption of an iconic greedy capitalist. Almost two centuries after Ebenezer Scrooge opened his heart for Tiny Tim, we are still debating the possibility of redemption for this particular economic system.

Few love capitalism, but many are resigned to its reign because they believe that there is no alternative. As Jim Stanford explains in *Economics for Everyone: A Short Guide to the Economics of Capitalism*, though many of us own stocks, either directly or in our pension plan portfolios, the capitalist class, constituting only about 5 percent of the population, own and control the lion's share of productive assets.[48] Through the limited liability corporation—Ford, Cargill, Exxon, Amazon and the like—capitalists put these assets to work.

What makes capitalism such a dynamo? Its defining features are greed, growth, and the valuation of human beings solely on the basis of what they can produce. Capitalism is driven by greed. It cannot comprehend the concept of "enough." Greed is undoubtedly a part of human nature, but so are compassion and co-operation. Capitalism nurtures greed and makes of it a virtue, celebrating those who master it—the likes of Elon Musk, Bill Gates, Richard Branson, and Jeff Bezos.

Capitalism demands that every corner of the planet, every community, every ecosystem be available for exploitation. Like a vampire seeking blood, capitalism withers without access to cheap resources, land, and labour, and will do whatever it takes to acquire them. Colonialism is one manifestation of this insatiable drive. Another is the constant hunt for a good deal on collectively owned assets—health care being a prime example—with the threadbare argument that private enterprise is always and everywhere more efficient than collective ownership.

Capitalism dehumanizes. Individuals are simply one factor of production whose cost is to be minimized. At the extreme, as Andrew Nikiforuk documents in *The Energy of Slaves*, abolition of slavery was fought to the bitter end by plantation owners who feared it would lower return on investment.[49] Unliveable minimum wages are a contemporary manifestation of this dehumanization.

Capitalism is relentless in its subversion of democracy in pursuit of self-interest. In *The Trouble with Billionaires*, Linda McQuaig and Neil Brooks chronicle the endemic collusion between the Canadian political establishment and the capitalist class—for example, enshrining capital gains policies so that wealthy investors pay less tax on what their money earns than real working people do on their earnings.[50] In the US, democracy is under siege as a result of court decisions granting corporations rights of persons to spend unlimited amounts for favoured candidates.

Blind growth is the lifeblood of capitalism. Profit leads to investment, leading to more profit, and so it goes. A CEO who ignores the profit-investment-growth formula is likely to be devoured by competitors. What is gained in efficiency is merely ploughed back into still more resource exploitation and production—a variation on the Jevons paradox first postulated by W. S. Jevons in 1865, after observing that more efficient coal burning actually led to increased consumption of coal. Efforts at energy conservation increase profits, which are then invested into still more production. Faced with the looming satiation of needs in the 1950 and 1960s, the advertising industry, so adeptly portrayed in *Mad Men*, had to be created to manufacture desire and sustain the growth.

Thomas Piketty's *Capital in the Twenty-First Century* is perhaps the most celebrated contemporary critique of capitalism.[51] Piketty argues that capitalism, left to its own devices, generates staggering levels of inequality, demanding an ever-increasing share of the growth it generates. In another well-known critique, *This Changes Everything*, Naomi Klein states her position unambiguously—capitalism is the problem and no less than the survival of human civilization depends on finding a better way.[52]

Celebrated environmental journalist Elizabeth Kolbert and energy expert Mark Jaccard, both well-known climate change crusaders, are dismissive of Klein's argument.[53] Climate change is the existential threat, they say. There is no time for anti-capitalist ideological diversions. And if capitalists such as the Waltons—the first family of Walmart—can pitch in to save the planet by outfitting their stores with solar panels, so be it. Klein argues that we will never build a global consensus to meet the challenge of climate change if we remain guided by an economic system that breeds inequality and, by definition, must grow relentlessly at a compound rate or wither.

Capitalism has proven to be an amazing engine of economic growth and has brought humanity unimagined material abundance—but at the expense of equality and the debasing of the rest of creation. In an era of uneconomic growth and soul-destroying excesses of material consumption, we need a new economic operating system, one capable of confronting the existential crises of our time—inequality and ecological collapse.

So where do you stand on this chicken-and-egg question—capitalism or climate change? Naomi Klein has done us a great service by putting the question on the table. There's no room for sacred cows in the confrontation with climate change. God bless us one and all!

NOTES

1   "Alberta at Noon," *CBC Radio*, 4 March 2015, https://www.cbc.ca/albertaatnoon/episode/2015/03/04/an-for-wednesday-march-4-2015/.

2   "Canadian Income Tax Rates for Individuals—Current and Previous Years," *Government of Canada, Canada Revenue Agency*, last modified 21 January 2020, https://www.canada.ca/en/revenue-agency/services/tax/individuals/frequently-asked-questions-individuals/canadian-income-tax-rates-individuals-current-previous-years.html#provincial.

3   "Canadian Income Tax Rates For Individuals."

4   Shannon Stunden Bower, Trevor Harrison, and Greg Flanagan, *Stabilizing Alberta's Revenues: A Common Sense Approach* (Edmonton: Parkland Institute, February 2013), https://www.parklandinstitute.ca/stabilizing_albertas_revenues.

5   Bev Dahlby and Greg Flanagan, "Should Alberta Have Higher Taxes?" *Alberta Views*, 1 May 2019, https://albertaviews.ca/alberta-higher-taxes/.

6   Adam Smith, *The Wealth of Nations* (London, 1776; New York: Bantam Dell, 2003), 2065.

7   Sean A. Cahill, *Corporate Income Tax Rate Database: Canada and Provinces, 1960–2005* (Ottawa: Agriculture and Agri-Food Canada, March 2007), Appendix A, Table A1.

8   "Alberta Tax Overview," *Government of Alberta*, 2020, https://www.alberta.ca/taxes-levies-overview.aspx.

9   Kevin Taft, *Follow the Money: Where Is Alberta's Wealth Going?* (Calgary: Detselig, 2012).

10   "2020 Canadian Federal/Provincial Marginal Tax Rates," *Mackenzie Investments*, 2020, https://www.mackenzieinvestments.com/en/services/tax-and-estate-planning/tax-rates; Canada, "Canada Has Lowest Tax Rate on New Business Investment in G7," news release, 18 July 2019, https://www.canada.ca/en/department-finance/news/2019/07/canada-has-lowest-tax-rate-on-new-business-investment-in-g7.html.

11   "A Primer on Capital Gains Taxes in Canada," *CBC News*, 18 October 2000, https://www.cbc.ca/news/business/a-primer-on-capital-gains-taxes-in-canada-1.231145.

12   "HSBC Documents Show Bank Helped Clients Hide Billions from Tax Man," *CBC News*, 9 February 2015, https://www.cbc.ca/news/business/hsbc-documents-show-bank-helped-clients-hide-billions-from-tax-man-1.2950062.

13 "Tackle Tax Havens," *Canadians for Tax Fairness*, 2019, https://www.taxfairness.ca/en/news/tackle-tax-havens-0.

14 Linda McQuaig, "The Harper Government's Tough Posture and Weak Rules on Tax Havens," *Rabble*, 9 April 2013, https://rabble.ca/columnists/2013/04/harper-governments-tough-posture-and-weak-rules-tax-havens.

15 James Tobin, "The Tobin Tax: The Case for a Tax on International Monetary Transactions," *Canadian Centre for Policy Alternatives*, 1 April 2011, https://www.policyalternatives.ca/publications/monitor/tobin-tax.

16 Linda McQuaig and Neil Brooks, *The Trouble with Billionaires* (Toronto: Viking, 2010).

17 Trevor Tombe, "Alberta's Long-Term Fiscal Future," University of Calgary, School of Public Policy Research Paper 11, November 2018, 31, https://www.policyschool.ca/wp-content/uploads/2018/11/AB-Fiscal-Future-Tombe.pdf.

18 "How Canada Performs: Income per Capita," *Conference Board of Canada*, accessed 9 September 2020, https://www.conferenceboard.ca/hcp/provincial/economy/income-per-capita.aspx.

19 Taft, *Follow the Money*, 101.

20 "Table C.3.2b: Annual Statutory Teachers' Salaries in Public Institutions, by Level of Education Taught and Teaching Experience, Canadian Dollars, Canada, Provinces and Territories, 2016–2017," Education Indicators in Canada: An International Perspective, *Statistics Canada*, 2018, https://www150.statcan.gc.ca/n1/pub/81-604-x/2018001/t/tblc.3.1b-eng.htm.

21 "Here Are the Top 10 Sovereign Wealth Funds in the Arab World," *Al Arabiya*, 10 September 2020, https://english.alarabiya.net/en/business/economy/2019/08/28/Here-are-the-top-10-sovereign-wealth-funds-in-the-Arab-world.

22 "Top 89 Largest Sovereign Wealth Fund Rankings by Total Assets," *Sovereign Wealth Fund Investor*, 2020, https://www.swfinstitute.org/fund-rankings/sovereign-wealth-fund.

23 Taft, *Follow the Money*, 127.

24 Taft, *Follow the Money*, 129.

25 Rick Bell, "Alberta Premier Jim Prentice Says Fiscal Crisis Means Rollbacks on Table for Public Sector . . . and Him," *Edmonton Sun*, 26 January 2015, https://edmontonsun.com/2015/01/25/alberta-premier-jim-prentice-says-fiscal-crisis-means-rollbacks-on-table-for-public-sector--and-him/wcm/61e41a87-6eb1-4b6e-a3da-27d0f59e5580./.

26 Francis Fong, *Income Inequality in Canada: The Urban Gap* (Ottawa: Chartered Professional Accountants of Canada, 2017), https://www.cpacanada.ca/en/the-cpa-profession/about-cpa-canada/key-activities/public-policy-government-relations/economic-policy-research/income-inequality-canada.

27 "High Income Tax-Filers in Canada, Table: 11-10-0055-01," *Statistics Canada*, last modified 13 November 2020, https://www150.statcan.gc.ca/t1/tbl1/en/tv.action?pid=1110005501.

28 "How Canada Performs."

29   Noel Keough, Bob Morrison, and Celia Lee, *State of Our City 2020: An Urgent Call for a Just Transition* (Calgary: Sustainable Calgary Society, 2020), 25, http://www.sustainablecalgary.org/publications.

30   Robert Reich, "The Flat-Tax Fraud, and the Necessity of a Truly Progressive Tax," *Robert Reich*, 21 October 2011, https://robertreich.org/post/11753807617.

31   Keough, Morrison, and Lee, *State of Our City 2020*, 21.

32   Keough, Morrison, and Lee, *State of Our City 2020*, 46.

33   Taionrén:hote Dan David, "Point of View: The Oka Crisis—Looking Forward after 30 Years," *CBC News*, 10 July 2020, https://www.cbc.ca/news/canada/montreal/pov-taionrén-hote-dan-david-on-oka-crisis-after-30-years-1.5644082; Deb Steel, "Chiefs Call for Calm and Dialogue as Canada Seeks Resolution to Wet'suwet'en Solidarity Demonstrations," *Windspeaker*, 18 February 2020, https://windspeaker.com/news/windspeaker-news/chiefs-call-calm-and-dialogue-canada-seeks-resolution-wetsuweten-solidarity; "The Wet'suwet'en and B.C.'s Gas-Pipeline Battle: A Guide to the Story So Far," *Globe and Mail*, 11 January 2019, https://www.theglobeandmail.com/canada/british-columbia/article-wetsuweten-bc-lng-pipeline-explainer/.

34   Christine Dell'Amore, "Species Extinction Happening 1,000 Times Faster Because of Humans?" *National Geographic*, 30 May 2014, https://www.nationalgeographic.com/news/2014/5/140529-conservation-science-animals-species-endangered-extinction/.

35   UN Environment, *GEO-6 Key Messages* (Nairobi: UN Environment Programme, 2019), https://wedocs.unep.org/bitstream/handle/20.500.11822/28774/GEO6_keymessages_EN.pdf?sequence=1&isAllowed=y.

36   Keough, Morrison, and Lee, *State of Our City 2020*, 21.

37   Fong, *Income Inequality in Canada*, 16.

38   Thomas Piketty, *Capital in the Twenty-First Century*, trans. Arthur Goldhammer (Cambridge, MA: Belknap, 2014).

39   Keough, Morrison, and Lee, *State of Our City 2020*, 33.

40   Piketty, *Capital in the Twenty-First Century*, 368.

41   UN Framework Convention on Climate Change, *UN Climate Change Annual Report 2019* (Bonn, Germany: UNFCCC, 2019), 6, https://unfccc.int/sites/default/files/resource/unfccc_annual_report_2019.pdf. For the 800,00 years, see Lisa V. Alexander et al., "Summary for Policymakers," 11, in *Climate Change 2013: The Physical Science Basis. Contribution of Working Group I to the Fifth Assessment Report of the Intergovernmental Panel on Climate Change*, ed. T. F. Stocker et al. (Cambridge: Cambridge University Press), https://www.ipcc.ch/report/ar5/wg1/.

42   Ed Broadbent, "Equality or Barbarism," Charles R. Bronfman Lecture, University of Ottawa, 14 October 2010, *Toronto Star*, 16 October 2010, https://www.thestar.com/opinion/editorials/2010/10/16/equality_or_barbarism.html.

43   Jane Jacobs, *Dark Age Ahead* (Toronto: Vintage Canada, 2005).

44   Carl von Clausewitz, trans. J. J. Graham, *On War* (New York: Barnes and Noble, 2004), first published 1873, 28.

45   Gwynne Dyer, *War: The New Edition* (New York: Random House, 2004), 445.

46   William Rees, "End Game: The Economy as Eco-Catastrophe and What Needs to Change," *Real-World Economics Review* 87 (March 2019): 132–48.

47   Christopher Clark, *The Sleepwalkers: How Europe Went to War in 1914* (New York: Harper, 2013), 562.

48   Jim Stanford, *Economics for Everyone: A Short Guide to the Economics of Capitalism*, 2nd ed. (Toronto: Fernwood, 2015), 93.

49   Andrew Nikiforuk, *The Energy of Slaves: Oil and the New Servitude* (Vancouver: Greystone, 2012).

50   McQuaig and Brooks, *Trouble with Billionaires*.

51   Piketty, *Capital in the Twenty-First Century*.

52   Naomi Klein, *This Changes Everything: Capitalism and the Climate* (New York: Simon and Schuster, 2014).

53   Naomi Klein and Elizabeth Kolbert, "Can Climate Change Cure Capitalism? An Exchange," *New York Review of Books*, 8 January 2015, https://www.nybooks.com/articles/2015/01/08/can-climate-change-cure-capitalism-exchange/; Mark Jaccard, "I Wish This Changed Everything," review of *This Changes Everything: Capitalism and the Climate*, by Naomi Klein, *Literary Review of Canada*, November 2014, https://reviewcanada.ca/magazine/2014/11/i-wish-this-changed-everything/.

Further Reading

Graeber, David. *Debt: The First 5,000 Years*. London: Melville House, 2014.

Magdoff, Fred, and John Bellamy Foster. "What Every Environmentalist Needs to Know about Capitalism: A Citizen's Guide to Capitalism and the Environment." *Monthly Review Press* 61, no. 10 (2010). https://monthlyreview.org/2010/03/01/what-every-environmentalist-needs-to-know-about-capitalism/.

Malm, Andreas. *Fossil Capital: The Rise of Steam Power and the Roots of Global Warming*. London: Verso, 2016.

Patel, Raj, and Jason Moore. *The History of the World in Seven Cheap Things: A Guide to Capitalism, Nature, and the Future of the Planet*. London: Verso, 2015.

Works Cited

"2020 Canadian Federal/Provincial Marginal Tax Rates." *Mackenzie Investments*, 2020. https://www.mackenzieinvestments.com/en/services/tax-and-estate-planning/tax-rates.

Alexander, Lisa V., Simon K. Allen, Nathaniel L. Bindoff, François-Marie Béon, John A. Church, Ulrich Cubasch, Seita Umori et al. "Summary for Policymakers." In *Climate Change 2013: The Physical Science Basis. Contribution of Working Group I* to the *Fifth Assessment Report of the Intergovernmental Panel on Climate Change*, edited by T. F. Stocker et al. (Cambridge: Cambridge University Press), https://www.ipcc.ch/report/ar5/wg1/.

"Alberta at Noon." *CBC Radio,* 4 March 2015. https://www.cbc.ca/albertaatnoon/episode/2015/03/04/an-for-wednesday-march-4-2015/.

"Alberta Tax Overview." *Government of Alberta*, 2020. https://www.alberta.ca/taxes-levies-overview.aspx.

Bell, Rick. "Alberta Premier Jim Prentice Says Fiscal Crisis Means Rollbacks on Table for Public Sector . . . and Him." *Edmonton Sun*, 26 January 2015. https://edmontonsun.com/2015/01/25/alberta-premier-jim-prentice-says-fiscal-crisis-means-rollbacks-on-table-for-public-sector--and-him/wcm/61e41a87-6eb1-4b6e-a3da-27d0f59e5580.

Bower, Shannon Stunden, Trevor Harrison, and Greg Flanagan. *Stabilizing Alberta's Revenues: A Common Sense Approach*. Edmonton: Parkland Institute, February 2013. https://www.parklandinstitute.ca/stabilizing_albertas_revenues.

Broadbent, Ed. "Equality or Barbarism." Charles R. Bronfman Lecture, University of Ottawa, 14 October 2010. *Toronto Star*, 16 October 2010. https://www.thestar.com/opinion/editorials/2010/10/16/equality_or_barbarism.html.

Cahill, Sean A. *Corporate Income Tax Rate Database: Canada and Provinces, 1960–2005*. Ottawa: Agriculture and Agri-Food Canada, March 2007.

Canada. "Canada Has Lowest Tax Rate on New Business Investment in G7." News release, 18 July 2019. https://www.canada.ca/en/department-finance/news/2019/07/canada-has-lowest-tax-rate-on-new-business-investment-in-g7.html.

"Canadian Income Tax Rates for Individuals—Current and Previous Years." *Government of Canada, Canada Revenue Agency*, last modified 21 January 2020. https://www.canada.ca/en/revenue-agency/services/tax/individuals/frequently-asked-questions-individuals/canadian-income-tax-rates-individuals-current-previous-years.html#provincial.

Clark, Christopher. *The Sleepwalkers: How Europe Went to War in 1914*. New York: Harper, 2013.

Clausewitz, Carl von. *On War*. Translated by J. J. Graham. New York: Barnes and Noble, 2004. First published 1873.

Dahlby, Bev, and Greg Flanagan. "Should Alberta Have Higher Taxes?" *Alberta Views*, 1 May 2019. https://albertaviews.ca/alberta-higher-taxes/.

David, Taionrén:hote Dan. "Point of View: The Oka Crisis—Looking Forward after 30 Years." *CBC News*, 10 July 2020. https://www.cbc.ca/news/canada/montreal/pov-taionrén-hote-dan-david-on-oka-crisis-after-30-years-1.5644082.

Dell'Amore, Christine. "Species Extinction Happening 1,000 Times Faster Because of Humans?" *National Geographic*, 30 May 2014. https://www.nationalgeographic.com/news/2014/5/140529-conservation-science-animals-species-endangered-extinction/.

Dyer, Gwynne. *War: The New Edition*. New York: Random House, 2004.

Fong, Francis. *Income Inequality in Canada: The Urban Gap*. Ottawa: Chartered Professional Accountants of Canada, 2017. https://www.cpacanada.ca/en/the-cpa-profession/about-cpa-canada/key-activities/public-policy-government-relations/economic-policy-research/income-inequality-canada.

"Here Are the Top 10 Sovereign Wealth Funds in the Arab World." *Al Arabiya*, 10 September 2020. https://english.alarabiya.net/en/business/economy/2019/08/28/Here-are-the-top-10-sovereign-wealth-funds-in-the-Arab-world.

"High Income Tax-Filers in Canada, Table: 11-10-0055-01." *Statistics Canada*, last modified 13 November 2020. https://www150.statcan.gc.ca/t1/tbl1/en/tv.action?pid=1110005501.

"How Canada Performs: Income per Capita." *Conference Board of Canada*. Accessed 9 September 2020. https://www.conferenceboard.ca/hcp/provincial/economy/income-per-capita.aspx.

"HSBC Documents Show Bank Helped Clients Hide Billions from Tax Man." *CBC News*, 9 February 2015. https://www.cbc.ca/news/business/hsbc-documents-show-bank-helped-clients-hide-billions-from-tax-man-1.2950062.

Jaccard, Mark. "I Wish This Changed Everything." Review of *This Changes Everything: Capitalism and the Climate*, by Naomi Klein. *Literary Review of Canada*, November 2014. https://reviewcanada.ca/magazine/2014/11/i-wish-this-changed-everything/.

Jacobs, Jane. *Dark Age Ahead*. Toronto: Vintage Canada, 2005.

Keough, Noel, Bob Morrison, and Celia Lee. *State of Our City 2020: An Urgent Call for a Just Transition*. Calgary: Sustainable Calgary Society, 2020. http://www.sustainablecalgary.org/publications.

Klein, Naomi. *This Changes Everything: Capitalism and the Climate*. New York: Simon and Schuster, 2014.

———, and Elizabeth Kolbert. "Can Climate Change Cure Capitalism? An Exchange." *New York Review of Books*, 8 January 2015. https://www.nybooks.com/articles/2015/01/08/can-climate-change-cure-capitalism-exchange/.

McQuaig, Linda. "The Harper Government's Tough Posture and Weak Rules on Tax Havens." *Rabble*, 9 April 2013. https://rabble.ca/columnists/2013/04/harper-governments-tough-posture-and-weak-rules-tax-havens.

McQuaig, Linda, and Neil Brooks. *The Trouble with Billionaires*. Toronto: Viking, 2010.

Nikiforuk, Andrew. *The Energy of Slaves: Oil and the New Servitude*. Vancouver: Greystone, 2012.

Piketty, Thomas. *Capital in the Twenty-First Century*. Translated by Arthur Goldhammer. Cambridge, MA: Belknap, 2014.

"A Primer on Capital Gains Taxes in Canada." *CBC News*, 18 October 2000. https://www.cbc.ca/news/business/a-primer-on-capital-gains-taxes-in-canada-1.231145.

Rees, William. "End Game: The Economy as Eco-Catastrophe and What Needs to Change." *Real-World Economics Review* 87 (March 2019): 132–48.

Reich, Robert. "The Flat-Tax Fraud, and the Necessity of a Truly Progressive Tax." *Robert Reich*, 21 October 2011. https://robertreich.org/post/11753807617.

Smith, Adam. *The Wealth of Nations*. New York: Bantam Dell, 2003. First published 1776 by W. Strahan and T. Cadell (London).

Stanford, Jim. *Economics for Everyone: A Short Guide to the Economics of Capitalism*. 2nd ed. Toronto: Fernwood, 2015.

Steel, Deb. "Chiefs Call for Calm and Dialogue as Canada Seeks Resolution to Wet'suwet'en Solidarity Demonstrations." *Windspeaker*, 18 February 2020. https://windspeaker.com/news/windspeaker-news/chiefs-call-calm-and-dialogue-canada-seeks-resolution-wetsuweten-solidarity.

"Table C.3.2b: Annual Statutory Teachers' Salaries in Public Institutions, by Level of Education Taught and Teaching Experience, Canadian Dollars, Canada, Provinces and Territories, 2016–2017." Education Indicators in Canada: An International Perspective. *Statistics Canada*, 2018. https://www150.statcan.gc.ca/n1/pub/81-604-x/2018001/t/tblc.3.1b-eng.htm.

"Tackle Tax Havens." *Canadians for Tax Fairness*, 2019. https://www.taxfairness.ca/en/news/tackle-tax-havens-0.

Taft, Kevin. *Follow the Money: Where Is Alberta's Wealth Going?* Calgary: Detselig, 2012.

Tobin, James. "The Tobin Tax: The Case for a Tax on International Monetary Transactions." *Canadian Centre for Policy Alternatives*, 1 April 2011. https://www.policyalternatives.ca/publications/monitor/tobin-tax.

Tombe, Trevor. "Alberta's Long-Term Fiscal Future." University of Calgary, School of Public Policy Research Paper 11, November 2018. https://www.policyschool.ca/wp-content/uploads/2018/11/AB-Fiscal-Future-Tombe.pdf.

"Top 89 Largest Sovereign Wealth Fund Rankings by Total Assets." *Sovereign Wealth Fund Investor*, 2020. https://www.swfinstitute.org/fund-rankings/sovereign-wealth-fund.

UN Environment. *GEO-6 Key Messages*. Nairobi: UN Environment Programme, 2019. https://wedocs.unep.org/bitstream/handle/20.500.11822/28774/GEO6_keymessages_EN.pdf?sequence=1&isAllowed=y.

UN Framework Convention on Climate Change. *UN Climate Change Annual Report 2019*. Bonn, Germany: UNFCCC, 2019. https://unfccc.int/sites/default/files/resource/unfccc_annual_report_2019.pdf.

"The Wet'suwet'en and B.C.'s Gas-Pipeline Battle: A Guide to the Story So Far." *Globe and Mail*, 11 January 2019. https://www.theglobeandmail.com/canada/british-columbia/article-wetsuweten-bc-lng-pipeline-explainer/.

14

Five Reasons Why Sustainability Matters

In this book, we acknowledge the spectacular nature of cities and the processes of urbanization. We also identify some of the most challenging aspects of urban life and some disturbing trends in cities around the world that became topics of conversation in our essay series. These themes include limits to growth, the machine metaphor versus the organic metaphor, and the undeniable reality that cities are the engines of the consumption that has brought us to the edge of catastrophe via climate change and biodiversity and ecosystem loss. Though cities provide unparalleled opportunities for an enriching, cosmopolitan lifestyle, they also isolate us from the rest of nature. While we celebrate diversity in cities around the world, city dwellers are also witnessing the most devastating effects of climate change and of war and violence. In this chapter, we take up these themes in a global context and propose a reframing of sustainability, with five propositions of why sustainability matters.

As was noted in chapter 2, some people, with justification, consider the term *sustainable development* oxymoronic. They interpret it as an exhortation to society to sustain a form of development that is demonstrably unsustainable and that is, in fact, the very reason why we have had to focus our attention on strategies to sustain human civilization in the first place. Critics point out that all too often, the capitalist expansionist project continues, with the adjective *sustainable* attached to whatever noun we are qualifying—"sustainable growth" being the most egregious example. I would concur with those critics.

However, I believe the concept of sustainability still holds potential. As we have seen, those who originally sought to define and popularize the concept did envision sustainability as a radical challenge to infinite economic expansion and growth at all costs. In my teaching, research, and advocacy work, I am often confronted by the question, Why does sustainability matter? I would like to propose that embedded in the emergence of the sustainability discourse in general and the recurring themes in this book's essays are five key reasons why sustainability matters—reasons that show the concept of "sustainability" to be a radical alternative to the capitalist expansionist project.

1. Endless Economic Growth on a Finite Planet

Growth is considered the sine qua non of modern capitalist economies. No nation-state exists that does not pursue the holy grail of economic growth. To propose an economic policy of no growth or degrowth would certainly be the death knell for any modern Western government. Adam Smith is credited with describing, in *The Wealth of Nations*, the economic logic of markets as the engine of growth, along with the famous metaphor of the hidden hand. Self-interested individual behaviour and the market are assumed to be the surest path to prosperity for all.[1] But markets are not exclusive to capitalism. Karl Marx's *Das Kapital* is the seminal description of the capitalist system, arguing that capitalism is, by design, exploitive of nature and workers.[2] In *Economics for Everyone*, Canadian economist Jim Stanford describes capitalism as a system built on greed and competition and the belief that individuals acting in their own self-interest will magically ensure the common good.[3] Stanford notes that though capitalism is the foundation of modern economies, it is rarely referred to by name. Yet even the left-leaning Stanford is obliged to see capitalism, with all its faults, as the only viable economic model for modern industrial economies.

Though hegemonic, the growth doctrine of capitalism is not without its challengers. Herman Daly was one of the first to describe our current state of affairs, with diminishing social and environmental returns from capitalism, as "non-economic growth" and to articulate an alternative steady-state economy.[4] Contemporary ecological economists, including Tim Jackson and Giorgos Kallis, now propose a degrowth economy, along with a framework for such a contracting economy that nevertheless delivers livelihoods and well-being.[5]

While some pursue the idea of capitalism without growth, I am persuaded that an economic system without growth will no longer resemble capitalism. A capitalist invests capital in order to produce profit via the production and sale of goods and services, and then takes that profit (a larger sum of capital) and invests it yet again to produce even more profit. For this endless chain of increased profit to work, ever-greater human and natural resources need to be exploited and put to work. On a finite planet, it is obvious that an infinitely expanding economy is an impossibility. At some point, the system fails: resources are depleted, ecosystems destroyed, and human labour exhausted. The question remains, of course, whether we are now at this point in history, or whether capitalism can continue expanding into the foreseeable future. Some claim that we can extend capitalist growth long into the future by developing new and more efficient technologies and processes. This is referred to as dematerialization. Factor four—reducing the material input per unit of output fourfold—is one model of dematerialization proposed by von Weizsäcker, Lovins, and Lovins.[6] The jury is out as to whether such a theoretical model can be achieved in practice. Ultimately, such a strategy can at best extend the life of capitalist growth.

Sustainability contradicts the idea of infinite growth on a finite planet. It puts the onus on capitalism to demonstrate that it can function in a no-growth world. Given the evidence of climate change, soil loss, biodiversity loss, and ocean depletion, sustainability's proposition is that we have reached the limits to growth.

2. War and Violence

On War, by Carl von Clausewitz, is considered by many to be the quintessential book on war-making. Clausewitz argued that "war is merely a continuation of policy by other means."[7] Colin Powell, Secretary of State under President G. W. Bush, described *On War* as "a beam of light from the past, still illuminating present day military quandaries."[8] It was Powell's application of the Clausewitzian "strategy of annihilation" in carrying out George Bush's disingenuous desire to use war to advance democracy in the 1992 invasion of Iraq that led to the horrors of Iraq, Afghanistan, Yemen, and Syria in the subsequent twenty-five years. It was the application of these same ideas by European generals that led to the horrors of trench warfare in the First World War.

According to the Stockholm International Peace Research Institute's (SIPRI) *Opportunity Cost of Military Spending*, humanity spent, collectively, $1.8 trillion on the military in 2018.[9] The United States alone spent almost $650 billion—as much as the next twenty-six nations combined. (Canada spent $21.6 billion on the military in 2018.)[10] According to the Brookings Institute, just $54 billion could fund all public school education in the forty-six poorest countries in the world.[11] In 2016 SIPRI researchers estimated that just 4 percent of annual military spending globally could fund the estimated annual costs to achieve all seventeen UN Sustainable Development Goals.[12]

SIPRI reports that US weapons manufacturers, like Boeing and Lockheed, account for over half of the arms sold internationally.[13] From 2011 to 2013, Eastern Europe, North Africa, and the Middle East all spent more on the military than on health.[14] The UN High Commission on Refugees reports that there are over twenty-one million refugees in the world today—most of them displaced by war and state-sponsored violence. Countries like Jordan and Lebanon, who host enormous numbers of refugees, find their own social, economic, and ecological stability threatened.

In his review of Christopher Clark's *The Sleepwalkers*, Ian Pindar writes that the author "suggests that European elites who vied to prove their virility in battle were suffering from a 'crisis of masculinity.'"[15] Clark himself states that they were "blind to the reality of the horror they were about to bring into the world."[16] Canadian anthropologist Wade Davis, in *Into the Silence*, gives one of the most visceral accounts of the horrors of the First World War. Davis describes the "quartered limbs hanging from shattered branches of burnt trees, bodies swollen and blackened with flies, skulls gnawed by rats, corpses stuck in the sides of trenches that aged with each day into the colors of the dead."[17]

In *War*, Gwynne Dyer challenges the idea of the utility of war as a tool of diplomacy for nation-states, arguing that with the power of weapons at our disposal today, and the urgency of existential threats such as climate change, war has no practical political value. Dyer writes, "We have reached a point where our moral imagination must expand again to embrace the whole of mankind or else we will perish."[18]

A sustainability perspective begins with a belief that violence in any form—domestic, schoolyard, against nature, or war—is intolerable. War is not heroic. It should not be celebrated. It should never be deployed in cold hard calculation as political strategy. War is a tragic failure of civilization, and the abolition of war is vital for the vision of a sustainable world.

3. Global Justice and Equity

The growth doctrine of capitalism has always relied on the notion of trickle-down economics, wherein the benefits of capitalism are supposedly realized by making the pie bigger and allowing everyone to benefit from growth, even if the lucky or ambitious few continue to take more and more of the pie. In *Capitalism in the Web of Life*, Jason Moore demonstrates that capitalism has flourished and come to dominate the planet through violence, slavery, racism, and the marginalization of others—whether it be based on ethnicity, gender, or religion.[19] The slave trades from West Africa provided the human labour for the industrialization of the cotton industry in North America, the sugar industry in the Caribbean, and the precious metal mines of South America. Moore argues that capitalism flourishes with, and in fact requires, exploitation of nature and human labour on a global scale as it relentlessly seeks out and appropriates new frontiers of cheap labour and resources. On a finite planet, he contends, we have probably reached the end point of this model of exploitation. There are no more frontiers to exploit.

We are all familiar with the notion of the 1 percent of the population who hold almost all of society's wealth. Recent research has produced startling statistics: eight men own the same wealth as 3.6 billion people (half of humanity); seven out of ten people live in countries that have seen rising inequality over the past thirty years; the two richest Canadians own the same wealth as the bottom third (eleven million) Canadians.[20]

There is a growing list of renowned mainstream economists, including Thomas Piketty, Robert Reich, and Nobel economists such as Paul Krugman and Joseph Stiglitz, who argue that inequality is perhaps the most problematic characteristic of today's capitalist economies, and unless addressed, it threatens the stability of capitalism.[21] Most of these authors demonstrate the links between economic inequality, deteriorating democracy, evaporating trust in our democratic institutions, and health and social outcomes. In *The Spirit Level*, Richard Wilkinson and Kate Pickett demonstrate that inequality explains uneven social and health outcomes better than any other factor and that in unequal societies, wellness suffers—even for the wealthiest.[22]

Sustainability demands attention to inequality and recognizes that making a more just world requires robust democracies. Many would argue that the disturbing emergent trends in global politics, including the distrust of institutions of government and the search by marginalized groups for even more marginalized scapegoats, is a direct result of growing inequality in the world's democracies. Human societies suffering from extreme and growing inequality cannot sustain themselves.

4. Human Exceptionalism

Our species, *Homo sapiens*, has generally considered itself superior to the rest of nature. We tell ourselves a story about evolution being a process toward ever more complex life forms, with humans at the top of the pyramid or the "great chain of being."[23] At worst, we tell ourselves that the rest of nature exists as nothing more than a resource for our development and progress. At best, enlightened religious doctrine calls on us to be responsible stewards over God's creation.

The writing of *On the Origin of Species* by Charles Darwin, inspired by his famous voyage on *HMS Beagle*, was a watershed moment in this story of human exceptionalism.[24] Darwin demonstrated a truth that many found hard to accept—that humans, like all other species, co-evolved over millions of years of the existence of life on earth, and that we are in fact relative newcomers on this planet. That we had most recently evolved from the apes was heresy when first proposed. Very few dispute this fact today.

We do, however, continue to search for attributes that make us exceptional. Frans de Waal and Derrick Jensen are two prominent writers who explore this issue in depth.[25] Many theories have been proposed—only humans feel pain; only humans grieve the loss of others of our species; only humans use technology; humans have the biggest brain to body ratio; only humans are capable of language; only humans are problem solvers; no other species can conceive of the future. One by one, these theories have been challenged. Even more crucially, environmental philosophers point out that the attributes by which we have compared ourselves are self-servingly chosen. We have deemed ourselves to be exceptional based on attributes for which we consider ourselves to be exceptional.

But why not consider others' attributes as defining superiority—longevity, numbers, sight, hearing, speed, or size? Other species are clearly superior to us in all of these attributes. Humans are certainly unique, as is every one of the millions of species on the planet. But as the Indigenous peoples of North America have insisted from first contact, other species are "all our relations." The emerging field of biomimicry recognizes that other species have evolved ingenious "technologies" to assist in making their way in the world.[26] Sustainability challenges us to look beyond the myth of exceptionalism and to find ways of living in harmony with the diversity of life on earth.

5. The Clockwork Universe

The beginnings of Western science are often traced back four hundred years to the mid-1600s. Immediately preceding this period, Europe was just emerging from the Dark Ages. Plagues had ravaged the continent and killed a large portion of the population, and nation-states did not yet exist. Europe had not yet embarked upon the Age of Discovery. Asian and Middle Eastern societies rivalled those of Europe. Science ultimately came to embody and enable the Age of Discovery, the rise of capitalism, the Industrial Revolution, and imperialist and colonial aggression.

The giants of the emerging scientific world view included Nicolaus Copernicus, who first challenged religious doctrine in claiming that the earth was not at the centre of the universe; Johannes Kepler, who mathematically described the motion of planets around the sun; and Francis Bacon, who first proposed the scientific method of observation as the secret to understanding our world. In his *Meditations on First Philosophy*, René Descartes penned his famous dictum "I think, therefore I am," proposing that our rational minds and our untrustworthy sensuous bodies are completely separate. He claimed that it was our minds that separate us from animals and enable us to understand and exercise control over the natural world. He proposed our exceptionalism to be not so much about our special relationship with God but about the power of our mind.[27]

But it is through Isaac Newton and his formulation of the laws of motion in *Philosophiae Naturalis Principia Mathematica* that our scientific understanding has been most profoundly shaped by the metaphor of the clockwork universe. Since Newton, the disciplines of Western science have sought to advance based on this machine metaphor. The iconic laboratory experiment underlay the belief that any organism or natural phenomenon could be described by methodically isolating and studying its parts.[28] In the early 1800s, French scholar Pierre-Simon Laplace, author of *Celestial Mechanics*, dreamed of the discovery of the one equation that would allow us to describe all change in the universe with omniscient precision.[29] Western science assumed that the world was ultimately orderly and predictable. Even the brilliant Albert Einstein, who challenged our belief in the uniform unfolding of time, held to the belief that God does not play dice and that the universe is ultimately predictable, even as evidence in modern physics mounted in support of a random and unpredictable universe.

German scientist Ernst Haeckel first coined the term *ecology* in 1866.[30] Ecology is the study of the interactions between living beings and their environment. Ecologists understand that any phenomenon—whether it is a human being, another living creature, an entire ecosystem, or a city—is more than the sum of its parts. The base metaphor in ecology is not the inanimate machine but the complex evolving living system.

The science of ecology is founded on two key ideas. First, living systems evolve over time. Darwin's concept of species evolution through natural selection offered some of the first empirical evidence of this critical insight. Darwin challenged the commonly held belief that the earth and all its life forms had always inhabited the earth, remaining unchanged through time. Early ecologists focused on an encyclopedic description of the existing world, but over time, the emphasis has shifted to the processes of change that govern the planet and all its diverse systems and life forms.

Second, the most profound elements of study are not discrete objects but the relationships among components of living systems. Ecology is more interested in the processes by which life and systems evolve than in describing how an object or life form exists at any particular point in time. In the early 1970s, Barry Commoner, one of the founders of the modern environmental movement, captured the systems view in *The Closing Circle* with the simple phrase "everything is connected to everything else."[31] More recently, our ecological world view has been advanced through the science of complexity, through which we now understand the world to be not only relational but profoundly unpredictable.[32] In such a world, "predict and control" is of limited value. We need to be more attuned to the ecological processes in which we are embedded and be ready to adapt to those processes as they unfold.

Sustainability matters because it invites us to question the hubris, violence, and assumed power and certainty of the deterministic Western scientific understanding of the world and to embrace, with a measure of humility, an indeterministic, evolutionary, relational, and process-oriented ecological world view.

NOTES

1   Adam Smith, *The Wealth of Nations* (London, 1776; New York: Bantam Dell, 2003).

2   Karl Marx, *Marx's Capital: A Student Edition,* ed. and intro. C. J. Arthur (London, UK: Electric Books, 2001).

3   Jim Stanford, *Economics for Everyone: A Short Guide to the Economics of Capitalism,* 2nd ed. (Toronto: Fernwood, 2015).

4   Herman Daly, *Beyond Growth: The Economics of Sustainable Development* (Boston: Beacon Press, 1997).

5   Tim Jackson, *Prosperity without Growth: Economics for a Finite Planet* (New York: Routledge, 2009); Giorgos Kallis, *Degrowth* (New York: Agenda, 2018).

6   Ernst von Weizsäcker, Amory B. Lovins, and L. Hunter Lovins, *Factor Four: Doubling Wealth and Halving Resource Use* (London, UK: Earthscan, 1998).

7   Carl von Clausewitz, trans. J. J. Graham, *On War* (New York: Barnes and Noble, 2004), first published 1873, 28.

8   Colin Powell, *My American Journey,* with Joseph E. Persico (New York: Ballantine Books, 1995), 207.

9   Nan Tian et al., *Trends in Military Expenditure, 2018,* SIPRI Fact Sheet, April 2019, 1, https://reliefweb.int/sites/reliefweb.int/files/resources/fs_1904_milex_2018.pdf.

10 Tian et al., *Trends in Military Expenditure,* 2.

11 Liesbet Steer, "Seven Facts about Global Education Financing," *Brookings Institution,* 20 February 2014, https://www.brookings.edu/blog/education-plus-development/2014/02/20/seven-facts-about-global-education-financing/.

12 Sam Perlo-Freeman, "The Opportunity Cost of World Military Spending," *Stockholm International Peace Research Institute,* 5 April 2016, https://www.sipri.org/commentary/blog/2016/opportunity-cost-world-military-spending.

13 "Arms Production," *Stockholm International Peace Research Institute,* 2020, http://www.sipri.org/research/armaments/production/recent-trends-in-arms-industry.

14	Sam Perlo-Freeman, "The Opportunity Cost of World Military Spending," *Stockholm International Peace Research Institute*, 5 April 2016, https://www.sipri.org/commentary/blog/2016/opportunity-cost-world-military-spending.

15	Ian Pindar, "The Sleepwalkers by Christopher Clark: Review," *The Guardian*, 19 July 2013, https://www.theguardian.com/books/2013/jul/19/sleepwalkers-christopher-clark-review.

16	Christopher Clark, *The Sleepwalkers: How Europe Went to War in 1914* (New York: Harper, 2013), 562.

17	Wade Davis, *Into the Silence: The Great War, Mallory, and the Conquest of Everest* (Toronto: Vintage, 2012), 5.

18	Gwynne Dyer, *War: The New Edition* (New York: Random House, 2004), 445.

19	Jason W. Moore, *Capitalism in the Web of Life: Ecology and the Accumulation of Capital* (New York: Verso, 2015).

20	Deborah Hardoon, *An Economy for the 99%*, Oxfam Briefing Paper (Oxford: Oxfam International, January 2017), https://www.oxfam.org/sites/www.oxfam.org/files/file_attachments/bp-economy-for-99-percent-160117-en.pdf.

21	Thomas Piketty, *Capital in the Twenty-First Century*, trans. Arthur Goldhammer (Cambridge, MA: Belknap, 2014); Robert Reich, *Aftershock: The Next Economy and America's Future* (New York: Knopf, 2010); Paul Krugman, *End This Depression Now* (New York: W. W. Norton, 2012); Joseph E. Stiglitz, *The Price of Inequality: How Today's Divided Society Endangers Our Future* (New York: W. W Norton, 2012).

22	Richard Wilkinson and Kate Pickett, *The Spirit Level: Why Greater Equality Makes Societies Stronger* (London: Bloomsbury, 2009).

23	Arran Gare, *Nihilism Inc.: Environmental Destruction and the Metaphysics of Sustainability* (Sydney, Australia: Eco-Logical Press, 1996).

24	Charles Darwin, *On the Origin of Species by Means of Natural Selection, or the Preservation of Favoured Races in the Struggle for Life* (London, 1859; New York: Bantam Classics 1999).

25	Frans de Waal, *Are We Smart Enough to Know How Smart Animals Are?* (New York: W. W. Norton, 2016); Derrick Jensen, *The Myth of Human Supremacy* (New York: Seven Stories Press, 2016).

26	Janine Benyus, *Biomimicry: Innovation Inspired by Nature* (New York: William Morrow, 2002).

27	Desmond Clarke, *Descartes: A Biography* (Cambridge: Cambridge University Press, 2006).

28	David Lindberg, *The Beginnings of Western Science* (Chicago: University of Chicago Press, 1992).

29	Charles Coulston Gillispie, *Pierre-Simon Laplace 1749–1827: A Life in Exact Science* (Princeton, NJ: Princeton University Press, 1997).

30   Donald Worster, *The Shaky Ground of Sustainability in the Wealth of Nature: Environmental History and the Ecological Imagination* (Oxford: Oxford University Press, 1993).

31   Barry Commoner, *The Closing Circle: Nature, Man and Society* (New York: Knopf, 1971).

32   John Holland is one of the pioneers in the science of complexity. See John H. Holland, *Complexity: A Very Short Introduction* (Oxford: Oxford University Press, 2014). For a survey of the development of the science of complexity, its key concepts, and its most influential exponents, see M. Mitchell Waldrop, *Complexity: The Emerging Science at the Edge of Order and Chaos* (New York: Simon and Schuster, 1992).

Works Cited

"Arms Production." *Stockholm International Peace Research Institute*, 2020. http://www.sipri.org/research/armaments/production/recent-trends-in-arms-industry.

Benyus, Janine. *Biomimicry: Innovation Inspired by Nature*. New York: William Morrow, 2002.

Clark, Christopher. *The Sleepwalkers: How Europe Went to War in 1914*. New York: Harper, 2013.

Clarke, Desmond. *Descartes: A Biography*. Cambridge: Cambridge University Press, 2006.

Clausewitz, Carl von. *On War*. Translated by J. J. Graham. New York: Barnes and Noble, 2004. First published 1873.

Commoner, Barry. *The Closing Circle: Nature, Man and Society*. New York: Knopf, 1971.

Daly, Herman. *Beyond Growth: The Economics of Sustainable Development*. Boston: Beacon Press, 1997.

Darwin, Charles. *On the Origin of Species by Means of Natural Selection, or the Preservation of Favoured Races in the Struggle for Life*. New York: Bantam Classics, 1999. First published 1859 by John Murray (London).

Davis, Wade. *Into the Silence: The Great War, Mallory, and the Conquest of Everest*. Toronto: Vintage, 2012.

De Waal, Frans. *Are We Smart Enough to Know How Smart Animals Are?* New York: W. W. Norton, 2016.

Dyer, Gwynne. *War: The New Edition*. New York: Random House, 2004.

Gare, Arran. *Nihilism Inc.: Environmental Destruction and the Metaphysics of Sustainability*. Sydney, Australia: Eco-Logical Press, 1996.

Gillispie, Charles Coulston. *Pierre-Simon Laplace, 1749–1827: A Life in Exact Science*. Princeton, NJ: Princeton University Press, 1997.

Hardoon, Deborah. *An Economy for the 99%.* Oxfam Briefing Paper. Oxford, UK: Oxfam Great Britain, January 2017. https://www.oxfam.org/sites/www.oxfam.org/files/file_attachments/bp-economy-for-99-percent-160117-en.pdf.

Holland, John H. *Complexity: A Very Short Introduction.* Oxford: Oxford University Press, 2014.

Jackson, Tim. *Prosperity without Growth: Economics for a Finite Planet.* New York: Routledge, 2009.

Jensen, Derrick. *The Myth of Human Supremacy.* New York: Seven Stories Press, 2016.

Kallis, Giorgos. *Degrowth.* New York: Agenda, 2018.

Krugman, Paul. *End This Depression Now.* New York: W. W. Norton, 2012.

Lindberg, David. *The Beginnings of Western Science.* Chicago: University of Chicago Press, 1992.

Marx, Karl. *Marx's Capital: A Student Edition.* Edited and introduction by C. J. Arthur. London, UK: Electric Books, 2001.

Moore, Jason W. *Capitalism in the Web of Life: Ecology and the Accumulation of Capital.* New York: Verso, 2015.

Perlo-Freeman, Sam. "The Opportunity Cost of World Military Spending." *Stockholm International Peace Research Institute,* 5 April 2016. https://www.sipri.org/commentary/blog/2016/opportunity-cost-world-military-spending.

Piketty, Thomas. *Capital in the Twenty-First Century.* Translated by Arthur Goldhammer. Cambridge, MA: Belknap, 2014.

Pindar, Ian. "The Sleepwalkers by Christopher Clark: Review." *The Guardian,* 19 July 2013. https://www.theguardian.com/books/2013/jul/19/sleepwalkers-christopher-clark-review.

Powell, Colin. *My American Journey.* With Joseph E. Persico. New York: Ballantine Books, 1995.

Reich, Robert. *Aftershock: The Next Economy and America's Future.* New York: Knopf, 2010.

Smith, Adam. *The Wealth of Nations.* New York: Bantam Dell, 2003. First published 1776 by W. Strahan and T. Cadell (London).

Stanford, Jim. *Economics for Everyone: A Short Guide to the Economics of Capitalism.* 2nd ed. Toronto: Fernwood, 2015.

Steer, Liesbet. "Seven Facts about Global Education Financing." *Brookings Institution,* 20 February 2014. https://www.brookings.edu/blog/education-plus-development/2014/02/20/seven-facts-about-global-education-financing/.

Stiglitz, Joseph E. *The Price of Inequality: How Today's Divided Society Endangers Our Future.* New York: W. W Norton, 2012.

Tian, Nan, Aude Fleurant, Alexandra Kuimova, Pieter D. Wezeman, and Siemon T. Wezeman. *Trends in Military Expenditure, 2018.* SIPRI Fact Sheet, April 2019. https://reliefweb.int/sites/reliefweb.int/files/resources/fs_1904_milex_2018.pdf.

Von Weizsäcker, Ernst, Amory B. Lovins, and L. Hunter Lovins. *Factor Four: Doubling Wealth and Halving Resource Use.* London, UK: Earthscan, 1998.

Waldrop, M. Mitchell. *Complexity: The Emerging Science at the Edge of Order and Chaos.* New York: Simon and Schuster, 1992.

Wilkinson, Richard, and Kate Pickett. *The Spirit Level: Why Greater Equality Makes Societies Stronger.* London: Bloomsbury, 2009.

Worster, Donald. *The Shaky Ground of Sustainability in the Wealth of Nature: Environmental History and the Ecological Imagination.* Oxford: Oxford University Press, 1993.

Bibliography

"2 Schools on Closure List, 5 Saved." *CBC News*, 21 January 2004. https://www.cbc.ca/news/canada/calgary/2-schools-on-closure-list-5-saved-1.498204.

"2019 Civic Census Results." *City of Calgary*, 2019. https://www.calgary.ca/ca/city-clerks/election-and-information-services/civic-census/censusresults.html.

"2019 Human Development Index Ranking." *UN Development Programme: Human Development Reports*, 2019. http://hdr.undp.org/en/content/2019-human-development-index-ranking.

"2020 Canadian Federal/Provincial Marginal Tax Rates." *Mackenzie Investments*, 2020. https://www.mackenzieinvestments.com/en/services/tax-and-estate-planning/tax-rates.

"68% of the World Population Projected to Live in Urban Areas by 2050, Says UN." *UN Department of Economic and Social Affairs*, 16 May 2018. https://www.un.org/development/desa/en/news/population/2018-revision-of-world-urbanization-prospects.html.

ABC Life Literacy Canada. *What Is Life Literacy?* Toronto: ABC Life Literacy Canada. Accessed 5 January 2021. https://abclifeliteracy.ca/wp-content/uploads/2019/11/ABC-Life-Literacy.pdf.

"A Bold Vision for Calgary's Cultural and Entertainment District." *Calgary Municipal Land Corporation*, 5 April 2018. https://www.calgarymlc.ca/news-full/2018/4/5/a-bold-vision-for-calgarys-cultural-and-entertainment-district.

"A Primer on Capital Gains Taxes in Canada." *CBC News*, 18 October 2000. https://www.cbc.ca/news/business/a-primer-on-capital-gains-taxes-in-canada-1.231145.

"About Passive House." *Passive House Canada*, 2020. https://www.passivehousecanada.com/about-passive-house/.

"About the Canadian Index of Wellbeing." *Canadian Index of Wellbeing*. Accessed 25 November 2020. https://uwaterloo.ca/canadian-index-wellbeing/about-canadian-index-wellbeing.

"About the SGI: Questionnaire." *Sustainable Governance Indicators*, 2020. https://www.sgi-network.org/2020/Questionnaire.

"About the SGI: Survey Structure." *Sustainable Governance Indicators*, 2020. https://www.sgi-network.org/2020/Survey_Structure.

Acemoglu, Daron, and James A. Robinson. "Economics Versus Politics: Pitfalls of Policy Advice." NBER Working Paper 18921. National Bureau of Economic Research, Cambridge, MA, March 2013.

ActiveCITY Collective. *Playbook 2030: A Guide to Building Canada's Most Liveable Region*. Calgary: ActiveCITY Collective, 2020. https://static1.squarespace.com/static/5a668a99bce1765a27495af0/t/5fc14fdf4e98326c024109a0/1606504451803/Playbook+2030+FINAL-compressed.pdf.

Adler, David. "Stories of Cities #37: How Radical Ideas Turned Curitiba into Brazil's 'Green Capital.'" *The Guardian*, 6 May 2016. https://www.theguardian.com/cities/2016/may/06/story-of-cities-37-mayor-jaime-lerner-curitiba-brazil-green-capital-global-icon.

Adomaitis, Kasparas. "Top Developed World Cities with Low Reliance on Car-Based Mobility." *Euromonitor International*, 31 August 2015. https://blog.euromonitor.com/top-developed-world-cities-with-low-reliance-on-car-based-mobility/.

Agence France-Presse. "'We Will Be Toasted, Roasted and Grilled': IMF Chief Sounds Climate Change Warning." *The Guardian*, 25 October 2017. https://www.theguardian.com/environment/2017/oct/25/we-will-be-toasted-roasted-and-grilled-imf-chief-sounds-climate-change-warning.

Agora Energiewende and Sandbag. *The European Power Sector in 2018: Up-to-Date Analysis on the Electricity Transition*. Berlin, Germany: Agora Energiewende and Sandbag, January 2019. https://www.agora-energiewende.de/fileadmin2/Projekte/2018/EU-Jahresauswertung_2019/Agora-Energiewende_European-Power-Sector-2018_WEB.pdf.

Agyeman, Julian. *Introducing Just Sustainabilities: Policy, Planning and Practice*. London: Zed Books, 2013.

"Alberta at Noon." *CBC Radio*, 4 March 2015. https://www.cbc.ca/albertaatnoon/episode/2015/03/04/an-for-wednesday-march-4-2015/.

"Alberta Tax Overview." *Government of Alberta*, 2020. https://www.alberta.ca/taxes-levies-overview.aspx.

Alberta Transportation. *Fuel Use Relative to Population: A Provincial Analysis*. Edmonton: Government of Alberta, n.d.

Alberta Wilderness Association. "Continuing the Sacrifice of the Eastern Slopes to Old King Coal." Press release, 4 December 2020. https://albertawilderness.ca/continuing-the-sacrifice-of-the-eastern-slopes-to-old-king-coal/.

Alexander, Lisa V., Simon K. Allen, Nathaniel L. Bindoff, François-Marie Béon, John A. Church, Ulrich Cubasch, Seita Umori et al. "Summary for Policymakers." In *Climate Change 2013: The Physical Science Basis. Contribution of Working Group I to the Fifth Assessment Report of the Intergovernmental Panel on Climate Change*, edited by T. F. Stocker et al. (Cambridge: Cambridge University Press), https://www.ipcc.ch/report/ar5/wg1/.

Alini, Erica. "Own a Car? You Won't Believe How Much That's Costing You Every Year." *Global News*, 9 November 2017. https://globalnews.ca/news/3832649/car-ownership-costs-public-transit-canada/.

Allen, Duncan W., and Timothy H. White. "North American Light-Rail Transit Ridership and Operating Costs: A Basis for Comparison." In *Seventh National Conference on Light-Rail Transit* 2:27–35. Conference Proceedings 8. Baltimore, Maryland, 12–15 November 1995. Washington, DC: National Academy Press, 1997. http://onlinepubs.trb.org/Onlinepubs/conf/1995/cp8/cp8v2-003.pdf.

Alvarez, Claude. *Science, Development and Violence: The Revolt against Modernity.* Oxford: University of Oxford Press, 1992.

"An Evening with Jan Gehl at the Calgary Public Library." *Canadian Architect*, 2 April 2011. https://www.canadianarchitect.com/an-evening-with-jan-gehl-at-the-calgary-public-library/.

Anderson, Drew. "Calgary's Tough Choices: Gamble on Growth or Gamble on Retreat." *CBC News*, 12 June 2020. https://www.cbc.ca/news/canada/calgary/calgary-tough-choices-economy-growth-shrinkage-1.5609548.

Anderson, Kristi, Tim Weis, Ben Thibault, Farrah Khan, Beth Nanni, and Noah Farber. *A Costly Diagnosis: Subsidizing Coal Power with Albertans' Health.* Prepared for Pembina Foundation for Environmental Research and Education by the Pembina Institute, Canadian Association of Physicians for the Environment, Asthma Society of Canada, and Lung Association, Alberta and Northwest Territories, March 2013.

Anielski, Mark. *The Economics of Happiness: Building Genuine Wealth.* Gabriola Island, BC: New Society, 2007.

"Arms Production." *Stockholm International Peace Research Institute*, 2020. http://www.sipri.org/research/armaments/production/recent-trends-in-arms-industry.

Arvai, Joe. "This Canadian City Could Be the Next Detroit." *Globe and Mail*, 9 December 2013. https://www.theglobeandmail.com/opinion/this-canadian-city-could-be-the-next-detroit/article15820368/.

Arya, Neil. "Pesticides and Human Health: Why Public Health Officials Should Support a Ban on Non-Essential Residential Use." *Canadian Journal of Public Health* 96 (2005): 89–92.

Atwood, Margaret. *The Handmaid's Tale.* Toronto: McClelland and Stewart, 1985.

Austin, Sam, and Lisa Young. "Political Finance in City Elections: Toronto and Calgary Compared." Paper prepared for presentation at the 2006 Annual Meeting of the Canadian Political Science Association, York University, 1–3 June 2006. https://www.cpsa-acsp.ca/papers-2006/Austin-Young.pdf.

Averill, Nancy. *Diversity Matters: Changing the Face of Public Boards.* Toronto: Maytree Foundation, 2009.

Bahar, Heymi. "Solar PV: Tracking Report." *International Energy Agency*, June 2020. https://www.iea.org/reports/solar-pv.

Baldus-Jeurson, C., Y. Poissant, and Wes Johnston. *National Survey Report of PV Power Applications in Canada 2018*. Paris: International Energy Agency, 2018. https://iea-pvps.org/wp-content/uploads/2020/01/2019-223_RP-ANU_DER-PVNORD_CBaldus-Jeursen_YPoissant_EN.pdf.

Bamburg, Jill. "Mondragon through a Critical Lens." *Employee Ownership News*, 3 October 2017. https://medium.com/fifty-by-fifty/mondragon-through-a-critical-lens-b29de8c6049.

Banerjee, Preet. "Our Love Affair with Home Ownership Might Be Doomed." *Globe and Mail*, 18 January 2012. https://www.theglobeandmail.com/real-estate/mortgages-and-rates/our-love-affair-with-home-ownership-might-be-doomed/article4179012/.

Banerji, Gunjan. "Dow Drops 600 Points on Global Growth Concerns." *Wall Street Journal*, 31 January 2020. https://www.wsj.com/articles/global-stocks-drift-lower-on-economic-growth-concerns-11580466790.

Bausells, Marta. "Superblocks to the Rescue: Barcelona's Plan to Give Streets Back to Residents." *The Guardian*, 17 May 2016. https://www.theguardian.com/cities/2016/may/17/superblocks-rescue-barcelona-spain-plan-give-streets-back-residents.

Beatley, Timothy. *Green Urbanism Down Under*. With Peter Newman. Washington, DC: Island Press, 2008.

———. *Green Urbanism: Learning from European Cities*. Washington, DC: Island Press, 2000. https://www.academia.edu/10399646/Green_Urbanism_Learning_From_European_Cities.

Beck, Julie. "The Decline of the Driver's License." *The Atlantic*, 22 January 2016. https://www.theatlantic.com/technology/archive/2016/01/the-decline-of-the-drivers-license/425169/.

Beck, Ulrich, Anthony Giddens, and Steve Lash. *Reflexive Modernization: Politics, Tradition and Aesthetics in the Modern Social Order*. Chicago: University of Chicago Press, 1995.

Becker, Sophia, Scott Bernstein, and Linda Young. *The New Real Estate Mantra: Location Near Public Transportation*. Chicago: Center for Neighborhood Technology, 2013. https://www.cnt.org/sites/default/files/publications/CNT_TheNewRealEstateMantra.pdf.

Bell, Rhonda. "Understanding Streetcar Costs, Funding, Operations and Partnerships." *Metro Magazine*, 2 August 2017. https://www.metro-magazine.com/10002957/understanding-streetcar-costs-funding-operations-and-partnerships.

Bell, Rick. "Alberta Premier Jim Prentice Says Fiscal Crisis Means Rollbacks on Table for Public Sector . . . and Him." *Edmonton Sun*, 26 January 2015. https://edmontonsun.com/2015/01/25/alberta-premier-jim-prentice-says-fiscal-crisis-means-rollbacks-on-table-for-public-sector--and-him/wcm/61e41a87-6eb1-4b6e-a3da-27d0f59e5580.

Bellefontaine, Michelle. "$260B Liability Figure for Abandoned Energy Infrastructure an 'Error in Judgement': AER." *CBC News*, 1 November 2018. https://www.cbc.ca/news/canada/edmonton/alberta-energy-regulator-liability-figure-error-1.4888532.

Bennet, Dean. "Alberta Finance Minister Says No Money Available for Teacher Salary Increases." *Edmonton Journal*, 4 March 2020. https://edmontonjournal.com/news/local-news/alberta-finance-minister-says-no-money-available-for-teacher-salary-increases.

Bentein, Jim. "Alberta Coal Mining Activity Rebounds in 2018." *Canadian Mining Journal*, 1 April 2019. https://www.jwnenergy.com/article/2019/4/1/coal-mining-activity-alberta-rebounds-2018/.

Benyus, Janine. *Biomimicry: Innovation Inspired by Nature.* New York: William Morrow, 2002.

Berry, Thomas. *The Dream of the Earth.* San Francisco: Sierra Club Books, 1990.

Black, Matthew. "'Ralph Bucks' 14 Years Later: Could the Prosperity Bonus Have Saved Alberta's Bottom Line?" *CTV News*, 14 January 2020. https://edmonton.ctvnews.ca/ralph-bucks-14-years-later-could-the-prosperity-bonus-have-saved-alberta-s-bottom-line-1.4767107.

Bland, Amy R., Jonathan P. Rosier, Mitul A. Mehta, Thea Schei, Barbara J. Sahakian, Trevor W. Robbins, and Rebecca Elliott. "Cooperative Behavior in the Ultimatum Game and Prisoner's Dilemma Depends on Players' Contributions." *Frontiers in Psychology*, 16 June 2017. https://www.frontiersin.org/articles/10.3389/fpsyg.2017.01017/full.

Blunden, Jessica. "2013 State of the Climate: Carbon Dioxide Tops 400 ppm." *National Oceanic and Atmospheric Association*, 13 July 2014. https://www.climate.gov/news-features/understanding-climate/2013-state-climate-carbon-dioxide-tops-400-ppm.

Bombeck, Aaron, Pat Dudar, Erica Hansen, Sarah Christensen, and Oghentega Odogu. *Laneway Housing in Calgary: A GIS Methodology for Site Suitability.* Calgary: University of Calgary, Faculty of Environmental Design, December 2016.

Bower, Shannon Stunden, Trevor Harrison, and Greg Flanagan. *Stabilizing Alberta's Revenues: A Common Sense Approach.* Edmonton: Parkland Institute, February 2013. https://www.parklandinstitute.ca/stabilizing_albertas_revenues.

Braid, Don. "UCP Cancels Doctor Pay Contract, Imposes Radical Change." *Calgary Herald*, 21 February 2020. https://calgaryherald.com/opinion/columnists/braid-ucp-cancels-doctor-pay-contract-imposes-radical-change.

Brennan, Jordan. *A Shrinking Universe: How Concentrated Corporate Power Is Shaping Income Inequality in Canada.* Ottawa: Canadian Centre for Policy Alternatives, November 2012. https://www.policyalternatives.ca/sites/default/files/uploads/publications/National%20Office/2012/11/Shrinking_Universe_0.pdf.

Brenner, Neil, David Marcuse, and Margit Mayer. *Cities for People, Not for Profit: Critical Urban Theory and the Right to the City.* New York: Routledge, 2011.

Broadbent, Ed. "Equality or Barbarism?" Charles R. Bronfman Lecture, University of Ottawa, 14 October 2010. *Toronto Star*, 16 October 2010. https://www.thestar.com/opinion/editorials/2010/10/16/equality_or_barbarism.html.

Buliung, Ron, Raktim Mitra, and Guy Faulkner. "Active School Transportation in the Greater Toronto Area, Canada: An Exploration of Trends in Space and Time (1986–2006)." *Preventive Medicine* 48, no. 6 (2009): 507–12.

Bussard, Lawrence. "Early History of Calgary." Master's thesis, University of Alberta, 1935. https://archive.org/details/earlyhistoryofca00buss/page/n1/mode/2up.

Cadan, Yossi, Ahmed Mokgopo, and Clara Vondrich. *$11 Trillion and Counting*. Boston: 350.org, 2019. https://631nj1ki9k11gbkhx39b3qpz-wpengine.netdna-ssl.com/divestment/wp-content/uploads/sites/52/2019/09/FF_11Trillion-WEB.pdf.

Cahill, Sean A. *Corporate Income Tax Rate Database: Canada and Provinces, 1960–2005*. Ottawa: Agriculture and Agri-Food Canada, March 2007.

Calgary Airport Authority. *YYC Strategic Operating Plan 2009–2013*. Calgary: CAA, November 2008. https://www.yyc.com/portals/0/15_2009031710575YYC StratPlan[1].pdf.

"Calgary Developers Lose 'Sprawl Subsidy' on Water, Road Costs." *CBC News*, 11 January 2016. https://www.cbc.ca/news/canada/calgary/developer-levy-increase-city-council-1.3399577.

Calgary Economic Development. *Calgary in the New Economy: The Economic Strategy for Calgary*. Calgary: CED, 2020. https://calgaryeconomicdevelopment.com/assets/Calgary-in-the-New-Economy/Calgary-in-the-New-Economy-Final.pdf.

———. *Economy*. Calgary: CED. Accessed 4 January 2021. https://calgaryeconomic development.com/dmsdocument/87.

———. *Fact Sheet: Calgary Wealth*. Calgary: CED, 2019. https://calgaryeconomic development.com/research-and-reports/report-library/report-library/?q= FactSheet-Wealth-2018-Edition-2019-07.pdf&sort=LastChanged%20DESC.

"Calgary Facts: Who Is a Calgarian?" *Life in Calgary*. Accessed 27 November 2020. https://www.lifeincalgary.ca/moving/calgary-facts#demographics.

Calgary Food Committee and Serecon Management Consulting Inc. *Calgary Eats! A Food System Assessment and Action Plan for Calgary*. Calgary: City of Calgary, May 2012. https://www.calgary.ca/ca/cmo/calgary-food-system-assessment-and-action-plan.html.

Calgary Homeless Foundation. *10 Year Plan to End Homelessness: 2008–2018*. January 2011 Update. Calgary: CHF, 2011. https://aventa.org/wp-content/uploads/2017/02/10-Year-Plan-Update.pdf.

Calgary Public Library. *Potential Realized: Calgary Public Library—Strategic Plan 2019–2022*. Calgary: CPL, 2019. https://calgarylibrary.ca/assets/PDFs/2020/2019-2022-strategic-plan-2020-initatives.pdf.

"Calgary Ring Road Deal Good for All." *NationTalk*, 25 October 2015. https://nationtalk.ca/story/calgary-ring-road-deal-good-for-all.

"Calgary Ring Road: Overview." *Government of Alberta*, 2020. https://www.alberta.ca/calgary-ring-road-overview.aspx.

Calgary Transportation Department. *Step Forward: A Strategic Plan for Improving Walking in Calgary*. Calgary: City of Calgary, August 2016. https://www.calgary.ca/pedestrianstrategy.

"Calgary Transportation Plan." *City of Calgary*, 2021. https://www.calgary.ca/transportation/tp/planning/calgary-transportation-plan/calgary-transportation-plan-ctp.html.

"Calgary Wins International Award for Pedestrian Strategy." *Canadian Consulting Engineer*, 14 September 2017. https://www.canadianconsultingengineer.com/transportation/calgary-wins-international-award-pedestrian-strategy/1003406086/.

Canada Mortgage and Housing Corporation. *Accessory Apartments: Characteristics, Issues and Opportunities*. Research and Development Highlights: Socio-Economic Series No. 3. Ottawa: CMHC, October 1991.

——. *Ontario Secondary Suite Research Study*. Research Insight. Ottawa: CMHC, May 2017. https://assets.cmhc-schl.gc.ca/sf/project/cmhc/pubsandreports/pdf/69095.pdf?rev=394642f2-9564-489e-8258-2fdc4bdc8446.

——. *The Secondary Rental Market in Canada: Estimated Size and Composition*. 2011 Census/National Household Survey Housing Series: Issue 11. Ottawa: CMHC, April 2016. https://assets.cmhc-schl.gc.ca/sf/project/cmhc/pubsandreports/pdf/68565.pdf?rev=960c40f1-b6d7-4cf0-ae6a-a832159ee503.

"Canada Pulls Out of Kyoto Protocol." *CBC News*, 12 December 2011. https://www.cbc.ca/news/politics/canada-pulls-out-of-kyoto-protocol-1.999072.

Canada. "Canada Has Lowest Tax Rate on New Business Investment in G7." News release, 18 July 2019. https://www.canada.ca/en/department-finance/news/2019/07/canada-has-lowest-tax-rate-on-new-business-investment-in-g7.html.

——. *Greenhouse Gas Emissions: Canadian Environmental Sustainability Indicators*. Ottawa: Environment and Climate Change Canada, 2020. https://www.canada.ca/content/dam/eccc/documents/pdf/cesindicators/ghg-emissions/2020/greenhouse-gas-emissions-en.pdf.

——. *Greenhouse Gas Emissions from Large Facilities: Canadian Environmental Sustainability Indicators*. Ottawa: Environment Canada, 2018. https://www.canada.ca/content/dam/eccc/documents/pdf/cesindicators/greenhouse-gas-emissions-large-facilities/2020/greenhouse-gas-emissions-large-facilities-en.pdf.

Canadian Association of Chiefs of Police. "The Link between Low Literacy and Crime." *Literacy and Policing in Canada: Target Crime with Literacy*, ch. 2, Fact Sheet 2. Kanata, ON: CACP. Accessed 5 January 2021. http://policeabc.ca/files/factsheets_englishPDFs/Ch02FactSheet02.pdf.

"Canadian Consulting Engineer Award of Excellence: Esplanade Riel." *Canadian Consulting Engineer*, 1 November 2014. https://www.canadianconsultingengineer.com/features/award-of-excellence-esplanade-riel/.

"Canadian Income Tax Rates for Individuals—Current and Previous Years." *Government of Canada, Canada Revenue Agency*, last modified 21 January 2020. https://www.canada.ca/en/revenue-agency/services/tax/individuals/frequently-asked-questions-individuals/canadian-income-tax-rates-individuals-current-previous-years.html#provincial.

Canadian Index of Wellbeing. *How Are Canadians Really Doing? The 2016 CIW National Report*. Waterloo, ON: CIW and University of Waterloo, 2016. https://uwaterloo.ca/canadian-index-wellbeing/sites/ca.canadian-index-wellbeing/files/uploads/files/c011676-nationalreport-ciw_final-s.pdf.

———. "New Evidence Reveals Canadian Wellbeing on the Decline." Press release, 23 October 2012. https://www.newswire.ca/news-releases/new-evidence-reveals-canadian-wellbeing-on-the-decline-511009361.html.

Canadian Press. "Concordia University Says It Will Divest Entirely from Coal, Oil and Gas by 2025." *CBC News*, 8 November 2019. https://www.cbc.ca/news/canada/montreal/concordia-divests-1.5353808.

———. "Key Facts in Canada's Robocalls Controversy." *CBC News*, 14 August 2014. https://www.cbc.ca/news/politics/key-facts-in-canada-s-robocalls-controversy-1.2736659.

"Car-Sharing Rolls Back into Calgary as Communauto Offers 150 Vehicles in Some Inner City Neighbourhoods." *CBC News*, 26 August 2020. https://www.cbc.ca/news/canada/calgary/calgary-car-share-return-negotiations-fleet-1.5701573.

"Car2Go to Shut Down in Montreal—And across North America." *CBC News*, 18 December 2019. https://www.cbc.ca/news/canada/montreal/car2go-montreal-north-america-1.5401130.

Caradonna, Jeremy. *Sustainability: A History*. Oxford: Oxford University Press, 2014.

Carbon Trackers. "Accounting for Hidden Reserves." Press release, 4 December 2013. https://carbontracker.org/accounting-for-hidden-reserves-press-release-2/.

———. "Nine out of Ten Barrels in Undeveloped Oil Sands Projects at Risk from Eroding Oil Price." Press release, 4 November 2014. https://carbontracker.org/nine-out-of-ten-barrels-in-undeveloped-oil-sands-projects-at-risk-from-eroding-oil-price/.

Carleton University. "Carleton Releases 2012 National Survey on Balancing Work and Caregiving in Canada: Linda Duxbury to Talk about Findings at Building Healthier Workplaces Conference." Press release, 25 October 2012. https://newsroom.carleton.ca/archives/2012/10/25/carleton-releases-2012-national-study-on-balancing-work-and-caregiving-in-canada-linda-duxbury-to-talk-about-findings-at-building-healthier-workplaces-conference/.

Carson, Rachel. *Silent Spring*. 40th anniversary ed. 1962. Reprint, New York: Houghton Mifflin, 2002.

Cathcart-Keays, Athlyn. "Two-Wheel Takeover: Bikes Outnumber Cars for the First Time in Copenhagen." *The Guardian*, 30 November 2016. https://www.theguardian.com/cities/2016/nov/30/cycling-revolution-bikes-outnumber-cars-first-time-copenhagen-denmark.

Cattaneo, Claudia. "King of Pain: Steve Williams Seizes on Price Pangs to Prepare Suncor for Oilsands Dominance." *Financial Post*, 9 October 2015. https://financialpost.com/commodities/energy/king-of-pain-steve-williams-seizes-on-price-pangs-to-prepare-suncor-for-oilsands-dominance.

Cavanagh, John, Daphne Wysham, and Marcos Arruda, eds. *Beyond Bretton Woods: Alternatives to the Global Economic Order*. Boulder, CO: Pluto Press, 1994.

Cayley-Daoust, Daniel, and Richard Girard. *Big Oil's Oily Grasp: The Making of Canada as a Petro-State and How Oil Money Is Corrupting Canadian Politics*. Ottawa: Polaris Institute, 2012. https://www.polarisinstitute.org/big_oil_s_oily_grasp.

CBE Communication and Engagement Services. *Shaping the Future of High School Spring Survey, 2019*. Calgary: Calgary Board of Education, 2019. https://www.cbe.ab.ca/get-involved/public-engagement/Documents/01082019-full-survey-report-public.pdf.

Celis-Morales, Carlos A., Donald M. Lyall, Paul Welsh, Jana Anderson, Lewis Steell, Yibing Guo, Reno Maldonado et al. "Association between Active Commuting and Incident Cardiovascular Disease, Cancer, and Mortality: Prospective Cohort Study." *British Medical Journal* 357 (April 2017).

Center for Neighborhood Technology. *Penny Wise Pound Fuelish: New Measures of Housing and Transportation Affordability*. Chicago: CNT, 2010. https://www.cnt.org/sites/default/files/publications/CNT_pwpf.pdf.

Cervero, Robert, and Mark Hansen. "Induced Travel Demand and Induced Road Investment: A Simultaneous Equation Analysis." *Journal of Transport Economics and Policy* 36, no. 3 (2002): 469–90. https://www.jstor.org/stable/20053915.

Charlton, Emma. "New Zealand Has Unveiled Its First 'Well-Being' Budget." *World Economic Forum*, 30 May 2019. https://www.weforum.org/agenda/2019/05/new-zealand-is-publishing-its-first-well-being-budget/.

Chen, Simiao, Michael Kuhn, Klaus Prettner, and David E. Bloom. "The Global Macroeconomic Burden of Road Injuries: Estimates and Projections for 166 Countries." *Lancet Planet Health* 3 (2019): e390–98. https://www.thelancet.com/action/showPdf?pii=S2542-5196%2819%2930170-6.

Chesterton, Andrew. "How Many Cars Are There in the World?" *Carsguide*, 6 August 2018. https://www.carsguide.com.au/car-advice/how-many-cars-are-there-in-the-world-70629.

Chiland, Elijah. "Metro CEO Supports Congestion Pricing, Free Fares on Public Transit." *CURBED Los Angeles*, 6 December 2018. https://la.curbed.com/2018/12/6/18129258/congestion-pricing-free-fares-metro-los-angeles.

"Cities and Neighbourhoods." *Walk Score*, 2020. https://www.walkscore.com/cities-and-neighborhoods/.

City of Calgary. *2017 Infrastructure Status Report*. Calgary: City of Calgary, 2017.

———. *2019 Quality of Life and Citizen Satisfaction Survey*. Calgary: City of Calgary, 2019. https://newsroom.calgary.ca/2019-citizen-satisfaction-survey-results/.

———. "Walkable and Transit Friendly Communities in Calgary." *Mobility Monitor*, May 2011. https://www.calgary.ca/transportation/tp/planning/transportation-data/transportation-monitoring-reports.html.

———. *Changing Travel Behaviour in the Calgary Region.* Travel Behaviour Report Series: Vol. 1. Calgary: City of Calgary, June 2013. https://www.calgary.ca/Transportation/TP/Documents/forecasting/Changing%20Travel%20Behaviour%20in%20the%20Calgary%20Region_v1_forWeb_2013-06-04.pdf?noredirect=1.

———. *Cycling Strategy.* Calgary: City of Calgary, June 2011. https://www.calgary.ca/transportation/tp/cycling/cycling-strategy/cycling-strategy.html.

———. *Fall 2020 Quality of Life and Citizen Satisfaction Survey.* Calgary: City of Calgary, 2020. https://www.calgary.ca/cfod/csc/citizen-satisfaction.html?redirect=/citsat.

———. *Foundations for Home: Calgary's Corporate Affordable Housing Strategy 2016–2025.* Calgary: City of Calgary, 2016. https://www.calgary.ca/cs/olsh/affordable-housing/affordable-housing.html.

———. *Hillhurst Sunnyside Area Redevelopment Plan.* Calgary: City of Calgary, 2018. https://d3aencwbm6zmht.cloudfront.net/asset/399111/hillhurst-sunnyside-arp.pdf.

———. *Housing in Calgary: An Inventory of Housing Supply, 2015–2016.* Calgary: City of Calgary, Affordable Housing Division. Accessed 14 November 2020. https://www.calgary.ca/cs/olsh/affordable-housing/learning-about-affordable-housing.html.

———. *Investing in Mobility: Transportation Infrastructure Investment Plan.* Calgary: City of Calgary, 2014.

———. *Keystone Hills Area Structure Plan.* Calgary: City of Calgary, 2012. https://www.calgary.ca/pda/pd/current-studies-and-ongoing-activities/keystone-hills.html.

———. *Keystone Hills Area Structure Plan: Ecological Footprint.* Report to Calgary Planning Commission. CPC212-041, Attachment 3, Appendix II, 12 April 2012.

———. *Municipal Development Plan.* Calgary: City of Calgary, 2009. https://www.calgary.ca/pda/pd/municipal-development-plan/municipal-development-plan-mdp.html.

———. *Municipal Development Plan/Calgary Transportation Plan 2018 Monitoring Progress Report.* Calgary: City of Calgary, 2018. https://www.calgary.ca/pda/pd/municipal-development-plan/municipal-development-plan-and-calgary-transportation-plan-2018-monitoring-progress-report.html.

———. *One Calgary: 2019–2022 Service Plans and Budgets.* Calgary: City of Calgary. Accessed 11 November 2020. https://www.calgary.ca/cfod/finance/plans-budgets-and-financial-reports/plans-and-budget-2019-2022/service-plans-and-budgets.html.

———. *Resilient Calgary.* Calgary: City of Calgary, 2019. https://www.calgary.ca/cs/calgary-resilience.html.

———. *Step Forward: A Strategic Plan for Improving Walking in Calgary.* Calgary: City of Calgary, August 2016. https://www.calgary.ca/transportation/tp/planning/calgary-transportation-plan/pedestrian-strategy.html?redirect=/pedestrianstrategy.

———. *Transit Oriented Development: Policy Guidelines.* Calgary: City of Calgary, 2005. https://www.calgary.ca/pda/pd/current-studies-and-ongoing-activities/transit-oriented-development-tod.html.

City of Kamloops. *Residential Suites Policy Update: Community Engagement Summary Report.* Kamloops, BC: City of Kamloops, March 2019. https://letstalk.kamloops.ca/7728/documents/15030.

Clark, Christopher. *The Sleepwalkers: How Europe Went to War in 1914.* New York: Harper, 2013.

Clarke, Desmond. *Descartes: A Biography.* Cambridge: Cambridge University Press, 2006.

Clausewitz, Carl von. *On War.* Translated by J. J. Graham. New York: Barnes and Noble, 2004. First published 1873.

"Coal Plants Cost Alberta $300M in Health Costs: Report." *CBC News*, 26 March 2013. https://www.cbc.ca/news/canada/edmonton/coal-plants-cost-alberta-300m-in-health-costs-report-1.1326727.

Commoner, Barry. *The Closing Circle: Nature, Man and Society.* New York: Knopf, 1971.

Conan Doyle, Arthur. "Cycling Notes." *Scientific American*, 18 January 1896. http://wheelbike.blogspot.com/2011/04/sir-arthur-conan-doyle-on-benefits-of.html.

Conceição, Pedro. *Beyond Income, Beyond Averages, Beyond Today: Inequalities in Human Development in the 21st Century.* Overview: Human Development Report 2019. New York: United Nations Development Programme, 2019. http://hdr.undp.org/sites/default/files/hdr_2019_overview_-_english.pdf.

Condon, Patrick M., Sigrid Gruenberger, and Marta Klaptocz. *The Case for the Tram: Learning from Portland.* Foundational Research Bulletin No. 6. Vancouver: University of British Columbia, Design Centre for Sustainability, May 2008. http://www.sxd.sala.ubc.ca/8_research/sxd_FRB06_tram.pdf.

"Confirmed Minutes 2012-10-15, Regular." Available at "Council and Committee Meetings and Bylaws." *City of Calgary*, 2017. https://publicaccess.calgary.ca/searchCCProc/index.htm.

Cotter, Adam. *Public Confidence in Canadian Institutions.* Spotlight on Canadians: Results from the General Social Survey. Catalogue no. 89-652-X2015007. Ottawa: Statistics Canada, December 2015. https://www150.statcan.gc.ca/n1/en/pub/89-652-x/89-652-x2015007-eng.pdf?st=ZAcCmKdF.

"Country Overshoot Days." *Earth Overshoot Day*, 2020. https://www.overshootday.org/newsroom/country-overshoot-days/.

"COVID-19 Coronavirus Pandemic: Reported Case of Death by Country, Territory or Conveyance." *Worldometer*, 2020. https://www.worldometers.info/coronavirus/.

Cox, Ethan. "Laval Becomes First University in Canada to Divest from Fossil Fuels." *Ricochet*, 15 February 2017. https://ricochet.media/en/1684/laval-becomes-first-university-in-canada-to-divest-from-fossil-fuels.

Coyne, Andrew. "New Brunswick Provides More Ammunition for Blowing Up First Past the Post." *National Post*, 27 September 2018. https://nationalpost.com/opinion/

andrew-coyne-n-b-election-provides-still-more-reasons-for-blowing-up-first-past-the-post.

Crawford, J. H. *Carfree Cities*. Utrecht, Netherlands: International Books, 2002.

"The 'Creative Class' Were Just the Rich All Along." *Long Reads*. Accessed 12 January 2021. https://longreads.com/2017/08/23/the-creative-class/.

Crowshoe, Lorna, and Fraser McLeod. *Indigenous Policy Framework for the City of Calgary*. Calgary: City of Calgary, Calgary Aboriginal Urban Affairs Committee, 2017. https://www.calgary.ca/csps/cns/first-nations-metis-and-inuit-peoples/first-nations-metis-inuit-peoples.html.

"Cuban Hurricane Preparation Offers Lessons in Organization." *Los Angeles Times*, 10 September 2005. https://www.latimes.com/archives/la-xpm-2005-sep-10-na-cuba10-story.html.

CUPE-BC and Civic Economics. *Independent BC: Small Business and the British Columbia Economy*. Chicago: Civic Economics, February 2013. https://ccednet-rcdec.ca/sites/ccednet-rcdec.ca/files/ccednet/pdfs/independant_bc_small_and_the_british_colombia_economy.pdf.

D'Alisa, Giacomo, Federico Demaria, and Giorgos Kallis, eds. *Degrowth: A Vocabulary for a New Era*. New York: Routledge, 2014.

Dabbs, Frank. "Ralph Klein's Real Legacy." *Alberta Views*, 1 September 2006. https://albertaviews.ca/ralph-kleins-real-legacy/.

Dahlby, Bev, and Greg Flanagan. "Should Alberta Have Higher Taxes?" *Alberta Views*, 1 May 2019. https://albertaviews.ca/alberta-higher-taxes/.

Daly, Herman. "Economics for a Full World." *Great Transition Initiative*, June 2015. http://www.greattransition.org/publication/economics-for-a-full-world.

——. *Beyond Growth: The Economics of Sustainable Development*. Boston: Beacon Press, 1997.

——. *From Uneconomic Growth to a Steady-State Economy*. Advances in Ecological Economics Series. Cheltenham, UK: Edward Elgar, 2014.

DARA and Climate Vulnerable Forum. *A Guide to the Cold Calculus of a Hot Planet*. Climate Vulnerability Monitor, 2nd ed. Madrid: Fundación DARA Internacional, 2012. https://daraint.org/wp-content/uploads/2012/09/CVM2ndEd-FrontMatter.pdf.

Darwin, Charles. *On the Origin of Species by Means of Natural Selection, or the Preservation of Favoured Races in the Struggle for Life*. New York: Bantam Classics, 1999. First published 1859 by John Murray (London).

Daseking, Wulf, Babette Köhler, and Götz Kemnitz. *Freiburg Charter: Requirements on Urban Development and Planning for the Future*. Freiburg: Academy of Urbanism and City of Freiburg, 2012. http://www.wulf-daseking.de/files/8214/0110/4795/Charta_Freiburg_2012en.pdf.

"Data Tables, 2016 Census." *Statistics Canada*, last modified 2019. https://www12.statcan.gc.ca/census-recensement/2016/dp-pd/dt-td/Rp-eng.cfm?TABID=2&Lang=E&APA-

TH=3&DETAIL=0&DIM=0&FL=A&FREE=0&GC=0&GID=1341679&GK=0&G
RP=1&PID=110531&PRID=10&PTYPE=109445&S=0&SHOWALL=0&SUB=0&-
Temporal=2017&THEME=120&VID=0&VNAMEE=&VNAMEF=&D1=0&D2=0
&D3=0&D4=0&D5=0&D6=0.

David, Taionrén:hote Dan. "Point of View: The Oka Crisis—Looking Forward after 30 Years." *CBC News*, 10 July 2020. https://www.cbc.ca/news/canada/montreal/pov-taionrén-hote-dan-david-on-oka-crisis-after-30-years-1.5644082.

Davis, Julie, David Merriman, Lucia Samayoa, and Brian Flanagan. *The Impact of an Urban Wal-Mart Store on Area Businesses: An Evaluation of One Chicago Neighborhood's Experience*. Chicago: Loyola University, Center for Urban Research and Learning, December 2009. https://ecommons.luc.edu/cgi/viewcontent. cgi?article=1002&context=curl_pubs.

Davis, Mike. *Planet of Slums*. New York: Verso, 2007.

Davis, Wade. *Into the Silence: The Great War, Mallory, and the Conquest of Everest*. Toronto: Vintage, 2012.

Davison, Aidan. *Technology and the Contested Meanings of Sustainability*. Albany: SUNY Press, 2001.

"Day 9: Tuesday, September 6." *PBS Frontline*, "14 Days: A Timeline," 22 November 2005. https://www.pbs.org/wgbh/pages/frontline/storm/etc/cron.html.

De Blasio, Bill, and Sadiq Khan. "As New York and London Mayors, We Call on All Cities to Divest from Fossil Fuels." *The Guardian*, 10 September 2018. https://www. theguardian.com/commentisfree/2018/sep/10/london-new-york-cities-divest-fossil-fuels-bill-de-blasio-sadiq-khan.

De Waal, Frans. *Are We Smart Enough to Know How Smart Animals Are?* New York: W. W. Norton, 2016.

Deberry, Jarvis. "Today's a Day to Remember Those Killed by Hurricanes Katrina and Maria." *New Orleans Advocate*, 29 August 2018. https://www.nola.com/opinions/ article_cb104aaa-aadf-5e90-b3a1-1413c51f85e2.html.

Deer, Brian. "There Is No Such Thing As Society." *Brian Deer: Award-Winning Investigations*. Accessed 6 February 2020. https://briandeer.com/social/thatcher-society.htm.

Dell'Amore, Christine. "Species Extinction Happening 1,000 Times Faster Because of Humans?" *National Geographic*, 30 May 2014. https://www.nationalgeographic. com/news/2014/5/140529-conservation-science-animals-species-endangered-extinction/.

Dembicki, Geoff. "The Emperor Kenney's New Clothes." *The Tyee*, 24 April 2020. https:// thetyee.ca/Analysis/2020/04/24/The-Emperor-Kenneys-New-Clothes/.

Dempsey, Hugh. *Calgary: Spirit of the West: A History*. Saskatoon: Fifth House, 1994.

Descamps, Philippe. "Copenhagen, Cycle City." *Le Monde diplomatique*, March 2020. https://mondediplo.com/2020/03/13copenhagen-bikes.

"Divestment: Overview." *Fossil Free*. Accessed 6 September 2020. https://gofossilfree.org/divestment/commitments/.

Dodge, David, and Duncan Kinney. "Calgary's Wind-Powered LRT an Incredibly Successful System: Nenshi." *Pembina Institute* (blog), 6 July 2015. https://www.pembina.org/blog/calgary-s-wind-powered-lrt-an-incredibly-successful-system-nenshi.

Doherty, Jeff. "Secondary Suites: Can Calgary Put This Debate to Bed?" *Alberta Views*, 1 April 2016. https://albertaviews.ca/secondary-suites/.

Downs, Anthony. "The Law of Peak-Hour Expressway Congestion." *Traffic Quarterly* 16, no. 3 (1962): 393–409. https://hdl.handle.net/2027/ucl.$b3477?urlappend=%3Bseq=457.

Dryzek, John. "Growth Unlimited: The Promethean Response." In *The Politics of the Earth: Environmental Discourses*. Oxford: Oxford University Press, 2013.

Duany, Andres, Elizabeth Plater-Zyberk, and Jeff Speck. *Suburban Nation: The Rise of Sprawl and the Decline of the American Dream*. New York: North Point Press, 2010.

Duxbury, Linda. *Dealing with Work-Life Issues in the Workplace: Standing Still Is Not an Option*. 2004 Don Wood Lecture in Industrial Relations. Kingston, ON: Queen's University, Industrial Relations Centre, 2004.

———, and Christopher Higgins. *Revisiting Work-Life Issues in Canada: The 2012 National Study on Balancing Work and Caregiving in Canada*. Report 1. Ottawa: Carleton University, 2012. https://newsroom.carleton.ca/wp-content/files/2012-National-Work-Long-Summary.pdf.

———, Maggie Stevenson, and Christopher Higgins. "Too Much to Do, Too Little Time: Role Overload and Stress in a Multi-Role Environment." *International Journal of Stress Management* 25, no. 3 (2018): 250–66.

Dyer, Gwynne. *War: The New Edition*. New York: Random House, 2004.

E. D. Hovee and Company. *Streetcar-Development Linkage: The Portland Streetcar Loop*. Prepared for City of Portland Office of Transportation, February 2008. http://www.reconnectingamerica.org/assets/Hovee-Report-Eastside-2008.pdf.

"Ecological Footprint." *Global Footprint Network: Advancing the Science of Sustainability*, 2003–20. https://www.footprintnetwork.org/our-work/ecological-footprint/.

Eisler, Riane. *The Chalice and the Blade: Our History, Our Future*. San Francisco: Harper, 1988.

"The End of Coal." *Government of Ontario*. Accessed 6 September 2020. https://www.ontario.ca/page/end-coal.

Energy Efficiency Alberta. *2019–2020 Annual Report*. Calgary: Energy Efficiency Alberta, 2020.

Escobar, Arturo. *Encountering Development: The Making and Unmaking of the Third World*. Princeton, NJ: Princeton University Press, 1995.

Eskins, Julia, and Karen Burshtein. "Step inside the World's 9 Most Futuristic Libraries." *Architectural Digest*, 5 December 2018. https://www.architecturaldigest.com/story/futuristic-libraries.

"Evolution of Solar PV Module Cost by Data Source, 1970–2020." *International Energy Agency*. Last updated 30 June 2020. https://www.iea.org/data-and-statistics/charts/evolution-of-solar-pv-module-cost-by-data-source-1970-2020.

Fanon, Frantz. *The Wretched of the Earth*. Translated by Richard Philcox. New York: Grove Press, 1963.

"February 2020 Price Index Results Released." *AutoTrader*, 5 March 2020. https://www.autotrader.ca/newsfeatures/20200305/february-2020-price-index-results-released.

Ferguson, Eva. "Parents Worry As New S.E. High School Fills Up, Turning Beaverbrook into a 'Ghost Town.'" *Calgary Herald*, 24 January 2019. https://calgaryherald.com/news/local-news/suburban-high-schools-overflow-as-inner-city-buildings-start-to-empty.

Fisher, Marc. "Cruising toward Oblivion." *Washington Post,* 2 September 2015. https://www.washingtonpost.com/sf/style/2015/09/02/americas-fading-car-culture/.

Florida, Richard. *The New Urban Crisis: How Our Cities Are Increasing Inequality, Deepening Segregation, and Failing the Middle Class—And What We Can Do about It*. New York: Basic Books, 2017.

———. *The Rise of the Creative Class: Revisited*. 10th anniversary ed. Philadelphia: Basic Books, 2014.

Fodor, Eben. *Better Not Bigger: How to Take Control of Urban Growth and Improve Your Community*. Gabriola Island, BC: New Society, 2007.

Fong, Francis. *Income Inequality in Canada: The Urban Gap*. Ottawa: Chartered Professional Accountants of Canada, 2017. https://www.cpacanada.ca/en/the-cpa-profession/about-cpa-canada/key-activities/public-policy-government-relations/economic-policy-research/income-inequality-canada.

Foran, Max. *Expansive Discourses: Urban Sprawl in Calgary, 1945–78*. Athabasca, AB: Athabasca University Press, 2009.

———, and Heather Foran. *Calgary: Canada's Frontier Metropolis*. Los Angeles: Windsor, 1982.

Ford Motor Company. "Looking Further with Ford: 2020 Trends." Accessed 3 September 2020. https://media.ford.com/content/dam/fordmedia/North%20America/US/2019/12/11/2020-Ford-Trends.pdf.

"Foreign Born Population %." *World Cities Culture Forum*. Accessed 7 September 2020. http://www.worldcitiescultureforum.com/data/foreign-born-population.

"Fort Edmonton Footbridge and Trails Fact Sheet." *City of Edmonton*. Accessed 3 September 2020. https://www.edmonton.ca/projects_plans/parks_recreation/fort-edmonton-footbridge-and-trails-fact-sheet.aspx.

Fournier, Philippe. "338Canada: The Urban-Rural Divide, Right along Party Lines." *Maclean's*, 29 September 2019. https://www.macleans.ca/politics/ottawa/338canada-the-urban-rural-divide-right-along-party-lines/.

Frangoul, Anmar. "Swedish Pension Fund with Billions of Assets under Management to Stop Fossil Fuel Investments." *CNBC*, 17 March 2020. https://www.cnbc.com/2020/03/17/swedish-pension-fund-to-stop-fossil-fuel-investments.html.

Franklin, Michael. "Voter Turnout Highest in 40 Years in Calgary." *CTV News*, 17 October 2017. https://calgary.ctvnews.ca/voter-turnout-highest-in-40-years-in-calgary-1.3636034.

Freire, Paolo. *Pedagogy of the Oppressed*. 30th anniversary ed. Translated by Myra Bergman Ramos. New York: Continuum, 2005.

French, Janet. "Alberta's Heritage Savings Trust Fund Hits Lowest Value in Eight Years." *CBC News*, 13 July 2020. https://www.cbc.ca/news/canada/edmonton/alberta-s-heritage-savings-trust-fund-1.5648392.

Gare, Arran. *Nihilism Inc.: Environmental Destruction and the Metaphysics of Sustainability*. Sydney, Australia: Eco-Logical Press, 1996.

Gehl, Jan. *Cities for People*. Washington, DC: Island Press, 2010.

German Advisory Council on Global Change. *Humanity on the Move: Unlocking the Transformative Power of Cities*. Berlin: WBGU, 2016.

Getaround. "Getaround Becomes Global Carsharing Leader with $300 Million Acquisition of European Platform Drivy." Press release, 24 April 2019. https://www.getaround.com/media/public/press/Getaround_Announces_300M_Acquisition_of_European_Platform_Drivy.pdf.

Gilligan, Melissa. "1 in 3 Canadians Suffer from Road Rage Each Month: Survey." *Global News*, 14 July 2015. https://globalnews.ca/news/2109293/1-in-3-canadians-suffer-from-road-rage-each-month-survey/.

Gillispie, Charles Coulton. *Pierre-Simon Laplace, 1749–1827: A Life in Exact Science*. Princeton, NJ: Princeton University Press, 1997.

"Gini Index (World Bank Estimate)—Country Ranking." *IndexMundi*. Accessed 21 August 2020. https://www.indexmundi.com/facts/indicators/SI.POV.GINI/rankings.

Giovannetti, Justin. "Kenney Seeks Nearly $1.7-Billion from Ottawa after Collapse in Alberta Oil Prices." *Global and Mail*, 13 November 2019. https://www.theglobeandmail.com/canada/alberta/article-alberta-premier-jason-kenney-seeks-nearly-17-billion-bailout-from/.

Gismondi, Mike, and Debra Davidson. *Challenging Legitimacy at the Precipice of Energy Calamity*. New York: Springer, 2011.

"Global Advertising Revenue from 2012–2024." *Statista*. Accessed 29 November 2020. https://www.statista.com/statistics/236943/global-advertising-spending/.

"Global New Installed Solar PV Capacity from 2000 to 2019." *Statista*, 14 July 2020. https://www.statista.com/statistics/280200/global-new-installed-solar-pv-capacity/.

Global Retail Strategies Inc. *Recommended Direction for City-Wide Commercial/ Retail Policy (Macro/Micro Final Report)*. Calgary: City of Calgary, December 2008. Amended 5 March 2009. https://kempton.files.wordpress.com/2009/03/commercial_study_final_macro_section.pdf.

Golden, Mark. "Sacrifice and Luck Help Japan Survive without Nuclear Power, Stanford Visiting Scholar Says." *Stanford University News*, 4 January 2013. https://news.stanford.edu/news/2013/january/japan-nuclear-power-010413.html.

Goodbrand, Pernille, Tamara Humphreys, and Jyoti Gondek. "Relatives or Rentals? Secondary Suites through a Multi-Generational Family Lens." *Canadian Geographer* 61, no. 4 (2017): 525–39.

Gordon, David. *Still Suburban? Growth in Canadian Suburbs, 2006–2016*. With Lyra Hindrich and Chris Willms. Council for Canadian Urbanism Working Paper #2, August, 2018. http://www.canadiansuburbs.ca/files/Still_Suburban_Monograph_2016.pdf.

Gould, Tim, and Neil Atkinson. "The Global Oil Industry Is Experiencing a Shock Like No Other in Its History." *International Energy Agency*, 1 April 2020. https://www.iea.org/articles/the-global-oil-industry-is-experiencing-shock-like-no-other-in-its-history.

Grant, Andrew. *Mind the Gap: The $1.6 Trillion Investment Risk*. London: Carbon Trackers, 2018. https://carbontracker.org/reports/mind-the-gap/.

Gray, Alex. "Estonia Is Making Public Transport Free." *World Economic Forum*, 1 June 2018. https://www.weforum.org/agenda/2018/06/estonia-is-making-public-transport-free/.

Green Party of Canada. "May Clarifies Deliberately Confusing Bill-C38." Press release, 10 May 2012. https://www.greenparty.ca/en/media-release/2012-05-10/may-clarifies-deliberately-confusing-bill-c-38.

Greene, Gregory, dir. *The End of Suburbia: Oil Depletion and the Collapse of the American Dream*. Belleville, ON: Electric Wallpaper Co., 2004.

Greenfield, Adam. *Radical Technologies: The Design of Everyday Life*. New York: Verso, 2017.

Grober, Ulrich. *Sustainability: A Cultural History*. Translated by Ray Cunningham. Cambridge, UK: UIT Cambridge, 2013.

"Guadalajara Light Rail System." *Railway Technology*. Accessed 31 August 2020. https://www.railway-technology.com/projects/guadalajara-light-rail-system/.

Guevara, Ernesto Che. *The Motorcycle Diaries: A Journey around South America*. London: Verso, 1995.

Gunnar, Astrid. "The Secret of Their Success: The Nordic Countries Are Probably the Best-Governed in the World." *The Economist*, 31 January 2013. https://www.economist.com/special-report/2013/01/31/the-secret-of-their-success.

Hafner, Marco, Martin Stepanek, and Wendy Troxel. *Later School Start Times in the US: An Economic Analysis*. Cambridge, UK: Rand Corporation, 2017. https://www.

rand.org/content/dam/rand/pubs/research_reports/RR2100/RR2109/RAND_
RR2109.pdf.

Haider, Murtaza, and Stephen Moranis. "Renters in Canada Are Three Times More Likely
to Be in Need of Adequate Housing Than Owners." *Financial Post,* 13 October
2020. https://financialpost.com/real-estate/renters-in-canada-are-three-times-
more-likely-to-be-in-need-of-adequate-housing-than-owners.

Haines, Andy, and Kristie Ebi. "The Imperative for Climate Action to Protect Health." *New
England Journal of Medicine* 380 (2019): 263–73.

Harari, Yuval Noah. *Homo Deus: A Brief History of Tomorrow.* Oxford: Signal Books, 2017.

———. *Sapiens: A Brief History of Humankind.* Oxford: Signal Books, 2016.

Harcourt, Mike, and Ken Cameron. *City Making in Paradise: Nine Decisions That Saved
Vancouver.* With Sean Rossiter. Vancouver: Douglas and McIntyre, 2007.

Hardoon, Deborah. *An Economy for the 99%.* Oxfam Briefing Paper. Oxford, UK: Oxfam
Great Britain, January 2017. https://www.oxfam.org/sites/www.oxfam.org/files/
file_attachments/bp-economy-for-99-percent-160117-en.pdf.

Harris, Michael. *Lament for an Ocean: The Collapse of the Atlantic Cod Fishery.* Toronto:
McClelland and Stewart, 2011.

Harris, Richard, and Kathleen Kinsella. "Secondary Suites: A Survey of Evidence and
Municipal Policy." *Canadian Geographer* 61, no. 4 (2017): 493–509.

Harvey, David. "Possible Urban Worlds." Megacities Lecture 4. Amersfoort,
Netherlands: Twynstra Gudde Management Consultants, 2009. https://
www.kas.de/c/document_library/get_file?uuid=1463ff93-1eab-8877-edfc-
ccef8540c262&groupId=252038.

———. *Rebel Cities: From the Right to the City to the Urban Revolution.* London: Verso,
2013.

———. *Spaces of Capital: Towards a Critical Geography.* London: Routledge, 2012.

Hatuka, Tali, Issachar Rosen-Zvi, Michael Birnhack, Eran Toch, and Hadas Zur. "The
Political Premises of Contemporary Urban Concepts: The Global City, the
Sustainable City, the Resilient City, the Creative City, and the Smart City." *Planning
Theory and Practice* 19, no. 2 (2018): 160–79.

Helliwell, John, Richard Layard, Jeffrey D. Sachs, and Jan Emmanuel De Neve, eds. *World
Happiness Report 2020.* New York: Sustainable Development Solutions Network,
2020. https://happiness-report.s3.amazonaws.com/2020/WHR20.pdf.

Henbest, Seb, Matthias Kimmel, Jef Callens, Tifenn Brandily, Meredith Annex, Julia
Attwood, Melina Bartels et al. *Bloomberg 2019 New Energy Outlook.* New York:
Bloomberg New Energy Finance, 2019. https://about.bnef.com/new-energy-
outlook/.

Henton, Darcy. "MSA Seeks Ban against Energy Traders in TransAlta Case."
Calgary Herald, 3 January 2014. http://www.calgaryherald.com/business/
seeks+against+energy+traders+TransAlta+case/9565197/story.html.

———, and Chris Varcoe. "Alberta Launches $3-Billion Cimate Change Strategy with Carbon Tax." *Calgary Herald,* 23 November 2015. https://calgaryherald.com/news/politics/alberta-unveils-details-of-its-climate-plan.

"Here Are the Top 10 Sovereign Wealth Funds in the Arab World." *Al Arabiya*, 10 September 2020. https://english.alarabiya.net/en/business/economy/2019/08/28/Here-are-the-top-10-sovereign-wealth-funds-in-the-Arab-world.

Herremans, Irene, and Jing Lu. "Board Gender Diversity and Environmental Performance: An Industries Perspective." *Business Strategy and the Environment* 28, no. 7 (2019): 1449–64.

"High Income Tax-Filers in Canada, Table: 11-10-0055-01." *Statistics Canada*, last modified 13 November 2020. https://www150.statcan.gc.ca/t1/tbl1/en/tv.action?pid=1110005501.

Hiller, Harry H., ed. *Urban Canada*. 3rd ed. Don Mills, ON: Oxford University Press, 2014.

Hillier, Jean, and Emma Rooksby, eds. *Habitus: A Sense of Place*. 2nd ed. London: Routledge, 2005.

Hirji, Zahra. "Stanford, Once Hailed for Divesting from Coal, Criticized for Not Going Further." *Inside Climate News*, 26 April 2016. https://insideclimatenews.org/news/26042016/stanford-divestment-coal-oil-gas-fossil-fuels-climate-change.

"History of the Marshall Plan." *George C. Marshall Foundation*. Accessed 6 September 2020. https://www.marshallfoundation.org/marshall/the-marshall-plan/history-marshall-plan/.

Holland, John H. *Complexity: A Very Short Introduction*. Oxford: Oxford University Press, 2014.

Holloway, Andy. "FP500: The Premier Ranking of Corporate Canada." *Financial Post*, 13 June 2019. https://financialpost.com/feature/fp500-the-premier-ranking-of-corporate-canada.

Hourdajian, Dara. "Introduced Species Summary Project: Dandelion (*Taraxacum officinale*)." *Columbia University*. Last edited 13 November 2006. http://www.columbia.edu/itc/cerc/danoff-burg/invasion_bio/inv_spp_summ/Taraxum_officinale.htm.

House, Rosemary, dir. *Rain, Drizzle, and Fog*. Ottawa: National Film Board, 1998. https://www.nfb.ca/film/rain_drizzle_and_fog/.

"Household Debt-to-Income Ratio Near Record High." *Canada Mortgage and Housing Corporation*, 13 December 2018. https://www.cmhc-schl.gc.ca/en/housing-observer-online/2018-housing-observer/household-debt-income-ratio-near-record-high.

"Household Spending, Canada, Regions and Provinces." *Statistics Canada,* last modified 3 January 2021. https://www150.statcan.gc.ca/t1/tbl1/en/cv.action?pid=1110022201.

"Housing + Transportation Index." *Center for Neighborhood Technology*. Accessed 29 November 2020. https://htaindex.cnt.org.

"How Canada Performs: Income per Capita." *Conference Board of Canada.* Accessed 9 September 2020. https://www.conferenceboard.ca/hcp/provincial/economy/income-per-capita.aspx.

"How Many Ads Do You See Each Day?" *Gradschools.com*, 2020. https://www.gradschools.com/programs/marketing-advertising/how-many-ads-do-you-see-each-day.

Howell, Trevor Scott. "Update: Business Throw Backing behind Secondary Suites." *Calgary Herald,* 13 December 2014.

———, and Annalise Klingbeil. "Data Reveals Pedestrian Danger: One Hit Per Day, and Most Had the Right of Way." *Calgary Herald*, 19 February 2016. https://calgaryherald.com/news/local-news/oh-no-not-again-city-data-shows-one-pedestrian-collision-a-day-most-had-right-of-way-20-hit-and-run.

"HSBC Documents Show Bank Helped Clients Hide Billions from Tax Man." *CBC News*, 9 February 2015. https://www.cbc.ca/news/business/hsbc-documents-show-bank-helped-clients-hide-billions-from-tax-man-1.2950062.

Hudson, C. A. *Poverty Costs 2.0: Investing in Albertans.* Calgary: Vibrant Communities Calgary and Action to End Poverty in Alberta, 2013. http://vibrantcalgary.com/wp-content/uploads/2016/06/PCosts_2_Investing_In_Albertans_web.pdf.

IBI Group. *The Implications of Alternative Growth Patterns on Infrastructure Costs.* Calgary: City of Calgary, April 2009. http://www.reconnectingamerica.org/assets/Uploads/planitcalgarycoststudyanalysisaprilthird.pdf.

Illich, Ivan. *Energy and Equity.* London: Marion Boyers, 2000.

imagineCalgary. "imagineCalgary Plan for Long Range Urban Sustainability." Calgary: City of Calgary, September 2007. https://www.calgary.ca/pda/pd/office-of-sustainability/imaginecalgary.html.

"Improving Energy Efficiency in Alberta's Buildings." *Pembina Institute* (blog), 13 February 2013. https://www.pembina.org/blog/improving-energy-efficiency-alberta-s-buildings.

International Institute for Sustainable Development. *Costs of Pollution in Canada: Measuring the Impacts on Families, Businesses and Governments.* Winnipeg: IISD, 2017. https://www.iisd.org/story/costs-of-pollution-in-canada/.

International Transport Forum. *Urban Mobility System Upgrade: How Shared Self-Driving Cars Could Change City Traffic.* Paris: Organisation for Economic Co-operation and Development, 2015. https://www.itf-oecd.org/sites/default/files/docs/15cpb_self-drivingcars.pdf.

International Union for the Conservation of Nature and Natural Resources, World Wildlife Fund, and UN Environment Program. *The World Conservation Strategy: Living Resource Conservation for Sustainable Development.* Gland, Switzerland: IUCN, 1980.

Irazabal, Clara. *City Making and Urban Governance in the Americas: Curitiba and Portland.* London: Routledge, 2017.

"The Italian Region Where 30% of GDP Comes from Cooperatives." *Apolitical*, 8 January 2018. https://apolitical.co/en/solution_article/italian-region-30-gdp-comes-cooperatives.

Jaccard, Mark. "The Accidental Activist: How an Energy Economist and Former Government Advisor Found Himself Blocking a Coal Train." *The Walrus*, 13 April 2020. https://thewalrus.ca/the-accidental-activist/.

———. *The Citizen's Guide to Climate Success: Overcoming Myths That Hinder Progess.* Cambridge: Cambridge University Press, 2020.

———. "I Wish This Changed Everything." Review of *This Changes Everything: Capitalism and the Climate*, by Naomi Klein. *Literary Review of Canada*, November 2014. https://reviewcanada.ca/magazine/2014/11/i-wish-this-changed-everything/.

Jackson, Tim. *Prosperity without Growth: Economics for a Finite Planet.* New York: Routledge, 2009.

Jacobs, Jane. *Dark Age Ahead.* Toronto: Vintage Canada, 2005.

———. *The Death and Life of Great American Cities.* New York: Random House, 1961.

Janssen, Ian. "Health Care Costs of Physical Inactivity in Canadian Adults." *Applied Physiology, Nutrition, and Metabolism* 37, no. 4 (June 2012): 803–6.

Jaskolka, Bryan. "What Is a Location Efficient Mortgage?" *Canadian Mortgages Inc.*, 29 April 2013. https://canadianmortgagesinc.ca/2013/04/what-is-a-location-efficient-mortgage.html.

Jensen, Derrick. *The Myth of Human Supremacy.* New York: Seven Stories Press, 2016.

Jones, Nicola. "How the World Passed a Carbon Threshold and Why It Matters." *YaleEnvironment360*, 26 January 2017. Yale School of the Environment. https://e360.yale.edu/features/how-the-world-passed-a-carbon-threshold-400ppm-and-why-it-matters.

Jun, Myung-jin. "The Effects of Portland's Urban Growth Boundary on Housing Prices." *Journal of the American Planning Association* 72, no. 2 (2006): 239–43.

Kail, Ellyn. "Photos of the New Orleans Neighborhood That Disappeared." *Feature Shoot*, 27 January 2017. https://www.featureshoot.com/2017/01/photos-new-orleans-neighborhood-disappeared/.

Kallis, Giorgos. *Degrowth.* New York: Agenda, 2018.

Kangasoja, Jonna, and Harry Schulman, eds. *Arabianranta: Rethinking Urban Living.* Helsinki: City of Helsinki Urban Facts, 2007.

Kaufmann, Bill. "Vulcan Solar Farm—Canada's Largest—Receives Key $500-Million Investment." *Calgary Herald*, 4 February 2020. https://calgaryherald.com/business/local-business/greengate-secures-partner-to-finance-countrys-largest-solar-project.

Kelbaugh, Douglas. *The Urban Fix: Resilient Cities in the War against Climate Change, Heat Islands and Overpopulation.* New York: Routledge, 2019.

Kell, John. "Avis to Buy Car-Sharing Service Zipcar." *Wall Street Journal*, 2 January 2013. https://www.wsj.com/articles/SB10001424127887324374004578217121433322386.

Keough, Noel. *Action Research on Transportation Housing Affordability: Final Report to Canada Mortgage and Housing Corporation.* CR File No. 6585-K090. Ottawa: CMHC, 2011. https://static1.squarespace.com/static/5ab716b9ee1759b04ca2703e/t/5ee0063c22b445748442fe51/1591739967822/Housing%2BTransport+Affordable+Living+-+FinalReport.pdf.

——. *State of Our City Report 2011: Sustainability in a Generation.* Calgary: Sustainable Calgary Society, 2011. https://static1.squarespace.com/static/5ab716b9ee1759b04ca2703e/t/5bff5fd970a6ad4f2ff729e0/1543462882064/2011-SOOC-Report.pdf.

——, Bob Morrison, and Celia Lee. *State of Our City 2020: An Urgent Call for a Just Transition.* Calgary: Sustainable Calgary Society, 2020. http://www.sustainablecalgary.org/publications.

——, Maryam Nabavi, and Jeff Loomis. *A Citizens' Agenda: For a More Healthy, Caring and Vibrant Calgary.* Calgary: Sustainable Calgary Society, 2005. https://static1.squarespace.com/static/5ab716b9ee1759b04ca2703e/t/5ee004c3984cb602a4c8a2c9/1591739598060/Citizens%27+Agenda+2006.pdf.

Klaszus, Jeremy. "Paying for It: Calgary's 14 New Communities: What Was City Council Thinking?" *The Sprawl*, 10 February 2020. https://www.sprawlcalgary.com/sprawlcast-calgarys-14-new-communities.

——. "Sprawlcast: Plan It Calgary, 10 Years Later." *The Sprawl*, 6 February 2020. https://www.sprawlcalgary.com/sprawlcast-plan-it.

Klein, Naomi. *This Changes Everything: Capitalism and the Climate.* New York: Simon and Schuster, 2014.

——, and Elizabeth Kolbert. "Can Climate Change Cure Capitalism? An Exchange." *New York Review of Books*, 8 January 2015. https://www.nybooks.com/articles/2015/01/08/can-climate-change-cure-capitalism-exchange/.

Knabb, Richard, Jamie Rhome, and Daniel Brown. *Tropical Cyclone Report: Hurricane Katrina 23–30 August 2005.* Miami: National Hurricane Center, 20 December 2005. https://www.nhc.noaa.gov/data/tcr/AL122005_Katrina.pdf.

Komarnicki, Jamie. "Voter Turnout Drops from Last Election." *Calgary Herald,* 22 October 2013. http://www.calgaryherald.com/news/voter+turnout+drops+from+last+election/9064000/story.html.

Korten, David C. *Change the Story, Change the Future: A Living Economy for a Living Earth.* Oakland, CA: Berrett-Koehler, 2015.

——. *The Post-Corporate World: Life after Capitalism.* West Hartford, CT: Kumerian Press and Berrett-Koehler, 1997.

Krugman, Paul. *End This Depression Now.* New York: W. W. Norton, 2012.

Kury de Castillo, Carolyn. "Construction Worker Shot in Suspected Road Rage Case in Calgary." *Global News*, 1 July 2019. https://globalnews.ca/news/5449633/construction-worker-shot-calgary-road-rage/.

"Kurzarbeit: Germany's Short-Time Work Benefit." *IMF News*, 15 June 2020. https://www. imf.org/en/News/Articles/2020/06/11/na061120-kurzarbeit-germanys-short-time-work-benefit.

Lachapelle, Erick, Christopher Borick, and Barry G. Rabe. *Key Findings Report for the 2013 Canada–US Comparative Climate Opinion Survey*. Ottawa: Canada 2020.

Leach, Andrew, and Blake Shaffer. "Opinion: Alberta's Shift Away from Coal Power Is a Climate Action Success Story." *CBC News*, 15 October 2020. https://www.cbc.ca/ news/canada/calgary/road-ahead-alberta-coal-power-electricity-decline-1.5761858.

"LEED Certification Process." *Canada Green Building Council*. Accessed 5 September 2020. https://www.cagbc.org/CAGBC/Programs/LEED/LEED_Certification_Process.aspx.

Lees, Loretta, Tom Slater, and Elvin Wyly. *Gentrification*. London: Routledge, 2007.

Lefebvre, Henri. *The Production of Space*. Hoboken, NJ: Wiley-Blackwell, 1992.

"Levelized Cost of Energy and Levelized Cost of Storage 2019." *Lazard*, 7 November 2019. https://www.lazard.com/perspective/lcoe2019.

Lewis, Mike, and Pat Conaty. *The Resilience Imperative: Cooperative Transitions to the Steady-State Economy*. Gabriola Island, BC: New Society, 2012.

Ley, David, and Cory Dobson. "Are There Limits to Gentrification? The Contexts of Impeded Gentrification in Vancouver." *Urban Studies* 45, no. 12 (2008): 2471–98.

Lindberg, David. *The Beginnings of Western Science*. Chicago: University of Chicago Press, 1992.

Lindgren, Richard L. *Legal Analysis of the Report of the Standing Committee on Environment and Sustainable Development Regarding the Canadian Environmental Assessment Act*. Edmonton: Canadian Environmental Law Association, March 2012. https://cela.ca/wp-content/uploads/2019/07/826CELA-Analysis-CEAA-ReportMarch-2012.pdf.

Litman, Todd. *Generated Traffic and Induced Travel: Implications for Transport Planning*. Victoria, BC: Victoria Transport Policy Institute, July 2020. https://www.vtpi.org/ gentraf.pdf.

"Living Building Challenge 4.0 Basic." *International Living Future Institute*, 2020. https:// living-future.org/lbc/basics4-0/.

Lo, Andrea. "Luxembourg Makes All Public Transit Free." *CNN*, 1 March 2020. https:// www.cnn.com/travel/article/luxembourg-free-public-transport/index.html.

Lombrana, Laura Millan. "An Urban Planner's Trick to Making Bikeable Cities." *Bloomberg News*, 5 August 2020. https://www.bloomberg.com/news/ articles/2020-08-05/an-urban-planner-s-trick-to-making-bike-able-cities.

"London Bike Commuters Will Outnumber Cars by 2018." *The Energy Mix*, 9 May 2016. https://theenergymix.com/2016/05/09/london-bike-commuters-will-outnumber-cars-by-2018/.

Lucas, Jack, and Zack Taylor. "Political Science and City Elections: Local Campaign Finance." *University of Calgary, School of Public Policy*, 5 October 2017. https://www.policyschool.ca/political-science-city-elections-local-campaign-finance/.

Lysack, Mishka. "Effective Policy Influencing and Environmental Advocacy: Health, Climate Change, and Phasing Out Coal." *International Social Work* 58, no. 3 (2015): 435–47.

Macdonald, David. *Fail Safe: CEO Compensation in Canada*. Ottawa: Canadian Centre for Policy Alternatives, 2020. https://www.policyalternatives.ca/sites/default/files/uploads/publications/National%20Office/2020/01/Fail%20Safe.pdf.

MacDougall, Andrew, and John Valley. *2019 Diversity Disclosure Practices: Women in Leadership Roles at TSX-Listed Companies*. Toronto: Osler, Hoskin and Harcourt, 2019. https://www.osler.com/osler/media/Osler/reports/corporate-governance/2019-Diversity-Disclosure-Practices-Women-in-leadership-roles-at-TSX-listed-companies.pdf.

Mackenzie, Hugh. *Canada's CEO Elite 100: The 0.01%*. Ottawa: Canadian Centre for Policy Alternatives, January 2012. https://www.policyalternatives.ca/sites/default/files/uploads/publications/National%20Office/2012/01/Canadas%20CEO%20Elite%20100FINAL.pdf.

MacLeod, Meredith. "Made-in-Canada Buy Nothing Day Takes Aim at Black Friday Consumer Excess." *CTV News*, 29 November 2019. https://www.ctvnews.ca/canada/made-in-canada-buy-nothing-day-takes-aim-at-black-friday-consumer-excess-1.4708081.

MacQueen, Ken. "Canada's Most Dangerous Cities: Newfoundland's Other Boom." *MacLean's*, 15 December 2011. https://www.macleans.ca/news/canada/newfoundland-the-rocks-other-boom/.

Malthus, Thomas. *An Essay on the Principle of Population, As It Affects the Future Improvement of Society, with Remarks on the Speculations of Mr. Godwin, M. Condorcet, and Other Writers*. Anonymously published, London, 1798.

"Managing Planet Earth." *Scientific American*, September 1989.

Mandel, Charles. "Canadian Climate Denial Group, Friends of Science, Named as Creditor in Coal Giant's Bankruptcy Files." *National Observer*, 20 June 2016. https://thenarwhal.ca/canadian-climate-denial-group-friends-science-named-creditor-coal-giant-s-bankruptcy-files/.

Marcuse, Peter. "Critical Planning: An Interview with Peter Marcuse." *Critical Planning* 15 (Summer 2008): 111–20.

———. "From Critical Urban Theory to the Right to the City." *City* 13, nos. 2–3 (2010): 185–97.

Markusoff, Jason. "By the Numbers: What You Need to Know about the Airport Tunnel." *Calgary Herald,* 22 May 2014. https://calgaryherald.com/news/local-news/by-the-numbers-what-you-need-to-know-about-the-airport-tunnel.

———. "Calgary Tax Increases Not Enough to Cover Growth Costs, Council Told." *Calgary Herald*, 28 October 2014. https://calgaryherald.com/news/local-news/calgary-tax-increases-not-enough-to-cover-growth-costs-council-told.

———. "WinSport 'Extremely Disappointed' in Council's Rejection of Plan to Sell Land." *Calgary Herald*, 31 July 2012. http://www.calgaryherald.com/news/calgary/winsport+extremely+disappointed+council+rejection+plan+sell+land/7020115/story.html.

Marmoreo, Jean. "We're Still Not As Fit As Swedes, but We Shouldn't Stop Trying." *Globe and Mail*, 28 January 2015. https://www.theglobeandmail.com/opinion/were-still-not-as-fit-as-swedes-but-we-shouldnt-stop-trying/article22674881/.

Martellozzo, Federico, Navin Ramankutty, Ron Hall, David T. Price, Brett Purdy, and Mark A. Friedl. "Urbanization and the Loss of Prime Farmland: A Case Study in the Calgary-Edmonton Corridor of Alberta." *Regional Environmental Change* 15 (2015): 881–93.

Martin, Elliot, and Susan Shaheen. "Impacts of Car2Go on Vehicle Ownership, Modal Shift, Vehicle Miles Traveled, and Greenhouse Gas Emission: An Analysis of Five North American Cities." Working Paper, Transportation Sustainability Research Center, University of California Berkeley, 12 July 2016. https://tsrc.berkeley.edu/publications/impacts-car2go-vehicle-ownership-modal-shift-vehicle-miles-traveled-and-greenhouse-gas.

Martínez, Marcos. "Merwede's Future: 12,000 Residents and Zero Parking Spaces." *Ferrovial* (blog), 19 October 2020. https://blog.ferrovial.com/en/2020/10/merwedes-future-12000-residents-and-zero-parking-spaces/.

Marx, Karl. *Marx's Capital: A Student Edition*. Edited and introduction by C. J. Arthur. London, UK: Electric Books, 2001.

Mason, Paul. "Alberta Is About to Learn How the Other Half Lives." *Globe and Mail*, 25 October 2019. https://www.theglobeandmail.com/canada/british-columbia/article-alberta-is-about-to-learn-how-the-other-half-lives/.

Massey, Doreen. *Space, Place and Gender*. Oxford: Polity Press, 1994.

Matsumura, Wataru, and Zakia Adam. "Fossil Fuel Consumption Subsidies Bounced Back Strongly in 2018." *International Energy Agency*, 13 June 2019. https://www.iea.org/commentaries/fossil-fuel-consumption-subsidies-bounced-back-strongly-in-2018.

May, Elizabeth. "When Canada Led the Way: A Short History of Climate Change." *Policy Options*, 1 October 2006. https://policyoptions.irpp.org/magazines/climate-change/when-canada-led-the-way-a-short-history-of-climate-change/.

McDonough, William, and Michael Braungart. *Cradle to Cradle: Remaking the Way We Make Things*. New York: North Point Press, 2002.

———. *The Upcycle: Beyond Sustainability—Designing for Abundance*. New York: North Point Press, 2013.

McGlade, Christophe, and Paul Ekins. "The Geographical Distribution of Fossil Fuels Unused When Limiting Global Warming to 2°C." *Nature* 517 (2015): 187–90.

McIntyre, Gordon. "Ten Years of Bike Lanes in Vancouver: Life Goes On, Chaos Averted." *Vancouver Sun*, 16 July 2019. https://vancouversun.com/news/local-news/ten-years-of-bike-lanes-in-vancouver-life-goes-on-chaos-averted.

McKeever, Pamela Malaspina, and Linda Clark. "Delayed High School Start Times Later Than 8:30 a.m. and Impact on Graduation Rates and Attendance Rates." *Sleep Health* 3, no. 2 (2017): 119–25.

McKibben, Bill. "Global Warming's Terrifying New Math." *Rolling Stone*, 19 July 2012. https://www.rollingstone.com/politics/politics-news/global-warmings-terrifying-new-math-188550/.

McLuhan, Marshall. *Understanding Media: The Extensions of Man*. With new introduction by Lewis H. Lapham. Cambridge, MA: MIT Press, 1994. First published 1964, McGraw-Hill (New York).

McQuaig, Linda. "The Harper Government's Tough Posture and Weak Rules on Tax Havens." *Rabble*, 9 April 2013. https://rabble.ca/columnists/2013/04/harper-governments-tough-posture-and-weak-rules-tax-havens.

McQuaig, Linda, and Neil Brooks. *The Trouble with Billionaires*. Toronto: Viking, 2010.

Mead, Rebecca. "Margaret Atwood, the Prophet of Dystopia." *The New Yorker,* 10 April 2017. https://www.newyorker.com/magazine/2017/04/17/margaret-atwood-the-prophet-of-dystopia.

Meadows, Donella H. *Thinking in Systems: A Primer*. Edited by Diana Wright. White River Junction, VT: Chelsea Green, 1998.

Meyer, Robinson. "The Cataclysmic Break That (Maybe) Occurred in 1950." *The Atlantic*, 16 April 2019. https://www.theatlantic.com/science/archive/2019/04/great-debate-over-when-anthropocene-started/587194/.

Mies, Maria. *The Subsistence Perspective: Beyond the Global Economy*. New York: Zed Books, 2000.

Miller-Maleschuk, Natalie. "Goats Return to Calgary Parks to Deal with Invasive Weeds." *CTV News*, 14 July 2020. https://calgary.ctvnews.ca/goats-return-to-calgary-parks-to-deal-with-invasive-weeds-1.5023865.

Miller, Byron. "Sustainability Fix Meets Growth Machine: Attempting to Govern the Calgary Metropolitan Region." In *Governing Cities through Regions: Canadian and European Perspectives*, edited by Roger Keil, Pierre Hamel, Julie-Anne Boudreau, and Stefan Kipfer, 213–38. Waterloo, ON: Wilfrid Laurier University Press, 2016.

Misra, Tanvi. "The Social Costs of Driving in Vancouver in 1 Chart." *Bloomberg CityLab*, 7 April 2015. https://www.bloomberg.com/news/articles/2015-04-07/an-interactive-tool-measures-the-social-costs-of-driving-and-transit-in-vancouver.

Mitchell, Stacy. *Big-Box Swindle: The True Cost of Mega-Retailers and the Fight for America's Independent Businesses*. Boston: Beacon Press, 2007.

———. "Local Stores Create Triple the Economic Activity of Chains." *Institute for Local Self-Reliance*, 1 February 2003. https://ilsr.org/local-stores-create-triple-economic-activity-chains/.

Mol, Arthur P. J., and David A. Sonnenfeld. "Ecological Modernization and the Global Economy." *Global Environmental Politics* 2, no. 2 (2002): 92–115.

Mol, Arthur P. J., David A. Sonnenfeld, and Gert Spaargaren. *The Ecological Modernization Reader: Environmental Reform in Theory and Practice*. London: Routledge, 2009.

Molotch, Harvey. "The City As a Growth Machine: Toward a Political Economy of Place." *American Journal of Sociology* 82, no. 2 (1976): 309–32.

Monbiot, George. *Heat: How to Stop the Planet from Burning*. San Francisco: South End, 2009.

"Monthly Ranking of Women in National Parliaments." *Interparliamentary Union Parline*, 2020. https://data.ipu.org/women-ranking?month=8&year=2020.

Moore, Jason W. *Capitalism in the Web of Life: Ecology and the Accumulation of Capital*. New York: Verso, 2015.

Morrison, Bob. "2012–2014 City Budget Submission by Governance, Finance, and Infrastructure Group." Unpublished. Calgary: CivicCamp, 2012.

Mössner, Samuel, Tim Freytag, and Byron Miller. "Editorial: Cities and the Politics of Urban Sustainability." *Die Erde: Journal of the Geographical Society of Berlin* 48, no. 4 (2017): 195–96.

Mumford, Lewis. *The City in History: Its Origins, Its Transformations, Its Prospects*. New York: Harvest Books, 1968.

Nace, Trevor. "Carbon Dioxide Levels Just Hit 417 ppm, Highest in Human History." *Forbes*, 1 June 2020. https://www.forbes.com/sites/trevornace/2020/06/10/carbon-dioxide-levels-just-hit-417ppm-highest-in-human-history/#5ee942ca229f.

Nader, Ralph. *Unsafe at Any Speed: The Designed-In Dangers of the American Automobile*. Boston: Knightsbridge, 1991.

"Natural Cultural Districts Exchange Toolkit." *Americans for the Arts*. Accessed 4 January 2021. https://www.americansforthearts.org/by-program/reports-and-data/toolkits/national-cultural-districts-exchange-toolkit.

Needham, Richard J. "The Happiest Canadians." *Maclean's*, 2 November 1964. https://archive.macleans.ca/article/1964/11/2/the-happiest-canadians.

Nenshi, Naheed. "Bad Optics: Alberta Confronts Its Wild West Municipal Election Campaign Funding Rules—the Laxest in the Country." *Alberta Views*, 1 April 2010. https://albertaviews.ca/bad-optics/.

Neruda, Pablo, and Ilan Stavans, eds. *All the Odes: A Bilingual Edition*. New York: Farrar, Strauss and Giroux, 2017.

Neumayer, Eric. *Weak Versus Strong Sustainability: Exploring the Limits of Two Opposing Paradigms*. 4th ed. Cheltenham, UK: Edward Elgar, 2013.

Newman, Peter, and Jeff Kenworthy. *The End of Automobile Dependence: How Cities Are Moving beyond Car-Based Planning*. Washington, DC: Island Press, 2015.

Newman, Peter, Timothy Beatley, and Heather Boyer. *Resilient Cities: Responding to Peak Oil and Climate Change*. Washington, DC: Island Press, 2009.

"NHS Focus on Geography Series, 2016 Census." *Statistics Canada*, modified 18 July 2019. https://www12.statcan.gc.ca/census-recensement/2016/as-sa/fogs-spg/Facts-cma-eng.cfm?LANG=Eng&GK=CMA&GC=825&TOPIC=7.

Nikiforuk, Andrew. *The Energy of Slaves: Oil and the New Servitude*. Vancouver: Greystone, 2012.

Niranjan, Ajit. "Falling Solar Panel Prices Spell Sunny Future for Clean Energy." *Deutsche Welle*, 28 May 2020. https://www.dw.com/en/cheap-solar-energy-prices-explained/a-53590607.

Nkrumah, Kwame. *Neo-Colonialism: The Last Stage of Imperialism*. London: Thomas Nelson, 1965.

"November 26, 2012 By-Elections, Poll-by-Poll Results, Alberta, Calgary Centre." *Elections Canada*. Accessed 8 September 2020. https://www.elections.ca/res/rep/off/ovr_2012b/9635_e.html.

Nugmanova, Assel, Wulf-Holger Arndt, Md Aslam Hossain, and Jong Ryeol Kim. "Effectiveness of Ring Roads in Reducing Traffic Congestion in Cities for Long Run: Big Almaty Ring Road Case Study." *Sustainability* 11, no. 18 (2019): 4973.

O'Neill, Paul. *The Oldest City: The Story of St. John's, Newfoundland*. Boulder, CO: Boulder, 2013.

O'Sullivan, Feargus. "Norway Will Spend Almost $1 Billion on New Bike Highways." *Bloomberg CityLab*, 3 March 2016. https://www.bloomberg.com/news/articles/2016-03-03/norway-s-national-transit-plan-will-spend-almost-1-billion-on-new-bike-highways.

O2 Planning and Design. *Bow to Bluff Urban Design Framework*. Calgary: Bow to Bluff, 2011. https://www.cip-icu.ca/Files/Awards/Planning-Excellence/2013-16-Bow-to-Bluff-FULL-PLAN.aspx.

"OECD Better Life Index." *Organisation for Economic Co-operation and Development*. Accessed 4 September 2020. http://www.oecdbetterlifeindex.org/#/11111111111.

"Official Voting Results Forty-First General Election 2011." *Elections Canada*. Accessed 8 September 2020. https://www.elections.ca/scripts/ovr2011/default.html.

"Oil Sands Fact and Statistics." *Government of Alberta*, 2020. https://www.alberta.ca/oil-sands-facts-and-statistics.aspx.

Oliver, Joe. "An Open Letter from Natural Resources Minister Joe Oliver." *Globe and Mail*, 9 January 2012. https://www.theglobeandmail.com/news/politics/an-open-letter-from-natural-resources-minister-joe-oliver/article4085663/.

Organisation for Economic Co-operation and Development. *Growing Unequal? Income Distribution and Poverty in OECD Countries*. Geneva: OECD, October 2008. https://www.oecd.org/els/soc/growingunequalincomedistributionandpoverty inoecdcountries.htm.

———. *Road Safety Annual Report 2019: Canada.* Geneva: OECD International Transport Forum, 2019. https://www.itf-oecd.org/sites/default/files/canada-road-safety.pdf.

———. *Trust and Public Policy: How Better Governance Can Help Rebuild Public Trust.* OECD Public Governance Reviews. Paris: OECD, March 2017. http://www.oecd.org/corruption-integrity/reports/trust-and-public-policy-9789264268920-en.html.

Ostrom, Elinor. *Governing the Commons: The Evolution of Institutions for Collective Action.* Cambridge: Cambridge University Press, 2015.

Owen, David. *Green Metropolis: Why Living Smaller, Living Closer, and Driving Less Are the Keys to Sustainability.* New York: Riverhead Books, 2010.

Owens, Brian. "Half of Canada's Government Scientists Still Feel Muzzled." *Science Magazine,* 21 February 2018. https://www.sciencemag.org/news/2018/02/half-canada-s-government-scientists-still-feel-muzzled.

Packer, George. "Doublethink Is Stronger Than Orwell Imagined: What 1984 Means Today." Review of *The Ministry of Truth: The Biography of George Orwells's 1984,* by Dorian Lynskey. *The Atlantic,* July 2019. https://www.theatlantic.com/magazine/archive/2019/07/1984-george-orwell/590638/.

Parent, Michael. "What the MEC Sale Might Really Be About." *The Tyee,* 6 October 2020. https://thetyee.ca/Analysis/2020/10/06/What-MEC-Sale-Is-Really-About/.

Paris, Max. "Greens Leader Accuses Tories of Sabotaging Climate Talks." *CBC News,* 29 November 2012. https://www.cbc.ca/news/politics/greens-leader-accuses-tories-of-sabotaging-climate-talks-1.1130619.

"Paskapoo Slopes Development Plan Approved by City Council." *CBC News,* 27 July 2015. https://www.cbc.ca/news/canada/calgary/paskapoo-slopes-development-plan-approved-by-city-council-1.3169706.

"Peace Bridge Builders Want More Money." *CBC News,* 13 March 2013. https://www.cbc.ca/news/canada/calgary/peace-bridge-builders-want-more-money-1.1392311.

Peck, Jamie. "Struggling with the Creative Class." *International Journal of Urban and Regional Research* 29, no. 4 (2005): 740–70.

Pegels, Anna. "Germany: The Energy Transition as a Green Industrial Development Agenda." In *Green Industrial Policy: Concept, Policies, Country Experiences,* edited by T. Altenburg and C. Assmann, 166–84. Bonn, Germany: UN Environment; German Development Institute, 2017. https://www.un-page.org/files/public/green_industrial_policy_book_aw_web.pdf.

Pembina Institute. "Pembina Reacts to Energy Efficiency Alberta Announcement." Media release, 27 October 2016. https://www.pembina.org/media-release/pembina-reacts-to-energy-efficiency-alberta-announcement.

———. "Pembina Reacts to Passage of Bill C-38." Media release, 19 June 2012. https://www.pembina.org/media-release/2351.

Perlo-Freeman, Sam. "The Opportunity Cost of World Military Spending." *Stockholm International Peace Research Institute,* 5 April 2016. https://www.sipri.org/commentary/blog/2016/opportunity-cost-world-military-spending.

"Pesticide-Free Parks in Calgary." *City of Calgary*, 2020. https://www.calgary.ca/csps/parks/planning-and-operations/pest-management/pesticide-free-parks-in-calgary.html.

Peters, Adele. "What Happened When Oslo Decided to Make Its Downtown Basically Car-Free?" *Fast Company*, 24 January 2019. https://www.fastcompany.com/90294948/what-happened-when-oslo-decided-to-make-its-downtown-basically-car-free.

Piketty, Thomas. *Capital in the Twenty-First Century*. Translated by Arthur Goldhammer. Cambridge, MA: Belknap, 2014.

Pindar, Ian. "The Sleepwalkers by Christopher Clark: Review." *The Guardian*, 19 July 2013. https://www.theguardian.com/books/2013/jul/19/sleepwalkers-christopher-clark-review.

Ponto, Jason. "Cycling through Intersections: Regimes of Velomobility in Calgary and Amsterdam." PhD diss., University of Calgary, 2017. http://hdl.handle.net/11023/3760.

Potkins, Meghan. "Growth, Climate Change Could Push Calgary's Water Intake to the Limit by 2036." *Calgary Herald*, 14 May 2019. https://calgaryherald.com/news/local-news/calgary-could-reach-daily-water-licence-limit-by-2036.

Powell, Colin. *My American Journey*. With Joseph E. Persico. New York: Ballantine Books, 1995.

Pressreader. "Landlord Loopholes: Condo Conversion Rules Too Loose to Protect Renters." *Calgary Herald*, 24 January 2008. https://www.pressreader.com/canada/calgary-herald/20080124/281736970133548.

Priday, Richard. "London's Cycling Boom Is Slowing. And It's Still Mostly White Men." *WIRED*, 21 March 2018. https://www.wired.co.uk/article/cycling-london-city-centre-bikes-cycle-superhighway.

"Public Transportation Ridership Report: Fourth Quarter 2018." *American Public Transportation Association*, 12 April 2019. https://www.apta.com/wp-content/uploads/2018-Q4-Ridership-APTA-3.pdf.

"Public Trust and Spending Concerns on Agenda for Calgary Council Next Year." *CBC News*, 9 December 2019. https://www.cbc.ca/news/canada/calgary/public-trust-spending-calgary-council-strategy-1.5390001.

Punter, John. *The Vancouver Achievement: Urban Planning and Design*. Vancouver: University of British Columbia Press, 2003.

Qualman, Darrin. "Home Grown: 67 Years of US and Canadian House Size Data." *Darrin Qualman*, 8 May 2018. https://www.darrinqualman.com/house-size/.

Rand, Ayn. *Anthem*. Project Gutenberg. First published 1938. https://www.gutenberg.org/files/1250/1250-h/1250-h.htm.

———. *The Fountainhead*. New York: Signet, 1952.

Raworth, Kate. *Doughnut Economics: 7 Ways to Think Like a 21st Century Economist*. Vermont: Chelsea Green, 2017.

Redclift, Michael. *Sustainable Development: Exploring the Contradictions*. London: Routledge, 1987.

Rees, William. "Achieving Sustainability: Reform or Transformation?" *Journal of Planning Literature* 9, no.4 (1995): 343–61.

———. "The Ecology of Sustainable Development." *Ecologist* 20, no. 1 (1990): 18–23.

———. "End Game: The Economy as Eco-Catastrophe and What Needs to Change." *Real-World Economics Review* 87 (March 2019): 132–48.

———. "Is 'Sustainable City' an Oxymoron?" *Local Environment* 2, no. 3 (1997): 303–10.

———. "What's Blocking Sustainability? Human Nature, Cognition and Denial." *Sustainability: Science, Practice and Policy* 6, no. 2 (2010): 13–25.

"Registered Secondary Suites." *City of Calgary*. Accessed 7 September 2020. https://secondarysuites.calgary.ca.

Reguly, Eric. "Is the Car Dead?" *Globe and Mail*, 30 August 2012. https://www.theglobeandmail.com/report-on-business/rob-magazine/is-the-car-dead/article4510125/.

Reich, Robert. *Aftershock: The Next Economy and America's Future*. New York: Knopf, 2010.

———. "The Flat-Tax Fraud, and the Necessity of a Truly Progressive Tax." *Robert Reich*, 21 October 2011. https://robertreich.org/post/11753807617.

Reiger, Sarah. "Calgary's Airport Faces $67M Deficit This Year." *CBC News*, 7 July 2020. https://www.cbc.ca/news/canada/calgary/calgary-airport-1.5641441.

———. "CBE Retroactively Scraps Fee-Free Busing, Calgary Transit Rebate for 2019–20 School Year." *CBC News*, 10 December 2019. https://www.cbc.ca/news/canada/calgary/cbe-bus-costs-1.5391732.

The Republic of Doyle. Toronto: Canadian Broadcasting Corporation, 2014. https://www.imdb.com/title/tt1297754/.

Reuters. "Norway Wealth Fund Hits Record 10 Trillion Kroner As Stocks Rise." *Al Jazeera*, 25 October 2019. https://www.aljazeera.com/ajimpact/norway-wealth-fund-hits-record-10-trillion-kroner-stocks-rise-191025095606511.html.

Roberts, David. "Shared Vehicles Could Make Our Cities Dramatically More Livable." *Vox*, 28 July 2016. https://www.vox.com/2016/7/28/12294214/shared-vehicles-livable-cities.

Rodrigo. "What Does Raymond Williams Mean When He Describes Culture As Being 'a Whole Way of Life'?" *The WritePass Journal*, 21 November 2016. https://writepass.com/journal/2016/11/what-does-raymond-williams-mean-when-he-describes-culture-as-being-a-whole-way-of-life-what-are-the-merits-and-limitation-of-this-perspective/#_ftn10.

Row, Jesse, Erin Welk, Nathan Lemphers, and Paul Cobb. *Options for Reducing GHG Emissions in Calgary: Research Report*. Calgary: City of Calgary, February 2011. https://www.pembina.org/reports/calgary-ghg-main-report.pdf.

Rubin, Jeff. *The End of Growth.* Toronto: Random House, 2012.

———. "Why Saudi Arabia Can No Longer Temper Oil Prices." *Globe and Mail*, 23 February 2011. https://www.theglobeandmail.com/report-on-business/industry-news/energy-and-resources/why-saudi-arabia-can-no-longer-temper-oil-prices/article623163/.

———. *Why Your World Is About to Get a Whole Lot Smaller.* Toronto: Vintage, 2010.

Ruttan, Susan. "A Home for the Homeless." *Alberta Views*, 1 January 2011. https://albertaviews.ca/a-home-for-the-homeless/.

Sachs, Jeffrey D. *The Age of Sustainable Development.* New York: Columbia University Press, 2017.

Sachs, Wolfgang. *The Development Dictionary: A Guide to Knowledge as Power.* London: Zed Books, 2010.

———. *For the Love of the Automobile: Looking Back into the History of Our Desires.* Berkeley: University of California Press, 1992.

———. *Planet Dialectics: Explorations in Environment and Development.* Toronto: Zed Books, 2000.

Said, Edward. *Orientalism.* London: Penguin Books, 1985.

Salus, Jesse. "The Origins of the Southwest Ring Road." *The History of a Road* (blog), 5 March 2016. https://calgaryringroad.wordpress.com/2016/03/05/the-origins-of-the-southwest-ring-road/.

Sánchez-Bayo, Francisco, and Kris A. G. Wyckhuys. "Worldwide Decline of the Entomofauna: A Review of Its Drivers." *Biological Conservation* 232 (April 2019): 8–27.

Sandercock, Leonie. "Out of the Closet: The Importance of Stories." *Planning Theory and Practice* 4, no. 1 (2003): 11–28.

Sanzillo, Tom, and Kathy Hipple. "IEEFA Report: Additional $320 Million in Subsidies Used to Finance Trans Mountain Pipeline in First Half of 2019." Press release, Institute for Energy Economics and Financial Analysis, Lakewood, ON, 19 November 2019. https://ieefa.org/ieefa-report-additional-320-million-in-subsidies-used-to-finance-trans-mountain-pipeline-in-first-half-of-2019/.

Satterthwaite, David, ed. *The Earthscan Reader in Sustainable Cities.* London: Earthscan, 1999.

Schmela, Michael. "EU Market Outlook for Solar Power/2019–2023." Brussels: SolarPower Europe, 2019. https://www.solarpowereurope.org/wp-content/uploads/2019/12/SolarPower-Europe_EU-Market-Outlook-for-Solar-Power-2019-2023_.pdf?cf_id=7181.

Schneider, Aaron, and Sangit Roy. *Policy from the People: A North-South NGO Policy Dialogue.* Ottawa: Canadian Council for International Cooperation, 1992.

Schumacher, Nick, Victoria Goodday, Blake Shaffer, and Jennifer Winter. *Energy and Environmental Policy Trends*. Calgary: University of Calgary, 2020. https://www. policyschool.ca/wp-content/uploads/2020/11/Energy-Trends-Renewables-Nov.pdf.

Schwartz, John. "Rockefellers, Heirs to an Oil Fortune, Will Divest Charity of Fossil Fuels." *New York Times*, 22 September 2014. https://www.nytimes.com/2014/09/22/ us/heirs-to-an-oil-fortune-join-the-divestment-drive.html.

Seba, Tony. *Clean Disruption of Energy and Transportation: How Silicon Valley Is Making Oil, Nuclear, Natural Gas, and Coal Obsolete*. Silicon Valley, CA: Clean Planet Ventures, 2014. https://tonyseba.com/wp-content/uploads/2014/05/book-cover-Clean-Disruption.pdf.

"Secondary Suites (Completed Permits)." *City of Edmonton*. Accessed 7 September 2020. https://data.edmonton.ca/Sustainable-Development/Secondary-Suites-Completed-Permits-/q3qs-7g3d.

Sen, Amartya. *The Idea of Justice*. Cambridge, MA: Belknap Press, 2009.

Serageldin, Ismail. "The Eye of the Storm: The Library of Alexandria and the Egyptian and Global Revolutions." In *Bibliotheca Alexandrina Annual Report, July 2010–June 2011*, 137–46. Alexandria, Egypt: Bibliotheca Alexandrina, 2011. https:// www.bibalex.org/Attachments/Publications/Files/201208091245249995_ AnnualReport20102011English982012small.pdf.

Seskus, Tony, and Renata D'Aliesio. "Voter Turnout Lowest in Alberta's History." *Edmonton Journal*, 5 March 2008. https://edmontonjournal.com/news/voter-turnout-lowest-in-albertas-history.

"SGI 2020 Scores." At "Downloads SGI 2020," *Sustainable Governance Indicators*, 2020. https://www.sgi-network.org/2020/Downloads.

Shiva, Vandana. *Staying Alive: Women, Ecology and Development*. New York: South End Press, 2010.

Siekierska, Alicja. "Canada among Only Seven Countries to See Rise in Pedestrian Deaths, OECD Study Reveals." *Financial Post*, 25 May 2018. https://financialpost.com/ transportation/canada-among-only-seven-countries-to-see-rise-in-pedestrian-deaths-oecd-study-finds.

Smith, Adam. *The Wealth of Nations*. New York: Bantam Dell, 2003. First published 1776 by W. Strahan and T. Cadell (London).

Smith, Alanna. "Car2Go Can't Make It Go in Calgary, Pulling out of 'Highly Volatile' Market." *Calgary Herald*, 27 September 2019. https://calgaryherald.com/news/ local-news/car2go-leaving-calgary-in-light-of-highly-volatile-transportation-market-limited-success.

Smith, Madeline. "New Local Election Rules Would Let City Council Hopefuls Disclose Donors after Election Day." *Calgary Herald*, 25 June 2020. https://calgaryherald. com/news/politics/alberta-rolls-out-proposed-changes-to-municipal-election-funding-rules.

———, and Jason Herring. "Magliocca's False Expenses Included Flight Upgrades, Hotel Stays, Meals and Booze: Report." *Calgary Herald*, 30 July 2020. https://calgaryherald.com/news/local-news/magliocca-expense-investigation-shows-years-of-problematic-spending-nenshi-says.

Soja, Edward. *Thirdspace: Journeys to Los Angeles and Other Real-and-Imagined Places.* Toronto: Wiley-Blackwell, 1996.

Soroye, Peter, Tim Newbold, and Jeremy Kerr. "Climate Change Contributes to Widespread Declines among Bumble Bees across Continents." *Science* 367 (February 2020): 685–88.

Sparrow, Andrew. "Firms Must Justify Investment in Fossil Fuels, Warns Mark Carney." *The Guardian*, 30 December 2019. https://www.theguardian.com/business/2019/dec/30/firms-must-justify-investment-in-fossil-fuels-warns-mark-carney.

Stamp, Robert. *Suburban Modern: Postwar Dreams in Calgary.* Calgary: Touchwood, 2004.

Standing, Guy. "Coronavirus Has Shown Us Why We Urgently Need to Make a Basic Income a Reality." *World Economic Forum*, 13 April 2020. https://www.weforum.org/agenda/2020/04/coronavirus-made-basic-income-vital/.

Stanford, James. *Economics for Everyone: A Short Guide to the Economics of Capitalism.* 2nd ed. Toronto: Fernwood, 2015.

Staples, David. "Has Edmonton Hit a Home Run with Its New Footbridge at Fort Edmonton Park?" *Edmonton Journal*, 16 August 2011. https://edmontonjournal.com/news/local-news/has-edmonton-hit-a-home-run-with-its-new-footbridge-at-fort-edmonton-park.

Startup Sauna. Accessed 8 September 2020. http://startupsauna.com.

Statistics Canada. "Canada's Population Estimates: Subprovincial Areas, July 1, 2019." *Statistics Canada*, released 13 February 2020. https://www150.statcan.gc.ca/n1/daily-quotidien/200213/dq200213a-eng.htm.

———. "Literacy—Comparative Distributions of Proficiency Levels of Population Aged 16 and 65, Countries, Provinces and Territories." In *Skills in Canada: First Results from the Programme for the International Assessment of Adult Competencies*, chart 1.2, 17. Catalogue no. 89-555-X. Ottawa: Statistics Canada, 2013. https://www150.statcan.gc.ca/n1/pub/89-555-x/2013001/c-g/c-g1.2-eng.htm.

———. *The Shift to Smaller Households over the Past Century.* Canadian Megatrends. Catalogue no. 11-630-X. Ottawa: Statistics Canada, 2017. https://www150.statcan.gc.ca/n1/en/pub/11-630-x/11-630-x2015008-eng.pdf?st=UY-2ok55.

———. "Table 11-10-0055-01, High Income Tax Filers in Canada." Ottawa: Statistics Canada, 2020. https://www150.statcan.gc.ca/t1/tbl1/en/tv.action?pid=1110005501.

"Staying on Track to Realize the Sustainable Development Goals." *United Nations: Department of Economic and Social Affairs*, 3 January 2019. https://www.un.org/development/desa/en/news/sustainable/sustainable-development-goals.html.

Steel, Deb. "Chiefs Call for Calm and Dialogue as Canada Seeks Resolution to Wet'suwet'en Solidarity Demonstrations." *Windspeaker*, 18 February 2020. https://

windspeaker.com/news/windspeaker-news/chiefs-call-calm-and-dialogue-canada-seeks-resolution-wetsuweten-solidarity.

Steer, Liesbet. "Seven Facts about Global Education Financing." *Brookings Institution*, 20 February 2014. https://www.brookings.edu/blog/education-plus-development/2014/02/20/seven-facts-about-global-education-financing/.

Steffen, Will. *Unburnable Carbon: Why We Need to Leave Fossil Fuels in the Ground*. Potts Point, Australia: Climate Council of Australia, 2015. https://www.climatecouncil.org.au/uploads/a904b54ce67740c4b4ee2753134154b0.pdf.

Stephenson, Amanda. "Energy Efficiency Alberta Programs Scrapped by UCP." *Calgary Herald*, 31 October 2019. https://calgaryherald.com/business/local-business/energy-efficiency-alberta-programs-scrapped-by-ucp.

Stiglitz, Joseph E. *The Price of Inequality: How Today's Divided Society Endangers Our Future*. New York: W. W Norton, 2012.

Stilwell, Victoria, and Wei Lu. "The 10 Most Unequal Big Cities in America." *Bloomberg*, 10 November 2015. https://www.bloomberg.com/news/articles/2015-11-10/the-10-most-unequal-big-cities-in-america.

Stone, Clarence N. *Regime Politics: Governing Atlanta 1946–1988*. Lawrence: University of Kansas Press, 1989.

Sudamant, Andrew, Matt Tierney, Eduard Cubi, Effie Papargyropoulou, Andy Gouldson, and Joule Bergerson. *The Economics of Low Carbon Development*. Calgary: City of Calgary, 2019. https://climate.leeds.ac.uk/wp-content/uploads/2018/03/Calgary-Exec-Sum-draft-4_Web.pdf.

Suderman, Peter. "Blade Runner's 2019 Los Angeles Helped Define the American City of the Future." *Vox*, 2 October 2017. https://www.vox.com/culture/2017/10/2/1637 5126/blade-runner-future-city-ridley-scott.

Surowiecki, James. *The Wisdom of Crowds*. New York: Anchor Books, 2005.

"Survey of Household Spending, 2014." *Statistics Canada*, last modified 2017. https://www150.statcan.gc.ca/n1/daily-quotidien/160212/dq160212a-eng.htm.

"Sustainable City." *ICLEI (International Council for Local Environmental Initiatives)*. Accessed 4 September 2020. http://old.iclei.org/index.php?id=35.

"Sustainable Development Goals." *United Nations*. Accessed 2 September 2020. https://sustainabledevelopment.un.org/?menu=1300.

Synge, M. B. *A Book of Discovery: The History of the World's Exploration, from the Earliest Times to the Finding of the South Pole*. London: T. C. and E. C. Jack, 1912. Released 20 October 2007, Project Gutenberg. https://archive.org/stream/abookofdiscovery23107gut/pg23107.txt.

"Table C.3.2b: Annual Statutory Teachers' Salaries in Public Institutions, by Level of Education Taught and Teaching Experience, Canadian Dollars, Canada, Provinces and Territories, 2016–2017." Education Indicators in Canada: An International Perspective. *Statistics Canada*, 2018. https://www150.statcan.gc.ca/n1/pub/81-604-x/2018001/t/tblc.3.1b-eng.htm.

"Tackle Tax Havens." *Canadians for Tax Fairness*, 2019. https://www.taxfairness.ca/en/news/tackle-tax-havens-0.

Taft, Kevin. *Follow the Money: Where Is Alberta's Wealth Going?* Calgary: Detselig, 2012.

———. *Oil's Deep State: How the Petroleum Industry Undermines Democracy and Stops Action on Global Warming—in Alberta and in Ottawa.* Toronto: Lorimer, 2017.

Thompson, Derek, and Jordan Weissmann. "The Cheapest Generation: Why Millennials Aren't Buying Cars or Houses, and What That Means for the Economy." *The Atlantic*, September 2012. https://www.theatlantic.com/magazine/archive/2012/09/the-cheapest-generation/309060/.

Thompson, Martha. *Lessons in Risk Reduction from Cuba.* "Case Studies 2007." *UN-Habitat,* 2007. https://mirror.unhabitat.org/content.asp?typeid=19&catid=555&cid=5403.

Thomson, Graham. "NDP Tightens Election Financing Rules, but Leaves Government a Loophole." *Calgary Herald*, 30 November 2016. https://calgaryherald.com/opinion/columnists/thomson-ndp-tightens-election-financing-rules-but-leaves-government-a-loophole.

"Three Central Banks Take Action in Sign of Alarm." *Reuters*, 5 July 2012. https://ca.reuters.com/article/us-centralbanks-action/three-central-banks-take-action-in-sign-of-alarm-idUSBRE8640RN20120705.

Tian, Nan, Aude Fleurant, Alexandra Kuimova, Pieter D. Wezeman, and Siemon T. Wezeman. *Trends in Military Expenditure, 2018.* SIPRI Fact Sheet, April 2019. https://reliefweb.int/sites/reliefweb.int/files/resources/fs_1904_milex_2018.pdf.

Tobin, James. "The Tobin Tax: The Case for a Tax on International Monetary Transactions." *Canadian Centre for Policy Alternatives*, 1 April 2011. https://www.policyalternatives.ca/publications/monitor/tobin-tax.

Toma and Bouma Management Consultants. *Alberta REA Strategic Review: Rural Economic Impacts.* Prepared for Alberta Rural Electrification Associations, January 2013. https://ccrnrcrc.files.wordpress.com/2014/05/rea-report-f-2.pdf.

Tombe, Trevor. "Alberta's Long-Term Fiscal Future." University of Calgary, School of Public Policy Research Paper 11, November 2018. https://www.policyschool.ca/wp-content/uploads/2018/11/AB-Fiscal-Future-Tombe.pdf.

"Top 89 Largest Sovereign Wealth Fund Rankings by Total Assets." *Sovereign Wealth Fund Investor*, 2020. https://www.swfinstitute.org/fund-rankings/sovereign-wealth-fund.

"Tram and Light Rail Transit Systems." *Wikipedia*. Last edited 28 October 2020. https://en.wikipedia.org/wiki/Tram_and_light_rail_transit_systems.

"Transit Yearly Ridership." *City of Calgary*, 2020. https://data.calgary.ca/Transportation-Transit/Yearly-Ridership-current-year-is-year-to-date-/n9it-gzsq.

Treaty 7 Elders and Tribal Council. *The True Spirit and Original Intent of Treaty 7.* With Walter Hildebrandt, Dorothy First Rider, and Sarah Carter. Montreal/Kingston: McGill-Queen's University Press, 1996.

Treuhaft, Sarah. *All-In Cities: Building an Equitable Economy from the Ground Up.* Washington, DC: PolicyLink, 2016. https://www.policylink.org/aic-building-an-equitable-economy-from-the-ground-up.

Truman, Harry S. "Inaugural Address of Harry S. Truman." 20 January 1949. *The Avalon Project: Documents in Law, History and Diplomacy.* Yale Law School, Lillian Goldman Law Library, 2008. https://avalon.law.yale.edu/20th_century/truman.asp.

Turner, Chris. "The Greenprint: Checking on Germany's Transition to Renewable Energy." *Globe and Mail*, 1 June 2019. https://www.theglobeandmail.com/opinion/article-the-greenprint-checking-up-on-germanys-transition-to-renewable/.

"UBC Votes to Divest $380M from Fossil Fuels, but Students Demand More." *CBC News*, 24 November 2019. https://www.cbc.ca/news/canada/british-columbia/ubc-divestment-vote-1.5371719.

UN Department of Economics and Social Affairs. *United Nations Demographic Yearbook 2015.* New York: United Nations, 2016. https://unstats.un.org/unsd/demographic-social/products/dyb/dybsets/2015.pdf.

UN Environment. *GEO-6 Key Messages.* Nairobi: UN Environment Programme, 2019. https://wedocs.unep.org/bitstream/handle/20.500.11822/28774/GEO6_keymessages_EN.pdf?sequence=1&isAllowed=y.

———. *Global Biodiversity Outlook 5: Summary for Policymakers.* Montreal: Secretariat of the Convention on Biological Diversity, UN Environment Programme, 2020. https://www.cbd.int/gbo/gbo5/publication/gbo-5-spm-en.pdf.

———. *Global Environmental Outlook 5: Environment for the Future We Want.* Nairobi: UN Environment Programme, 2012. https://sustainabledevelopment.un.org/index.php?page=view&type=400&nr=546&menu=35.

———. *Global Environmental Outlook 6: Healthy Planet, Healthy People.* Nairobi: United Nations Environment Programme, 2019.

———. *The GEO-5 Process: End Matter.* Nairobi: UN Environment Programme, 2012. https://issuu.com/christinadianparmionova/docs/geo5_endmatter.

———. "Human Health in Dire Straits If Urgent Actions Are Not Made to Protect the Environment, Warns UN Landmark Report." Press release, 13 March 2019. https://www.unenvironment.org/news-and-stories/press-release/human-health-dire-straits-if-urgent-actions-are-not-made-protect.

UN Framework Convention on Climate Change. *Canada's Withdrawal from the Kyoto Protocol and Its Effects on Canada's Reporting Obligations under the Protocol: Note by the Secretariat.* Bonn, Germany: UNFCCC Compliance Committee, August 2014. https://unfccc.int/files/kyoto_protocol/compliance/enforcement_branch/application/pdf/cc-eb-25-2014-2_canada_withdrawal_from_kp.pdf.

———. *The Kyoto Protocol.* Geneva: United Nations, December 1997. https://unfccc.int/kyoto_protocol.

———. *UN Climate Change Annual Report 2019.* Bonn, Germany: UNFCCC, 2019. https://unfccc.int/sites/default/files/resource/unfccc_annual_report_2019.pdf.

UN-Habitat. *World Cities Report 2016: Urbanization and Development—Emerging Futures.* Nairobi, Kenya: United Nations Human Settlement Programme, 2016. https://unhabitat.org/world-cities-report.

United Nations. *The Sustainable Development Goals Report 2019.* New York: United Nations, 2019. https://unstats.un.org/sdgs/report/2019/The-Sustainable-Development-Goals-Report-2019.pdf.

"UQAM Halts Investment in Fossil Fuels." *CTV News,* 17 May 2019. https://montreal.ctvnews.ca/uqam-halts-investments-in-fossil-fuels-1.4426978.

Vaessen, Doug, and Lisa Geddes. "Mayor Calls for Investigation of Civic Election Campaign Contributions." *Global News,* 23 April 2013. https://globalnews.ca/news/504916/mayor-calls-for-investigation-of-civic-election-campaign-contributions/.

Van der Poorten, Kylee, and Byron Miller. "Secondary Suites, Second-Class Citizens: The History and Geography of Calgary's Most Controversial Housing Policy." *Canadian Geographer* 61, no. 4 (2017): 564–78.

Van der Zee, Renate. "How Amsterdam Became the Bicycle Capital of the World." *The Guardian,* 5 May 2015. https://www.theguardian.com/cities/2015/may/05/amsterdam-bicycle-capital-world-transport-cycling-kindermoord.

Vanderklippe, Nathan. "Bonuses Soar in the Oil Patch 'Bubble.'" *Globe and Mail,* 1 May 2012. https://www.theglobeandmail.com/report-on-business/streetwise/bonuses-soar-in-oil-patch-bubble/article4103979/.

Vaughan, Adam. "World Council of Churches Rules Out Fossil Fuel Investments." *The Guardian,* 11 July 2014. https://www.theguardian.com/environment/2014/jul/11/world-council-of-churches-pulls-fossil-fuel-investments.

Växjö: The Sustainable City Frontrunner." *Nordregio,* 29 June 2018. https://nordregio.org/sustainable_cities/europes-greenest-city-vaxjo/.

Veal, A. J. *Whatever Happened to the Leisure Society?* New York: Routledge, 2018.

"Vehicle Buyers in the United States in 2017, by Age Group." *Statista.* Accessed 21 August 2020. https://www.statista.com/statistics/987393/age-distribution-of-vehicle-buyers-united-states/.

Vibrant Communities Calgary. *A Snapshot of Poverty in Calgary 2019.* Calgary: VCC, August 2019. http://enoughforall.ca/wp-content/uploads/2019/08/A-Snapshot-of-poverty-in-Calgary-in-2019.pdf.

———. *A Snapshot of Poverty in Calgary 2019.* Calgary: VCC, August 2019. http://enoughforall.ca/wp-content/uploads/2019/08/A-Snapshot-of-poverty-in-Calgary-in-2019.pdf.

Victor, Peter, and Tim Jackson. "Towards an Ecological Macroeconomics." Prepared for INET Annual Plenary Conference "Paradigm Lost: Rethinking Economics and Politics," Berlin, April 2012. https://www.ineteconomics.org/uploads/papers/victor-peter-berlin-paper-draft-w-Tim-Jackson.pdf.

Vimmerstedt, Laura, Sertaç Akar, Philipp Beiter, Wesley Cole, David Feldman, Parthiv Kurup, Ashwin Ramdas et al. *Annual Technology Baseline: The 2020 Electricity Update*. Golden, CO: National Renewable Energy Laboratory, July 2020. https://www.nrel.gov/docs/fy20osti/76814.pdf.

Vincanne, Adam, Sharon Kaufman, Taslim van Hattum, and Sandra Moody. "Aging Disaster: Mortality, Vulnerability, and Long-Term Recovery among Katrina Survivors." *Medical Anthropology* 30, no. 2 (May 2011): 247–70.

Von Weizsäcker, Ernst, Amory B. Lovins, and L. Hunter Lovins. *Factor Four: Doubling Wealth and Halving Resource Use*. London, UK: Earthscan, 1998.

"Voter Turnout at Federal Elections and Referendums 1867–2015." *Elections Canada*, last modified 12 May 2020. https://www.elections.ca/content.aspx?section=ele&dir=turn&document=index&lang=e.

Waldrop, M. Mitchell. *Complexity: The Emerging Science at the Edge of Order and Chaos*. New York: Simon and Schuster, 1992.

Walks, R. Alan. "The Causes of City-Suburban Political Polarization? A Canadian Case Study." *Annals of the Association of American Geographers* 96, no. 2 (2006): 390–414.

Watkins, Mel. "Comment Staples Redux." *Studies in Political Economy* 79, no. 1 (2007): 213–26.

Watts, Jonathan. "Belt and Road Summit Puts Spotlight on Chinese Coal Funding." *The Guardian*, 25 April 2019. https://www.theguardian.com/world/2019/apr/25/belt-and-road-summit-puts-spotlight-on-chinese-coal-funding.

"We Can End Poverty: Millennium Development Goals and Beyond 2015." *United Nations*. Accessed 2 September 2020. https://www.un.org/millenniumgoals/.

"The Wet'suwet'en and B.C.'s Gas-Pipeline Battle: A Guide to the Story So Far." *Globe and Mail*, 11 January 2019. https://www.theglobeandmail.com/canada/british-columbia/article-wetsuweten-bc-lng-pipeline-explainer/.

"What Is Net Zero?" *World Green Building Council*, 2016–20. https://www.worldgbc.org/advancing-net-zero/what-net-zero.

"What's Copenhagen's Magic Formula to Reduce CO_2 Levels?" *Euronews*, 10 October 2019. https://www.euronews.com/2019/10/10/what-s-copenhagen-s-magic-formula-to-reduce-co2-levels.

Wheeler, Stephen M., and Timothy Beatley, eds. *The Sustainable Urban Development Reader*. 3rd ed. New York: Routledge, 2014.

"When Buying Cars, Millennials Choose Used and Practical over New and Flashy." *Financial Post*, 21 September 2015. https://financialpost.com/personal-finance/young-money/when-buying-cars-millennials-choose-used-and-practical-over-new-and-flashy.

Wilkinson, Richard, and Kate Pickett. *The Spirit Level: Why Greater Equality Makes Societies Stronger*. London: Bloomsbury, 2009.

Williams, Raymond. *Culture and Society: 1780–1950*. New York: Columbia University Press, 1983.

Willsher, Kim. "Paris Mayor Unveils '15-Minute City' Plan in Re-Election Campaign." *The Guardian*, 7 February 2020. https://www.theguardian.com/world/2020/feb/07/paris-mayor-unveils-15-minute-city-plan-in-re-election-campaign.

"Wind Facts: Affordable Power." *Canadian Wind Energy Association*. Accessed 6 September 2020. https://canwea.ca/wind-facts/affordable-power/.

"Wind Markets: Wind Energy in Alberta." *Canadian Wind Energy Association*. Accessed 6 September 2020. https://canwea.ca/wind-energy/alberta/.

Wingrove, Josh. "'Bitumen Bubble' Means a Hard Reckoning for Alberta, Redford Warns." *Globe and Mail*, 24 January 2013. https://www.theglobeandmail.com/news/national/bitumen-bubble-means-a-hard-reckoning-for-alberta-redford-warns/article7833915/.

Wodrich, Nigel, and Aidan Worswick. *Estimating the Top Tail of the Family Wealth Distribution in Canada*. Ottawa: Office of the Parliamentary Budget Officer, 17 June 2020. https://www.pbo-dpb.gc.ca/web/default/files/Documents/Reports/RP-2021-007-S/RP-2021-007-S_en.pdf.

Wood, James. "Alberta Government Commits to West Leg of Calgary's Ring Road." *Edmonton Journal*, 5 July 2015. https://edmontonjournal.com/news/politics/ndp-government-commits-to-west-leg-of-ring-road/wcm/cf3fce83-6e09-4a0d-992f-346808286719.

World Commission on Environment and Development. *Our Common Future*. Oxford: Oxford University Press, 1987. https://sustainabledevelopment.un.org/content/documents/5987our-common-future.pdf.

"World Energy Outlook 2020." *International Energy Agency*, 2020. https://www.iea.org/reports/world-energy-outlook-2020.

World Health Organization. *Global Status Report on Road Safety 2018*. Geneva: WHO, 2018. https://www.who.int/violence_injury_prevention/road_safety_status/2018/en/.

"World Vehicles in Use, by Country, Region, and Type, 2005–2015." *International Organization of Motor Vehicle Manufacturers (OICA)*. Accessed 31 August 2020. http://www.oica.net/category/vehicles-in-use/.

Worster, Donald. *The Shaky Ground of Sustainability in the Wealth of Nature: Environmental History and the Ecological Imagination*. Oxford: Oxford University Press, 1993.

Yergin, Daniel. *The Prize: The Epic Quest for Oil, Money and Power*. New York: Free Press, 2008.

Young, Robert. *Postcolonialism: A Very Short Introduction*. Oxford: Oxford University Press, 2003.

Zeidler, Maryze. "How the B.C. Election of '96 Changed Provincial Politics." *CBC News*, 29 April 2017. https://www.cbc.ca/news/canada/british-columbia/how-the-b-c-election-of-96-changed-provincial-politics-1.4089562.

Zhu, Jing, and Yingling Fan. "Daily Travel Behavior and Emotional Well-Being: A Comprehensive Assessment of Travel-Related Emotions and the Associated Trip and Personal Factors." In *Happy Cities: Role of Transportation*. Minneapolis: University of Minnesota, 2017. https://conservancy.umn.edu/handle/11299/185433.

Zickefoose, Sherri. "Mayor Seeks Clarity on Gift Policy." *Calgary Herald*, 11 December 2012. https://www.pressreader.com/canada/calgary-hera ld/20121211/281878705685855.

Zimonjic, Peter. "Liberals Detail $40B for 10-Year National Housing Strategy, Introduce Canada Housing Benefit." *CBC News*, 22 November 2017. https://www.cbc.ca/news/politics/housing-national-benefit-1.4413615.

Zinc Research. *Calgary Secondary Suites Survey*. Calgary: Students Union, University of Calgary, 3 March 2011. https://www.yumpu.com/en/document/read/26865862/report-for-press-release-secondary-suites-students-union-.

"Zipcar Overview." *Zipcar*, 2021. https://www.zipcar.com/press/overview.

Further Reading

Blais, Pamela. *Perverse Cities: Hidden Subsidies, Wonky Policy, and Urban Sprawl*. Vancouver: University of British Columbia Press, 2010.

Bohm, Steffen, Campbell Jones, Chris Land, and Matthew Paterson, eds. *Against Automobility*. Oxford: Blackwell, 2006.

Bruegmann, Robert. *Sprawl: A Compact History*. Chicago: University of Chicago Press, 2005.

Condon, Patrick. "Portland Just Showed Vancouver How to Fix Its Housing Crisis." *The Tyee*, 28 August 2020. https://thetyee.ca/Analysis/2020/08/28/Portland-Showed-Vancouver-Fix-Housing-Crisis/?fbclid=IwAR07mvtiPUA3B9oAQROtswmBhVUY 2tlxWzG6a1Q-1SJaTVewPNGcUoZVkXc.

———. *Seven Rules for Sustainable Communities: Design Strategies for a Post-Carbon World*. Washington, DC: Island Press, 2010.

Crawford, J. H. *Carfree Cities*. Utrecht, Netherlands: International Books, 2002.

Dennis, Kingsley, and John Urry. *After the Car*. Cambridge, UK: Polity, 2009.

Dietz, Rob, and Dan O'Neill. *Enough Is Enough: Building a Sustainable Economy in a World of Finite Resources*. San Francisco: Brett-Koehler, 2013.

Flint, Anthony. *Wrestling with Moses: How Jane Jacobs Took on New York's Master Builder and Transformed the American City*. New York: Random House, 2011.

Flyvbjerg, Bent. *Rationality and Power: Democracy in Practice*. Chicago: University of Chicago Press, 1998.

Gardiner, Stephen M. *A Perfect Moral Storm: The Ethical Tragedy of Climate Change.* Oxford: Oxford University Press, 2011.

Gismondi, Mike, Sean Connelly, Mary Beckie, and Mark Roseland. *Scaling Up: The Convergence of Social Economy and Sustainability.* Athabasca, AB: Athabasca University Press, 2016.

Graeber, David. *Debt: The First 5,000 Years.* London: Melville House, 2014.

Hanson, Lorelei, ed. *Public Deliberation on Climate Change: Lessons from Alberta Climate Dialogue.* Athabasca, AB: Athabasca University Press, 2018.

Jaccard, Mark. *The Citizen's Guide to Climate Success: Overcoming Myths That Hinder Progress.* Cambridge, UK: Cambridge University Press, 2020.

Krier, Leon. "The Future of Cities: The Absurdity of Modernism." Nikos Salingaros: Interview with Leon Krier. *Planetizen,* 5 November 2001. https://www.planetizen.com/node/32.

Latour, Bruno. *Down to Earth: Politics in the New Climatic Regime.* Cambridge, UK: Polity, 2017.

Lees, Loretta, Tom Slater, and Elvin Wyly. *Gentrification.* London: Routledge, 2007.

Magdoff, Fred, and John Bellamy Foster. "What Every Environmentalist Needs to Know about Capitalism: A Citizen's Guide to Capitalism and the Environment." *Monthly Review Press* 61, no. 10 (2010). https://monthlyreview.org/2010/03/01/what-every-environmentalist-needs-to-know-about-capitalism/.

Malm, Andreas. *Fossil Capital: The Rise of Steam Power and the Roots of Global Warming.* London: Verso, 2016.

McKibben, Bill. *Oil and Honey: The Education of an Unlikely Activist.* New York: Henry Holt, 2013.

McNeill, J. R., and Peter Engelke. *The Great Acceleration: An Environmental History of the Anthropocene Since 1945.* Cambridge, MA: Harvard University Press, 2014.

Meslin, Dave. *Teardown: Building Democracy from the Ground Up.* Toronto: Penguin, 2019.

Monbiot, George. *Feral: Rewilding the Land, the Sea, and Human Life.* Chicago: University of Chicago Press, 2014.

———. *Out of the Wreckage: A New Politics for an Age of Crisis.* London: Verso, 2017.

Nikiforuk, Andrew. *Slick Water: Fracking and One Insider's Stand against the World's Most Powerful Industry.* Vancouver: Greystone Books, 2015.

Patel, Raj, and Jason Moore. *The History of the World in Seven Cheap Things: A Guide to Capitalism, Nature, and the Future of the Planet.* London: Verso, 2015.

Peredo, Ana Maria, and Murdith McLean. "Decommodification in Action: Common Property as Countermovement." *Organization* (July 2019): 1–23.

Post-Growth Institute. https://www.postgrowth.org.

Quarter, Jack, Laurie Mook, and Ann Armstrong. *Understanding the Social Economy: A Canadian Perspective.* 2nd ed. Toronto: University of Toronto Press, 2017.

Restakis, John. *Humanizing the Economy: Co-operatives in the Age of Capital.* Gabriola Island, BC: New Society, 2010.

Shell, Ellen Ruppel. *Cheap: The High Cost of Discount Culture.* New York: Penguin, 2009.

Smil, Vaclav. *Energy and Civilization: A History.* Cambridge, MA: MIT Press, 2018.

Subhabrata, Bobby Banerjee, John M. Jermier, Ana Maria Peredo, Robert Perey, and André Reichel. "Special Issue: Theoretical Perspectives on Organizations and Organizing in a Post-Growth Era." *Organization* (2020): 1–21.

Turner, Chris. *The Patch: The People, Pipelines and Politics of the Oil Sands.* Toronto: Simon and Schuster, 2017.

Wohlleben, Peter. *The Hidden Life of Trees: What They Feel, How They Communicate.* Vancouver: Greystone Books, 2015.

Acknowledgements

A heartfelt thanks to the many people who helped bring this book into being.

To Craig Gerlach with the Certificate in Sustainability Studies Program at the University of Calgary for generous support for the publication of *Sustainability Matters*. I am grateful to all of my colleagues and co-instructors in the Sustainability Studies Program who supported my efforts to help shape the program while introducing early versions of the book into the curriculum—Craig Gerlach, Sarah Skett, Dianne Draper, Allan Habib, and Brian Sinclair.

To my friend and colleague Ana Maria Peredo at the University of Victoria for her encouragement and invitations to test my ideas in her classroom and with wider audiences at the University of Victoria.

To my friends and colleagues in the Department of Geography, including Byron Miller and Eliot Tretter. Byron's knowledge of and insight into processes of urbanization, as well as the many discussions and book club debates that he hosted over several years, have been invaluable in shaping my understanding of the dynamics of change in Calgary. Eliot's generosity and keen eye in reviewing my manuscript and his willingness to share his knowledge of urban and critical geography literature were much appreciated.

To my partner in life, Linda Grandinetti, always ready to review the most drafty of chapters and to encourage me onward when the task seemed too daunting.

To Jo Hildebrand, my friend and incomparable editor, whose ability to decipher and transform my opaque and awkward words into pleasurable and precise prose at times seemed like a magic trick.

To my colleagues at the University of Calgary Press, Brian Scrivener and Helen Hajnoczky, for saying yes to this book and for working with me to make it a reality.

To Drew Anderson, a passionate journalist whose work continues to inspire me and the *Fast Forward Weekly* managing editor at the time we began our series of essays that became the kernel of this book.

To my friends at PLAN:NET—Phil Cox, Stan Benjamin, and Bruce Smedley. My ideas on sustainability were shaped during endless hours of conversation over coffee at Peppino's Deli.

To the many, many champions of Sustainable Calgary over the years with whom I have had the pleasure to do the at times frustrating but important work of sustainability research, education advocacy, and action in Calgary. To my friend Bob Morrison, a long-time board member of Sustainable Calgary, a tireless researcher, and an advocate for a more just and sustainable city. In particular, my greatest thanks to those with whom I co-founded Sustainable Calgary many years ago—Jan Ingles, Linda Grandinetti, Monica Pohlmann, and Carol Spring. Our work together has been invaluable in shaping my understanding of sustainability.

Authors

Noel Keough

Given that we present this book as a work of reflective practice, it is important to say a few words about our personal narratives. My early adulthood and first career as a drilling engineer working for a multinational oil and gas company was marked by a foggy but discomforting disenchantment with the technocratic status quo. My second career was in the field of international development, where my critical stance to the world was formed by experiences in post-revolution Nicaragua, in the Philippines after Ferdinand Marcos, and in the Middle East during the ongoing conflict in the region. Eventually, my attention turned back to my own community, where I engaged with issues of urban sustainability, first as a citizen activist and then as an academic. My sense of urgency about the ecological crisis was awakened by my witness to poverty, social injustice, and ecological devastation in countries of the Global South. It was solidified by my recognition that these issues are of a kind with the ecological, social, and economic devastation wrought in Newfoundland (where I was born and raised) with the collapse of the North Atlantic cod fishery and the closure of that fishery in 1992. Having been directly affected by the 2013 Calgary flood (my entire community flooded, with six feet of water in our basement), I also feel a visceral sense of urgency to address the mitigation of and adaptation to climate change through a sustainability transition in Alberta in both my city, Calgary, and my neighbourhood of Sunnyside.

Geoff Ghitter

Like Noel, I did not come to the study of urban systems in a straight line. My first training was in physical geography with a specialty in remote sensing. Essentially, I used computer algorithms to decipher satellite data of the earth with the goal of finding "hotspots" of biological diversity.

Identifying the sorts of habitat to which fauna is attracted is an essential first step in protecting both common and at-risk species. After ten years of public and private practice, I returned to university to do a doctorate based on two realizations: first, "good data" does not by itself bring about "good practice," and second, the mechanics and evolution of biological systems like the forests that I studied apply generally to all sorts of systems, including cities. The scenarios described in this book reflect a broad sampling of the sorts of issues that, only when addressed together as a system, work to create sustainable places. As a species, we are socially and technically equipped to move forward and to bring with us, as we go, an environment that can properly and abundantly sustain us. But we are not on that pathway. The only true constraint to developing cities sustainably is political.

Index

A

affordable housing: co-ops, 90, 168; one of many sustainability solutions, 162; policy, 12, 78, 85; secondary suites, 222, 224; strategy, 165, 175, 225
affordable living, 105, 225–27
Age of Sustainable Development, The (Sachs, Jeffrey), 30
agenda, 21, 23, 30, 39
Alaska Permanent Fund, 197
Alberta Heritage Fund, 197
Alexandria, Egypt, 151
Alvarez, Claude, 26
Amsterdam, 56, 107–8
Anthropocene, 14, 16
Arabianranta, Helsinki, 53, 67
art, public, 58, 67
arts: and culture, 4, 6, 143, 163, 228; economic activity, 67, 90; participation in, 4, 6, 88, 150
Arvai, Joe, 254
Atlanta, 62
Atwood, Margaret, 252
Austin, Texas, 80
auto dependence, 2, 119–20, 126. *See also* car dependent
automobile: age of the, 38–39, 57, 110; cost of, 9, 98, 121, 124, 198, 130, 146; death and injury, 9, 14, 120, 122, 123, 125; dependence on, 10, 43, 49–50, 82; life beyond the, 90, 98, 125; pre-automobile, 98, 104, 109
autonomous vehicles, 13, 124

B

Barcelona, 57, 62, 108
Beatley, Timothy, 10, 63–65
bees, 6, 152

bicycle: health and, 56, 98, 106, 109; infrastructure, 51, 53, 90, 124, 194; mode share, 107–8
big box retail, 79–81, 110, 148
Big Box Swindle (Mitchell, Stacy), 80
Bill C-38, 196–97, 254
biodiversity: loss of, 30, 52, 68, 276, 289, 291; targets, 154
bitumen bubble, 195
Black Lives Matter, 44
Blackfoot, 37
Bowness (community of), 79, 81
Broadbent, Ed, 16, 278
Bronconnier, Dave (mayor), 82–83, 40–41
Brundtland Report, 4, 6, 10, 23–25, 28, 30. *See also Our Common Future*; Rio Earth Summit; World Commission on Environment and Development
Buy Nothing Day, 230, 232

C

Calgary Airport Authority (CAA), 127–30
Calgary Economic Development (CED), 82, 174–76, 255
Calgary Homeless Foundation (CHF), 175, 224, 225
Calgary Public Library (CPL), 149–51
Calgary Regional Partnership (CRP), 89
Calgary Transportation Planning (CTP), 39–41, 82. *See also* Plan It Calgary
Canada Mortgage and Housing Corporation (CMHC), 223
Canadian Association of Petroleum Producers (CAPP), 253
Canadian Association of Physicians for the Environment (CAPE), 207
Canadian Energy Pipeline Association (CEPA), 253

Canadian Index of Wellbeing (CIW), 162–63, 166

Canadians for Tax Fairness, 272

capital, 6, 277. *See also* capital gains; capital investment; cultural capital; financial capital; natural capital; political capital; social capital

capital gains, 272, 275, 280

Capital in the Twenty-First Century (Piketty, Thomas), 134, 277, 281, 293

capital investment, 100, 255

capitalism: alternatives to, 24, 31, 290; and climate change, 282; critique of, 23, 277, 279–81, 293; future of, 26, 291; green, 28; and urbanization, 11, 16; and Western civilization, 295

Capitalism in the Web of Life (Moore, Jason), 293

capitalist: class, 280; and climate change, 281; modus operandi of, 13, 245, 289; system, 5, 23–24, 30, 270, 290–91, 293

car dependent, 2, 14, 66, 227, 256. *See also* auto dependence

car share, 120, 123, 126, 176, 233

carbon tax, 166, 198,

Carbon Tracker, 204–5

Carney, Mark, 202

Carson, Rachel (*Silent Spring*), 27, 259

Ceci, Joe (city councilor), 82

Center for Neighborhood Technology (CNT), 226

Chicago, 80

citizen(s): activism, 89–91, 106, 146, 169; capacity of, 4, 55, 149, 175; consultation with and engagement of, 3, 6, 40, 42, 66, 67, 245; engaged, 3, 80, 82, 84, 128; global, 15, 196, 204; responsibility, 5, 192, 244; rights of, 59, 83, 87, 144, 246, 270

Citizen Satisfaction Survey, 250–52

Citizens' Agenda, A (Sustainable Calgary Society), 175

Citizen's Guide to Climate Success, The (Jaccard, Mark), 10, 208, 281

city (cities): creative, 6, 150; eco-, 67; and eco-footprint, 16; examples of, 50, 66, 90, 127, 249; and governance, 15; healthy, 56; inclusive, 14, 150; liveable, 10, 56, 88, 131, 280; organizations of, 11; post-carbon, 10, 174–75; resilient, 10, 45, 58,

61–62, 98, 107; smart, 13, 30; and sprawl, 82; sustainable, 10–11; vibrant, 10

City in History, The (Mumford, Lewis), 13

City Making in Paradise (Harcourt, Mike), 89–90

Clark, Christopher (*The Sleepwalkers*), 279, 292

climate change: air travel, 128–29; capitalism, 281–82; cities, 61–62, 68, 289; denial, 128; economy, 163, 175, 291; fossil fuels, 5, 132, 166, 196, 198, 201–4, 207; global negotiations, 196; governance, 251–51; inequality and justice, 13, 16, 231; least developed countries, 231; local drivers, 2, 124, 178; reports, 52, 128, 278; war, 17, 292

climate emergency, 98, 106, 154

Climate Vulnerability Monitor (DARA), 231–32

clockwork universe, 14, 295

Closing Circle, The (Commoner, Barry), 296

coal: divestment, 204; Jevons paradox, 281; jobs, 202; mining, 174; phase-out, 192, 196, 200, 206–8; stranded assets, 203

colonialism, 6, 280

colonization, 37

Commoner, Barry (*Closing Circle, The*), 296

commons, enclosure of the, 26

community gardens, 43, 58, 67

community land trust, 175

Condon, Patrick, 100

congestion: induced demand, 98, 101, 131; policy solutions to, 103, 108; school busing, 78; traffic, 4, 61, 98

consumer: activism, 90, 120; choice, 80, 232; co-op, 167; of energy, 193, 201, 206, 193, 201; goods, 38, 279; spending, 256, 279

consumerism, 163, 222, 230, 232

consumerist, 6, 9, 222, 231

consumption: cities and, 6, 289; energy, 43, 50, 52, 163,170–71; patterns of, 63–64, 148, 171, 232, 256, 276; resource, 15, 24, 28, 174, 281; water, 43

co-operative(s), 6, 90, 120, 167–68

Copenhagen, 57, 62, 107, 249

cosmopolitan(ism), 2, 14, 151, 289

creativity, 3, 10, 15–16, 249

Cuba, 50, 58–60, 229

cultural capital, 14, 144

culture (cultural), 143–44, 151, 162–63, 228

Culture and Society (Williams, Raymond), 143

Curitiba, 50, 66–67

D

Daly, Herman, 162, 164, 174, 258, 290
dandelions, 61, 151–54
DARA (*Climate Vulnerability Monitor*), 231–32
Dark Age Ahead (Jacobs, Jane), 149, 279
Darwin, Charles, 294, 296
Das Kapital (Marx, Karl), 290
Daseking, Wulf, 65–66
Davis, Wade (*Into the Silence*), 292
Davison, Aidan (*Technology and the Contested Meaning of Sustainability*), 23, 27–29
deficit: budget, 9, 130; ecological, 9; of imagination, 125; infrastructure, 9; social, 9
degrowth, 171, 290. *See also* non-economic growth; uneconomic growth
dematerialization, 291
density: automobiles, 54; comparisons, 57; human scale, 55; population, 43, 50, 126, 131–32, 148, 223; and transit, 53, 56, 105
Descartes, René (*Meditations on First Philosophy*), 13, 295
design: ecological, 10; urban, 3, 10, 76, 120, 131, 194
development: critiques of, 10, 75, 87, 131; greenfield, 38, 41, 52–53, 173; industry, 5, 82, 83, 86–88, 146, 252–53 (*see also* Urban Development Institute); international, 4, 23, 25–26, 349; and Plan It, 41, 173; real estate, 15, 90, 171; urban, 10, 38, 65, 84, 86, 149. *See also* green urbanism; suburban development: cost of
diabetes, 9
divestment, 192, 203–4
Duany, Andres, 10
Duxbury, Linda, 163–64, 179, 185–86, 310
Dyer, Gwynne, 279, 292

E

Earth Overshoot Day, 231
eco-efficiency, 29
ecological: collapse, 281; crisis, 257–58; economics, 258, 290; restoration, 259; stability, 292; world view, 296–97
ecological footprint: of Calgary, 9, 40, 42–43, 52; of Canada, 163, 279; of cities, 15–16, 56; green urbanism 64–65
ecological integrity, 45

ecological modernization, 23, 28–30
ecology: age of, 5; of the earth, 203; global, 64; industrial, 10; science of, 192, 296; women and, 26
economic diversification, 2, 175, 193
economic growth: alternatives to, 163, 171; in Calgary, 42, 164, 174, 254; and climate change, 11; critiques of, 7, 27, 162; and ecological well-being, 161, 281, 290; and energy, 169, 275, 276; externalities of, 9, 12; ideology of, 2, 6, 17, 31, 129; and sustainable development, 30, 257–59. *See also* degrowth; non-economic growth; uneconomic growth
Economics for Everyone (Stanford, Jim), 280, 290
efficiency, 14, 39, 67, 200, 207, 243, 281
End This Depression Now (Krugman, Paul), 257
energy: green, 65; transition, 192. *See also* renewable(s)
Energy and Equity (Illich, Ivan), 123
Energy Efficiency Alberta (EEA), 207
Energy of Slaves, The (Nikiforuk, Andrew), 280
engaged intellectuals, 1
environment(al)(ist): active transportation, 98, 100, 105–6; activism, 41; biodiversity loss, 52, 154; built, 50, 61,63–67, 88, 98, 145; climate change, 128, 196, 207; economy, 161–62, 164, 167, 169, 171, 203, 206, 209; First Nations, 37; human exceptionalism, 294; indicators, 42, 163, 230, 232, 248; politics, 44, 56, 60, 84, 196, 250; in popular non-fiction, 279, 281, 296; poverty and inequality, 16, 23, 49; sustainable development, 4, 11, 23–30, 165, 257, 259
evolution(ary), 294, 296–97, 350
expansionist paradigm, 28
Expansive Discourse (Foran, Max), 49, 57
externalities, 9
extinction, 6, 152, 276

F

Farrell, Druh (city councilor), 146
financial capital, 162, 205
First Nations, 37, 42, 149, 197, 276
first-past-the-post, 246, 252–53
fiscal cliff, 9, 81, 83

flood, 17, 50, 60, 67, 89, 349

Florida, Richard (*Rise of the Creative Class, The*), 6, 10, 13, 255

Follow the Money (Taft, Kevin), 173, 272–74

food bank, 12, 167, 255, 275

Foran, Max (*Expansive Discourse*), 49, 57

fossil fuels: climate change, 9, 171, 192, 202; demand for, 193; dependence on, 269, 275; divestment from, 204–6; ecological impacts, 279; health impacts, 231

400 ppm, 174, 192, 201

Freiburg, Germany, 50, 65–66, 120, 127, 199

Freire, Paulo, 3

G

Gehl, Jan, 13, 50, 56–57, 131

gentrification, 6

Global Environmental Outlook (GEO), 52, 232, 258

global village, 2, 3, 5, 9, 45, 222, 231, 270

global warming, 14, 44, 64. *See also* climate change

governance: effective, 165; good, 14, 15, 243, 245, 247–49, 252; indicators of, 247–48; municipal, 15; within a systems analysis, 2–4, 29; trust in, 250; urban, 6, 76

Granville Island, Vancouver, 90

green: belt, 84; building design, 54, 176; capitalism, 28; community, 67; energy, 65; metropolis, 56; space(s), 58, 67, 153; urbanism, 10, 50, 62–67; zone, 84

Green Line, 126

Green Metropolis (Owen, David), 56–57

Green Party, 196, 198, 202

Greenfield, Adam (*Radical Technologies*), 29

greenhouse gases (GHGs), 9, 78, 128–29, 206–7

growth machine, 6, 13, 161–62, 172–73, 256

H

habitat: car, 13, 49, 120, 122; human, 13, 15, 109, 120; wildlife, 9, 153–54, 196, 350

Haeckel, Ernst, 296

hailstorm, 60

Harari, Yuval Noah (*Sapiens*), 17, 29

Harcourt, Mike (*City Making in Paradise*), 89–90

Harper, Stephen (prime minister), 166, 196, 232

Harvey, David, 6, 11

heart disease, 9, 108

Heat (Monbiot, George), 128–29

Helsinki, 50, 53, 56, 67–68, 151, 194, 248–49

Hillhurst-Sunnyside (community of), 54–55, 57, 132, 154, 168, 227, 349

homelessness, 12, 90, 123, 165, 167, 223, 255, 276; *10 Year Plan to End Homelessness*, 175, 225

housing: choice, 79, 148, 226; co-housing, 176; co-operative, 90, 168; non-market, 6; price, 255; rental, 224

housing affordability. *See* affordable housing

human settlement, 2, 13, 15, 37

hurricane, 17, 50; Katrina, 58–59

hydro power, 206

I

ideological, 9, 147, 193, 278, 281

ideology, 66, 147, 151, 196, 207

Illich, Ivan (*Energy and Equity*), 123

imagineCalgary, 40–41, 52, 54, 91, 128, 146; industry resistance to, 82–83, 88

immigrant, 14, 42, 56, 176, 224, 251

immigration, 38

imperialist, 295

income inequality, 2, 162, 178, 257. *See also* inequality

Indigenous, 37–38, 222, 295

induced demand, 98, 101, 103

Industrial Revolution, 14, 295

industry: energy, 5; industrial ecology, 10

inequality: in Calgary, 12, 42, 149, 162, 177, 276; Canadian Index of Wellbeing, 163; CEO compensation, 162, 167, 178; and climate change, 16; and democracy, 175, 293; Global Environmental Outlook, 232; income, 2, 178, 257, 277, 281, 294

infrastructure: automobile, 98; bicycle, 53, 90, 103, 107, 108, 145, 227; deficits, 9, 256; education, 76, 165; energy, 198; pedestrian, 145–46; social, 177; suburban, 39, 50, 83, 173; transit, 51, 53, 100; transportation, 13, 120–21, 127, 132; urban, 56, 58–60, 63, 83, 102, 173

injustice, 12, 221–22, 231, 349

innovation, 15–16; cultural, 6; political, 6; social, 175; technological, 10, 27–30, 164, 174, 192, 249, 251

International Council for Local
  Environmental Initiatives (ICLEI), 11
international development. *See* development:
  international
International Energy Agency, 201, 205. *See
  also* World Energy Outlook
Into the Silence (Davis, Wade), 292

J

Jaccard, Mark (*Citizen's Guide to Climate
  Success, The*), 10, 208, 281
Jacobs, Jane (*Dark Age Ahead*), 13, 16, 50, 55,
  131, 149, 151, 279
Jane's Walk, 55, 57
Jevons paradox, 281
Johannesburg, 30
justice: economic, 257; global, 13, 248, 293;
  idea of, 233; social, 4, 6, 148, 151, 178

K

Kenney, Jason (premier), 147, 172, 203, 247,
  259, 271–73
Keystone Hills, 50–53
Klein, Naomi (*This Changes Everything*), 13,
  281–82
Klein, Ralph, 39, 82, 89, 147, 200
Krugman, Paul (*End This Depression Now*), 13,
  85, 257, 293
Kyoto Protocol, 12, 128, 197

L

land use planning, 2, 39, 41, 50, 79, 89–90
laneway housing, 175, 225
Leduc oil discovery, 38
Lefebvre, Henri, 5
leisure society, 163
lifestyles: sedentary, 9, 52, 146
light rail transit (LRT): alternative to ring
  road, 119, 126, 132, 136n59; and climate
  change, 100, 199; industrial retooling,
  166; North American ridership, 99;
  policy and planning, 52, 55, 226–27;
  Portland revitalization, 104; compared
  to tram/streetcar, 98–101, 105
limits to growth, 24–25, 258, 289, 291
local: business, 58, 79–81, 102; retail, 81
London, England, 108–9, 204

M

Maathai, Wangari, 233
Malthus, Thomas, 170
Marcuse, Peter, 5
marginalization, 5, 11, 42, 293
Marx, Karl (*Das Kapital*), 290
Marxist, 11
Mauna Loa, 201
maximum sustained yield (MSY), 23, 25
May, Elizabeth, 196
McDonough, William, 10
McQuaig, Linda (*Trouble with Billionaires,
  The*), 270, 272, 280
media: cities in popular, 13; and governance,
  243, 250; mass media, 14, 44, 145–46,
  247; personalities, 229; reactionary, 146,
  254; social, 29, 44, 230, 250–51
Meditations on First Philosophy (Descartes,
  René), 13, 295
Melbourne, Australia, 98, 102, 104–6, 126
militarization, 24
military, 278–79, 291–92
Millennium Development Goals. *See* UN
  Millennium Development Goals
Mitchell, Stacy (*Big Box Swindle*), 80
Moh' kinsstis, 37
Mol, Arthur, 28–29
Molotch, Harvey, 6, 162, 172, 256,
Monbiot, George (*Heat*), 128–29
Montgomery (community of), 79, 81
Moore, Jason (*Capitalism in the Web of Life*),
  293
moratorium: North Atlantic cod fishery, 258;
  tar sands, 174
Mumford, Lewis (*City in History, The*), 13,
  15, 18
Municipal Development Plan (MDP), 12,
  39–41, 50–53, 68, 79, 81–84

N

Nader, Ralph (*Unsafe at Any Speed*), 120, 122,
  125
natural capital, 162, 166
Nenshi, Naheed (mayor), 15, 51, 82, 84, 228,
  247
neocolonial(ism), 6–7
neocolonialist, 27
neoliberal, 3, 9, 15, 23, 144
New Orleans, 50, 58–60
new urbanism, 10, 41

Newman, Peter (*Resilient Cities*), 61–62
Newton, Isaac (*Philosophiae Naturalis Principia Mathematica*), 13, 295
Nikiforuk, Andrew (*Energy of Slaves, The*), 280
NIMBYism, 224
1984 (Orwell, George), 252
non-economic growth, 290. *See also* degrowth; uneconomic growth
non-market housing, 6
Norwegian Sovereign Wealth Fund, 197
Notley, Rachel (premier), 89, 130, 132, 203, 247
nuclear energy, 170, 193

O

obesity, 9, 77, 257
oil and gas: clean-up, 259; dependence on, 255; executive compensation, 205; industry lobbying, 253–54; pipelines, 44; sovereign wealth, investment and profit, 191, 197, 200, 270, 273
Oil and Gas Reliance Index, 275
oil price, 193; crash of, 42; faltering, 203; high, 205; soaring, 166; triple digit, 129, 170
oil sands, 200, 205. *See also* tar sands
Oil's Deep State (Taft, Kevin), 44
Oka, 276
1.5°C, 278
Orwell, George (*1984*), 128, 252
Oslo, 108, 194
Our Common Future, 4, 161, 278. *See also* Brundtland Report; Rio Earth Summit; World Commission on Environment and Development
Owen, David (*Green Metropolis*), 56–57

P

pandemic, 44, 56, 107–8, 129, 231, 277; COVID, 165, 231; plagues, 295
Paris, 15, 56–57, 107, 109, 194
Paris Accord (Agreement), 204, 278
participation, 14, 25, 163, 175, 246; citizen, 45, 82; democratic, 45; elections, 244; governance, 243; voter, 178
Peace Bridge, 144–47
pedestrian, 110; infrastructure, 50, 67, 90, 105, 145–46; injury and death, 124; preferences, 109; strategy, 91, 106
Pembina Institute, 196, 206–7

Philosophiae Naturalis Principia Mathematica (Newton, Isaac), 295
Pickett, Kate (*Spirit Level, The*), 61, 248, 257, 293
Piketty, Thomas (*Capital in the Twenty-First Century*), 134, 277, 281, 293
Pincott, Brian (city councilor), 81
pipelines: oil and gas, 44, 198; Keystone XL, 191, 195; TransMountain, 174, 195, 198
Plan It Calgary, 40–41, 52–55, 81–82, 91, 128, 146, 193. *See also* Municipal Development Plan
planning: affordable housing, 176; ecological limits, 28; economics of, 39, 55, 129; of energy infrastructure, 199; and governance, 76; participatory, 40, 45, 66; policy and practice, 4, 12, 40–41, 50, 59, 76; politics of, 82–84; regional, 89, 91; and resilience, 59–60; and schools, 78; transportation, 100, 106, 109, 131; in Vancouver, 89–91. *See also* land use planning
Plater-Zyberk, Elizabeth, 10
political capital, 23, 41, 106
Pope, Carl, 195
Portland, Oregon, 76, 84–85, 98–99, 104–6
post-colonialist, 26
poverty: in Calgary, 12, 167, 275; and disabilities, 167; global, 23–25, 279, 349; inequality, 174, 176–77, 276; *Poverty Costs*, 172; trap, 125, working poor, 12, 275
praxis, 3
Prentice, Jim (premier), 130, 203, 270–74
Promethean response, 27
public health, 9, 56, 88, 149, 153, 207
Public Interest Alberta, 271
public transit, 4, 101–4, 121–22, 126, 131, 148, 226

R

Radical Technologies (Greenfield, Adam), 29
Redford, Alison (premier) 131, 195
Rees, William, 16, 28, 279
refugee, 292
regime theory, 6
renewable(s): co-operatives, 168; cost of, 200–2, 205, 207–8; electricity, 105, 162, 166, 176; politics of, 198, 207; transition strategy, 5, 162, 192, 205, 208

Resilient Cities (Newman, Peter), 61–62
ring road, 79, 119, 130–32, 137, 146
Rio de Janeiro, 5, 23, 24, 39, 42, 257
Rio Earth Summit, 10, 42, 244, 259, 278
Rio+20, 30, 259
Rise of the Creative Class, The (Florida,
    Richard), 13, 255
Rubin, Jeff (*Why Your World Is About to Get a
    Whole Lot Smaller*), 129, 169–71, 175

S

Sachs, Jeffrey (*Age of Sustainable
    Development, The*), 30
Sachs, Wolfgang, 25, 27
Sandercock, Leonie, 3
Sapiens (Harari, Yuval Noah), 17, 29
schools, 57, 76, 78, 80, 248
Seba, Tony, 124
secondary suites, 222–25
Sen, Amartya, 221
Shiva, Vandana (*Staying Alive*), 26
Silent Spring (Carson, Rachel), 27, 244, 257,
    259
silos, 2, 15, 165
Singapore, 56
Sleepwalkers, The (Clark, Christopher), 279,
    292
smart growth, 41
Smith, Adam (*Wealth of Nations, The*), 176,
    271, 290
social capital, 58, 88, 162, 165–66, 203, 230,
    251
social housing, 67
social justice. *See* justice
solar energy: Alberta's potential, 176, 199,
    200; and climate change, 281; cost of,
    201–2; in Germany, 65–66, 199–200; and
    industrial retooling, 124, 166, 204–5,
    281; limitations of, 170
Spirit Level, The (Wilkinson and Pickett), 61,
    248, 257, 293
sprawl: alternatives to, 10; in the automobile
    age, 49, 57, 82, 120, 131; definition of, 50;
    ecological impacts of, 9; and energy, 61;
    and the growth machine, 75, 256; policy
    to combat, 50, 105, 222, 225; political
    economy of, 5, 39, 255, 256; rural, 84, 89,
    110, 164; schools, 76, 78; subsidization
    of, 56, 81, 130, 173, 174, 255; as a

systemic problem, 2, 4, 75; urban growth
    boundary, 84, 89–90
Sprawl, The, 81
St. John's, Newfoundland, 98, 109–11, 250
Stanford, Jim (*Economics for Everyone*), 280,
    290
State of Our City, 42–43, 177, 198, 229, 275
Staying Alive (Shiva, Vandana), 26
Stockholm International Peace Research
    Institute (SIPRI), 292
Stone, Clarence, 6, 256
stranded assets, 192, 203–4
streetcars, 98, 102–3, 124, 126, 226. *See also*
    trams
substitutability, 6, 28
suburb(s), 147–48, 193–94; auto-oriented, 57,
    63, 66, 84, 122, 126, 131. *See also* sprawl;
    Sustainable Suburbs Study
suburban, 194, 225–26; votes, 148. *See also*
    infrastructure: suburban; sprawl
suburban development, 10, 75, 87; cost of, 51,
    146, 164, 173; policy response to, 41, 53,
    56; politics of, 39, 50. *See also* sprawl
suburbanization, 38–39. *See also* sprawl
suburbia, 53, 57, 122. *See also* sprawl
sustainability: principles of, 4, 45; strong 7,
    11–12, 24; transition, 5, 9, 270, 349; weak,
    6, 28
Sustainable Calgary: *Citizens' Agenda, A*,
    175; and cultural diversity in Calgary,
    222, 229; energy data, 198; formation
    of, 42, 348; in a global context, 2;
    good governance, 244–45; and green
    urbanism, 68; *Housing + Transportation*
    research, 105, 226; and imagineCalgary,
    82; income inequality, 177, 275; Oil and
    Gas Reliance Index, 275; principles of
    sustainability, 45, 270. *See also State of
    Our City*
sustainable development: Brundtland Report,
    24, 161, 165, 259; Canadian leadership,
    278; coal phase-out, 207; co-optation
    of, 27; critique of, 23, 26, 29, 289; and
    ecological modernization, 23, 28–30;
    expansionist paradigm, 28; maximum
    sustained yield, 25; North/South policy
    divergence, 24; origins and evolution of
    global discourse, 4–6, 10, 23, 29–30; Plan
    It Calgary, 193. *See also* UN Sustainable
    Development Goals

Sustainable Development Goals (SDGs). *See* UN Sustainable Development Goals
Sustainable Governance Index (SGI), 247
Sustainable Suburbs Study, 39
systems thinking, 2, 40

T

Taft, Kevin (*Follow the Money, Oil's Deep State*), 44, 173, 272–74
tar sands: and economic growth, 164, 173; ethical dilemma of, 149, 198–99, 201; politics of, 254; social and ecological impacts, 166, 174, 203, 206; stranded assets, 192, 195, 205
tax, 66, 80, 87, 255, 270, 273–74, 280; avoidance, 272; bracket, 271–72, 275; break, 245; business, 61; capital gains, 272; carbon, 166, 198; corporate, 259, 271–72; cut, 246, 259; education, 77; energy, 170; flat, 271; graduated, 271; havens, 272; and income, 271; and inequality, 177; municipal, 121; neoliberalism, 147–48, 164; -payer, 56, 78, 83, 130, 146, 173; policies, 247; progressive, 271; property, 256; revenue, 51, 81; savings, 57; taxation (fair), 251, 271; Tobin tax, 272
technical fix, 27
technocentric, 6
technocratic, 349
technological, 25–26, 29-30, 144, 150, 192, 251
technology: and anthropocentrism, 294; and the automobile, 120, 127; dystopia, 16, 28–30; energy, 124, 200, 202; panacea, 1, 27, 193; resource substitutability, 6, 28; transfer to developing countries, 24; urban life, 62, 66, 10; work-life balance, 164. *See also* bicycle; Center for Neighborhood Technology; smart cities
Technology and the Contested Meaning of Sustainability (Davison, Aidan), 23, 27–29
techno-systemic, 23, 29
Teck Resources Frontier, 174, 197, 200
10 Year Plan to End Homelessness (Calgary Homeless Foundation), 175, 225
This Changes Everything (Klein, Naomi), 13, 281–82
trams, 66, 97–106, 126. *See also* streetcars
transition. *See* energy; sustainability

transit-oriented design (TOD), 41, 105
transportation. *See* automobile; bicycle; car dependent; light rail transit; pedestrian; walkability
Transportation Housing Affordability Index, 226–27
Treaty 7, 37
Trinity Hills, 79
Trouble with Billionaires, The (McQuaig and Brooks), 280
Trudeau, Justin (prime minister), 165–66, 197, 278
Truman, Harry (president), 26
trust: Alberta Heritage Trust Fund, 274; community land trust, 175; governance, 84, 229, 246, 249–52; lack of, 245, 247, 272–73, 293–95; as marketing strategy, 123; in Nordic countries, 244, 248–49; reliable city infrastructure, 100; social and cultural capital, 14, 165, 243–44, 247, 257
Turner, Chris, 202

U

UN Climate Change Annual Report, 278
UN-Habitat, 11, 40
UN Millennium Development Goals (MDGs), 23, 30
UN Sustainable Development Goals (SDGs), 24, 30, 154, 257, 292
uneconomic growth, 9, 162, 164, 256. *See also* degrowth; non-economic growth
Unsafe at Any Speed (Nader, Ralph), 122
urban: planning, 4, 50, 55, 131, 222; theory, 4. *See also* design; governance; growth machine; regime theory
Urban Development Institute (UDI), 41
Urban Growth Boundary (UGB), 76, 84–86, 90
urbanization, 4, 6, 10–11, 30, 38, 289, 347

V

Vancouver: 40, 64, 76, 82, 125, 131; *City Making in Paradise*, 84–91; cost of cars, 108; cultural diversity, 228; Granville Island and the Seawall, 90; Walk Score, 125
Vauban, Freiburg, 127
Vaxjo, Sweden, 50
visible minority, 14, 222, 228–29
Von Clausewitz, Carl, 279, 291

W

walkability, 79, 111, 125, 131
walkable, 56–57, 82, 85, 122, 146, 227;
    Keystone Hills, 51; Peace Bridge, 144; St.
    John's, 109
Walk Score, 125
Walks, Alan, 148
walkshed, 102
Wealth of Nations, The (Smith, Adam), 176,
    271, 290
Wet'suwet'en, 276
*Why Your World Is About to Get a Whole Lot
    Smaller* (Rubin, Jeff), 129
wildfire, 17
Wilkinson, Richard (*Spirit Level, The*), 61, 248,
    257, 293
Williams, Raymond (*Culture and Society*), 143
wind energy: Alberta's potential, 176,
    198–200, 206–7; global growth, 200, 202;
    industrial retooling, 124, 166; limitations
    of, 170; rail-based transportation, 126
Winsport, 79
World Commission on Environment and
    Development, 4
World Energy Outlook, 200. *See also*
    International Energy Agency
World Happiness Report, 232, 249

a PROUD
PARTNER in

Campus
Alberta

A book in the **Campus Alberta Collection**, a collaboration of Athabasca University Press,
University of Alberta Press, University of Calgary Press.

 UNIVERSITY OF CALGARY
Press

◊AU PRESS

 UNIVERSITY *of* ALBERTA PRESS

University of Calgary Press

press.ucalgary.ca

Athabasca University Press

aupress.ca

University of Alberta Press

uap.ualberta.ca

Sustainability Matters:
Prospects for a Just Transition in
Calgary, Canada's Petro-City

Noel Keough with Geoff Ghitter

978-1-77385-248-5 (pb)

Creating the Future of Health:
The History of the Cumming School of
Medicine at the University of Calgary,
1967–2012

Robert Lampard, David B. Hogan,
Frank W. Stahnisch, and
James R. Wright, Jr.

978-1-77385-164-8 (pb)

Intertwined Histories:
Plants in Their Social Contexts

Edited by Jim Ellis

978-1-77385-090-0 (pb)

Water Rites:
Reimagining Water in the West

Edited by Jim Ellis

978-1-55238-997-3 (pb)

Writing Alberta:
Building on a Literary Identity

Edited by George Melnyk
and Donna Coates

978-1-55238-890-7 (pb)

The Frontier of Patriotism:
Alberta and the First World War

Edited by Adriana A. Davies
and Jeff Keshen

978-1-55238-834-1 (pb)

So Far and Yet So Close:
Frontier Cattle Ranching in Western
Prairie Canada and the Northern
Territory of Australia

Warren M. Elofson

978-1-55238-794-8 (pb)

A Sales Tax for Alberta: Why and How

Edited by Robert L. Ascah

978-1-77199-297-8 (pb)

Regime of Obstruction:
How Corporate Power Blocks
Energy Democracy

Edited by William K. Carroll

978-1-77199-289-3 (pb)

Fish Wars and Trout Travesties:
Saving Southern Alberta's
Coldwater Streams
in the 1920s

George Colpitts

978-1-927356-71-5 (pb)

The Medium Is the Monster:
Canadian Adaptations of
Frankenstein and the Discourse
of Technology

Mark A. McCutcheon

978-1-77199-236-7 (cl)

978-1-77199-224-4 (pb)

Public Deliberation on
Climate Change:
Lessons from Alberta
Climate Dialogue

Edited by Lorelei L. Hanson

978-1-77199-215-2 (pb)

Visiting With the Ancestors:
Blackfoot Shirts in Museum Spaces

Laura Peers and Alison K. Brown

978-1-77199-037-0 (pb)

Alberta Oil and the Decline of
Democracy in Canada

Edited by Meenal Shrivastava
and Lorna Stefanick

978-1-77199-029-5 (pb)

Situating Design in Alberta

Edited by Isabel Prochner
& Tim Antoniuk

978-1-77212-578-8 (pb)

Dissonant Methods:
Undoing Discipline in the
Humanities Classroom

Edited by Ada S. Jaarsma
and Kit Dobson,

978-1-77212-489-7 (pb)

Feminist Acts:
Branching Out Magazine and the
Making of Canadian Feminism

Tessa Jordan

978-1-77212-484-2 (pb)

Keetsahnak / Our Missing and
Murdered Indigenous Sisters

Edited by Kim Anderson,
Maria Campbell and Christi Belcourt

978-1-77212-367-8 (pb)

Trudeau's Tango:
Alberta Meets Pierre Elliott
Trudeau, 1968–1972

Darryl Raymaker

978-1-77212-265-7 (pb)

Seeking Order in Anarchy:
Multilateralism as State Strategy

Edited by Robert W. Murray

978-1-77212-139-1 (pb)

Upgrading Oilsands:
Bitumen and Heavy Oil

Murray R. Gray

978-1-77212-035-6 (hc)